THE LONELY

Alistair Horne is the author of the bestselling biography of Macmillan, and several prize-winning military histories such as *A Savage War of Peace* and *The Price of Glory*. His most recent book was *A Bundle From Britain*, a memoir of his childhood in wartime America.

David Montgomery is the only son of the Field Marshal, and succeeded his father as Viscount Montgomery of Alamein in 1976. His papers provide a new light on Monty's life.

Also by Alistair Horne

Back into Power
The Land is Bright
Canada and the Canadians
The Price of Glory: Verdun 1916
The Fall of Paris: The Siege and the Commune 1870–71
To Lose a Battle: France 1940
The Terrible Year: The Paris Commune 1871
Death of a Generation
Small Earthquake in Chile
Napoleon: Master of Europe 1805–1807
The French Army and Politics 1870–1970
A Savage War of Peace: Algeria 1954–1962
Macmillan: 1894–1956
Macmillan: 1957–1986
A Bundle from Britain

THE LONELY LEADER

MONTY

1944–1945

ALISTAIR HORNE

WITH

DAVID MONTGOMERY

PAN BOOKS

First published 1994 by Macmillan London

This edition published 1995 by Pan Books Ltd
an imprint of Macmillan General Books
Cavaye Place London SW10 9PG
and Basingstoke

Associated companies throughout the world

ISBN 0 330 34249 5

1 3 5 7 9 8 6 4 2

A CIP catalogue record for this book is available from the British Library

Phototypeset by Intype, London
Printed and bound in Great Britain by
Cox & Wyman Ltd, Reading, Berkshire

In memory of all Monty's men who 'went over the Jordan'
in north-west Europe, June 1944–May 1945

CONTENTS

List of Illustrations

1. Ceremonial March of 47 (London) Division at Lille in September 1918.
2. David with his mother in Lenk, Switzerland, at Christmas 1936.
3. Monty leaves the City Chambers in Glasgow on 22 April 1944.
4. Planning for the invasion in London, 1 February 1944. (Courtesy of the Imperial War Museum)
5. Monty addressing US infantry troops in April 1944.
6. Monty accompanied by Kit Dawnay, his Military Assistant during April 1944.
7. The actor Clifton James inspects the Guard of Honour at Gibraltar.
8. Field Marshal Rommel inspecting the Atlantic Wall. (Imperial War Museum)
9. Royal Marine Commandos leaving the landing craft to go ashore at St-Aubin-sur-Mer.
10. The second wave of 9 Canadian Brigade coming ashore on 6 June. (Imperial War Museum)
11. Men of the 2nd Battalion Royal Warwickshire during the final assault on Caen, 8 July 1944. (Imperial War Museum)
12. British troops and vehicles during the first week following the invasion. (Imperial War Museum)
13. The Prime Minister arrives in Normandy on 12 June 1944.
14. Watching an air battle near HQ 8 Corps on 12 June 1944.
15. The King arrives in Normandy and is greeted on the beach by the C-in-C, 16 June 1944.
16. Sir James Grigg, Secretary of State for War, at the Château de Creullet, 18 June 1944.

17. Monty with his puppies, Rommel and Hitler, at TAC Headquarters at Blay. (Imperial War Museum)
18. Crossing the Seine at Vernon on 1 September 1944.
19. Conversation piece painted by James Gunn at the Château Everberg outside Brussels in September 1944.
20. Monty examining the remains of a V2 bomb which fell near HQ 79th Armoured Division. (Imperial War Museum)
21. Paratroopers in a shellhole at Arnhem. (Imperial War Museum)
22. Ike leaving after a stormy conference on 29 November 1944 at Zonhoven. (Imperial War Museum)
23. Monty with the much-respected General Guy Simonds of the Canadian Army. (Imperial War Museum)
24. Lieutenant-General George S. Patton, commander of US 3rd Army. (Imperial War Museum)
25. Troops of the US 83rd Infantry Division in the northern part of the Ardennes salient. (Imperial War Museum)
26. A shattered German tank at the end of December 1944. (Imperial War Museum)
27. Soldiers of the US 26th Infantry Division (Yankee) working their way through a town during the Battle of the Ardennes. (Imperial War Museum)
28. Sherman tanks of the US 3rd Army Division in action during the Ardennes offensive. (Imperial War Museum)
29. Monty, Eisenhower and Bradley in Holland on 2 March 1945.
30. Churchill, Brooke and Monty have lunch on the banks of the Rhine on 26 March 1945.
31. Monty briefing his liaison officers at Ostenwalde in April 1945. (Imperial War Museum)
32. Monty receives the representatives of Doenitz and Keitel at TAC Headquarters 21 Army Group on Lüneburg Heath on 3 May 1945.

All the above illustrations not credited to the Imperial War Museum are from the private collection of David Montgomery. Nos. 13 and 15, belonging to the Field Marshal's private collection, were signed by Churchill and the King respectively.

List of Maps

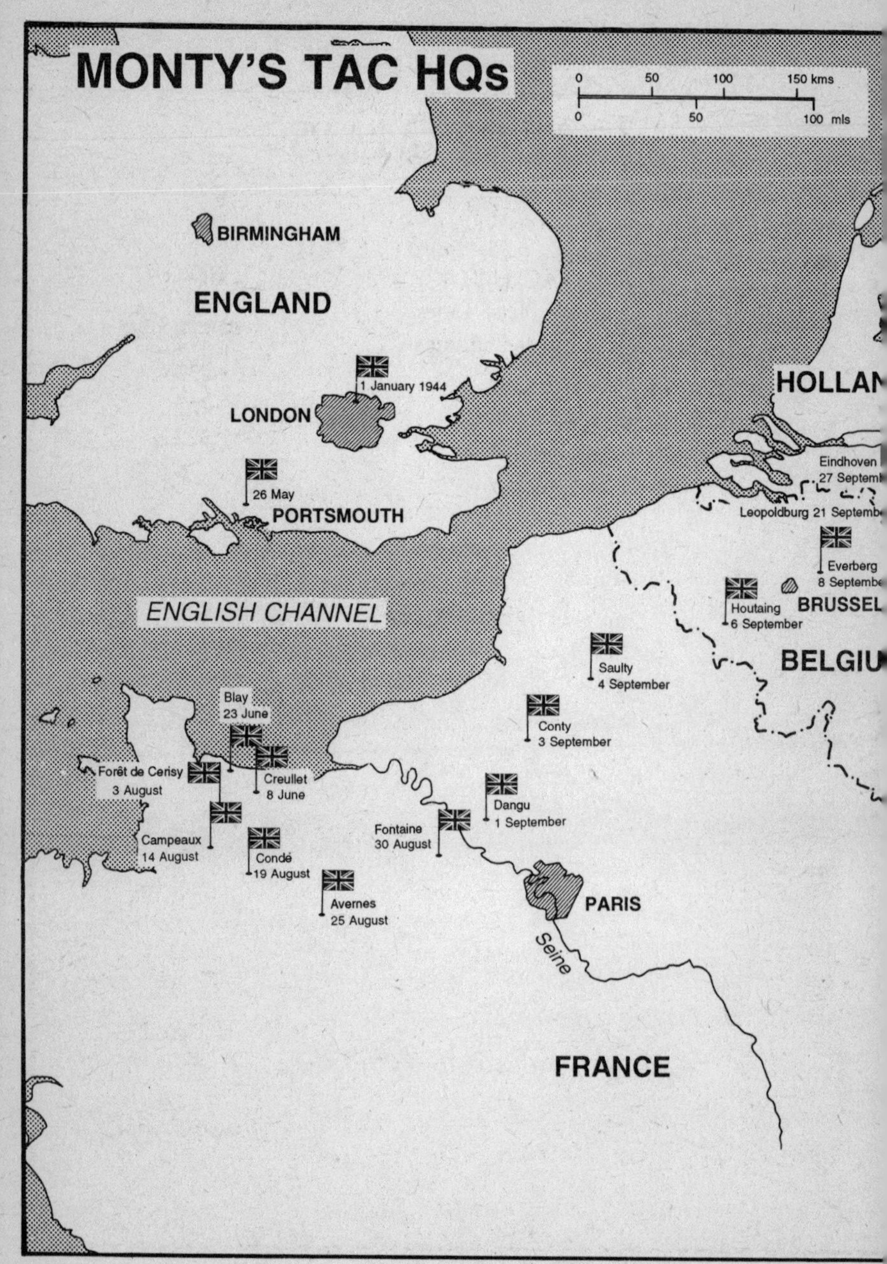
MONTY'S TAC HQs
0 50 100 150 kms
0 50 100 mls
BIRMINGHAM
ENGLAND
1 January 1944
LONDON
26 May
PORTSMOUTH
HOLLAN
Eindhoven
27 Septem
Leopoldburg 21 Septemb
Everberg
8 Septembe
Houtaing
6 September
BRUSSEL
BELGIU
ENGLISH CHANNEL
Saulty
4 September
Conty
3 September
Blay
23 June
Forêt de Cerisy
3 August
Creullet
8 June
Dangu
1 September
Fontaine
30 August
Campeaux
14 August
Condé
19 August
Avernes
25 August
PARIS
Seine
FRANCE

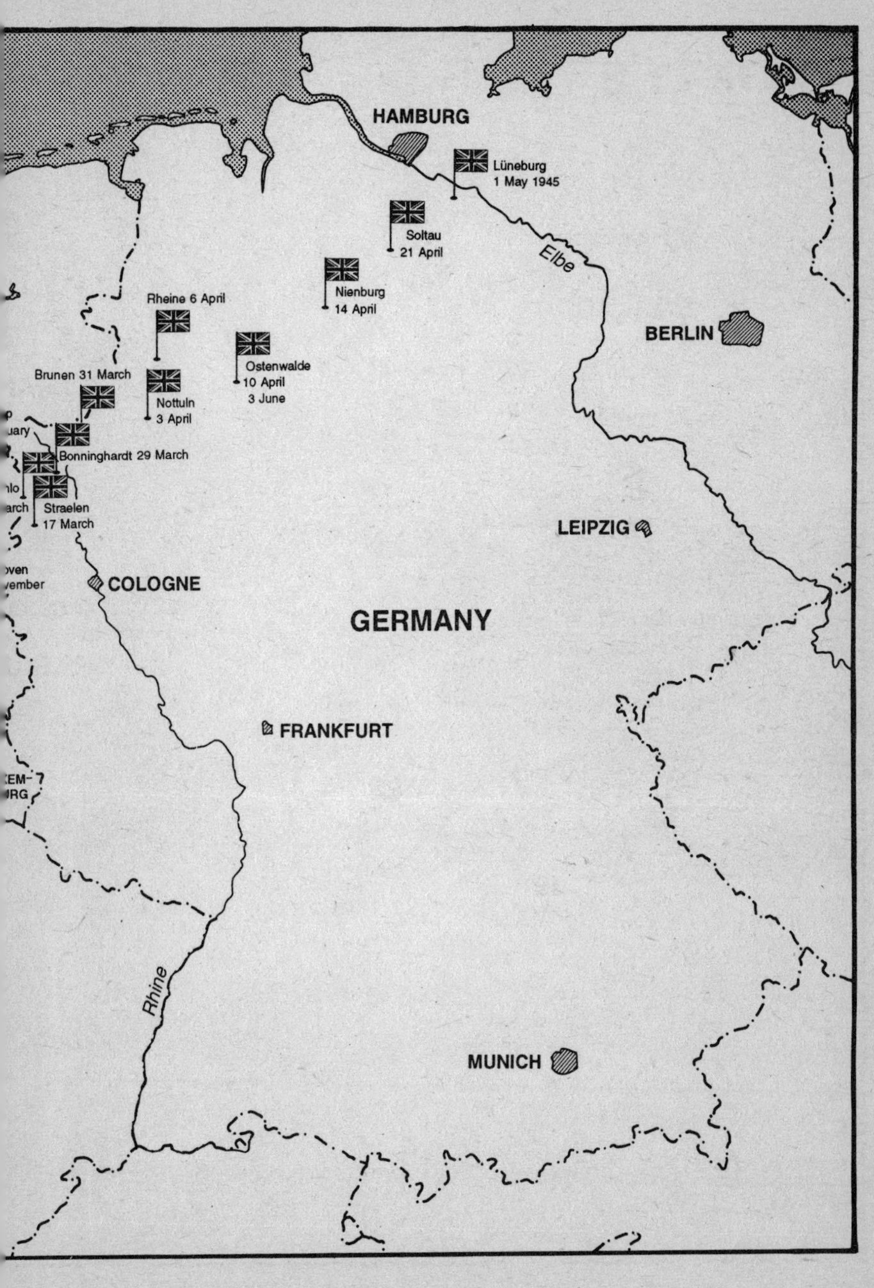
HAMBURG
Lüneburg
1 May 1945
Soltau
21 April
Elbe
Nienburg
14 April
Rheine 6 April
BERLIN
Ostenwalde
10 April
3 June
Brunen 31 March
Nottuln
3 April
Bonninghardt 29 March
Straelen
17 March
LEIPZIG
COLOGNE
GERMANY
FRANKFURT
Rhine
MUNICH

Foreword

By David Montgomery

During the ten years that elapsed from my father's death in 1976 to the publication of the third and final volume of the outstanding biography by Nigel Hamilton, I was often asked when, or indeed if, I would write about my father. I replied that the subject had been so comprehensively covered that there was no immediate need but that, in due course, a new opportunity might occur. About three years ago I conceived the idea that it would be most interesting to retrace the journey of my father through north-west Europe from the beaches in Normandy to Lüneburg Heath, by following the itinerary of TAC HQ (Tactical Headquarters) 21 Army Group – the small headquarters around the three caravans which, though I never visited it, had for so long been part of my life.

The notion of a mobile headquarters separated from main head-quarters was implemented by my father as soon as he took command of the Eighth Army in August 1942, and at that time comprised two caravans which had been captured from the Italians. These, together with the map wagon which was added for the invasion of north-west Europe, are now a feature exhibit in the Imperial War Museum at Duxford. The story of how the caravans were acquired and the part they played in my father's concept of command will appear later in this book.

I felt that it should be possible to identify almost all the twenty-seven sites and locations in France, Belgium, Holland and Germany (as well as the first site, near Portsmouth) at which TAC HQ had stopped between June 1944 and May 1945. My idea was to visit them all and undertake what I considered would be a filial pilgrimage. However, it was obvious that it would be much better to combine this historical peregrination with personal anecdotes and other documentary material. All biography needs to be revised from time to time with different perspectives on the personalities and new judgements made from the historian's own analysis of events, as viewed from another angle. The question was how to achieve it.

I decided to put the proposition to Alistair Horne, not only a distinguished historian but a long-time friend dating back to Cambridge days. I suggested that we could combine by my contributing with contacts, personal anecdotes and previously unpublished archive material, and that he should use these to take a new look at my father from an entirely different viewpoint. This would inevitably involve us both in controversial issues, as my father has no shortage of critics anxious to pick over the bones! A good example was the attempt to dislodge him from command in July 1944 when the campaign appeared to be stalled. Unfortunately my father did his own cause little good by always insisting, largely out of consideration for the morale of his troops, that everything was developing exactly according to plan. In truth very little ever goes exactly to plan, and certainly not after immensely complicated landings on a hostile defended shore. I believe that my father was always flexible, adapting to circumstances and making new disposals as the situation required, but seldom admitting it.

As a result of this and other matters of great historical debate, I insisted that Alistair should have complete freedom to criticize and comment as he felt, and that I would object only if there were clear errors of fact, and would request no changes to matters of opinion or judgement, even if I took a dissenting view.

Thus it was that we set off in June 1992 on a fascinating and most enjoyable two-stage reconnaissance, with Alistair as captain and pilot, and myself as staff officer and navigator. It was a memorable journey which gave a completely new insight into the campaign and its problems. More particularly it provided an opportunity to review the inadequacy of British equipment, the political relationships between the Allies and many aspects of the last stage of the war which had hitherto been dealt with tangentially. This in itself was a most instructive and rewarding experience.

But if this is a more personal appraisal of my father I cannot avoid touching on my own relationship with him during my early life. As was normal in pre-war army days, our family life was almost entirely nomadic. Born in England in 1928, by the time I was six I had already lived for extensive periods in Jerusalem, Alexandria and Quetta, near the north-west frontier of Imperial India. After the

Quetta earthquake, a major natural disaster and a quite unforgettable experience, following which the children were evacuated to facilitate the clear-up work, I returned to England and, on a bitterly cold day in January 1936, at the tender age of seven and a half, went to boarding school.

From then until I finished military service at twenty and went to university, life was almost entirely institutional. In October 1937 my mother died when I had just turned nine years old, following which my father had to make special arrangements for me. In theory, my eldest half-brother, John, although away much of the time as a serving sapper officer, was my guardian. His fiancée Jocelyn had taken care of me while my mother was dying, inspiring a lifelong devotion. In practice, I moved from place to place each school holiday until August 1942, when my father was appointed to command the Eighth Army and transferred at short notice to the desert. He then decided to make more permanent arrangements, and Tom Reynolds, the headmaster of the preparatory school, which I had left the previous term, was appointed my guardian. I then lived with his family until my father created his own family home at Isington Mill in 1948.

All this may seem rather an odd upbringing, although I never felt in the least deprived; in fact to begin with my father was a most assiduous and devoted parent. However, this changed dramatically when, almost overnight, he became internationally famous and in two and a half years had become a living legend. To be an only child with no mother in these circumstances is undoubtedly rather complicated and confusing for a teenager, but, like most things, one becomes accustomed and adjusts accordingly. Although proud of his achievement I was always conscious that our relationship would never be quite normal, as it had been when I was a child and my mother was alive.

In retrospect it must have been far worse for him – preoccupied with great affairs but equally concerned, as his letters reveal, with the welfare of his only son. I now believe that my youthful exuberance and at times rather excessively wild behaviour must have been a sore trial, and one which he could well have done without. The Reynolds family, to whom I owe an enormous debt of gratitude, took much of the burden and concern away, although it would have been all much easier if my mother had survived.

It has been suggested that my father's single-minded purpose and ambition to succeed derived from her death. However, any serious analysis of my father's approach to military matters, starting with his experience in the First World War, reveals that he was totally dedicated to his profession from an early age and way in front of his contemporaries, especially in all aspects of training and preparation for war. What is more certain is that my mother's early death had an impact on my circumstances and on our relationship.

I remain convinced that as a general, both in the desert and in north-west Europe, my father was the right man at the right time in the right place. Unfortunately in the post-war world the adulation had its effect upon his character, with no one close enough to mitigate this and bring him back to reality. Although he welcomed heated debate on almost any subject with his personal staff and numerous protégés, with his only son this produced friction and irritation. He was a soldier's general with a capacity to inspire at a time when it was most needed and this, above all else, will be his lasting memorial.

Montgomery of Alamein
December 1993

PREFACE

BY ALISTAIR HORNE

In defeat, unbeatable; in victory, unbearable.

(Winston Churchill, quoted in Edward Marsh, *Ambrosia and Small Beer*)

It has been a damned nice thing – the nearest run thing you ever saw in your life. . . . By God! I don't think it would have done if I had not been there.

(Duke of Wellington, *Creevey Papers*, vol. X, p. 236)

I don't know if we could have done it without Monty. It was his sort of battle. Whatever they say about him, he got us there.

(Major-General Walter Bedell Smith, speaking of D-Day in March 1976)

I FIRST MET Monty just after the war. I was a young officer with MI5 attached to GHQ Middle East; Field Marshal Viscount Montgomery of Alamein was Chief of the Imperial General Staff (CIGS) and had come out to what was then Palestine with the unpalatable task of telling us that exigencies of the world situation demanded the postponement of our demobilization. The venue for this distressing encounter was a large, partially covered squash court. The moment the great soldier began speaking, volleys of flapping pigeons took off, making a mockery of his speech. The Field Marshal turned to the General with the command 'Get those pigeons out of here!' The General turned to the Major-General, who turned to the Brigadier . . . The order passed all the way down the line to an embarrassed subaltern who ineffectually endeavoured to catch the pigeons with a butterfly net. The birds were unmoved; nobody dared laugh. With mounting irritation, Monty persisted against a backdrop of flapping. We all sat there stonily, our mirth suppressed only by the grimness of the tidings he pronounced. I remember reflecting long afterwards on the Canute-like disbelief of this small general that a flock of pigeons should possibly interrupt his delivery. It seemed quite arrogant.*

The second time I saw Monty was about ten years later, when he had just retired from the army but was instructing the current British government on how to conduct its foreign relations with the Russians and Chinese. He was speaking after dinner in a room with phenomenally bad acoustics; a few seats away from him was the distinguished blind journalist, T. E. Utley. Someone at the end of the table complained of not being able to hear him, at which Monty snapped back, 'I can see one of you is blind, but are the rest of you deaf, too?' It was a savage remark, and the two incidents combined left me long with an impression of both cruelty and arrogance.

Later, as I became a military historian, we corresponded. Through his son David, my friend from Cambridge days, I would visit him down at his retreat in Isington Mill. He reacted with unexpected warmth to my early books on French military history, and I became aware – under those fiercely penetrating blue eyes – of a much kindlier, but also intensely lonely human being. It was this loneliness which made a particular impression on me. But never for a moment did it occur to me during my visits to Isington Mill three decades ago that I might one day write a biography of him.

As an armoured man educated in America during the early part of the Second World War, my original sympathies were instinctively with the dashing Patton rather than with the cautious Monty. These were later reinforced by books, such as Correlli Barnett's *The Desert Generals*, critical of Monty's performance in the pursuit after Alamein. All too often he seemed to be dogged by that besetting sin of the British Army, the Gallipoli instinct to pause and 'regroup' whenever success seemed within reach. But perhaps the passage of years brings caution to military analysts too. David Montgomery in his Foreword describes the genesis of this book, the unpublished material he has provided and the extensive 'recce' of all his father's twenty-eight TAC HQs which we jointly undertook in 1992. With it also came, at least for me, valuable new insights into the man and the wartime commander. While writing the official life of Harold Macmillan, I was constantly reminded of the loneliness at the top,

* Forty-five years later I was reminded of this episode when I learned the story of the Schloss Ostenwalde frogs (see Epilogue).

whether of a prime minister or a commander-in-chief. In Monty it seemed to acquire another dimension (by comparison, Macmillan was a positively gregarious figure), and David and I instinctively agreed on *The Lonely Leader* as a natural title.

If there is a justification for a new study of Montgomery, coming on top of all that has already been published (and notably the imposing and exhaustive three-volume biography, in which few details are spared, written by Nigel Hamilton in the 1980s), it should be on the basis of new interpretations even more than of new material. In the two post-atomic generations that have grown up since D-Day 1944, the whole concept of war has also subtly altered; now it has to be short, painless, without casualties (at least for the 'good guys') and, above all, suitably adaptable for television. What would have happened if television cameramen had been present on OMAHA Beach on 6 June 1944, providing the kind of live coverage that so influenced American public opinion during Vietnam, and threatened to call the shots during the Gulf War, confounds the imagination. Most probably there would have been no D + 1. Equally, could Monty conceivably have survived his very bad press during the weeks of apparent stalemate of June–July 1944 if he had been subjected to a nightly grilling by those semi-informed, instant pundits of television, so eager for immediate results, as were the coalition generals during the (fortunately) brief Gulf War of 1991? It was once said of Verdun, 1916, that it could never 'be done again'. Happily – at least on the Western Front in 1939–45 – it never was. Fifty years on, one asks oneself, could D-Day ever be done again? The acquired wisdom always was that, because of nuclear weapons, the answer was no. Then, in the lingering moments of pessimism that prefaced the Gulf War, it looked briefly as if it might *have* to be – against Iraq's Saddam Hussein.

On reopening the files on OVERLORD, 1944, one's immediate reaction is: what a staggering risk! Across the years, it now comes across as a much nearer-run thing, to use Wellington's famous dictum, than one had previously realized. There was absolutely no margin for error, and penalties for failure would have been inestimable. It was once said of the First World War that there was only one man on either side who could have lost it in an afternoon: Admiral Lord Jellicoe, Commander-in-Chief of the Royal Navy. Had Jellicoe forfeited Britain's margin of superiority over the Kaiser's fleet, Britain would have been starved into submission, her French and Russian allies then conquered at ease. It seems to me that, in the Second World War, once Eisenhower as Allied Supreme Commander had given that majestically courageous decision of 5 June, 'OK, let's go,' Monty then comes closest to sharing Jellicoe's reputation in his war. The responsibility resting on those narrow shoulders, the 'what-ifs?' of failure, were simply colossal. Granted the huge preponderance of Allied material power arrayed against Germany by mid-1944 – supremacy in the air, the U-boats defeated, the gigantic US military build-up since Pearl Harbor, the seemingly unstoppable might of the Soviet steamroller – with the brilliance of hindsight it seems inconceivable today that the Allies could then still actually have lost the war. Yet history has a way of springing surprises. There were at least three ways in which the OVERLORD landings could have been defeated: by misfortune, by lack of resolve or by a bad plan incompetently executed. In the first instance, through no human agency, an evil change in the weather could have swept away the Allied landing forces as surely as it did the Spanish Armada of 1588, or as the ancient Greeks were mercilessly harried to the edge of destruction by Poseidon on their way to and from the siege of Troy.

In June 1944, however, failure through a lack of resolve, or a bad plan, would have reflected on one man, and one man only – Bernard Law Montgomery.

Consider the consequences of defeat on D-Day. The Allies would have lost their almost irreplaceable fleet of landing craft, in which even by June 1944 the margin was uncomfortably small. Britain would have sacrificed her last available army. It would have taken at least another year, well into the summer of 1945, before another invasion attempt could have been mounted; and that would then have had to be manned largely by Americans. In the meantime, Hitler would have been developing his deadly jet aircraft, and new technology would have enhanced the striking power of his U-boat fleet. Possibly (though improbably) his scientists might have developed an atomic bomb. But, with certainty, Britain would have been hammered mercilessly by Hitler's V-weapons, constantly increasing in numbers in the Pas de Calais and the Low Countries, and largely immune to air attack. By late summer of 1944, under the rain of the V-1 'doodlebugs' and after nearly five years of war, British morale was already shakier than it had been at any time in the Blitz; could it have held up after another devastating defeat, and for another year? What if the national hero, Monty, repulsed on the shores of Normandy, had joined the long, lugubrious ranks of the defeated and sacked British generals? In the US, a tremendous head of idealism had built up to smash Hitler, as the number-one priority; yet with a bloody catastrophe on the Normandy beaches, could the restless Americans have resisted the pressures of Admiral King and the 'Pacific Lobby' to transfer their main effort to defeating the hated Japanese enemy?

There then remains the unpredictable Russian card. In the course of their smashing spring offensive of 1944, which brought the Red Army sweeping into Poland, the Soviets looked irresistible, but supposing the bulk of the sixty German divisions pinned down in the West by OVERLORD had been released to hold the Eastern Front? Might they then have been able to fight the Russians, with their already colossal losses in men, to a bloody standstill? Since the *glasnost* opening of the Soviet archives in 1990, we are now aware, in addition to the Ribbentrop–Molotov Pact of 1939, of at least two (previously unknown) overtures for a separate peace from Stalin, giant with feet of clay, to Hitler in the terrible autumn of 1941. With the Allies defeated in the West in 1944, such a desperate remedy, though improbable, would not have been inconceivable. Certainly this was the hope that buoyed up Rommel and its probability would have been vastly increased had ROUNDUP, the invasion of Normandy scheduled for the summer of 1943, been attempted then, rather than a year later. This is what Roosevelt and Marshall had wanted, and what would have resulted in a premature effort with green troops doomed to almost certain failure, averted only under heaviest pressure from Churchill and his prudent CIGS, Brooke – who, a year later, was still privately wondering whether OVERLORD 'may well be the most ghastly disaster of the whole war'.

Thus, if an Allied repulse on D-Day did not actually lead to some form of victory for Hitler, at best it would have meant another bloody year of war, ruinous for Britain, the extinction of the last surviving remnants of European Jewry through completion of the Final Solution, culminating almost certainly with the employment of the first atomic bombs in the summer of 1945 on Germany, not Japan. Sweeping through a 'nuked' Germany, the victorious Red Army would have stopped nowhere short of the Rhine. Lost to Communism, Europe, and the world, would have been a very different place today.

This was what was involved on 6 June 1944. The risks facing Montgomery and his Anglo-American forces were truly gigantic. Of course, once the landings had been consolidated, these risks were substantially reduced and ultimate victory seemed but a matter of time. But there still lay ahead weeks of the most bitter fighting experienced in Europe by Americans, British and Canadians during the entire war. At various times, pundits of the Western press predicted Normandy bogging down into a grisly deadlock reminiscent of 1914–18. Every post-war study reveals Hitler's Wehrmacht of 1944, despite its losses in five years of war, to have been an even more formidable instrument than hitherto accepted; nothing attests this better than his eleventh-hour Ardennes offensive of December 1944, which, with Germany on the very threshold of collapse, came so close to inflicting a devastating defeat on the Americans. My own researches for this book further incline me to believe that Monty was fighting with a much more 'flawed weapon' in his hand than has been realized.

This in itself may have been one of the less apparent sources of his own disastrous relations with Eisenhower and the Americans.

There was 'a wrenching disproportion between the legend and the reality as Americans perceive it', writes one of Monty's harsher US critics, Eric Larrabee: 'The transatlantic view is not only less charitable than the homegrown one but alien, in a literal sense, to the world Montgomery inhabited.'* There was a fundamental truth here. Dating back to the days when the triumph of El Alamein had begun to fade away, Monty has never enjoyed a good press in the United States. For this he really had no one to blame but himself, compounding as he did the offence of what he said during the war with what he wrote subsequently in the post-war 'anecdotage' of his memoirs. Tragically, the superb joint Anglo-American achievements of the war became muddied in the self-justification and ripostes by

* Larrabee, *Commander in Chief*, p. 471.

Angry Old Men on both sides of the Atlantic. There were many things about the wartime Monty that were profoundly unpalatable to Americans: his smug boastfulness, his *ex post facto* insistence that all his operations had gone precisely according to plan, his supercilious treatment of Ike and Americans in general. Reading the wartime communications between him and his superior, Eisenhower, one feels Ike must have had a forbearance of heroic, if not saintly, proportions. But one has also to recall that, until Pearl Harbor, and in sharpest contrast to contemporary Anglo-American soldiers with two generations of NATO communal existence, a British officer of Monty's generation would have been as likely to have met a Martian as an American counterpart. After the liberation of France, Monty, given his prickly character, could never have put over to the Americans his second-phase strategy for the 'single thrust' into Germany – however sound militarily that might have been. An Alexander might have done, but then Alexander would almost certainly never have had the tactical skill to land half-a-million men in Normandy, nor the inspired touch to persuade men to slog on at Caen, nor the persistence to continue – in the teeth of all opposition – with a strategy that would lead to the greatest Allied victory of the war to date.

During the Normandy campaign, Monty's press in the States was far worse than he deserved; but today few major American historians deny that it could not have been won without him – any more than the Alliance could have been sustained under the command of a lesser man than Eisenhower. Yet, in his lonely isolation from SHAEF* and Ike, Monty's was truly a tragedy of personalities and failed communications. Here alone, it seemed to us, a reappraisal was overdue.

Originally, the Horne–Montgomery scheme was to carry the story through to the German surrender of May 1945, with a more proportionate share of the book devoted to the post-September 1944 sections of the campaign. But books in the writing have a way of taking over. Gradually the decisive victory of Normandy, and Monty's dominant role in it, seemed all-important, with everything that followed becoming little more than historical postscripts. The

* Supreme Headquarters Allied Expeditionary Force.

tragic story of Arnhem, the Battle of the Bulge, the crossing of the Rhine and the triumphant sweep across Germany have all been told many times, and are here peripheral. But Normandy was the key to it all; just as 1 September 1944, with Monty's promotion and demotion and Eisenhower's assumption of overall command, becomes a natural watershed of intense historic significance – beyond just the confines of the war.

Finally, perhaps, a word of appreciation is due to my fellow author. Nowhere were Monty's idiosyncrasies of character more evident than in his treatment of his son. Yet the initial idea of this book was his – to undertake, as he puts it, a 'filial pilgrimage'. We covered 2000 miles, all the way from Southwick House to Lüneburger Heide, rediscovering to our satisfaction (and some surprise) the sites of all the twenty-eight TAC HQs; only arriving finally at Lüneburger Heide did we unexpectedly encounter the greatest difficulty in finding the Holy Grail itself, the site of the German surrender of May 1945 – as will be related. Much unpublished material, in the form of letters and other documents, came from David Montgomery, but at no time was any restriction ever imposed on my total freedom to write what I wished about his father. In this sense, the result is perhaps hardly an 'official' or 'authorized' biography. The research was joint, the writing entirely by me – though it was commented on by David at every stage, and he generously shoulders responsibility for the final product. I am indebted to David for all this, as well as for his constant, long-suffering and amiable support.

Equally I am indebted to him for helping expose a number of *belles légendes* that have grown up over the years and have been accepted uncritically by other authors. For instance, there is the widely told story about ex-Sergeant Parker who stayed on at Isington Mill as odd-job man during the last years of the Field Marshal. The unfortunate Parker was said to have been attacked by a horde of infuriated water-rats when clearing weed out of the mill-race – and died as a result of his injuries. 'Most unfortunate' was supposed to have been Monty's callous comment. A horrifying tale – but 'total rubbish', says David: 'Parker died of cancer.' Equally fantastical was the notion given credence by, among others, Alun Chalfont in his biography that Monty had homosexual tendencies, as will be seen.

Both stories may illustrate the difficulties that face any biographer of Monty because of the mass of apocrypha that has grown up around him.

To avoid burdening the reader with a mass of footnotes, we have given source references that are indicative rather than exhaustive. Fuller details of those sources may be found in the Bibliography.

There are very many people to whom David Montgomery and I owe gratitude. In the realm of unpublished diaries and other material, in the first instance there is a particular debt to Johnny Henderson for so generously opening to us his personal wartime diaries. These had never been seen before outside his immediate circle, and provided a valuable and fresh view of Monty and his TAC HQ. We are also grateful to him for his unstinting help in the course of numerous interviews and queries. An indispensable treasury of material for any historian writing about the man or the period is, of course, the copious archive of oral interviews carried out by Nigel Hamilton in the course of writing his own monumental three-volume biography. The archive is now accessible in the Imperial War Museum.

For other unpublished written documents or recorded tapes, we are particularly indebted to the late Colonel Peter Earle (his diaries are deposited in the IWM), to Colonels Trumbull Warren of Ontario and Ray BonDurant of Florida, and to Major Paul Odgers for access to his invaluable 'Chronicle' of TAC HQ. My old friend, Lady Liddell Hart, widow of Sir Basil, was most helpful in giving me access to her private papers, while of course the Liddell Hart Archives in King's College, London, remain an essential quarry.

Mrs Mary Laurie and Mrs Susanna Cort, daughters of the late Major Noël Chavasse, were most generous in allowing free access to his correspondence and photograph albums. Sir William Mather kindly provided a valuable personal account of the Battle of Soltau; conversations taped at length between David Montgomery and Manfred Rommel also afforded much excellent new material on Monty's adversary in North Africa and Normandy, Erwin Rommel.

The following helped most graciously with interviews: Air Chief Marshal Sir Harry Broadhurst, Colonel John and Jocelyn Carver, Major T. Coverdale, Major R. Harden, the late Lord Hunter, Sir Richard O'Brien, Major Paul Odgers, the late General Sir Charles Richardson, Sir Hereward Wake, Sir E. Williams.

We are especially indebted to Sir Carol Mather, who not only agreed to be interviewed but most kindly checked the manuscript.

Both of us are personally grateful to the following for their kind hospitality and help in the course of the 'recce' carried out in two sections, in June and September of 1992: the Marquis de Canchy, C. Pozzo di Borgo, M. and Mme Pierre Dalle, M. André Coilliot, Princesse de Merode, Mme Henriette Claessen, the Mayor and Corporation of Zonhoven, Mme Mommen, Nick McCarthy, Colonel M. Craster, Sabine, Gräfin von Perponcher-Sedlnitzky. At Arnhem, we were most warmly welcomed by the curator of its excellent museum Adrian Groeneweg; and in the Ardennes by SE J. P. van Bellinghem, and by M. Guy Arend, through whose remarkable free enterprise two outstanding museums have arisen at Bastogne and Arlon.

For additional help and advice on various points, we are indebted to: Colonel Tom Bigland, the late Axel von dem Bussche, Field Marshal Lord Carver, General Sir John Hackett, Professor Sir Michael Howard, Dr Georg Meyer, Dr Jochen Thiess, Sir Brian Urquhart and the Defense Enquiry Office of the US Embassy in London.

Once again, the Imperial War Museum, under the directorship of Dr Alan Borg, Ted Inman at Duxford and Roderick Suddaby of the Department of Documents, together with Nigel Steel, rose marvellously and tirelessly to the occasion. We are equally indebted for illustrations to Mrs Hilary Roberts of the IWM.

By no means least, this book depended largely on access to the Montgomery Collection in the IWM, as well as to the copious unpublished files of correspondence and other material in the private possession of the present Lord Montgomery – the progenitor of the whole concept of *The Lonely Leader*. (Perhaps typical of this untapped treasure-trove was discovery of the original War Office top-secret file on the mini-drama of the looted pig. It now resides in the IWM.) I remain eternally beholden to David for his endless patience and good humour in dealing cheerfully with a multitude of queries and problems – as well as with the capacity of his co-author to lose documents – throughout the arduous work of preparing this book. We remain firm friends.

One thing, however, is quite certain: without the remarkable team of editor and copy-editor of Roland Philipps and Peter James, valiantly supported by Tanya Stobbs, this book would never have been completed on time. In other ways I owe a special debt to Roland, for his super-human calmness, something essential to a super-heated author. I hasten to add that any error of fact in answering the James–Philipps 800-point pre-Christmas questionnaire has to remain entirely the responsibility of this author. For other support of a similar nature, 'above and beyond the call', I am – once again – profoundly grateful to my saintly and superb research-assistant and secretary, Anne Whatmore.

And finally, inestimably, I owe a debt to my wife, Sheelin, who put up with an impossible author for far too many months.

Alistair Horne
Turville, Christmas Eve 1993

CHAPTER ONE

THE MAKING OF A SOLDIER

1887–1939

> The stern compression of circumstances, twinges of adversity, the spur of slights and taunts in early years, are needed to evoke that ruthless fixity of purpose and tenacious mother-wit without which great actions are seldom accomplished.
>
> (Winston Churchill, *Marlborough*)

> Montgomery was often tiresome and sometimes absurd. All the same, as so many have said, he was the greatest British field commander since Wellington. Perhaps this is not much of a compliment; there are few competitors for the title.
>
> (A. J. P. Taylor, *Observer*, 11 April 1976)

ON 2 JANUARY 1944, a small general arrived in London with a very big job: to lead the Anglo-American invasion of north-west Europe that spring. If he were to fail at D-Day, and were the Allies to be thrown back into the sea (as they had been at Dunkirk in 1940 and Dieppe in 1942), the extent of the disaster would be incalculable. Less than eighteen months previously, General Sir Bernard Law Montgomery had been a totally unknown figure outside his profession – and most emphatically not universally loved within it. To a young staff officer, he had then looked at first sight more like 'a very alert Parson Jack Russell terrier'* than a great warlord. Now, relinquishing his legendary Eighth Army after their victory in North Africa, he returned from the Mediterranean, to become almost overnight the best-known and most beloved British general since Wellington after Waterloo.

If, as Napoleon declared, every soldier carried with him in his great pack a marshal's baton, Bernard Law Montgomery would

* Goronwy Rees, *A Bundle of Sensations*, p. 135.

indeed be getting his before the summer was up; but in his pack he carried a great deal more of historic weight from the Mediterranean. In it he carried undeniable military genius, success (a substance so far denied British arms almost consistently since September 1939), extraordinary charisma – and a very difficult personality.

Bernard Law Montgomery was born in 1887, on 17 November (therefore a member of the curious zodiacal fellowship of Scorpio, genius allied with self-destruction), three and four years respectively before his adversaries Adolf Hitler and Erwin Rommel (the latter also a Scorpion), into a fairly representative Victorian family of slender means. Both sides of the family, the Montgomerys and the Farrars, had India and the Church in the background. Before Irish Protestant blood came into their veins, the Montgomerys originally stemmed from Normandy – where Bernard would fight his greatest battle. But, although with their innate pugnacity the Irish have provided some of Britain's finest soldiers of two world wars – Brooke, Alexander and Montgomery, just to cite the famous trio of 1939–45 – it seems that it was from the Farrar side of the family whence Monty inherited most the cutting edge of his personality, as well as its less pleasant aspects.

His maternal grandfather, Frederic William Farrar, was a remarkable Victorian by any standard. Originally a reforming schoolmaster of the Dr Arnold stamp, in the course of his life he published some seventy-five books, covering a vast range from Classics to what would now be called sociology. But it was his famous novel, *Eric, or Little by Little*, written when he was twenty-seven, that gained for him a certain literary immortality. Translated into innumerable languages and running to over fifty editions, with its mixture of high morality and excessive sentimentality cloying to the modern reader, as a bestseller about English school life in the nineteenth century it was second only to *Tom Brown's Schooldays*. It was also probably the only novel to make an impact on the author's grandson, at any rate in early life. Farrar was a man of most forceful personality, with total faith in his own judgement and a remarkable ability to simplify – all characteristics that were passed on in full to his grandson. He took orders, and having made a name for himself as a rebel (and a troublesome one at that) against the existing education, he was appointed honorary chaplain to Queen Victoria, an unusual honour for a school teacher. In 1871 he was made headmaster of Marlborough College, but four years later – at forty-five – Disraeli appointed him Rector of that prestigious church, St Margaret's, Westminster. There his powerful oratory had such an extraordinary success that his congregation had to reserve seats, often sitting on the steps of the pulpit itself. After his death, a nearby street in Westminster was named after him.

To St Margaret's Farrar also brought as curate a former pupil from Harrow, the Revd Henry Montgomery, sixteen years younger than himself, and son of an Indian civil servant, Sir Robert – who, during the Siege of Lucknow in 1858, had earned the reputation of being 'brave as a lion, and gentle as a lamb', and went on to become lieutenant-governor of the Punjab. Shortly after arriving at St Margaret's, the Revd Henry became engaged at the age of thirty-two to the Dean's daughter Maud, then aged only fourteen. They were married two years later. On Maud's own account, it was not an outstandingly happy marriage, although Henry adored her. Before she reached twenty-five, Maud had borne five of her nine children; Bernard was number four. It was, in his words, 'an uninteresting family, some might say'.* Certainly there was within it never the least breath of scandal; Henry came greatly under the influence of his father-in-law's tirades from the pulpit against 'Demon Drink', based on his observations during forays into the East End. Eventually he took the pledge, passing on his obsession with temperance down through the next two generations of the Montgomery family. In the not very kind words of Maud (she appears not to have been a notably kind person), compared to her brilliant father, Henry was 'a plodder'; his most distinguished recorded achievement being his ability to jump in one bound up the steps leading to Hall at Trinity College (an almost impossible feat).†

Nevertheless, at a relatively early age Henry in 1889 was appointed bishop of Tasmania. His first action was to rush to the Athenaeum Club to discover exactly where his diocese was. Bernard was two years old. For the next twelve years Tasmania was to be the Montgomerys' home, and it was there that Bernard grew up. It was

* Montgomery, *Memoirs*, p. 18.

† This agility was apparently inherited by his grandson David, who – in his day at Trinity – became one of the more redoubtable of the audacious night-climbers at Cambridge.

a spartan regime, though perhaps little more so than the norm of the times: the children were up at dawn, chopping firewood, with lessons beginning at 7.30, followed by a strict bedroom inspection and prayers, and only then breakfast. Money was very tight; Monty claimed he never owned a watch until the outbreak of the First World War. Henry was a gentle, rather saintly man, described as having a 'silky beard and kindly face'. Bernard adored him: 'He was always a friend. If ever there was a saint on this earth, it was my father. He got bullied a good deal by my mother and she could always make him do what she wanted.' Even late in the Bishop's life (he died in 1932, but his wife lived on long after him) when the family had returned to England, the parsimonious Maud:

> ran all the family finances and gave my father ten shillings a week; this sum had to include his daily lunch at the Athenaeum, and he was severely cross-examined if he meekly asked for another shilling or two before the end of the week. Poor dear man, I never thought his last years were very happy; he was never allowed to do as he liked. . . .*

All the siblings seemed to dislike the Farrars. In his memoirs, Monty stated categorically, 'Certainly I can say that my own childhood was unhappy,' and this was something he blamed largely on his mother. She seems, with little doubt, to have been a harsh parent, incapable of giving out much affection – least of all to young Bernard.

Maud's general principle was 'Go and find out what Bernard is doing and tell him to stop it.' There were constant 'defeats' and beatings with a cane – invariably administered not by the Bishop but by Maud. On one never forgotten occasion young Monty had been caught smoking. Sorrowfully his father took him into his study, knelt him down in prayer, then pronounced him forgiven. But outside the study door his mother was waiting, with a stick, and she gave him a savage beating, notwithstanding the Bishop's earlier absolution. By his own admission more rebellious and unmalleable than his siblings, as well as incapable of subterfuge, Bernard deserved much of what he got. Already a contemporary recalled him as being 'a difficult sort of chap'.† Perhaps illustrative is an oft retailed anecdote from later

* Montgomery, *Memoirs*, p. 19.

† Chalfont, *Montgomery of Alamein*, p. 32.

years when, at Moville, their home in Ireland, Monty deliberately cut away a precious clematis outside his mother's window – just to annoy.

Often we exaggerate the recollected horrors of childhood; just possibly, over the latter years Monty made his mother out to be blacker than she really was, if for no other reason than to explain his own shocking treatment of her (and, more inexplicably, of his sisters) once the mantle of fame had descended upon him. But there is no pardoning the cold lack of love which young Monty found there.

How much did this really shape his character, his later career – and his relationships with others? Certainly strong-minded women can have the most powerful and long-lasting effect on their sons. A case in point is that of Harold Macmillan and his excessively dominating American mother Nellie, who probably ruined his marriage – but without whose drive and ambition he would almost certainly never have become prime minister. Unlike Monty, he never ceased to venerate his mother, and it was to her that he wrote all his (deeply moving) letters from the trenches. Similarly with Monty: it was not to the beloved and gentle Bishop that he wrote in this time of terrible crisis, but to his unkind mother, some of the most emotive and intimate lines he ever penned, sixty letters in all. Therefore, one should perhaps treat with more caution than have some biographers the alleged hatred between the future Field Marshal and his mother.

In 1901, the family reluctantly left Tasmania for home, Henry to become secretary of the Society of the Propagation of the Gospel in Foreign Parts, which post he held until his retirement, aged seventy-four, in 1921. The family now divided their time between an over-crowded house in Chiswick and holidays at the family home in Moville, County Donegal, twenty miles from Londonderry, which an ancestor had purchased in the mid-eighteenth century. In London the Bishop would escape whenever he could to the tranquillity of the Athenaeum Club – on his ten-bob-a-week pocket money. Now aged thirteen, Bernard was sent off as a day boy to St Paul's School, which, some forty years on, he would select for his OVERLORD GHQ. In a school already academically distinguished, Bernard at first made no great mark; he dawdled and dreamed, and in his own words, 'did practically no work'. He was more interested in sport, though a report from a rugger coach stated, 'Runs strongly but takes too long to get away.' It was an observation that would be seized upon by later critics of Monty's mobility on the field of battle. Undersized and wiry, he earned the nickname 'Monkey', on which the school magazine dilated:

> This intelligent animal . . . is vivacious, of unflagging energy, and much feared by the neighbouring animals owing to its unfortunate tendency of trying to pull out the top hairs of the head. This it calls 'tackling'. To foreign fauna it shows no mercy, stamping on their heads and doing many other inconceivable atrocities, with a view, no doubt, to proving its patriotism. . . .

(This last line would doubtless have provoked wry smiles from Dwight D. Eisenhower and Bernard's American colleagues in distant years to come.)

Aged fourteen, Bernard won the first of his battles against his mother. To her intense rage he declared that he was going to enter the army, instead of the Church. (Subsequently he claimed that he had done it principally to annoy her.) But in his penultimate year at St Paul's his report warned that, 'rather backward for his age', to get into Sandhurst 'he must give more time for work'. According to his devoted youngest brother, Brian, he did, and entered Sandhurst in January 1907, when he was just over nineteen, with not more than satisfactory marks. He stood five foot seven inches tall, weighed 138 pounds and had a chest measurement of just thirty-four inches. In addition to the fees, Maud gave him an allowance of nine shillings a week. It was far less than any of Bernard's contemporaries had to spend, and undoubtedly affected his attitude both as a cadet and as a young officer. At the Royal Military College, there occurred an episode of which perhaps too much has been made in terms of Monty's adult character, but which undoubtedly came close to terminating his military career then and there. He was the ringleader in setting fire to the shirt-tails of an unpopular fellow cadet – for no better reason than that 'He was a dweadful chap!' The unfortunate victim suffered serious and painful burns and had to enter hospital. From this youthful prank gone badly wrong, it was subsequently deduced that Monty was a sadist at heart ('You have a cruel mouth, Monty!' once declared his wife, Betty – but at least partly in jest). He lost his cadet corporal's stripes and was retarded six months – generally regarded as a serious handicap for a future officer's career. Having lived it down, however, Monty received his commission in July 1908, but suffered a first bitter disappointment when rejected for the Indian Army – on the grounds that his marks were too low. He had opted for service in India, partly to follow in the steps of his grandfather, Sir Robert, but also because promotion and pay (always a vital factor with the hard-up young Monty) were that much better.

Instead he selected the not-very-grand Royal Warwickshire Regiment (because, he said, he liked the cap badge) and was posted off to India anyway, in December 1908. His straitened finances immediately set him apart from his fellow officers, in ways that were to mark out his future career. Not for him were polo or racing or the pursuit of women in those carefree peacetime days when 'talking shop' was strictly taboo in any officers' mess, and any display of 'keenness' the worst of all possible bad form; in any case, knowing only his stern mother and his sisters, he considered the pursuit of women a frivolous pastime. Instead, he dedicated himself to mastering his profession. His colleagues were a hard-drinking lot; one major, suffering in the early morning, insisted on sitting by himself at a small table, facing the wall and speaking to no one. In his memoirs Monty noted acidly, 'An expression heard frequently was that so-and-so was a "good mixer". A good mixer was a man who had never been known to refuse a drink. . . .'* Leaving aside Dean Farrar's influence and his natural aversion, Monty could not afford to become a 'good mixer'. Impressed on his memory was an early oral examination by an outside inquisitor with 'a face like a bottle of port' whose first question was 'How many times in each twenty-four hours are the bowels of a mule moved?'; the future Field Marshal duly failed. Such were the priorities of an average British line regiment on the eve of its most terrible test. By 1913 Monty was glad to return home, and glad to have failed for the Indian Army.

In the last remaining months of peace, Monty fell briefly under the influence of the first officer to broaden his understanding of *real* soldiering and who 'encouraged my youthful ambition', a Captain Lefroy who had just returned from Staff College. He made the young

* *Memoirs*, p. 29.

subaltern think about what was wrong with the British Army; sadly he was killed in the war, 'a great loss to me and to the Army', wrote Monty, putting first things first.

When war broke out in August 1914, Monty was a full lieutenant of twenty-six. On mobilization, he recalls, all officers were ordered to take their swords to the armourer to be sharpened; meanwhile, an immense German army was marching through Belgium equipped with the latest machine guns and heavy artillery. The Warwickshires found themselves caught up in the famous retreat from Mons at the end of August, counter-attacking into the irresistibly advancing Germans at Le Cateau – only a short distance from where Monty's later adversary, Erwin Rommel, was to make his reputation by his famous Panzer breakthrough into France in May 1940. Charging up a hill, Lieutenant Montgomery tripped and fell over his carefully sharpened sword. Under 'a perfect storm of shrapnel fire', as Bernard described it to his mother, the Warwickshires were dropping 'like ninepins' and this fall may well have preserved his life: 'by the time I had picked myself up and rushed after my men I found most of them had been killed . . .'. As he had accurately predicted in one of his earlier letters to his mother, they had gone into battle 'knowing absolutely nothing, not even where the enemy is until we bump against him'. Now a shocking thing happened. Having lost two of his companies in this suicidal charge, the commanding officer, Lieutenant-Colonel Elkington, turned and retreated fifteen miles to St Quentin, where he precipitately tried to arrange the surrender of his battalion. Disgraced, he was cashiered; later he joined the French Foreign Legion, won both the coveted Médaille Militaire and the Croix de Guerre, was subsequently reinstated in the British Army and was awarded the DSO. In the words of Monty's brother Brian, Le Cateau 'drove home the British Army's lack of training for modern war'.

In the confusion of this 'most unfortunate day', Monty was reported missing, just one month after war had begun. However, he was soon writing to his mother that he was alive and commanding:

> my own company now as my major got his leg broken in our first fight; so I ride a horse, as all company commanders are mounted. I have a big beard. I have not washed my face or hands for 10 days. . . . We get letters in strange situations; I eat the peppermints

> [sent by his sister Winsome] with a dead man beside me in the trench....

In October 1914, the Warwickshires found themselves thrown into the grim First Battle of Ypres. The Germans were occupying the nearby small village of Méteren, and Monty's company were detailed off to dislodge them. Today its attack line is now cut by the new A25 autoroute to Dunkirk, but the church spire atop a gentle slope, which would have been Monty's objective, is still clearly visible. Within a hundred yards of the village, he was hit by a sniper:

> the bullet entered at the back which was toward the enemy, and came out in front, having gone through my right lung.... A soldier from my platoon ran forward and plugged the wound with my field service dressing: while doing so, the sniper shot him through the head and he collapsed on top of me.... I lay there all afternoon; the sniper kept firing at me and I received one more bullet in the left knee. The man lying on me took all the bullets and saved my life....

It was not until nightfall that Monty finally reached a clearing station. By then his condition seemed so hopeless that orderlies had already begun to dig his grave. Had the bullet passed through the other lung, it would have pierced his heart too; as it was, it was a wound from which few recovered. However, with his iron will, Monty survived, though the wound was to leave him short of breath for the rest of his life. He remained a pipesmoker, and the wound – rather than any Cromwellian objection to the vice – was what, eventually, caused his passionate aversion to anyone (even the Supreme Allied Commander, Ike, his boss) smoking in his presence.

Méteren – once again – almost certainly preserved the young Monty's life for greater things. On Ypres' imposing Menin Gate, the names of the British Commonwealth fallen go on for ever and ever, outside and beneath the arch and up the stairs; of one British infantry regiment, the Royal Fusiliers, there are the names of thirty-eight young second-lieutenants alone, underlining the tragic statistic that in the Great War the life in action of a junior officer was calculated in minutes only. So the probability of Lieutenant Bernard Montgomery surviving through to 1918 would have been slight. For his exemplary courage at Méteren, he was awarded the DSO, a high distinction for a junior officer, and – after four months' recuperation – transferred to the staff. In swift order he found himself promoted to brigade major attached to one of the new units of Kitchener's volunteer army. His brigadier he described in his forthright manner as 'a very nice person but quite useless' (a phrase that was to become one of the most overworked in his simple vocabulary); 'and it would be true to say that I really ran the Brigade and they all knew'. The ancient Brigadier was nevertheless generous enough to write to Bishop Montgomery, predicting for his son 'a brilliant future in the army'. Returning to Flanders, Monty's first letters show him still far from being shocked by what he found, at least in terms of staff work: 'The organization of the army out here is quite wonderful.' But the treatment of the troops made a lasting impression on him: 'Altogether the conditions for the men living in the trenches are very bad. I go out every day round the trenches and posts. . . .'

Monty's capacity for hard work and his outstanding efficiency as a staff officer swiftly made their mark. His letters to his mother display an astonishing lack of security, revealing to her every detail of military activities. When the dreadful day of 1 July 1916 came, his 104th Brigade had the good fortune to be removed from the futile holocaust of the Somme. On that first day, Kitchener's new army lost nearly 20,000 in dead alone. In his later career, Monty was renowned for his determination to avoid unnecessary casualties; however, none of his letters from France yet reflect this. He shows himself philosophically acceptive, and not unduly impressed by the dreadful casualties being suffered all around them; perhaps that required a poet, a Blunden or a Sassoon. It was only in the aftermath of war that it was to have a most powerful impact on Monty's thinking. For the immediate future, however, it instilled in him a determination that, when opportunity knocked, he would ensure that things were at least better done.

What chiefly affected him was the wasteful inefficiency with which it was all carried out: 'It is no exaggeration to say that the majority of officers and men of the 23rd Manchester [one of the battalions belonging to his brigade] had but little idea of what they were attacking. The attack completely failed, although the officers and men went forward with great determination. . . .' Before

Field Marshal Haig, the Commander-in-Chief, called off the murderous Somme offensive in November 1916, after it had achieved no breakthrough, Monty's 104th Brigade had been in the line no less than three times.

At the beginning of 1917, the year of Passchendaele, Monty was promoted to G-2 (a staff officer, usually a major) of the 33rd Division, then in rapid succession to the key role of G-2 Ops of IX Army Corps. This was part of the Second Army commanded by General Sir Herbert Plumer, often regarded as the only British commander on the Western Front to begin to understand its lessons. Instead of launching costly general offensives like the Somme and Passchendaele, Plumer concentrated his army on limited attacks against specific and realizable objectives – all prepared with meticulous care. He was the first to use the principle of leap-frogging fresh units to replace the first-line attacking troops once these had lost their edge; it was a device Monty would employ when he commanded his own army at El Alamein. Plumer was the 'soldier's soldier' *par excellence* of the First World War, and Monty's education on his staff probably influenced his subsequent thinking more than any other experience on the Western Front. In 1917, a sixty-page training document emanated from the hand of Plumer's young G-2, the first of many that Monty would draw up in the course of his career. It set the scene for Plumer's autumn offensive, three separate attacks which by the detailed planning, the thorough training and the carefully timed creeping barrage to precede the infantry were models of their time.

All Plumer's objectives were achieved, at considerable cost to the enemy and relatively little to the attackers (at least compared with other British – and French – initiatives). Regrettably, the successes of Plumer, who was sent off to command in Italy, were squandered by Haig's obstinate persistence in extending the campaign. In the mud of Passchendaele that autumn, over a period of less than three weeks the fine Canadian Corps (with which Monty's brother Donald was serving) alone lost 12,000 men. Monty, at his most acid, was unimpressed. 'The Canadians are a queer crowd,' he wrote to his mother, perhaps displaying some insular prejudices that were to reappear a generation later; 'they seem to think they are the best troops in France.... They forget that the whole art of war is to gain your objective with as little loss as possible.... They are narrow-minded and lack soldierly instincts.'

March 1918 brought General Ludendorff's 'last-gasp' offensive, which came within inches of cracking the British front, backed by a mass of men and artillery released from the collapsed Russian front. Superbly well prepared, Ludendorff's forces struck in total surprise, accompanied by an unprecedented concentration of shellfire; instead of advancing in those steady straight lines that had typified most of Haig's costly offensives, packets of highly trained stormtroops infiltrated through selected breaches in the British lines, to be followed rapidly by a flood of fast-moving infantry, who then outflanked the defenders. Accorded the name 'expanding torrent', it was a natural development of Plumer's experiment of the previous year – about which more was to be heard in the inter-war years. For the first time since 1914, the Western Front erupted – disastrously for the Allies – into a war of movement. For a few nerve-wracking weeks, it looked as if Ludendorff would accomplish Hitler's triumph of 1940, by splitting the British and French armies from one another, and pinning the British up against the Channel. It fell to Monty's IX Corps to hold the key Kemmel Ridge, which, had it fallen, would have given Ludendorff the victory he sought. The corps lost an appalling 27,000 casualties; one battalion of the Devons was reported 'exterminated almost to a man'. But the front held; the German tide halted, and turned about – for the last time.

Promoted to lieutenant-colonel at the age of thirty, Monty now found himself in the all-powerful role of chief of staff of a division. His divisional commander, General Gorringe, believed in the principle followed by the German Army, whereby the actual implementation of orders was left almost entirely to the Chief of Staff. This arrangement suited Monty admirably; it was here, he said, that 'I learnt the value of the Chief-of-Staff system, which I used so successfully in the Second World War'. In the closing months of the war, from this junior staff officer emanated instructions ordering special training sessions, in which all battalion commanding officers were also required to take part – something unheard of in the British lines.

In October 1918, Monty's 47th Division took part in the victorious Allied advance as the defeated enemy was rolled back towards Germany. But he noted, with respect, how even in bankruptcy the German military machine conducted a most professional fighting retreat, beaten and hungry though it was. Even in those final months of the war, he appreciated that no risks could be taken. The 47th Division liberated Lille, and, by one of history's bizarre coincidences, at the Victory Parade there, a gaunt and deadly serious Lieutenant-Colonel Montgomery is photographed standing just one pace in front of his future boss, Mr Winston Churchill, currently Minister of Munitions. It was notably closer than he ever got to the Commander-in-Chief, Sir Douglas Haig, on whom (though more favoured than most of his contemporaries) he had set eyes only once during the whole war – and then only from a distance. The memory remained within him the rest of his career. 'Any future C-in-C has got to be well known, not only to the soldiers, but to their wives and mothers,' he would declare as a matter of ritual in the years ahead.

So the war ended for Monty. The flatness and lassitude of peacetime soldiering now recommenced. After all it had suffered, in the British officer corps (for those fortunate enough still to be retained by it) there was little enough incentive – indeed rather less than there had been before 1914 – to pursue vigorously the study of military innovations, or the art of killing, after so terrible a bloodletting. Lieutenant-Colonel Montgomery, just thirty-one, was at once one of the rare exceptions. Though he fundamentally disapproved of advancement via what was known in the Second World War as the 'old-boy network', it seems that it was a chance meeting at a tennis party with the ex-CIGS, General Sir 'Wully' Robertson, that secured him a coveted place at Staff College the year after hostilities ended. There, so the story went, a student in disgrace would be sentenced to sit next to Monty at breakfast for a month, while the Staff College magazine of December 1920 queried what weaponry or munitions might be required to stop him 'babbling at breakfast'. Noting in his memoirs the widespread urge to return to less arduous pleasures of pre-war, peacetime soldiering, Monty retails a music-hall joke. 'If bread is the staff of life, what is the life of the staff?' Answer: ' "One big loaf!" There was tremendous applause, in which I joined,' recorded Monty, but it 'made me think seriously, and from my own experiences I knew something was wrong'. To him the professional army was 'a life study and few officers seem to realize that'. Of his contemporaries at Staff College, he remarked to his brother Brian, 'Very few of them were any good.' This kind of Cromwellian dedication and intolerance made him little more popular among his contemporaries than he had been in pre-war regimental life, and he was certainly never at ease with them, even at this relatively early stage in his career.

It was already otherwise, however, with his young subordinates. He enjoyed taking groups of subalterns to visit the French battlefields, and they responded warmly to him as an outstanding teacher, even discovering in him (according to Brian Montgomery) an 'infectious sense of humour' that was suspected by few of his equals.

Among the latter, the rare friends of lasting consequence that he did make during his Staff College years included one of the senior instructors, a gunner colonel and fellow Ulsterman called Alan Brooke. Already tipped as a potential CIGS, curt in manner and precise to a fault, as critical of the failings of others as was Monty, Brooke at once impressed him by a professionalism that was at least equal to his own. His respect for Brooke was to endure throughout the rest of his career, and he was the one officer of whom he constantly walked in awe. Another who made a permanent mark was a very different personality, a *bon vivant* subaltern thirteen years Monty's junior, whom he met while both were training the Territorial Army. One of his outstanding talents was a capacity for never forgetting an officer's name, or ability, once met and – in the phrase of brother Brian – Freddie de Guingand was to become to Monty in the key years of command ahead what the inestimable Berthier was to Napoleon.

Of a very different hue was Monty's relationship, stemming from the early 1920s, with that prophet of the unorthodox, thorn in the side of the conventional British military mind – Basil Liddell Hart. Invalided out of the army with a lowly rank, Liddell Hart in his writings was busy trying to make sense of the lessons of the recent war and to devise antidotes (the 'Strategy of Indirect Approach', as it later became known) for the murderous stalemates on the Western Front. Physically, there could hardly have been a more incongruous couple. In contrast to Monty's compact figure, the gangly guru, 'the

Captain' – eight years his junior and seven inches taller – looked like an emaciated marabout stork. At their first encounter, an identity of interests – the shortcomings of the British Army – brought them together. Then fundamental disagreements on first principles (as well as the intense vanity and egotism of both men) set them apart for many years until, at the very end of their lives, they became the closest of friends, with Monty (belatedly) praising Liddell Hart as Britain's outstanding military thinker.

Monty's earliest correspondence with Liddell Hart, one of the world's most voluminous letter-writers, was prompted by the *Infantry Training Manual*, the drafting of which had made Liddell Hart's reputation as a twenty-four-year-old subaltern. In 1930, Monty was appointed to update it; by his proudly unrepentant admission, he arbitrarily scrapped all the other work done on it, 'omitting all the amendments the committee had put forward'. Liddell Hart was infuriated because Monty had expressly made no mention of 'exploitation', the theme of the 'expanding torrent' which had become the essence of Liddell Hart's thinking on offensive, mobile warfare. In his own memoirs, Liddell Hart claimed this was 'a persisting blind spot' in Monty's approach to tactics. (He was in fact quite dismissive of Monty then, referring to him in those memoirs less than half-a-dozen times; and then to remark that 'he did not show the natural signs of leadership, or a knack of handling men . . .'; that he had once brought his battalion 'to the verge of mutiny by misjudged handling'; that – much more serious – he never properly understood the idea of an armoured breakthrough, supported by infantry, the modern development of the 'expanding torrent' with which Liddell Hart conceived a future war should be won.) It was of course, alas, in Nazi Germany that the writings of Liddell Hart, true prophet without honour in his own country, were first taken seriously, forming the blueprint for the Panzer forces of General Heinz Guderian.

Liddell Hart's widow, Kathleen, was always emphatic that the pre-war rift between the 'Guru' (who later became special adviser to Hore-Belisha, Secretary for War, as Britain entered the Second World War) and the serving soldier was never as sharp as some biographers have made out, but their dispute over the employment of armour was fundamental. Monty, ever the infantryman, saw all war as a confrontation between bodies of infantry. Though he appreciated the potential of tanks, he saw them in a largely subsidiary role, punching holes in the enemy line for the infantry to move through, then retiring. 'Tanks are very blind and cannot reconnoitre by themselves,' he wrote to Liddell Hart. 'In mobile war they will normally move forward by bounds in support of the advancing infantry.' This philosophy, though modified by the painful lessons of 1940, was to remain fairly consistent in Monty right through the desert and Normandy; but it was certainly not how Liddell Hart, 'Bony' Fuller or the other apostles, saw modern armoured warfare developing. Nevertheless, devastating a critic as Liddell Hart could be, his recognition of Monty in the 1920s carries weight and was to hold good through the years: 'He was already one of the most thoroughly professional soldiers in the army. I was the more impressed because by then I had come to realize, through widening experience, how amateurish most "professional soldiers" still were.'*

In this context, it is essential never to lose sight of the fact that it was Monty, the serving infantry officer, not the historians and theoreticians, who would have the heavy responsibility, ultimately, of putting theory into practice. While they could afford to be radicals, if not revolutionaries, Monty – though always a *reformer* – was never either. It is an important distinction; if in the deeply conventional British Army of the 1920s he had been a revolutionary he would have ended either in a siding or – like the Liddell Harts, Fullers and Martels – out of the army altogether. In a letter to Liddell Hart of 1924, he set out his antipathy to teaching the 'exceptional', explaining, 'You will notice that I use the word "normal" a great deal. I am a great believer in giving people a "normal" to work on. . . .' In contrast to Liddell Hart's 'vision' of future warfare, Monty the pragmatist was committed to making the most secure army possible out of the available human material as presented by the ordinary soldier.

With two generations of NATO soldiering and mixed headquarters behind them, British army officers of today would find it hard to

* Liddell Hart, *Memoirs*, vol. I, p. 55.

imagine just how narrow and restrictive military life was in the 1920s and 1930s. After 1918, there would have been virtually no contact with foreign contemporaries – least of all Americans. If the Montgomerys and Brookes had any conceptions about their American opposite numbers (whom they almost certainly never met), they would hardly have been complimentary. America had come in at the end of the war, when most of the hard fighting had been done, had grabbed the laurels of victory, then run off home again, into the comforts of isolationism, abandoning Europe in a worse mess than it had been in before. British generals' ignorance about American military procedure, and thinking, was almost total – factors of some significance when it comes to OVERLORD, 1944. Hunting, polo and racing and restrained forays into philandering (for those who could afford any of these) constituted norms of military life, as they had been before 1914. Shop-talk in the mess was no less taboo, and discussion about commerce or the arts little less frowned upon. No officer's conversation, at this time, would have been more restricted than Monty's; 'for two months I had to sit next to this fellow at dinner', one of his second-in-commands once complained, 'and conversation was impossible; he could only talk about the army!'

For a bachelor already in his mid-thirties, Monty's conversational dexterity seemed hardly guaranteed to change his status, even if it were not for the deterring shadow of his bullying mother. His sister Una recalled, with affection, how 'absolutely wonderful' Bernard had been during his precious wartime leaves, telling her, 'Have a party and I will pay for it and look after you. . . . I don't dance, as you know, but I'll look after you.' Later he was heard dismissively to declare, 'I haven't got time for the preliminary reconnaissance.' Then, suddenly, aged thirty-eight, he fell in love – with a beautiful seventeen-year-old blonde called Betty Anderson. Apart from their great difference in age, this first Betty was clearly not seduced by Bernard's overtures, which consisted, while on holiday at Dinard, of tracing for her in the Brittany sand his ideas on military deployment. She liked him; he proposed; she turned him down; he pursued her, in vain, on a skiing holiday to Switzerland; still she said no. But, in the party at Lenk that January of 1926, was a second Betty, an army widow called Mrs Carver. Taking a Napoleonic *coup d'oeil*, Monty switched fronts with commendable dexterity. The following summer, on 27 July 1927, he and Betty Carver were married; a year later their only son, David, was born.

It seems, by all accounts, an instant love-match. The odds were distinctly against it. Here, on the one hand, was a bachelor already set in his ways, prematurely middle-aged, totally wedded to his profession, and – through the conflict with his mother – virtually a misogynist; she, on the other hand, was a fun-loving artist with Bohemian tastes, a thirty-nine-year-old widow of twelve years' standing who had been deeply in love with her first husband. Waldo Carver, from a Cheshire cotton family, had joined up at the beginning of the war and had been killed at Gallipoli in 1915. Inconsolable, she was left with two small boys – Dick and John – both of whom were to become regular officers. (Betty herself, *née* Hobart, had a brother Patrick, also a regular officer, who was to become an inventive genius in armour with a significant role in Monty's later career.) Setting up as an artist in a studio in Chiswick, she had become close friends with her neighbours, the humorist A. P. Herbert* and his wife Gwen; through them she developed a wide range of friends among artists and writers. Though he was only nine when she died, her son, David Montgomery, was left with 'a clear recollection of a most affectionate, charming, lovable person'. This was the general view of Betty Montgomery; she was warm and outgoing, instantly attracting everyone she met. What she saw in Monty may seem hard to judge, except that, with his instinctive affinity for the young, he was at once a hit with the young Carver boys, making their skiing holiday fun and generally 'organizing' them, in a manner which, though bossy and pronouncedly military, neither they nor their mother minded. (In fact, as Betty was to explain to a friend, after years of fending for herself as a naturally disorganized person she rather welcomed the way Monty took over – even the bossy daily 'orders' with which he would encompass her life.) She was grateful for the protective net he cast around her, which enabled her to get on with her painting (at which she was not unskilled) in tranquillity.

In this most unlikely union, 'a new world began to develop in front of Bernard', his brother Brian tells us: 'a world of people for whom the armed forces counted little, if at all, and yet were clearly

* Monty came to consider A. P. Herbert's novel *The Secret Battle* (1919) 'the best story of front-line war I have ever read'.

intelligent, hard working and highly talented. The memory of this was to stand him in good stead in the years ahead.'* With mock displeasure he would complain of Eric Kennington, the war artist famed for his masterly drawings of T. E. Lawrence, 'Dweadful fella! Eats peas off his knife,' but clearly he enjoyed – and was enriched by – *la vie bohème* that Betty brought into his life. She took him to the Italian Riviera, introducing him to the delights of picnics and bathing parties, which he would previously have written off as 'idle pursuits'. More than just bringing a degree of frivolity into his austere life, she showed him qualities of friendship, affection, support and even of deep love which his unhappy childhood had led him to believe no woman could provide. In the passage in which he himself describes their marriage in his memoirs, brief but heartrending in its understatement, he says, 'A time of great happiness then began; it had never before seemed possible that such love and affection could exist. We went everywhere, and did everything, together.'

The softening effects were not immediately apparent. Still only a lieutenant-colonel, fifteen years after he had held the rank in the war, he was at last given command of a battalion of the Warwickshires and sent to Poona – which was well nicknamed the 'Sloth Belt' of India. It was the worst imaginable fate for a keen soldier. His general, Sir George (or 'Ma') Jeffreys, was by legend the most 'regimental' officer in the Brigade of Guards, who had brought his Grenadiers out of the retreat from Mons almost without loss and in parade-ground order. But he had little interest in any form of training for modern warfare, while hours spent drilling on the parade ground were total anathema to Monty. The story, probably only marginally apocryphal, is told of this time how Monty, when informed by the redoubtable 'Ma' Jeffreys that his horse was seven paces too far to the left on parade, simply turned round and ordered the whole battalion of 800 men to move seven paces to the right. Probably only his early reappointment to be chief instructor at the Quetta Staff College saved Monty from a collision that might well have proved disastrous to his career. Despite Monty's ill-disguised contempt for him, 'Ma' Jeffreys, nothing if not fair, gave him a favourable report, but with the friendly caution: '(and this is meant for advice, *not*

* Brian Montgomery, *A Field Marshal in the Family*, p. 203.

adverse criticism), to bear in mind the frailties of average human nature, and remember that most others have neither the same energy nor the same ability as himself . . .'. But the interlude was to leave Monty with at best an ambivalent attitude towards elitist units like the Brigade of Guards, or the 'Cavalry amateurs'.

Brian Montgomery reckoned that the three years, 1934–7, that his brother spent at Quetta 'were among the happiest times of his life' – despite the terrible earthquake which devastated the town, leaving 30,000 dead buried under the ruins, and which enforced one of Monty's only two separations from Betty. It was also, he thought, possibly his most fruitful period professionally between the two wars. Monty thought deeply about the role of leadership at this time, reading extensively on the lives of great commanders, notably Wellington. His tactical concept of war matured; in the words of his biographer, Nigel Hamilton, it was 'not spectacular for its novel ideas, but for its unity of conception and the absolute clarity' with which he put it over. And so it would remain. That unquenchable self-confidence in his own star was in no way diminished. On separate occasions, he was recorded as anticipating that he would end as CIGS, and – convinced of the inevitability of war – that he would personally lead a victorious British Army into Berlin. Only the latter was to be denied him. At the same time, the softening influence of Betty made him noticeably a more amenable colleague, and more popular than ever among his students. On her side, Betty, with her small son, enjoyed life in Quetta to the full, as well as being an excellent 'Colonel's Lady'. On one occasion, after she had danced all night (of course, without Monty), a solemn servant brought in her earrings the following morning on a silver platter. Monty, the adored and adoring husband with no cause for jealousy, was only amused – perhaps a little charmed – by her distractedness.

In May 1937, the Montgomerys returned home. The shadows were closing in; Hitler had reoccupied the Rhineland and was about to move on Austria. Monty, to his delight, promoted, was to be given command of the 9th Infantry Brigade in Portsmouth. That August he was on Salisbury Plain, conducting as a new brigade commander exercises that were the most important in his career to date. He was trying out the notions he had recently developed in his article on the 'Encounter Battle'. 'We have got to develop new methods, and learn a new technique,' he insisted. 'If he [the commander] has no plan, he will find that he is being made to conform gradually to the enemy's plan.' Highly relevant to his own handling of far larger formations in the coming war was his emphasis that the commander had to have his headquarters 'well forward – he will then gain the earliest possible information . . . and issue orders to subordinates before their units arrive . . .'. The accent of the exercise, like almost all British army strategy since Marlborough, was naturally enough on the defensive, not offensive. In the course of the manoeuvres, Monty's newly appointed brigade major, Frank Simpson (nicknamed 'Simbo', another pre-war acquaintance who, 'picked up' by Monty subsequently, would play a most important part in his career in north-west Europe), records the Brigadier's stunned rage at the performance of a Yeomanry colonel. When told by a subaltern that he was being 'fired on' by a machine gun and therefore couldn't advance, the Colonel 'bellowed with rage and said: "Damn it, boy, you have a horse, go and catch the bloody gun!" ' To 'Simbo' Monty declared, 'these people didn't understand war'. It was yet another mark against the 'cavalry amateurs' noted down in Monty's elephantine memory.

Despite the war clouds, his married life with Betty seemed at a zenith. Then suddenly, out of the bluest of blue skies, tragedy struck. In the light of modern standards of medicine, what happened seems almost inconceivable. Betty had returned from India suffering from mild laryngitis; they had two months' leave, touring the Lake District, when Bernard noted that she 'seemed to be weaker than formerly and easily got tired', but was 'always cheerful and happy'. She then took nine-year-old David to the seaside, to Burnham-on-Sea. There, according to Monty's account, Betty 'was stung on the foot by some insect; she could not say what sort of insect it was, and this was never known. That night her leg began to swell and became painful; a doctor was called and he put her at once into the local Cottage hospital, and sent for me.'*

For what ensued, Monty has been open to censure. While he

* Montgomery, *Memoirs*, p. 43.

was away on his brigade manoeuvres, Betty's condition was rapidly worsening. With hindsight, it might be argued that Monty should have dropped everything to be at her side, or have had her moved to a hospital better qualified to cope with her exceptional malady. But his mind was totally on what was happening on Salisbury Plain – not solely on account of its importance, selfishly, to his own career, but also with his awareness of how close war now was. Equally, it is doubtful whether he (or anyone else) realized the gravity of her condition. In September, one of the few who came to see Betty regularly with little David was Jocelyn, the twenty-one-year-old fiancée of John Carver. Jocelyn recalled her lying 'in great pain':

> her trouble was not properly diagnosed by the very limited staff. I think there was only one visiting doctor, and I only saw the matron. . . . Monty did come to see his wife but he did not visit us until it was time to take David back to school. At the beginning he told me not to contact anyone about Betty's illness; of course I was in touch with my parents but I didn't know anyone else in the rest of the family at the time. I did wonder why no one got in touch; Betty was so lonely and Monty was totally involved with his new command. . . . Even I knew that she was extremely ill and needed a specialist, but I didn't even write to John about it because there was nothing he could do, and I suppose Monty felt the same.*

It was a gigantic responsibility for a young girl, still not even a member of the family. After David went back to school, Betty's cousin, Katie Hobart, rushed over from Ireland, deeply concerned, to take over. On 9 October, she wrote to the Carver sons:

> There is no straightforward progress – it's a very up and down business, and though today she is ever so much better – and she has been since Monday – she is still not as well as she was a week ago. . . . I think it is really the poison in her system . . . also the different serum injections which she gets have strange effects. . . . She has very severe pain in the good leg and one elbow. . . .
>
> Poor Monty. His cut and dried plans miscarry. He had 'time-tabled' that she was to be moved to Portsmouth last week, then it was to be today; I am quite certain she would not be fit for this,

* Interview 23 November 1992.

and the doctors forbade it. Monty, I feel, has still to learn that in serious illness things do not work out according to plan like ordering an advance at dawn!*

On the 15th, six days later, Katie was writing to Jocelyn:
I am terribly sorry to say that poor Betty is much worse; her lungs are now affected by the poisoning and she has great difficulty in breathing. She became so bad that night that the doctor sent for Bernard, who arrived yesterday. . . . I am sorry to give such depressing news but things are very serious at present. . . .

In an attempt to arrest the spread of the inexplicable blood poisoning through her system, Betty's leg was amputated. Monty began to prepare Ravelin House, the new army quarters at Portsmouth, for an invalid. But it was clear she was dying of septicaemia. On 19 October 1937, she died in his arms as he read the Twenty-third Psalm to her. As her life had ebbed away, the actions of Monty, totally distraught, became unnaturally obsessive to the point of derangement. He refused to let the Carver sons fly home from India and would not allow David to come to the hospital in his mother's last days or to attend the funeral. Many years later, he explained in his memoirs, '. . . I could not bring myself to let him see her suffering. He was only nine years old and was happy at school; after the funeral I went to his school and told him myself. Perhaps I was wrong, but I did what I thought was right.' It was ever his fall-back position, but in his sequestration of David now it was almost as if he blamed himself for her death – who can ever know? When his sister Winsome offered to take David immediately into her home, he replied, 'No thank you very much; I'll look after him myself.' Later, in the warm friendship of old age, Basil Liddell Hart once referred to Betty in a manner that might have seemed mildly critical of his treatment of her; Monty turned in icy rage and said, 'Never mention her name again.'

There now began for young David, motherless only child with a father henceforth wedded only to his profession, and moving constantly from army post to army post, a childhood as grim as any out

* Montgomery Collection.

of the Victorian era. He never complained. On the bonus side, the bereavement marked the beginning of an enormous affection for Jocelyn, shortly to marry John Carver, 'as she was with me at a very crucial time of my life'. That first Christmas, alone with his inconsolable father he remembered always as particularly 'dreadful', even though he was bought a new train set. 'There was a frightful atmosphere of gloom,' Jocelyn recalled. Monty would let none of the rest of the family anywhere near him. Many of his army colleagues put out helping hands; among the few whose hand he accepted was his brigade major, 'Simbo' Simpson, who had efficiently carried on the Salisbury Plain exercises during the times Monty was away at Betty's side and who 'now proved his worth', wrote Brian Montgomery, 'as a friend and counsellor also'. He was 'a tower of strength', recorded Monty himself. But Monty was knocked sideways. To Dick Carver in India, in one of those rare letters in which he opened his heart, he wrote:

> But, oh Dick, it is hard to bear and I am afraid I break into tears whenever I think of her. But I must try to bear up. I have come back alone to this big empty house for good now. And I get desperately lonely and sad. I suppose in time I shall get over it, but at present it seems that I never shall.

For days he remained alone in Ravelin House, and would see no one. 'I was utterly defeated,' he wrote in his memoirs:

> I began to search my mind for anything I had done wrong, that I should have been dealt such a shattering blow. I could not understand it; my soul cried out in anguish against this apparent injustice. I seemed to be surrounded by utter darkness; all the spirit was knocked out of me. I had no one to love except David and he was away at school.

As far as this study is concerned, the important question one has to ask is: to what extent did this 'shattering blow' affect Monty's future career? History has many examples of great leaders forged by reverses in their private lives, by imprisonment or by bereavement, by the frustration of long years in the political wilderness (like Winston Churchill and Charles de Gaulle), or by the infidelity of a wife (like Harold Macmillan). The question may properly be asked:

had he not lost so tragically the one person who had given him what he had always been denied by his *repoussante* mother – total love and belief in his own ability – would Monty still have ended up the indomitable general, the self-assured victor of Alamein and Normandy? Many of those who were closest to him challenge this hypothesis, insisting that his great professionalism would still have carried him through to the top; David Montgomery believes that he would have been subject to 'fewer ego trips, but otherwise the same'. But there is no doubt that, whether or not it sharpened his professional edge, the death of Betty left him emotionally impoverished. As it was, he returned to being much the same person that he had been before Betty – the self-contained solitary, awkward and unclubbable with his contemporaries. And here one detects the seeds of future conflict with his peers, most particularly with the clubbable Eisenhower, that were to have such baneful consequences in the coming war. With Betty still there to tease him and mollify him, can one not guess that he would have been a much less intractable colleague, less susceptible to that abrasive arrogance and intolerable intolerance which so clung to and muddied his reputation?

What is indisputable is that, in the words of brother Brian, he 'remarried his profession'. He was now a junior brigadier of fifty, an age at which, in Britain's post-1945 army, he would have had the prospect of imminent retirement. But, once he had got over his immediate grief, Monty threw himself into soldiering with a kind of frenzied dedication that those who suffered from it considered almost akin to madness. (One is, however, reminded of King George II's remark to similar detractors of James Wolfe of Quebec fame: 'Mad, is he? Then I hope he will *bite* some of my other generals!') Sane to a fault in one respect, though, he was motivated by an acute sense of just how little time there was. Germany, urged on by the maniacal Hitler to seek revenge for the humiliation of 1918, was forging the most lethal offensive apparatus in the history of war, utilizing and adapting the teachings of Liddell Hart to produce the new concept of the *Blitzkrieg*.

Meanwhile, the British Army went on its way, concentrating on the priorities of Imperial defence, concerning itself only tardily with the prospects of fighting a European war once again – with the exception of a few voices in the wilderness, like those of Monty and

Brooke, crying out for reform. Studying intelligence reports about current Wehrmacht training, Monty began to press his battalion commanding officers to train up their junior officers to take over larger units, even the battalion, in the event of heavy casualties. (Yet, one has to remind oneself again, he was essentially ever the *reformer*, not a radical or a revolutionary, and stopped short of German techniques of training up senior NCOs for such responsibilities; this even a Monty would have regarded in the 1930s as striking too deeply at the heart of the British Army's long-established caste system.)

In the summer of 1938, the last before the war, Brigadier Montgomery found himself down on Slapton Sands, in charge of the first joint-services amphibious operation since disastrous Gallipoli in 1915. What would have happened to this modest forerunner of OVERLORD, six years later, in the teeth of a defending Wehrmacht appals the imagination. Only one 'so-called landing craft' could be dug out for the exercise; for the rest, the troops landed in open rowing boats as they had done for the previous 200 years. But Monty's staff-work was impeccable; so was his detailed report at the end, though his naval opposite number in his commentary remarked acidly, 'This is not a report but a hymn of self-praise.' General Archibald Wavell, the general in charge of the exercise and not a man easily piqued, was evidently put out by one caustic shaft by Monty. An officer of the Scottish Black Watch, Wavell had enquired innocently about the disadvantages of the kilt in the event of contamination by a gas attack, to which Monty had retorted, 'I understand that the best Scotchmen do not wear drawers under the kilt; the result, therefore, might be very unpleasant.'

Nevertheless Wavell, who in just two years' time was to become one of Monty's unhappy predecessors in the Western Desert, wrote him a glowing report: 'one of the clearest brains we have in the higher ranks, an excellent trainer of troops . . .'. There followed the invariable caveat, though masterly in its understatement: 'He has some of the defects of the enthusiast, in an occasional impatience and intolerance when things cannot be done as quickly as he would like or when he meets brains less quick and clear than his own. . . .' It was on the basis of Wavell's recommendation that Monty was now appointed to take command of the 8th Division in strife-torn Palestine (then a British mandatory territory), to be followed – when the post became vacant, foreseeably in the near future – with that of the 3rd Division back in England. This was promotion, and a major breakthrough; in the event of war, the 3rd Division, an elite regular unit, would form part of the British Expeditionary Force (BEF) to be sent at once to France.

Before Monty embarked for Palestine, however, there took place in Portsmouth an episode which, parochial in itself, was typical of Monty's high-handedness, and came close to wrecking his career, now at last so clearly in the ascendant. To raise cash for his brigade's married families' welfare fund, off his own bat Monty rented the garrison football field to Portsmouth City Council for a fair. It was government property, and the Brigadier had sought no one's approval; the War Office was furious and demanded repayment of the money. Monty replied that it had already been spent. Fortunately he was able to show, naturally, that not a penny had gone into the coffers of the officers' mess or into his own pocket. It was nevertheless an irregularity for which lesser officers had been asked to leave the service, and momentarily his career hung in the balance – 'dicky on the perch', as he put it.

In October 1938 Monty set off for Palestine, having parked David on army friends, the Carthews, near Portsmouth. For the next ten years, father and son would be almost completely separated, and David would have no home that he could call his own. Palestine, where the Arabs were in revolt against British policy, limited as it was, of resettlement of the Jews, was largely an anti-terrorist police operation. This Monty handled with predictable efficiency during the few months he was there, all the time training up his officers for the bigger test ahead. Before relinquishing his command, he left behind him a detailed memorandum which was to form the basis for the future control of the Mandate – crucial as it would be to the British war effort.

In April 1939, one month after Hitler had moved into Czechoslovakia, Monty was called home – earlier than expected – to take over the 3rd Division. He replied that he was ready, and would forgo any leave owing to him: 'I am fit and well and thrive on plenty of work.' Once again fate intervened; a few days later he was stricken with a high fever and what seemed like pleurisy. In June X-rays suggested tuberculosis in his good lung. In a very bad way, he was shipped home on a stretcher, accompanied by two nurses and two male orderlies. Then a miracle occurred. At the end of the sea voyage, Monty 'walked off the ship at Tilbury in good health'. A three-day examination at Millbank Hospital revealed 'that nothing was wrong with me. I asked about the patch on my lung; it had disappeared. . . .' That there should have been two such wrong diagnoses in as many years, first Betty, then Monty, may say something about the doctors in those days; but the second may equally be taken as a proof of the wiry little soldier's extraordinary power of mind over matter. This was certainly how his sister Winsome saw it. She had travelled home on the same ship, anxiously watching over his recovery while the ship's doctor insisted that he would 'never see action' in the coming war. 'It was just sheer guts,' she reckoned. 'He wasn't going to give in. . . . He had Betty's photographs in the cabin. . . .' One decision, however, was enforced on Monty by this illness: he would never smoke again – nor would he permit any 'passive smoking' in his presence.

It was August 1939; Britain stood on the brink of war. But before Monty could take over the promised command of his new division there was yet another, bureaucratic hitch. Upon mobilization all previous appointments automatically lapsed. Monty's predecessor, though selected to be governor of Bermuda, was to remain nominally still in command. It was a ridiculous situation for one of Britain's all-too-few crack units to find itself in. 'Here is a division,' Monty fumed to 'Simbo' Simpson, 'getting ready for battle and it has no Divisional Commander at all. It is just drifting aimlessly at the moment. . . . The Divisional Commander is enjoying himself in Ireland. . . .' Just conceivably the procrastination in transfer of the 3rd Division to Major-General Montgomery also reflected, once more, his unpopularity in the higher military echelons. Monty appealed to the GOC (General Officer Commanding) Southern Command, who was now his old friend, Lieutenant-General Sir Alan Brooke. Not for the last time, Brooke intervened successfully on his behalf. Monty received his command on 28 August 1939. Four days later Hitler invaded Poland.

CHAPTER TWO

AT WAR AGAIN

1939–1943

Nations have passed away and left no traces,
And history gives the naked cause of it –
One single, simple reason in all cases;
They fell because their peoples were not fit.

(Rudyard Kipling, Preface to *Land and Sea Tales*)

no point in going into the cavalry nowadays. All these machines . . . there is a lot of damn-fool talk about this being a mechanized war and an air war and a commercial war. All wars are infantry wars, and always have been . . .

(Lieutenant-Colonel of the Bombardiers, in Evelyn Waugh, *Put Out More Flags*)

I was never embarrassed by the Germans, nor do I propose to be in the future . . .

(Montgomery, to XII Corps officers, 30 June 1941)

AT THE beginning of October 1939, the BEF's 3rd Division – already nicknamed the 'Iron Division' – took up its position around the key French city of Lille. It was only a short distance from Méteren, where Lieutenant Montgomery had been wounded almost exactly twenty-five years previously. In terms of cycles of history, the two world wars had succeeded each other with frightening swiftness. In purely military terms, Major-General Montgomery was as well prepared for the challenge as any other officer in the British Army. There was no more dedicated professional, and he had commanded every unit from a platoon upwards. He was a superb trainer of younger men, to whom he was able to impart his own extraordinary *esprit de corps* and sense of allegiance. His self-confidence was immeasurable; he was going to command the most effective division in the BEF – and he was going to win the war. Yet, to a psychiatrist, that indestructible self-confidence might have seemed to be covering up mountainous chips on the shoulder, the massive inferiority complex of a small man whose social life in the army had been stunted by lack of money, whose emotions remained atrophied from his mother's lack of maternal love, and who was still deeply bruised from the death of his wife only two years previously. He was a peacetime misfit, abrasive and awkward to his colleagues and his superiors alike.

In France, what Monty found filled him swiftly with contempt for both the Commander-in-Chief, Lord Gort VC ('the job was above his ceiling') and, more ferociously, the Secretary of State for War, Leslie Hore-Belisha, who was never to be forgiven his boast that 'Our army is as well if not better equipped than any similar army.' Palpably it was not, as events were swiftly to demonstrate. Fortunately for Monty (and for Britain) his corps commander, and immediate senior, was the man he respected most in the British Army: Lieutenant-General Alan Brooke. As a pugnacious Ulsterman, Monty says 'my soul revolted' when, during the Phoney War, 'France and Britain stood aside while Germany swallowed Poland,' and continued to stand while the Wehrmacht prepared its attack in the West. Little that Monty saw of his allies impressed him at this time. He deplored the way the French buried themselves beneath their 'invincible' Maginot Line, hoping they would not be attacked, just as he deplored the boastful slogans like 'Ils ne passeront pas' and 'Nous gagnerons parce que nous sommes les plus forts!', products of a grossly inflated false optimism that bore little reality to what acute observers like Monty and Brooke could see with their own eyes. It all spurred Monty on, regardless of weather conditions during a particularly harsh winter, to drive his Iron Division in exercise after exercise. He instituted modern co-ordinated operations of all arms, which were still curiously unfamiliar to British units. Having studied the terrible mayhem wreaked by the Luftwaffe on the Polish Army caught moving in daylight, in particular he made his tired troops repeatedly practise night movements, which he had perfected while in Egypt in 1932/33, and which in his later battles from Alamein to Normandy would bear the particular Monty hallmark. He also established his reputation for ruthlessly sacking senior officers whom he deemed 'useless, quite useless', sending them off to be railway transport officers on French railway stations, where their restricted talents were better employed.

It was during the Phoney War that Monty, consulting his little black book in which he entered the name of every officer who caught his fancy, made the first recruitments for his famous TAC HQ, his personal court that was to stay with him through the rest of the war. Having sacked his Divisional Intelligence Officer for incompetence, he ordered one of his brigadiers to send him his 'best young officer'. The Brigadier, a fierce Coldstreamer called Jack Whitaker, unafraid of Monty and determined not to lose his elite staff, sent him a temporary wartime soldier, a young merchant banker called Christopher 'Kit' Dawnay. Dawnay was amazed to be ordered to start by taking all his meals with the General in his mess; but he remained, later running TAC HQ right through to Lüneburg Heath.* Another early recruit was Charles Sweeny of the Ulster Rifles, to be his first ADC. In his memoirs, Monty wrote unashamedly, 'He was a delightful Irish boy and I loved him dearly.' The word 'love' occasionally misinterpreted in a subsequent, prurient age to mean something rather more, this affection for – and deep loyalty towards – his 'young men' was something profoundly characteristic of Monty. It was to provide the strength, and weaknesses, of his highly personal style of command.

Meanwhile, with his concern about the welfare of the troops being ever a top priority, he got himself once again into serious trouble, reminiscent of the Portsmouth football-field episode. This time it came over his rather insensitive wording of a detailed, five-point order dealing with venereal disease, the prevalence of which was causing alarm in the BEF. Laying down the need for readily accessible Early Treatment Rooms, Monty – with perfect reason – observed that 'the man who has a woman in a beetroot field near his coy. billet will not walk a mile to the battalion E.T. room'. But the senior chaplain at GHQ was outraged, passing on his indignation to Gort, who considered the order improper and told Brooke that the

* It is worth noting that in Dawnay, Monty chose an officer from the army elite, the 'amateurs' in whom he had found so much to criticize in peacetime days. Surprisingly many of his subsequent 'discoveries' would equally be non-regulars – guardsmen, like Carol Mather, or cavalrymen, like Johnny Henderson. And they served him well.

divisional commander should withdraw it. Such an action would have been almost tantamount to sacking him. Once again Brooke intervened to save Monty, while administering a severe 'blasting'. 'I informed him that I had a very high opinion of his military capabilities and an equally low one of his literary ones!' Brooke recorded. It was about the last occasion that Monty failed to take a 'blasting' from Brooke seriously. Incongruous as it may seem, given his subsequent reputation as a Cromwellian puritan, riding to battle with the Bible and John Bunyan, there was that underlying mischievous sense of humour (what brother Brian called an 'imp of mischief') that persisted in seeing the droll side of the row – where Brooke could see none. The incident also revealed in Monty, however, that essential lack of sensitivity that would later lead him into so much trouble with the Americans.

On 10 May 1940 came the German *Blitzkrieg* in the West, for which Monty had been training his division during the eight months of Phoney War. To keyed-up professional soldiers, it was in many ways almost a relief. The story of the next few weeks has been told elsewhere.* In accordance with the plan of the French Commander-in-Chief, General Gamelin, following the invasion of neutral Belgium the cream of the French Army and the BEF moved rapidly forward to the line of the River Dyle – straight into the trap which Hitler's General von Manstein had so cunningly laid. Meanwhile the Führer's ten crack Panzer divisions, including one brilliantly commanded by Monty's future opponent, Erwin Rommel, were hooking southwards through the supposedly impenetrable Ardennes. When they emerged from the forests, they struck with devastating force on the hinge of two French armies, Huntziger's Second and Corap's Ninth, comprised mainly of B divisions of elderly reservists. It was a perfect combination of Liddell Hart's 'indirect approach' and his doctrine – so little heeded in Britain – of the 'expanding torrent', and Monty's principle of concentrating all on one particular point. In the air, the Allies were seriously outclassed and outnumbered. In terms of armour, the crucial factor of the campaign, the French actually had more tanks – many of them with thicker armour and heavier guns – than the Germans. But they were dispersed in 'penny packets' and

* See Horne, *To Lose a Battle*.

were mopped up piecemeal. Though they managed, briefly, to upset Rommel in one minor action at Arras when the battle was already lost, the British were little better off in armour than the French. Had they been able to commit more armoured units, these too would only have been rounded up in the general humiliation.

The overriding fact was that General von Rundstedt, the German commander (whose triumph would encourage him to have 'another go' across the same terrain four-and-a-half years later), was marching to one of the most brilliant blueprints in the history of warfare – Manstein's *Sichelschnitt*. Most important, the young German soldiers were full of self-confidence – what Monty called 'binge'. Morale was high; in the French Army it was very low. Given all the ingredients, and the forces in hand, the issue was virtually decided by 15 May, the fifth day of battle when the Panzers burst across the Meuse at Sedan into open country.

Monty described his division as having executed its move forward to the River Dyle near Louvain 'perfectly', apart from a minor altercation when an officious Belgian frontier guard tried to halt its passage on the ground that it did not possess the necessary permits. There was still an element of unreality about it all – the older officers were retracing footsteps as if in a dream – and they advanced virtually unopposed by the Germans. With the BEF, a certain 'Kim' Philby, representing *The Times* and showing an astuteness which would later bring some advantage to another employer, remarked apprehensively to an American colleague, 'It went too damn well. With all that air power why didn't he bother us? What is he up to?' The answer soon came. Ordered to defend Louvain, Monty found an elderly Belgian general who refused to hand over to the 3rd Division. In a rare moment of tact (possibly he had learned something from his VD 'blasting'), Monty told him that he would 'unreservedly' place his unit under the Belgian's command. To an apprehensive Brooke he explained that, once the Germans had arrived, 'I then place the Division Commander under strict arrest and I take command!' Waiting for that attack on Louvain, Monty explains in his memoirs how it was there that he developed his habit of going to bed early and giving orders that he was 'never to be disturbed except in a crisis'. He was angered when, disregarding this instruction, an orderly officer had the nerve to wake him to report that the Germans had 'got into Louvain': 'The staff officer was amazed when I said: "Go away and don't bother me. Tell the brigadier in Louvain to turn them out." I then went to sleep again.'*

HQ 3rd Division had taken over the small château at nearby Everberg belonging to Prince de Merode, who was passionately attached to his excellent wines. Though it is improbable that the abstemious Monty should have been aware of it, members of his headquarters staff appear to have 'emptied the cellar', to the good Prince's rage. When the Germans arrived a few days later, so the Princesse recalls with loaded emphasis, they were 'très aimables, très corrects'. As the retreat began in May 1940, Monty assured the Princesse – like MacArthur – 'I shall return.' As good as his word, in September 1944 he returned, now a field marshal; this time his officers were 'impeccable'. In May 1940, however, the stay at Everberg was a short one for Monty. Within a matter of days, 3rd Division was on the move again, falling back on Dunkirk. Wrote Monty proudly in an unusually poetic passage in his memoirs, it did 'everything that was demanded of it; it was like a ship with all sails set in a rough sea, which rides the storm easily and answers to the slightest touch on the helm.' The most testing moment came on the 27th, when in the midst of a raging battle Monty had to move his division sideways to fill a gap left by the collapsing Belgians. He chose to move by night, putting into practice all the training of the past months, saving the BEF from being outflanked and incidentally creating something of a legend in the wretched saga of the retreat. 'There is no doubt', recorded Brooke, 'that one of Monty's strong points is his boundless confidence in himself. He was priceless on this occasion, and I thanked Heaven to have a commander of his calibre to undertake this march.'

In excellent fighting order, the 3rd Division reached Dunkirk. Among the sand-dunes, there took place a painfully emotional scene with General Brooke, ordered by the War Office to sail to England, leaving Monty to bring home his corps. Brooke wrote that he 'felt like a deserter, not remaining with it to the last'. This normally phlegmatic man was on the verge of tears when Monty met him, 'so I took him a little way into the sand hills and then he broke down

* Montgomery, *Memoirs*, p. 61.

and wept'. Brian Horrocks, then commanding a battalion of the Middlesex Regiment and later Monty's favourite corps commander, was astonished to find Brooke in this state: 'his shoulders were bowed and it looked as though he were weeping. Monty was patting him on the back. Then they shook hands and General Brooke walked slowly to his car and drove away.'*

While standing on those same beaches, Monty's young ADC, Charles Sweeny of the Ulster Rifles, was wounded in the head slightly by a shell-splinter: 'I cursed him soundly for not wearing his steel helmet, quite forgetting that I was not wearing one myself – as he pointed out!' The episode was significant in that it revealed Monty taking what might be considered 'cheek' from a very junior officer, which he would not have taken from one more senior – a phenomenon that would assume importance as the Monty legend unfolded.

Now (briefly) a temporary corps commander, Monty embarked for Dover on the morning of 1 June with the remains of Brooke's II Corps, but without any of their heavy equipment. He was later to claim that he had never been 'embarrassed by the Germans', but they had certainly embarrassed the BEF. Within three weeks, France had capitulated. Britain was left alone, and absurdly vulnerable. Alas, for all Churchill's caution about wars not being won by evacuations, the 'miracle of Dunkirk' was to obscure – from all but a few like Monty – the terrible inadequacy in the British Army which had led to what was in all reality a most humiliating defeat. Thus another miserable two years of evacuations and débâcles were to ensue before the lessons were learned and the tide of defeats turned. Coupled with what he found in England, the humiliation of Dunkirk sent Monty into a fierce rage and he set to tackling it with a ferocious single-mindedness that at times seemed to verge on the manic – particularly to those in his path. After Dunkirk, in the whole country there were just enough transport and heavy arms to equip *one* division; these were given to Monty's 3rd Division, to the command of which he returned on reaching England. He issued orders banning leave for personnel to go home to their families; the solitary widower, with no home to go to himself, he pointed the way by not even going to

* Horrocks, *A Full Life*, p. 85.

see his eleven-year-old son David after Dunkirk. In the aftermath of the nightmare of the retreat from Belgium, it was an insensitive and wildly unpopular order and soon had to be rescinded; but still he persisted in refusing to allow wives and families to live within the operational area.

Within two weeks of disembarking, Monty issued a five-page order analysing the 'Important Lessons' learned in France; three days later he summoned all 466 officers of the division to the first of his great wartime mass addresses. It was prefaced by a new rule: a three-minute interval for throat-clearing, then no coughing once he had begun to speak.

Transferred to defend the Sussex coast against the anticipated German invasion, Monty was appalled to discover that his division was supposed to dig in with a purely linear defence all along the beach. On 2 July, he had his first encounter with Prime Minister Churchill, who was paying an official visit to this crucial sector. He made an instant mark, at dinner, by refusing to drink or smoke, adding that he was therefore 'one hundred per cent fit', to which Churchill retorted 'in a flash that he both drank and smoked and was two hundred per cent fit'. Forthrightly – and rather courageously, given Churchill's known detestation for anything that might smack of defeatism – he remarked, 'I don't see how on earth we can win this war,' to which came the reply, 'Nor do I.' Monty followed up by pointing out that, now the best equipped in the whole army, his division was nevertheless condemned to a static defence. He recommended that it should be withdrawn behind the coast, provided with commandeered civilian buses to give it mobility and employed in a counter-attack role. Characteristically, Churchill liked the idea, and Monty got his buses. More important, he had made an important impression on the all-powerful warlord, and vice versa. Though the two events were probably no more than coincidental, three weeks later, on 22 July, he was promoted lieutenant-general and given command of a corps.

By his own account, his taking over of V Corps – located in Hampshire and Dorset – marked the beginning of his 'real influence in the training of the Army then in England'. From it were derived all the doctrines that he was to take out to Africa, and to bring back for D-Day in 1944. His first priority was fitness, 'physical and mental', quoting with relish his favourite lines from Kipling:

> Nations have passed away and left no traces,
> And history gives the naked cause of it –
> One single, simple reason in all cases;
> They fell because their peoples were not fit.

Officers had to be 'full of binge'; in the Monty context this meant that 'they must look forward to a good fight'. When inspecting troops, he requested that they should remove their steel helmets so that he could see whether or not their eyes were 'full of binge', the light of battle. Woe betide the commanding officer if they were not. In the worst of weathers, ancient members of the staff were turned out for their weekly seven-mile runs. With those he considered 'useless, quite useless', Monty was ruthless. To a stout colonel, whose doctor had warned that the run would kill him, he observed that he should get it over with, so that he 'could be replaced easily and smoothly'. Another ancient commanding officer who had seen service in the Boer War was 'a really decrepit sight . . . very old, frail, and looks very ill. He should be removed from command at once and sent away to end his life in peace somewhere. . . .' In the same unit, the unfortunate Quartermaster was damned as 'idle and has taken to drink. . . . his services should be dispensed with at once and he should be sent back to his farm . . .'.

These were the kind of remarks that would never be forgotten, or forgiven, and would later rebound to plague Monty. There were occasions when even some of his fans began to think the new corps commander might be a bit unhinged. By August even Brooke (now promoted to the key job of Commander-in-Chief Home Forces) appended a note of caution to a letter in which he congratulated Monty on his new post: 'I know you well enough also, Monty, to give you a word of warning against doing wild things. You have a name for annoying people at times with your ways, and I have found difficulties in backing you at times against this reputation.' The reproof would become standard fare over the years.

Nevertheless, it was unmistakable that the Monty medicine was working. Brian Urquhart, who later in the war had the dire responsibility of being the Airborne Intelligence Officer in the run-up to

Arnhem and thus had 'bitter cause to doubt Montgomery's judgement and to detest his egocentricity', nevertheless retained the most vivid memory of attending one of Monty's first mass pep-talks, in a Folkestone cinema in May 1941:

> when the war seemed endless and unwinnable, he made a tremendous impression. Whatever else he may have been, Montgomery was a genius at morale-building and training, and we desperately needed both. I don't remember exactly what he said, but he appeared to take us into his confidence, and we left the cinema with a feeling of at last having a leader in full charge. We also had the feeling that if we didn't shape up, he personally would find out and ship us out.*

By the end of 1940, V Corps had proved its battleworthiness in a series of massive exercises and was 'full of binge'. With his dread of the troops getting into trenches and becoming 'Maginot-minded', Monty had got it away from the coast and transformed it into an efficiently mobile force. It was still basically defence-minded, yet the immediate threat of Operation SEALION, the invasion of Britain, had passed as Hitler's mind moved eastwards.

On 10 January 1941, Monty was struck by another personal tragedy. Having closed down his last home at Ravelin House, Portsmouth, in 1938, he had stored all his furniture and family belongings in a warehouse. During an air raid that night, an incendiary bomb razed it to the ground, destroying all Monty's precious mementoes of his life with Betty. He had no home, and now no belongings. He took it philosophically: it was war – the loss was less serious, to him, than 3rd Division leaving all its guns behind in France. But that first Christmas after Dunkirk must have been another grim one for David. In the 1920s one of Monty's oft pronounced maxims had been 'You cannot make a good soldier and a good husband.' When his own engagement was announced, his surprised fellow officers (led by Freddie de Guingand) sent him a cable: 'Which is it to be, the soldier or the husband?' Monty may well have been unamused; no acknowledgement was forthcoming. But one thing was certain – in

* Urquhart, *A Life in Peace and War*, p. 43.

his own behaviour he was to provide the worst possible example for being a 'good soldier and a good father'. In all Monty's complex make-up, nowhere were his idiosyncrasies more evident than in his treatment of his son, which showed up some of the less pleasant sides of his character. It often seems as if he had learned nothing from what he had suffered from his own unloving mother, source – as he himself would claim – of so much misery and personality-distortion in his own life.

One of his closest collaborators, Bill Williams, later gave the opinion that he 'treated David terribly – it broke our hearts to see it'.* His possessiveness was extreme; on Betty's death, he had already peremptorily refused his sister Winsome's spontaneous offer to be surrogate mother to the small boy; when war began, he gave strictest orders to David's various guardians that he was on no account ever to visit his grandmother, the redoubtable Maud, or any other member of the family.

There was a suggestion that David might have been sent, along with other 'Bundles from Britain', as an evacuee to Canada, but Monty promptly vetoed that – 'I wanted him in England.' Instead he was dumped on a Major Carthew, a serving officer in the Black Watch. Life became 'very mobile . . . we moved from place to place', recalled David. In August 1939, he had been on holiday in France with the Carthews when mobilization took place, 'and the French were all moving up north-east and we were going north-west – diagonally across them, so there was chaos and everybody was trying to get back'. After Carthew was recalled to the colours, David was sent back to his prep school, Amesbury, under the charge of the headmaster Tom Reynolds and his wife Phyllis. There he heard that war had broken out and his father despatched to France. His life continued nomadic, spent in a series of 'holiday homes for children'. At one of these in Devon, in 1941, which was run by 'an extraordinary old trout called Lottie Hogg' and which 'I absolutely adored', he fell from a second floor while climbing a drainpipe (a prelude to his more adventurous post-war days in Cambridge) and

* In all the forty-odd years that he has known him, his co-author has never once heard David Montgomery complain about his childhood, austere even by wartime standards, though Monty in his memoirs went so far as to admit, mildly, that it was 'an unsatisfactory life'.

broke his leg. 'An ADC was despatched to fetch me and I was never allowed back there again.' Without family or home, he recalled (uncomplainingly) having no possessions; his beloved train set, given to console him after the death of his mother, disappeared in one of many wartime moves, having been placed in the care of an army colonel whose name David lost. For the ten, spartan years following his mother's death, he was to see virtually nothing of his father, growing up with the minimum rapport between them. Following the drain-pipe episode, he was transferred for an all-too brief spell into the care of his stepbrother's young wife, Jocelyn Carver, only twelve years older than himself.

At the end of 1940, General Wavell, Monty's GOC from pre-war days, brought Britain a much needed morale booster by his remarkable desert victories against Mussolini's forces, routing a far superior army and advancing deep into Cyrenaica. It was the kind of action, a colonial limited campaign, that the inter-war British Army had been trained for. But these were Italians, not Germans. In April 1941, Hitler lunged into Yugoslavia and Greece, pushing into the sea once again another British Expeditionary Force, troops which Wavell could ill lose but which Churchill had ordered to be sent to support the hard-pressed Greeks. In May, there was yet another humiliating evacuation, this time of Crete, which had been plucked from under the noses of the Royal Navy by German airpower and paratroopers. In the desert Rommel had appeared, sending Wavell's victorious forces reeling back into Egypt within two short weeks and capturing the commander, General O'Connor, Monty's contemporary and one of the brightest lights in the army. The whole tenor of war in the desert was now transformed: three separate sets of trained British troops joined the bag of prisoners lost at Dunkirk.

Then, on 22 June 1941, the most climactic day in the war to date, Hitler attacked the Soviet Union.

It was quite plain well before Operation BARBAROSSA began that Britain was now safe – at least temporarily – from invasion. Yet the emphasis still lay, nervously, on defence. In April 1941, Monty was transferred to command XII Corps in south-east England. Disappointingly, it was simply a sidestep and, with his aggressive instincts, he must have fretted that he had not been chosen to lead a unit to the Mediterranean battlefield.

On his departure from V Corps, he wrote to Kit Dawnay, explaining, 'One reason why I dislike going is that I shall not see so much of you. I have a very real affection for you, Kit, and I count you as a real friend.' He added that he was glad he had been able to get Dawnay to Staff College, and promised that he would later try to 'rope' him in to XII Corps. It was an extraordinary letter for a general in those days to write to a young major, but it perhaps typified the feeling Monty had already for his 'young men' and the powerful sense of loyalty that dominated their relationships – in both directions.

Within a fortnight, Monty was writing to Dawnay again, announcing with evident satisfaction:

> ... I rather fancy I burst in Kent like a 15″ shell, and it was needed!!
>
> Wives are being evacuated by train loads; it is just a matter as to whether the railways will stand the traffic....
>
> A number of heads are being chopped off – the bag to date is three brigadiers and six COs. The standard was very low.

This kind of boastfulness was hardly destined to increase his popularity. At the end of June, the week after Hitler invaded the Soviet Union, Monty launched his new, slothful corps on a four-day exercise with the revealing codename BINGE – to be succeeded by another called MORE BINGE. His verdict at the end of the first exercise was as damning as it could be: 'A great deal went wrong.... The army is not a mutual congratulation society; great issues are at stake; if we lose the battles in Kent we may lose the war.'

More heads rolled, to be replaced with more of his own cohorts – such as 'Simbo' Simpson, who had been so loyal at the time of Betty's death, to be his Brigadier General Staff (BGS), and Kit Dawnay, on his return from Staff College. Sometimes his excess of zeal led to unfairness, as when he sacked 'a perfectly good' intelligence officer because he was 'fat and had German connections'. The depressing fact was that good human material was spread very thin, as Brooke was to note in his diary for 31 March 1942: 'Half of our Corps and Divisional Commanders are totally unfit for their appointments; and yet if I were to sack them I could find no better.'

This was a terrible indictment on the state of the British Army after two-and-a-half years of war – drained as it was by all those men in prisoner-of-war camps. It was also perhaps indicative of the unpopularity acquired by Monty that so many months would go by without his name even being considered for promotion to a battlefield command. Not the least obstacle was the vicious, continuing row, reaching to Alamein and beyond, that he had with his superior, General Sir Claude Auchinleck.

All this hyperactivity of decapitation and new ideas might suggest that there was something frenzied in the atmosphere of a Monty headquarters. Far from it. Goronwy Rees (he who likened Monty to a Jack Russell terrier) was one of many to be impressed by the:

> air he had of extraordinary quietness and calm, as if nothing in the world could disturb his peace of mind. . . . And as one talked to him, one was aware all the time of the stillness and quietness that reigned all around him . . . as if even the birds were under a spell of silence; it was a kind of stillness one might associate more easily with a priest than a general.*

In November 1941, Monty was at last promoted (though he still maintained the rank of lieutenant-general) to an army command as GOC South-Eastern Command. The following month, with the Japanese attack on Malaya, Britain found herself confronted by a new enemy just as menacing as the Wehrmacht, and the world battlefield expanded yet again. Following the losses in Greece, Crete and the Western Desert, troops were rushed to defend Singapore and Hong Kong, only to arrive in time to be made POWs. The units being built up so laboriously in Britain were depleted of another hundred thousand men. Of the British forces sent to Burma Brooke noted gloomily that they 'don't seem to be fighting well there either'. For officers with less self-assurance than Monty it must have been a heartrending process, frustrating in that he was in no position to reverse it.

Meanwhile, in Russia, after being checked at the gates of Moscow in December 1941, Hitler's hordes, numbering at one point nearly 200 divisions – virtually the whole Wehrmacht, except for Rommel's

* Rees, *A Bundle of Sensations*, p. 136.

handful of highly professional veterans of the Afrika Korps – plunged on once again. By the end of the summer campaign of 1942, they had reached the high point of their advance – deep in the Caucasus and penetrating as far as Stalingrad on the Volga. All of them, on the vast Eastern Front and in the Western Desert alike, were gaining battle experience of inestimable value, something which was denied all but the few divisions of General Auchinleck's newly constituted Eighth Army.

In Britain, Monty's own training programme was reaching a new pitch of intensity, but what substitute could there be for the actual battlefield, with all its brutality, surprises and lessons? He became the first British commander to develop close tactical support with the air force, something which the Germans had already raised to a high state of perfection by 1940. In close conjunction with Brooke, he saw to it that each of the new British armoured divisions contained at least one lorry-borne infantry brigade – as had the Germans when they crossed the Meuse in 1940. He studied successful Soviet techniques of carrying infantry into the attack on the backs of tanks. (Meanwhile, in Russia, the Germans were now bringing up their infantry close behind the Panzers in cross-country armoured troop-carriers.) He developed the lessons he had gained in the First World War, the need for flexibility in regrouping – what later came to be closely linked with the key Monty formula of 'balance' – and the need to operate, on the offensive, by means of one or more concentrated attacks on relatively narrow fronts, instead of mass efforts against a wide front. 'Concentration – control – simplicity' was the secret formula he dinned into his officers. Above all, he was crystallizing his philosophy of leadership. The leader, as he developed the theme in his memoirs, has to see his objective clearly and let everyone else know what he wants; he must begin with a very firm 'grip' on his military machine; he must never bring his subordinates back to confer with him, he must go forward (a view that would cause much conflict with the Americans from Normandy onwards); he himself must live in tranquillity, removed from all the exhaustion imposed by detail;* he must be able to exercise 'direct and personal' command,

* Here, in later life, he was fond of quoting a notional epitaph to a high government official: 'Here lies the man who died of exhaustion brought about by preoccupation with detail. He never had time to think because he was always reading papers. He saw every tree, but never the whole wood.'

to which end would follow his famous system, like his hero Wellington's, of fast-moving young liaison officers.

Above all came his belief that the morale of the soldier was 'the greatest single factor in war'. Belittling prevailing notions of the importance of welfare, NAAFI canteens and suchlike, he reckoned that morale was best enhanced by the assurance that, in battle, the general would never sacrifice his men's lives 'wastefully'. (Fierce battles of position, like Alamein and around Caen, however, would not always make it realizable.) In this context especially, the choice of trustworthy commanders was paramount. 'Probably a third of my working hours were spent in the consideration of personalities,' wrote Monty,* and it was almost certainly no exaggeration. The little black book in which were written down the names of officers, good and bad, greater and lesser, was always busy.

Finally, having achieved a clear head through the virtues of abstemiousness, it was essential for a leader to have 'a proper sense of religious truth; he must be prepared to acknowledge it, and to lead his troops in the light of that truth. He must always keep his finger on the spiritual pulse of his armies.'†

In the British Army of 1940–2, however, there were strict limits to what one small, not very popular, general could achieve. Constantly aware of being up against the great deadweight of tradition, Monty was nevertheless, as has already been noted of the inter-war years, himself a product of it. As a typical infantry officer, he placed too low a priority on the employment of the tank – despite all the lessons given by the Germans from 1939 onwards. The First World War had taught him, so his biographer tells us, that it 'had been won not by guns, tanks, aircraft, trenches or barbed wire – but by the manipulation of reserves. . . . The war, he knew, would never be won by tank production.'‡ If so, that was a fundamental error which came close to losing the war. Rarely, if ever, does one find Monty protesting to Brooke or the War Office about standards of heavy equipment. Possibly it was not in his power to do so; but, when one considers

* Montgomery, *Memoirs*, p. 85.

† *Ibid.*, p. 9.

‡ Hamilton, *Monty*, vol. I, p. 429.

all the other areas where Monty never feared to tread, this issue seems not to have assumed sufficiently high priority in his book. Yet, throughout the Second World War, it was to remain one of Britain's most serious weaknesses.

In the air, when Britain faced extinction in 1940, it was only largely thanks to the genius of one man, the designer of the Spitfire, that the RAF had a fighter the equal of (or better than) the Luftwaffe's. Apart from the Hurricane, much of the rest was inferior, as heroic pilots discovered when they tried to demolish the German pontoons across the Meuse in May 1940 with their feeble, outclassed Fairey Battle bombers. But far more disgraceful, and consistently so, was the story of Britain's inferiority in tank design, from the beginning of the war through to the end. By the time of the French campaign, the Germans had realized that their main armoury of light tanks, Mark Is and IIs, were underarmed and too lightly armoured, so they produced the Mark III, then the IV, the V and the VI – the dreaded Panthers and Tigers. By contrast, the British would always be a tank and a battle behind; it was not an error that the Soviets, with their brilliant T-34s – possibly the most effective tank of the war – were to repeat. In the desert, many young British tankers would die because their Crusader armour plate could not resist the impact of a Mark III Panzer's 50mm shell; while their own, smaller 2pdr, aimed by a crude shoulder pad, could seldom reach, let alone penetrate, its adversary. When the 6pdr came along (at Alamein), the Germans had the long 75mm; when the Americans introduced the excellent Sherman with its (low-velocity) 75, the Germans countered it with their 88mm – the most lethal gun on either side during the entire war. (Ironically, it was not until the war was over that Britain produced a good tank, the Centurion – which was, *inter alia*, to help a revolted colony, Israel, to win many of its battles.)

The story of Britain's tank inferiority all through the Second World War is one of the great disgraces of her military history. The blame has never been properly apportioned or the 'guilty men' named, but it must have lain at the top, far out of the reach of a simple army commander, however zealous a reformer. There were distinguished tank commanders, 'apostles of mobility', who fought under Monty in both the desert and Europe, like the future field marshal Michael Carver, and who were sharply critical of his myopia in this connection.* In Normandy, the baneful influence of this disgrace of tank design would be felt again and again.

By the summer of 1942, as the Red Army reeled back to the Volga, uncovering the Caucasus oilfields as it went as well as the back door to the Middle East, fears in Britain reinforced by memories of the August 1939 Molotov–Ribbentrop Pact that Stalin might quit the war became ever more nightmarish. Pressures mounted for the opening of a Second Front in the West. To the simplest private, this could only mean a direct frontal assault across the Channel. With the forces in hand, even with Americans slowly arriving – and arriving not only slowly but green – could it possibly be achieved that year or even the following year? To date, as we have noted, all training exercises in Britain had been essentially defensive, preparing for the German invasion that never came. Only in May 1942 did Monty initiate the first large-scale offensive manoeuvres; it was to be his last before leaving for Egypt and Alamein. Appropriately christened Operation TIGER, he described it as a 'real rough-house lasting at least ten days', and twenty years later called it 'the most strenuous exercise ever held in England'. One hundred thousand troops were involved, Monty's old XII Corps set against the new and unblooded Canadian Corps. It was the first time he had had Canadian commanders under him, and the views he formed (which he made little effort to conceal) of some of them, such as McNaughton and Crerar, were not auspicious; he held them guilty of 'playing politics' and 'bellyaching' – one of the most damning epithets in the Monty vocabulary. This early tension with Crerar in particular would bear its repercussions from D-Day onwards.

Another transatlantic VIP spectator at TIGER, making a first walk-on appearance in Monty's career, was a Major-General (temporary) Dwight D. Eisenhower, sent from Washington to press the British to a cross-Channel invasion by April 1943, codenamed (ambitiously) ROUNDUP. That first meeting, on 27 May, was equally inauspicious. Eisenhower's biographer,

* Monty's claim, in his *History of Warfare*, to have been powerfully influenced by Liddell Hart's thinking on armour is dismissed acidly by Carver in his *Apostles of Mobility* in one short sentence: 'It is difficult to detect it' (p. 79). See also pp. 175–83.

Stephen Ambrose, describes how he first struck his new American allies:

> . . . Montgomery wore a field greatcoat which emphasized his own small physical stature and tiny steps. He had a permanent scowl that gave him a crabbed look. He was, by nature, condescending, especially toward Americans, most of whom regarded him with extreme distaste. While he lectured, Eisenhower [an uncontrollable chain-smoker] calmly lit a cigarette. He had taken about two puffs when Montgomery broke off in mid-sentence, sniffed the air with his nose held high, and demanded, 'Who's smoking?'
>
> 'I am,' Eisenhower replied.
>
> 'I don't permit smoking in my office,' Montgomery said sternly.*

Not knowing the reason for Monty's smoking ban, Eisenhower, a man with a very short fuse,† almost exploded. Afterwards Kay Summersby, his recently appointed driver, without knowing the cause of his rage overheard him fuming in the back of the car to General Mark Clark. His voice had:

> turned harsh. I heard something about 'that son of a bitch' and started listening. He meant Monty. . . . he was furious – really steaming mad. And he was still mad. It was my first exposure to the Eisenhower temper. I sneaked a look in the rear-view mirror. His face was flaming red, and the veins in his forehead looked like worms.‡

This minor episode was not lightly forgotten, with Kay claiming that the relationship between the two men 'never got any better'. At the time, however, Eisenhower restrained himself to reporting when he returned to the States, with consummate mildness, that '. . . General Montgomery is a decisive type who appears to be extremely energetic and professionally able'. Monty's sole com-

* Stephen Ambrose, *Eisenhower*, vol. II, p. 69.

† 'Ike's damn Dutch temper' was how Ike's equally incendiary contemporary, Douglas MacArthur, rated it. After an early row with his boss, General Marshall, Eisenhower in a recognition of this failing gives a preview of the remarkable wisdom and restraint he would later display as Allied Supreme Commander, by writing in his diary the words: 'Anger cannot win, it cannot even think clearly' (*Ibid.*, pp. 65–6).

‡ Kay Summersby, *Past Forgetting*, pp. 25–6.

ment, in his memoirs, was: 'He wrote his name in my autograph book.'

Apart from this small delayed-action bomb, TIGER ended as yet another vindication for the Monty technique. He was trying out an innovation that would play a historic role in his two great setpiece battles, at Alamein and around Caen: to destroy enemy armoured formations 'by forcing him to attack our own armour on previously selected and occupied ground'. But by comparison with the rather more practical training undergone by the three million German troops locked daily in the titanic engagements on the Eastern Front, the 'rough-housing' experienced by the six divisions in TIGER was, inevitably, a mere drop in the bucket. As ancient colonels continued to collapse and die on runs, and umpires bustled about hypothetically on Salisbury Plain, the problem remained: after three years of consistent defeats, how was an army which had not won a single battle against its main adversary since the beginning of the war going to be shifted into forward gear? After the dreadful shock, still lingering, of being hurled into the sea in 1940, how long would it take before it risked *attacking* Germans in a major confrontation? It is perhaps all too easy to forget that, like most of the men under him, Monty had seen no shot fired in anger for over two years. Strange as it may seem, for a soldier decorated with the DSO who had fought in two world wars and commanded every formation in the British Army from a platoon upwards, it was also a fact – because of the combination of Méteren in 1914 and Dunkirk in 1940 – that up to Alamein Britain's most victorious fighting general had seen less than a total of ten weeks in action in both wars. Again, it was a disturbing fact to set against the experience being logged up by the Rundstedts and the Rommels.

On 19 August, under powerful pressure from the Americans, underpinned by Churchill's own irresistible impatience for action, the first major landing in north-west Europe since 1940 took place. Conceived as a means of practising amphibious landings and intended to go some way to meeting Russian demands for a Second Front to divert German troops from the east, the Dieppe Raid was an unqualified disaster, the landing force – though backed by heavy tanks – being unable to get off the beach. The Canadian official history remarks:

> from a force of fewer than 5000 men engaged for only nine hours,* the Canadian Army lost more prisoners than in the whole eleven months of the later campaign in North-West Europe. . . . the total of fatal casualties was 56 officers and 851 other ranks. Canadian casualties of all categories aggregated 3369.

Canada mourned, and seethed. Why the raw Canadians were chosen, their training still not up to Monty standards, was never made clear; possibly others than Monty had been influenced by the pressures of 'bellyaching' and the demand for a role for restless, bored troops. Whatever, Dieppe provided the most terrible warning of what could happen to a premature ROUNDUP landing. Had it taken place the previous month, as originally scheduled, almost certainly Monty would have joined the ranks of the sacked, the name 'Alamein' never added to his name. The troops and the land-force side of the planning had come from his army. Like Arnhem, later, it was a fiasco for which some would always hold him responsible – he had been in the chair when the first crucial decision was taken and had not demurred. But it was a responsibility that he was always meticulous to eschew. Monty's own defence was that, once the raid had been postponed through bad weather, security was at risk and it should have been aborted 'for all time. . . . this advice was disregarded'; and 'there were far too many authorities with a hand in it; there was no . . . Task Force Commander'. One of those principally involved was an ambitious, and all-persuasive, young acting RN commodore; said Monty acidly of Mountbatten: 'very gallant sailor. Had three ships sunk under him. *Three* ships. . . . Doesn't know how to fight a battle.'

As far as Monty's own education was concerned, Dieppe taught him the salutary and not-to-be-forgotten lesson: never to underestimate the power of Germans on the defensive. But what in effect saved his bacon was that, nine days before Dieppe, on 10 August, he had left England to take command of the Eighth Army.

*

* The landing force also included 1000 British troops and a small number of American Rangers and Free French soldiers.

It was on 7 August that Monty, visiting exercises in Scotland, was telephoned by the War Office appointing him to command the Northern Task Force of Operation TORCH, the Anglo-American invasion of French North Africa scheduled to take place in October. His boss, the Supreme Allied Commander just nominated, was to be the nicotine-addicted General Eisenhower; Monty's fellow army commander was to be the flamboyant Californian millionaire, that pistol-packing, cavalry-man-turned-tankman, the unpredictable and independent-minded General George S. Patton, who for most of his army career had been Eisenhower's senior. The proposition did not entirely appeal to Monty: 'I knew very few American soldiers and did not know how my methods would appeal to him [Eisenhower].' The very next day another call came from the War Office, telling him to proceed immediately to Egypt, where General Gott, the new commander-designate of the Eighth Army, had just been shot down and killed. Its morale thoroughly shaken, the army had been on the retreat before Rommel ever since the ugly débâcle of May at Gazala, and now had its back to the Suez Canal at El Alamein. Monty was to take over the command, under General Alexander. He set off 'with a light heart and great confidence'.

First, however, there was David to deal with, who had just started public school at Winchester: 'I took a very quick decision and wrote to Major Reynolds, the retired army officer who was headmaster of David's former preparatory school.' Much in the manner of garaging a car for the duration, Monty – rather than entrust David to any member of the family – summarily requested headmaster Reynolds: 'Will you and your lady wife take charge of David for me until I return.' Once again, strictest instructions were given that he was not to visit his grandmother, Maud:

> She is an old lady and quite unable to take charge of anyone. She will want David to go and stay in Ireland for his holidays.
>
> *On no account is he to go.*
>
> She is a menace with the young.

Without even finding time to telephone David, he wrote a final hasty note to Reynolds emphasizing that he put David:

> in your *complete and absolute* charge. If any members of my family chip in and want to advise, see them right off. . . .

If I am killed his legal guardian is then John Carver. But I shall not be killed.

Goodbye to you.

When one reviews Monty's career to date – his reputation as the outstanding divisional commander in France, followed by his magnificent performance training up a corps, then an army – perhaps the extraordinary thing is that he had not been Brooke's immediate choice for the Eighth Army, after the sacking of Auchinleck in the summer of 1942 (Brooke had been CIGS since 1941). Yet all through 1942 until July, there is no mention whatever in Brooke's diaries of his name, no suggestion of promotion. This may well say something of the unpopularity which Monty had already aroused and which was to bedevil his subsequent career in Normandy. Equally, it may have been that Brooke, knowing his Monty, felt that without his being there to keep him under close control, Gott would have been the safer risk. So, for the great battle ahead, the little Jack Russell General was everybody's second choice.*

Within three months, his face was to become the most celebrated in the Western world, replacing that of Winston Churchill on the cover of *Time* magazine, to the astonishment of his colleagues and (perhaps somewhat less) to his own amazement. The story of El Alamein must be one of the best known in the history of war: the rushing of 300 of America's latest Sherman tanks round the Cape to replace the terrible losses inflicted by Rommel's Panzers; the revitalization of an exhausted, if not demoralized, Eighth Army; the triumphant stonewall defence against Rommel's final bid for Cairo and the Suez Canal at Alam Halfa (whether Monty pirated the blueprint from the sacked Auchinleck need not concern us here); the desperate, costly thirteen-day 'rough-house' of Alamein itself and the terrible thousand-a-day casualties that were the antithesis of everything Monty stood for; the narrow margin of success; the failure of the British armour; and, finally, the over-cautious pursuit all the way to Tripoli that was to permit the bulk of Rommel's broken army to escape. For their relevance to what lay ahead in 1944, we need only examine here these last two aspects

* Reputedly, Monty knew nothing of the horse-trading that had preceded his appointment until publication of the Alanbrooke diaries fifteen years later.

– apart from pausing, yet again, to consider Monty's greatest achievement of all, his instillation of fighting spirit into the Eighth Army.

Arriving still in thick battledress in the August heat of Egypt, Monty was immediately horrified by what he found. Exemplifying the state of morale in Auchinleck's GHQ was the fact that, covered with mosquito netting, it was abuzz with a million insects, 'a meat safe for flies'. He ordered the netting taken away, the headquarters removed into the open air by the more salubrious atmosphere of the sea. For the first time in British Army history, it would be placed right next to the RAF TAC HQ.* Commanders, deeply influenced by successive defeats and by the apparent invincibility of Rommel, had developed a habit of 'looking over their shoulders' – at the Suez Canal just behind them. It was perhaps worst in some of the tank regiments. Too many had seen friends 'brew up' in inferior tanks, constantly outclassed by the enemy – the nightmare of being trapped in burning machines, the frequent horror of commanders eviscerated by armour-piercing rounds, their entrails slopping down the necks of the crew beneath. Rommel's new long-barrelled 75s had taken a heavy toll, outmatching even the heavy American Grants and the latest Shermans that were just arriving.† At the opposite extreme, Monty found some of the crack cavalry units were just 'too brave', behaving as if they were in the shires. During one terrible Balaclava-style charge in July, the British had lost 118 tanks to 3 of the enemy. They 'really are', Monty complained to his infantry corps commander, Horrocks, 'hunting the whole time. They are after a fox. They'll go, they'll always attack. That's their one element.' It represented everything he most deplored about the army elite in the inter-war era. 'I am not going to have that,' he told Horrocks.

In this same conversation, as recorded by Horrocks, Monty revealed beyond shadow of doubt that he too realized the inferiority

* Regrettably, and with troubling consequences, this was something he could not achieve in the closer confines of Normandy.

† Field Marshal Lord Carver, who served with 7th Armoured through the Desert Campaign, and later commanded one of its brigades in Normandy, states that even as late as Alam Halfa in August 1942 Rommel had no more than 26 of the long-barrelled 75 Mk IVs.

of British armour: 'all the Germans do is withdraw their 88s behind the line and then knock out all our tanks. What's more their 88s have a far better range and the Germans have far better tanks than we've got.'*

But what did he do about it?

Immediately, all plans for withdrawal were countermanded. Setting into practice everything he had perfected during the long years of training, in one of those mass meetings that were to become part of the Monty legend, he told his officers: '... I want to impress on everyone that the bad times are over....' There were to be no 'doubters in this party', and 'no bellyaching'. His newly appointed Chief of Staff, de Guingand, recalled that the effect was 'electric – it was terrific! And we all went to bed that night with new hope in our hearts.' 'Bill' Williams, the young Oxford don who was to go with Monty all the way to Lüneburg Heath as his intelligence chief, found it was 'straight out of school speech day. And yet ... a feeling of great exhilaration.' By sheer showmanship, making himself and his plans known to every trooper, he set himself to replace the bogeyman of Rommel, by whom even Winston Churchill sometimes seemed to be hypnotized.

As one of Rommel's officers recognized, with Monty's takeover abruptly 'the war in the desert ceased to be a game'. The Afrika Korps' all-out attack on Alam Halfa was warded off. With great difficulty, Monty held the cavalry back from pursuit of the withdrawing German Panzers – with the usual disastrous consequences – thereby earning the lashes of critics for posterity. Instead, he allowed the Panzers to wear themselves down by attacking his armour 'on

* The German 88 had in fact started off life as a standard, high-velocity anti-aircraft gun. It had been used, on an *ad hoc* basis, with deadly effect, to knock out French bunkers along the Meuse in 1940; then it had become an anti-tank weapon, the deadliest of the entire war; and from there it was mounted in the Tiger tank, the dread scourge of Normandy in 1944. But the British too had a similar – if anything even more lethal – weapon in their armoury: the 3.7-inch ack-ack gun, which actually outranged the 88. This was employed, in dire emergency, firing over open sights during the defence of Tobruk, with deadly effect by Brigadier 'Mad Mac' Murray McIntyre (who died aged 100 in 1993). Because of War Office bureaucracy and rivalry between the two arms, anti-aircraft and armour, subsequent development of the 3.7 as an anti-tank weapon along the lines of the 88 was persistently discouraged – amazing as this may seem. Later in the war, 'Mad Mac' formed his own battery out of captured German 88s, which created havoc among the enemy.

ground of its own choosing'. A mistake was made, which would prove costly at Alamein, in letting the Germans hang on to the Himeimat Ridge. But Monty was not prepared to take any risks on the offensive with the still shaky Eighth Army. Nor would he at Alamein, two months later. Though by this time it was a force transformed, he was still writing in his diary in October:

> *But the training was not good* and it was beginning to become clear to me that I would have to be very careful . . . that formations and units were not given tasks which were likely to end in failure because of their low standard of training. . . . I must not be too ambitious in my demands.

It was a caveat that he would find himself repeating again and again, even in Normandy.

'Too ambitious', as it proved, was his creation of a new, armoured *corps de chasse*, X Corps, which – under Monty's first plans for Alamein – would have the job of destroying the enemy armour on 'ground of its own choice', after which, said Monty's orders ambitiously, 'the whole of the enemy army can be rounded up without any difficulty'. X Corps, with its tremendous responsibility, was to be placed under the redoubtable Horrocks. But Horrocks refused: as an infantryman who 'came from a very humble regiment [the Middlesex]', he knew that the smart cavalry would react badly. 'Put Lumsden in,' he recommended, because Lumsden was 'the great hero, he'd won the Grand National, God knows what else . . .'.* So Lieutenant-General Herbert Lumsden of the 12th Lancers got it. In the pre-Alamein desert battles, it would be hard to find anybody who exemplified better the polo-ground spirit: dashing, irresistible to women, good DSO won in France 1940, twice wounded and brave to a fault, he galloped around the battlefield in his white-painted tank (which he often drove himself), immaculately dressed (recalled Bill Mather, liaison officer with Lumsden at Alamein) in 'beautifully pressed cavalry trousers . . . white silk scarf and everything else', always conspicuously up with the forward tanks. But,

* Montgomery Collection.

the eager amateur to his fingertips, Lumsden was quite incapable of acting to a concerted, setpiece battle-plan, a failing that had doomed the Eighth Army's offensives again and again in the past. In the presence of Monty, who saw through the gloss, Lumsden froze up. On being told that his corps would have to 'force their way out of the minefields' at Alamein, he refused, reflecting less his own fearless instincts than the apprehensions of his squadron and troop leaders, who went into battle with a permanent dread of their thin-skinned tanks being taken in a trap by the 88s. But he did not refuse in Monty's presence. 'Tanks must be used as cavalry,' he told his officers, well out of Monty's hearing, 'and not be kept as supporters of infantry. So I don't propose to do that.'

It was a declaration verging on mutiny and nothing could have been more indicative of the essential fragility which Monty inherited in the Eighth Army. The few weeks between his arrival and Alamein were simply not enough to retrain a whole army. In the event, the performance of Lumsden and X Corps was nearly to cost the victory at Alamein, through their failure to exploit success. Monty was forced to withdraw the corps at a critical stage in the battle, because of its poor performance. Of Lumsden, fairly or unfairly, Monty wrote in an official report when he was CIGS after the war, 'At 2 a.m. on 25 October he lost his nerve; I had to take charge of his Corps for an hour and give orders to his Div Comds myself; he [Lumsden] said we could not win the battle and wanted to chuck it. After the battle was over, and we had removed the Germans from Egypt, I sent him back to England. I said in my report that he had done a great deal of fighting in the desert, possibly too much, without a rest.' After the Afrika Korps had begun to retreat, Lumsden's *corps de chasse*, on which Monty had placed such high hopes, failed to follow up and cut off its line of retreat. There ensued the long, disappointing pursuit across Africa, diminishing the superlative triumph of Alamein. Tripoli was captured, Tunisia reached, enabling Eighth Army to join hands with Eisenhower's TORCH forces pushing eastwards from Morocco. But Rommel escaped – to fight Monty again in Normandy. Montgomery cannot evade just criticism for his excessive caution during the post-Alamein pursuit, but the deficiency of Lumsden and the armour has to be regarded as a major contributory factor. The same problems would arise again, most banefully, in

Normandy – all, it might be said, because successive British governments and General Staffs and industry had failed – and continued to fail – so miserably to equip those heroic cavalrymen with proper tanks.

Not till years later did historians come to realize perhaps how close run a thing Alamein was in the light of the brittle fabric of the Eighth Army – despite that huge preponderance of British weaponry, the thousand-gun barrage that lit up the skies, all that new equipment rushed round the Cape. In the conflict between Monty and Lumsden,* which almost spoiled that stunning first victory against German forces of the Second World War, those who enjoy the congruencies of history may find a parallel with the two admirals from the previous war at Jutland: Jellicoe, the cautious Commander-in-Chief who could have 'lost the war in an afternoon', and Beatty, the battle-cruiser commander, the impetuous, jaunty huntsman with his rakish cap, who – after the third of his inadequately armoured leviathans had gone up with a roar – uttered that timeless complaint: 'There's something wrong with our bloody ships today, Chatfield.' Fortunately for civilization, however, Monty – excessively cautious as he might well have seemed at Alamein and after – was made of far more tenacious, more ruthless stuff than Jellicoe.

From August 1942 onwards, David had received regular letters in that clear, schoolboy hand with never a word crossed out, which had revealed something of his father's psychological pilgrim's progress. On 31 August: 'I am having a great time here; the Germans attacked this morning and I am enjoying fighting battles again. You must not worry about me; I am quite safe and can come to no harm. . . . I also enclose a photograph of myself, at my Desert HQ.' On 8 September: 'The battle I have been fighting with Rommel is over. I have defeated him and that is very good. I expect you will see a good deal about it in the papers. I have enjoyed it all tremendously.' His 'enjoyment' of battle was always something that was confounding, if not actually

* Michael Carver considers both Monty, and his biographer, Nigel Hamilton, to have been excessively prejudiced against Lumsden 'for disappointments during the battle' at El Alamein.

shocking, to his critics. On the eve of Alamein, on 23 October, he wrote:

> I write to you today as I shall be too busy to write for some time after today. I begin tonight a big battle which will help to end the war. We are all very well and my soldiers in great form. . . . I enclose for you a copy of a Personal Message I have issued to the army and it is being read to every man today. You should keep it carefully as one day it may be of value.

Nine days later, on 1 November:

> I am fighting a great battle with Rommel. It began on 23rd October and I do not think he can last much longer. I have great hopes that in another week I shall have defeated him. I am enjoying it very much. . . . I have now taken to wearing a black Tank Corps beret [to which he was never entitled!]. The Australian hat was very good in the summer but I do not need it now the weather is cooler.

On 10 November:

> This battle is really over and I have smashed Rommel and his army. It has been great fun and I have enjoyed it. Someday I will tell you all about it. . . . I expect the papers in England are full of it and contain a good deal about me. I am afraid Dick [Carver] was captured by the Germans at Matruh on 7th November. Poor Dick: he was so happy and was doing very good work.*
>
> We had very heavy rain after I had driven the Germans back and that saved them from complete annihilation as many of my troops were bogged in the desert and could not move. . . .

In between the two great desert battles, one letter survives (dated 12 October) which shows him writing to his son on more personal, family matters: '. . . I hear that you are now going to call the Reynolds Uncle and Aunt, and I think that is a first-class idea. I am going to call her Phyllis and she will call me Monty . . . and we will all now be a family party.' An extensive correspondence between the

* Carver escaped from his POW camp in Italy during the confusion surrounding the Italian surrender and was subsequently wounded in Normandy – fighting under his stepfather.

General and the schoolmaster's wife then ensued, with Monty writing to her often at greater length, and with less inhibition, than to his son.

David, an unusually outgoing boy, however, formed a warm attachment to the Reynolds, at whose school he now made his home in holiday time. But behind it lay an extraordinary and unpalatable little episode illustrative of Monty's obsessive paranoia about his family – which mounted in direct proportion to his fame. Staying with Jocelyn Carver at Littlewick Green the Christmas of 1942, David was taken out to lunch on Boxing Day, and 'had quite a lot to drink'. He then wrote to his father, saying 'I'd had a marvellous lunch and two glasses of sherry and two glasses of wine, etc. (Imagine writing this to a teetotal general in the desert!)' The offence appears to have been compounded, in Monty's eyes, by the fact that – after the Boxing Day excesses – David went down with 'flu, which prevented him being received by Winston Churchill. By return of post from GHQ Eighth Army came the edict that, under no circumstances, was he ever again to stay with the beloved Jocelyn, the one person to whom he felt close, and was henceforth to be solely in the charge of the Reynolds.

By the time of Alamein, Monty had pretty well established his private court, his headquarters staff – and particularly the inner entourage of his personal TAC HQ that was to serve him so well right up to May 1945. First there was Brigadier Freddie de Guingand, already BGS to the Eighth Army, noted down in the black book from pre-war acquaintance, but amazed to find Monty wanting to take him over from the despised and (in Monty's book) defeated Auchinleck team. Then there was 'Bill' Williams, the young, academic-looking history don from Balliol – another temporary wartime officer in the cavalry, who was to become Monty's trusted intelligence *éminence grise* in north-west Europe.

The way he chose his team is well revealed in the (unpublished) letters from Monty to Christopher Chavasse, Bishop of Rochester, a friend of Bishop Montgomery and father of Noël, a young officer serving in the desert. On 21 January 1943 Monty wrote:

> My dear Christopher
>
> I have just met a young son of yours who is a subaltern in the 1/7 Middlesex, and is now liaison officer 51 Div. HQ. . . . I discovered who he was, and had a long talk. He is a very nice lad and is doing well.
>
> It is very many years since we last met. I remember holidays in Moville a long time ago; I was at school and you and Noël* at the Varsity.
>
> Much has happened since then. Indeed much has happened since I began the battle of Egypt on 23rd October; we were then about 1600 miles from where we are now; I am now at the gates of Tripoli.

A few months later another letter followed, informing the Bishop that his son had done 'splendidly' and was getting a Military Cross: 'he has well earned it.' In September 1943, came the announcement, all in the round schoolboy hand of the Army Commander, that Noël was now serving on his personal staff as a liaison officer:

> I have been watching his work in the Highland Division very carefully for some time and when I saw how very good it was, I decided to bring him on to my own staff. I choose my staff with the greatest care and will have only the very best; and the fact that I have taken Noël on, implies that his work is of the highest class. Quite apart from this, he is a most charming and delightful boy, with a very fine character and a very high sense of duty; I am very fond of him. I thought you would like to know this.

Chavasse, too, stayed right through to the end. So did Johnny Henderson of the 12th Lancers, yet another wartime smart cavalryman, who became Monty's ADC aged twenty-three – having first asked to be released after a week's trial. From the late Gott, Monty took over his ADC, Captain John Poston, an exuberant and fearless officer who was to become perhaps his favourite. It was adventurous and often dangerous working as a liaison officer for 'Master', as they called him. Not all accepted the summons; later on, the commander

* The uncle of Lieutenant Chavasse, one of three double VCs from the First World War.

of his TAC HQ, Bill Mather,* of the Cheshire Yeomanry in Italy, (another family connection), alarmed by the Monty reputation declined at first, until accused of 'malingering'. Notwithstanding all that introverted egoism, however, it surely says something for Monty's extraordinary flair for sniffing out, and bringing on, young talent that so many stayed on with him to the bitter end.

By the end of 1942, as well as having formed his own personal entourage at TAC, Monty had largely completed the process of placing his 'men' in control of most of the key posts of Eighth Army.

The epic 1500-mile pursuit from Alamein to Tunis over, the longest in military history, in 1943 Monty found himself under the command of the inexperienced American General whom he had ordered to stop smoking a few months previously. To borrow an expression, for him particularly the war was about to enter into a whole new ball-game. He had already had, in the desert before Alamein, a further encounter with American top-brass, which had not been entirely fortunate. President Roosevelt's Republican opponent in the 1940 elections and now his roving personal emissary, the immensely likeable Wendell Willkie, had arrived to visit Monty in the middle of the Battle of Alam Halfa – accompanied by Major-General Brereton, commander of all the newly arriving US air-force squadrons. For Willkie, Monty had for once deviated from his golden rule of no VIPs to army headquarters, and FDR's emissary had left glowing with praise for Monty. But he had neglected to include Brereton in his invitation to dinner; only the timely intervention of the diplomatic Alexander averted a row. But Brereton, a chippy individual, never forgot. A few months later, in Tunisia, another unfortunate incident escalated from a light-hearted bet. Monty had boasted to Walter Bedell Smith, Ike's Chief of Staff, that he would reach Sfax by April; when Smith challenged this, Monty asked if he would give him a Flying Fortress B-17 bomber if he succeeded. The American agreed. Monty reached Sfax five days ahead of time – and insisted on claiming his pound of flesh. Bedell Smith at first treated it all as a joke, but

* Later Sir William Mather, CVO, OBE, MC, twice wounded, and Vice Lord Lieutenant of Cheshire. He was the brother of Carol Mather, who became a liaison officer with Monty in north-west Europe. Their father Loris was godfather to DM.

Monty, for all his puritanism in other directions, regarded a wager as something almost sacred. In the end, he got his Flying Fortress, complete with crew, which served him well and on many trips. But it displayed Monty's basic insensitivity when dealing with Americans, greatly embarrassed Bedell Smith and infuriated Eisenhower – once again; nor was Brooke greatly amused when he heard of it.

At the historic Casablanca Conference of January 1943, where Western strategy for the rest of the war was mapped out (and which Monty did not attend), the Americans were initially put out by the brusque, even curt manner of Monty's mentor, Brooke. Partly it belied the workings of an extremely precise, impatient mind, and his American counterparts came to recognize this. He was, throughout, much better able to conceal his deep reservations about American capabilities than was Monty – until his private thoughts were published in 1957, revealing him to have been at least as critical of the new partner, who was bound to become the dominant one. As it was, after the initial wariness had worn off, Casablanca was an almost unqualified success for British war aims – but it was the last such conference. With an entire liner packed with staff officers and typists, Brooke had arrived superbly well prepared, to the disconcertion of the Americans, but the conference had ended on the most harmonious of notes with almost every British point accepted. ROUNDUP would be postponed until September (eventually to June 1944); the main Allied war effort would be not in the Pacific (as desired by Admiral King and his powerful US Navy lobby) but in the Mediterranean. After North Africa was cleared (which happened three months later), it would be Sicily, then the Italian mainland.

Here Monty was largely at one with his new chief, Eisenhower. Both would have preferred the major effort to be mounted across the Channel, but – in view of the great build-up of forces in the Mediterranean – Eisenhower accepted that it had better be deployed there, though only until ROUNDUP was ready.

Meanwhile, at the hands of the dreaded German 88s in Tunisia's Kasserine Pass, the new Supreme Allied Commander had experienced his first operational setback; and it had been little short of a major disaster. It was, in effect, also Ike's first real battle, and the closest he had ever personally come to the front line.

Born in October 1890, three years after Monty, in a shack on the wrong side of the railway tracks in Texas, his father a labourer, Ike could hardly have had a background less like Monty's. He had graduated from West Point (where Omar Bradley had been his best friend) in June 1915, by which time Monty was already a severely wounded and decorated major. On that first day of the Somme, 1 July 1916, so terrible for Britain, Ike was marrying his sweetheart, Mary Geneva Doud, known as Mamie. After America had joined the Allies in 1917, Ike, already earmarked for his organizational ability, spent the rest of the First World War, in deep frustration, training American troops on a mock-up of the Western Front. In October 1918, he was all set to embark for France, in command of an armoured unit, but the Armistice beat him to it. (Meanwhile, his senior, George S. Patton Jr, was already a thirty-three-year-old lieutenant-colonel commanding two tank battalions at St Mihiel, riding into battle on a tank 'as if it were a polo pony'.)

In the inter-war period, Ike came to share Patton's enthusiasm for armoured warfare, but it got him nowhere. As Britain entered the war in 1939, he was just returning from four unhappy years in the shortly to be lost Philippines, serving under that great egocentric, General Douglas MacArthur. His efforts were, manifestly, of little help in saving the Philippines from Japanese conquest a few years later. By 1940, as Monty was bringing his division out of Dunkirk, Ike had just been promoted to command a battalion, while Colonel Patton was requesting that Ike should serve under him. With Pearl Harbor, the ascent of both suddenly became meteoric. Picked out – again for his talents as an organizer – by Roosevelt's Chief of Staff, the remote and austere George C. Marshall (right to the end of the war Marshall insisted on the formality of calling him 'Eisenhower'), by February 1943 he had soared to the rank of full general. Because of the extraordinary ability he was to develop for getting on with foreign leaders at all levels,* with that infectious, boyish American smile that could instantly reduce tensions, it would emerge as a

* Ike showed his mettle at a very early stage as Allied Supreme Commander by summarily dismissing senior American commanders caught boasting that they would show the British how to fight. Typical of this was when he sacked an American officer for calling a colleague a '*British* son-of-a-bitch'. Much given to using that particular sobriquet himself, Eisenhower explained that it was the qualifying word 'British' that was totally unacceptable.

choice of quite historic brilliance. Certainly, as a coalition leader he would prove to be 'the best we had'.

Yet, initially kept (in further frustration) to his desk by Marshall, Eisenhower had still never fought a battle, in any rank. When things went wrong, this was to be a constant source of condescension among his battle-hardened British opposite numbers, such as Brooke and Monty. 'Broadie' Broadhurst, Monty's much decorated TAC Air Force commander, recalled with detached amusement how, in Tunisia shortly after the fierce battle of Wadi Akarit, Ike's eyes had lit upon a dead guardsman still hanging on the barbed wire and had remarked with engaging candour, 'Say, Broadie, that's the first time I've seen a dead body!' The difference was that British officers like Monty and Brooke had seen just too many dead guardsmen hanging on the wire, in two world wars – and it was a fundamental difference dividing those who would lead the two nations back into Europe. Within the confines of his TAC HQ, Monty, who sometimes shocked his officers by his delight in making patronizing jokes about the Americans, was never beyond mocking Ike, the staff officer, for his lack of battle experience. 'Nice chap, no soldier' was how Monty apostrophized Eisenhower when he first appeared at his TAC HQ in Tunisia. It fairly summed up the depth of misunderstanding and what amounted to an enduring professional contempt for the American, which was shared by the CIGS, Brooke himself. Time would not noticeably amend their opinions, and this mistaken underrating of the qualities of Eisenhower was to prove a serious handicap during the campaign that lay ahead. Monty's first biographer, that inspired Australian, Alan Moorehead, possibly saw things more clearly when he wrote, in 1946, 'It is not suggested that Eisenhower and the Americans were amateurs, but their *emotions* were those of the amateur. . . .'*

In that first reverse at Kasserine Pass, where he showed himself at least as unwilling to take risks as Monty, Ike had – disquietingly – also evinced a lack of ruthless driving force, an inability, or unwillingness, to bully his subordinate commanders, in the way Monty had bullied, and sacked, the unfortunate Lumsden. After that defeat, Monty had been unsparing in his criticism of how the green US commanders had comported themselves.

* Moorehead, *Montgomery*, p. 212.

For the invasion of Sicily (Operation HUSKY), launched on 10 July 1943, Ike was the Supreme Commander, with the British Eighth Army and the US Seventh Army under command of Monty and Patton respectively. It was the first time the two had come into close contact, and the conflagration was spontaneous, the campaign marked throughout with heated wrangles between British and Americans. Monty damned Ike's seven consecutive plans for HUSKY as a 'mess' from beginning to end. Instead of the two armies being landed on separate coasts, as Patton wanted, the two were landed abreast, following Monty's preference for concentration. 'Blood and Guts' Patton fumed, and never forgave him. In the biggest airborne landing yet undertaken, nervous American pilots short-dropped 69 out of 144 gliders, carrying British paratroops, into the sea – with tragic losses. Once ashore, without warning him or getting Alexander's permission, Monty grabbed one of the principal routes assigned to Patton's US Seventh Army, pointing towards the Straits of Messina; then, in the vigorous words of Eisenhower's biographer, Stephen Ambrose:

> Montgomery did not drive for Messina; he hardly even crawled. He and Patton fought among themselves until Patton, furious at the passive role he had been assigned, struck out on his own, toward Palermo, in western Sicily, away from the Germans but toward the headlines.
>
> Then he turned right, to race Monty to Messina. On August 17, Patton's men won.*

The Americans were, justifiably, furious. In bitter fighting (it cost the British nearly 12,000 casualties against Patton's 7500) the Eighth Army became bogged down around Mount Etna, while 60,000 Germans, with their equipment, escaped across the Straits to fight another day in Italy. Sicily was far from being Monty's finest hour; but nor was it Patton's, for it was in Sicily that he slapped the face of a shell-shocked soldier, nearly terminating his own career there and then. But for his lifelong friend, admirer and protector, Ike, it would have done. Worse, for Monty the scars with Patton and the Americans would reopen insidiously the following year in France.

* Ambrose (2), p. 104.

Once into mainland Italy, in September, the early performance of Monty and his Eighth Army was not much better. Both were tired. The Americans, in their freshness, sometimes didn't seem to appreciate what nearly four years of war, reverses and privation had done to their British allies. A huge preparatory barrage, Alamein-style, across the Straits proved unnecessary: the Germans had all withdrawn. Ambling leisurely northwards, Monty's men found it 'like a holiday picnic after Sicily and Africa'. Meanwhile, the US Fifth Army landings at Salerno, just short of Naples to the north, had run into serious trouble. Momentarily it looked as if there might be another Dunkirk. Eisenhower even talked of parallels with Stalingrad, and there was deep bitterness in the American camp about Montgomery's slow advance to relieve the beleaguered beachhead. Salerno survived. But by November 1943 it was clear that the Germans had managed to impose a stalemate in Italy, horribly reminiscent of the First World War.

Was Italy the right place to be fighting at all, committed to slogging all the way up its mountainous length? Monty might well have wondered this, bogged down south of Rome at the end of 1943. With hindsight, military historians might argue that it would have been better to have stopped short of Naples, pinned down German divisions there by maintaining the minimum aggressive–defensive position and continued the strategic bombing of Germany from southern Italian airfields, while transferring all possible force in landing craft and men to concentrate on OVERLORD. At least, however, it could be said there was a British army, led by Monty, back in Europe after three wearisome and costly years.

CHAPTER THREE

'FROM TAC HQ I WILL COMMAND...'

December 1943–May 1944

The dread of the coming battle lay like a leaden weight on everyone's mind. Could it be anything else than an appalling 'blood bath'?

(Alan Moorehead, *Montgomery*, p. 186)

His conceitedness irked even those most devoted to him, but was tolerated because, in a world of muddle and confusion, his clarity of purpose and professional approach to the 'art of war' stood out like a beacon.

(Nigel Hamilton, *Monty*, vol. II, p. 479)

ON 27 DECEMBER 1943, Monty wrote to his friend the Bishop of Rochester:

> My dear Christopher – I shall be back in England shortly to take up my new job. It is a big job, probably the biggest I shall ever have to tackle. Noël [now an ADC] will come with me and I will send him to see you when we arrive. . . .
>
> P.S. Say nothing about my movements until Noël telephones you.

To speak of even a 'big job' was surely an understatement of historic proportions. Only four days previously, at his Eighth Army headquarters in Italy, Monty had received orders from Brooke that he was to return to England to take over command of 21 Army Group. This meant that, with Eisenhower as Supreme Allied Commander, he would now lead the invasion force into France; it also meant that on his shoulders would now rest perhaps the greatest responsibility of the entire war. Suddenly he was the man, the one man, who could win it – or lose it. In breaking the news of the 'big job' first to the father of one of his ADCs, there lay possibly a hint as to how Monty saw his priorities towards his new 'family' of young officers. It was only that same day that he wrote to Phyllis Reynolds so that she could pass on the news to his son David. His last letter to David had been a short note barely two weeks previously, with the P.S.: 'I hoped at one time I might have got home for Xmas. But now I fear not.'

The choice of Monty for this 'big job' had the same disturbing overtones of hesitance, doubts and second thoughts that had cast shadows over his despatch to the Eighth Army back in August 1942. The inter-Allied decisions prescribing OVERLORD for 1944 had been taken at the Cairo and Teheran conferences in November 1943, but at the latter, when Stalin had asked directly, 'Who will command?', both Churchill and Roosevelt had hedged. With so few months to go, all was still undecided. In Washington there was argument whether Marshall, FDR's indispensable equivalent to Brooke, should fill the number-one slot as Supreme Allied Commander. This was not resolved until the first week in December; another long ten days would pass before Monty received his orders. For, despite his historic triumph at El Alamein, despite his continuing reputation through Tripoli, Tunisia, Sicily and into Italy as the one Allied commander who consistently won battles, he was not the instant choice. Yet again it all reflected the animosities and enmities he had made on the way up. In his diplomatic way, Ike made it clear he would have preferred the gentlemanly – and malleable* – Alexander to be his British subordinate. In London, the Cabinet was split down the centre. Passing through the mud and cold of Italy on his way home from Cairo, Brooke noted with disquiet that Monty 'looked tired and definitely wants a rest and a change'. Was he the right man? And if he were not?

Certainly, with no prospect of moving on Rome before spring 1944 at the earliest, he had clearly reached the end of the line with his beloved Eighth Army. From his headquarters at Vasto on 30 December, he bade it an emotional farewell. As he shook hands with

* Shortly before the final decision was made, Monty sent off a long letter to Mountbatten, fiercely critical of Alexander's failure to 'grip the battle and co-ordinate' the armies under him in Italy.

his generals, de Guingand – unashamedly in tears – was reminded of Napoleon and his marshals. Less complimentary was the BBC correspondent listening to him, Denis Johnston:

> ... I thought to myself, what a headache, what a bore, what a bounder he must be to those on roughly the same level in the service. And at the same time what a great man he is as a leader of troops, and how right he is to wear funny hats so that the soldiers along the roads will know their general.

When he left TAC HQ, so Bill Mather recalled, 'the whole atmosphere went flat'. With him, in his kitbag, Monty carried from Italy worrying reservations about the battleworthiness of some of the Allied formations he might soon be commanding in Normandy:

> The Americans do not understand how to fight the Germans; they operate in regimental combat teams and the big idea is to have every combat team 'combating'; you do not get very far this way. They do not understand the great principles of surprise and concentration.

Also, he had noted under Alexander as supremo in Italy, 'there was no co-ordination, no plan, no grip; I did what I liked, Clark* did what he liked ...'.† These were misgivings that were to return to haunt him with force in the course of the next year.

On his way home, Monty spent New Year's Eve 1943 with Winston Churchill, recovering from pneumonia in Marrakech. Churchill gave Monty the COSSAC‡ plans for OVERLORD (then scheduled for 1 May, only four months away) for bedside reading and asked for an opinion. This was the first time Monty had seen them, and he responded sharply that 'I was not his military adviser,' but would nevertheless give his 'impressions' in the morning. These were, delivered forthrightly and with his habitual clarity: that the proposed beachhead was too narrow, the first attacking wave of three divisions far too small, that at best the plan would result in 'the

* General Mark Clark, commanding the US Fifth Army.

† Letter to Mountbatten, 23 December 1943, quoted in Hamilton, *Monty*, vol. II, p. 470.

‡ Standing for Chief of Staff, Supreme Allied Commander. This was the planning body established under Lieutenant-General Sir Frederick E. Morgan awaiting the appointment of Eisenhower.

most appalling confusion', and 'could hardly be considered a sound operation of war'. At worst, the landings could be 'roped off' by the Germans, and destroyed. Churchill was manifestly impressed by the instant authority of the commander whose appointment had been accompanied by so much reluctance. Of a trip together up into the Atlas mountains, he recorded, 'The General was in the highest spirits; he leaped about the rocks like an antelope, and I felt a strong reassurance that all would be well.' Certainly few generals of his age were so fit – and none so well equipped.

On New Year's Day 1944, Monty reached London, fêted universally as the conquering hero. In some quarters the acclaim was muted; the elitist Harold Nicolson growled disapprovingly in his diary for 5 January, 'Montgomery is the second most popular figure in England.' The England he found was entering its fifth year of war. Following the run of victories from Alamein and Stalingrad, morale was high, with the scent of victory in the air. But below the surface there was deep lassitude, a certain fragility that might surface unpredictably in the face of future reverses. The indiscriminate Luftwaffe bombing had resumed by night; in February a terrible panic at the entrance to an East End tube station resulted in 200 people being trampled to death, suggesting that nerves were not what they had been at the height of the Blitz. Food, clothing and petrol were savagely rationed and 'even the simplest commodities and services, now taken for granted, did not exist. Hard to evoke, it was a world without supermarkets, launderettes, plastic bags, biros, sellotape, long-playing records, transistors or tape recorders' – so we are reminded by Norman Kirby, who was to be charged with TAC HQ security in Normandy. There was no television; instead 'young people were still able to give vent to patriotic feelings by singing "There'll be blue birds over/The white cliffs of Dover", and "There'll always be an England" with a mixture of optimism and wistfulness'. The pro-Russian exhortations of 'Second Front Now' scribbled up on every wall provided a sense of the reality that lay so imminently ahead.

> The dread of the coming battle lay like a leaden weight on everyone's mind. Could it be anything else than an appalling 'blood bath'? There was something outrageous in this slow deliberate

> preparation for a massacre. The bombing of southern England went on. There were threats of rockets. Austerity followed one about like a lean and hungry dog

was how the Australian war correspondent, veteran of Alamein, Alan Moorehead, summed up the mood. Within the armed forces that Monty was returning to command, many still had memories of Dunkirk, while there were still those (not all that old) who recalled with horror the slaughter of the Somme from the previous war. Morale, he speedily discovered, was distinctly mixed.

Among the Americans – fresh, untried troops piling into England in ever increasing numbers – it was tremendous, but quite different in timbre. As their fathers had done in 1917, they marched in to the rousing, cocky optimism of George M. Cohan's 'Over There' ('We won't come back till it's over, over there . . .'). In that war there had been a wisecrack that AEF (American Expeditionary Force) stood for 'After England Failed'; for all those who admired Britain for standing up to Hitler alone in the dark days of 1940 there were also many who came with a similar sense of superior destiny now, mingled with the conviction that only America could 'make the world safe for democracy'. Impatience to get on with the invasion, smash Adolf Hitler and get home again combined with the exhilaration of a great adventure afoot. In their urgency to get across the Channel there was the temerity of inexperience, as they found more caution than they could understand in the war-battered, deprived island whose problems and priorities were so different from those of their own Fortress America, far removed from the realities of war.

In the succinct words of General de Gaulle, many Britons saw Ike's Yanks disturbingly as 'good natured, bad mannered'. From the staffs and the airmen in their East Anglian bases down to the simplest GI, they lived in comfort unheard of in Britain, remote from all but the most painless food-rationing, and with pay-packets several times those of their British and even Canadian counterparts. Though, with typical generosity, many spread their rations among their British friends (sometimes in return for favours in a different coin), in London particularly there was mounting resentment at the teeming, vastly inflated staffs bulging out of Grosvenor Square ('over-paid, over-sexed and over-here' went the acid joke; and it might have added, 'over-weight'), and at the USAAF aircrews whooping it up between ops, flashing those big white £5 notes with their girlfriends' telephone numbers scribbled on the back. But in that 'Ball before Waterloo' atmosphere of 1944 what the Londoners seldom saw were the American front-line troops, lean and tough infantrymen training down in the West Country, or the paratroopers of the 101st and 82nd Airborne Divisions round Newbury; nor were they always aware of the terrible losses suffered daily by the aircrews limping back to East Anglia from their non-stop daylight bombing raids.

Most of the Americans waiting and training in Britain were unmarried and their combination of high spirits, high pay and sheer novelty made them fairly irresistible. But equally the pressures of war and prolonged absence from home imposed heavy temptation upon the married, senior officers. Many of them established wartime liaisons; the swashbuckling Patton was seldom without comfort – later veiled from the sight back home of the only being he truly feared, his wife Beatrice, as a visiting 'niece'. Even that stern disciplinarian Walter Bedell Smith, Ike's Chief of Staff, had his Nurse Wilbur; while Ike himself was falling progressively in love with his driver/secretary, the attractive divorced Irishwoman, Kay Summersby,* sometimes described as his *chauffeuse*. Ike, nevertheless, strongly disapproved of the Babylonian high living and conspicuous consumption of many of his staff officers in London. A man of simple tastes in which reading westerns and playing gin-rummy predominated, he ran from the exigencies of the London hostesses (becoming 'almost as much of a recluse as Greta Garbo', according to Lieutenant Summersby), and hated life in a hotel. To get away from it all, he found a peaceable retreat at Telegraph Cottage, the least pretentious quarters of any general in his command, only half an hour from his GHQ in Grosvenor Square and minutes from Bushey Park, where the USAAF had its headquarters. Kay Summersby claimed that it was the nearest to a 'real home' that either had during the whole war; she also acquired for him a much

* Though she could only see her side of it, dying of cancer in 1973, Kay Summersby (who many years earlier had published a restrained account entitled *Eisenhower Was My Boss*) wrote her story of the love affair (*Past Forgetting*) which, given the circumstances, has a strong ring of truth to it – the last testament of a woman under sentence of death. Stephen Ambrose (2), however, questions whether it was ever 'a genuine love affair', or the sad fantasy of a dying woman. As he says, 'No one will ever know.'

loved Scottie that Ike christened Telek* ('a combination of Telegraph Cottage and Kay, two parts of my life that make me very happy,' said Ike).† With his personal staff constantly in attendance, their affair was largely a question of 'stealing a few kisses . . . more like teen-agers', and their few attempts to make love ended with Ike apologetically confessing impotence under all the prevailing stresses and strains of the war – and of being found out.

His affinity for dogs and for the seclusion afforded by Telegraph Cottage (though the motives may not all have been similar) must have been about the only characteristics Ike and Monty had in common. There were never two more different personalities on the same battlefield, and nobody has put the contrasts between them better than Alan Moorehead, who knew them both:

> Their very appearance displayed their opposing yet interlocking natures. On Eisenhower's broad and smiling face, everything was boyishness, frankness and enthusiasm. Even in his loose-limbed walk and his warm, full voice there was an air of friendliness and plain dealing. The heart warmed to him at once. Here was a man who was still the boy who once fished by the water-hole, an extrovert without any pretensions, a leader who knew and lived by all the weakness and failings and emotions of the ordinary human being.

In sharp contrast, wrote Moorehead,

> was set that 'intensely compacted hank of steel wire' that made up the troubled and complicated nature of Montgomery. It was the difference between the fire and the burning glass, the humanist and the individualist, the extrovert and the introvert, the determined amateur and the professional.

Ike was essentially gregarious and got on well with everybody – *especially* with his contemporaries; he drank, chain-smoked and blasphemed, and had a temper with a notoriously short fuse. And he was at ease with women. Meanwhile, as his antithesis, Kay Summersby came to hate Monty with a passion: 'the only person in the whole Allied Command whom I disliked. Not only was he a

* Telek survived, as Kay's pet, to the ripe old age of seventeen.

† Summersby, *Past Forgetting*, p. 62.

supercilious woman-hating little martinet, but he did things that used to make me so indignant that I would say to the General, "How can you stand it? Why don't you tell him off?" '* Monty's 'self-righteousness and rigidity often had the General actually gasping in anger', she claimed. But one may be entitled to wonder to what extent she fanned this anger – just as, *mutatis mutandis*, Brooke could work up Monty's disapprobation of Ike's professional shortcomings.

What really was to separate the two leaders, however, in the crucial months ahead, was their very different attitudes to warfare. Like his predecessor, Ulysses S. Grant, Ike favoured a strategy of constant attack, all along the line, with no component left idle. His was a policy of maximum utilization. As his biographer, Stephen Ambrose, explains,† 'He came from a mass-production society, and like any good general he wanted to use his nation's strengths on the battlefield,' whereas 'The British strength was brains, not brawn. Montgomery proposed to defeat the Germans in France by outthinking and outmanoeuvring them.' This was hardly anything to be ashamed of. There was also a sense, as of January 1944, that this great 'mass-production society' had greater reserves of manpower to be drawn upon for this strategy of maximum utilization.

With Ike as his immediate superior in the OVERLORD set-up, Monty would have under his command in 21 Army Group four army commanders. At the head of British Second Army was Miles Dempsey, rather delicate in appearance, with a service dress hat that always looked a size too big, but quietly competent and very much a Monty man. There was Crerar the Canadian, about whom Monty seldom had much good to say, considering him not up to the quality of the excellent men he commanded. Then there were Omar Bradley of the US First Army and – like a *deus ex machina* waiting in the wings to make a well-timed appearance – Patton of the US Third.

Almost until the last moment, a perennial question-mark hung over Patton's head – disgraced after the soldier-slapping incident in Sicily and repeatedly on the verge of disgrace for indiscretions in England. He was saved only by Ike's long-standing friendship, and by admiration for his unique qualities as the 'fastest with the mostest' commander America possessed. It was an admiration shared

* Summersby, *Past Forgetting*, p. 103.

† Ambrose (2), p. 145.

by none more than Patton himself: 'on reflection,' he wrote after the Sicily campaign, 'who is as good as I am? I know of no one.' Predictably, two such supreme egoists as Patton and Monty would not be long abiding each other. Even the modest and businesslike Bradley had expressed his reluctance to have Patton serve under him (Patton in return dubbed Bradley sneeringly 'Omar the tent-maker'). As far as 'Brad' himself was concerned, in Ike's view there was 'no position in the Army that he could not fill with success'; he was 'about the best rounded, well-balanced, senior officer that we have', Ike wrote to Marshall in 1943.* By 1944 this respect was widely shared by the British, while Bradley's relations with Monty all the way through Normandy – and right up to the dark days of 1945 – would remain about as good as they possibly could be.

Like Ike, with nowhere to live in London, in January 1944 Monty himself began by lodging at Claridge's, amid luxury that he had found, temporarily, not uncongenial during his visit to London of the previous spring – while a flat was being prepared for him at Latymer Court, West London. It lay next door to his old school of St Paul's, which, its students evacuated for the duration, had been chosen by Monty to be headquarters of 21 Army Group. Here, from the High Master's study – a room which he claimed he had never previously entered, even as a school prefect or captain of the 1st XV ('I had to become a Commander-in-Chief to do so')† – over the next five short months, all the plans for OVERLORD would be drawn up.

In the run-up to D-Day, apart from his temporary flat at Latymer Court, Amesbury School also became Monty's home, where he and his son kept their few belongings. Shortly after Alamein in November 1942 David had received the following: 'Great things have happened in the last few days and honours have been showered on me. My promotion to General and Knighthood – it is quite amazing.' From this moment of genuine and ingenuous delight at the honours being showered upon him, David noted a steady self-inflation of his father's

* Ambrose (1), p. 189.
† Montgomery, *Memoirs*, p. 213.

ego. Monty wrote on 15 February 1943, just after the capture of Tripoli:

> By the time you get this you may have received a portrait of myself. Take great care of it and it must go to Uncle Tom who has full instructions from me about getting it framed. Enclosed is a photo portrait, painted of me for the nation; it is by the same artist, Neville Lewis.

There was something almost touchingly childlike about his growing obsession with photographs and portraits of himself. The Reynoldses' small house became full to overflowing with trophies. To follow up the success of the Neville Lewis canvas in the desert, Monty charged Kit Dawnay with finding him a portrait painter in London. Improbably Dawnay chose that Bohemian satyr, Augustus John, then regarded as the best in the country. He was commissioned at £500 (a fairly handsome sum for a portrait in those days).

The encounter, however, was not a success, with the two forming an instant antipathy to each other and Monty complaining, 'Kit – I don't know where you found that chap. He's dirty, he drinks – and there are women in the background!' It was a considerable understatement. The painting gave Monty a long, narrow face and made him look like a greyhound. He rejected it; John was delighted, and promptly sold it for a vastly larger sum on the open market. The only benefit to emerge from the episode was an unexpectedly felicitous relationship between Monty and George Bernard Shaw, who had come to watch the sittings. Agreeing with Monty about the painting, the writer and the General hit it off to a surprising degree. Possibly Shaw evoked the lost world to which Betty had introduced him. 'Take that old petrol rag that wiped out so many portraits of me (all masterpieces),' Shaw told John,

> and rub out this one until the canvas is blank. Then paint a small figure looking at you straight from above, as he looks at me from the dais. . . . The present sketch isn't honestly worth more than the price of your keep while you were painting it. You really weren't interested in the man.

Meanwhile he informed the General, '. . . I'll tell you when the war is going to end.' Monty: 'Really?' Shaw: 'When money goes to five per cent – all wars end then!' 'Money' never did reach anything like 5 per cent. Shaw was out of touch.

For a fifteen-year-old schoolboy at Winchester, the return of the hero father, probably less well known to him than to millions of other Britons, was an extraordinary experience. David had last seen his father during his brief visit to London that had followed the victory in North Africa the previous May. Taken out to the theatre by him, he had been quite unprepared for the scene when the entire audience rose and clapped once the little General had been spotted taking his place in his box: 'They went wild. It was extraordinary – just like a pop star today!' With it came the speedy realization of what fame had done to his father's personality and of what it had imposed on the former recluse.

Anyone not in England at the time might find it almost impossible to imagine the degree of adulation which Monty received in 1944. It was quite unprecedented, far exceeding even that accorded Wellington after Waterloo, even Nelson at his peak of popularity. It meant that he could get his troops, American as well as British, to do anything for him. The downside was that it also marked 'the turning point in Monty's character', observed his devoted but dispassionate intelligence chief, Bill Williams: 'I really think it turned his head.'* The seeds of this almost Bonaparte-like vanity were already there, but they were to blossom into a fatal hubris.

Once again, Montgomery had the rare good fortune to have in Eisenhower – as he had had in Alexander – a superior who was willing to give him a free hand. Whatever Monty's reservations about his generalship, it was Eisenhower's style as overall commander to stand back, handing over to Monty all the detailed operational planning – which was eagerly accepted. Nevertheless, the final result was to reflect the combined output of many minds, British and American, working over many months and always within the limits allowed by the navy and the air force. Over the next five months identity of purpose, coupled to Eisenhower's greatness of spirit as a coalition commander, produced a rare amity between the generals of the two nations (even between Patton and Monty) that was not always to be found after 6 June 1944.

* Interview 25 November 1992.

As soon as Monty arrived back in London he set to demolishing the COSSAC plans, which had been constructed laboriously over the previous year and a half by Lieutenant-General Sir Frederick Morgan and his staff, but which – from the moment he had seen them in Marrakech – he had considered to be 'useless, quite useless'. The brief, and resources, given to the unfortunate Morgan had been well-nigh impossible (Brooke had told him, encouragingly, 'It won't work, but you must bloody well make it'). Nevertheless, the unfairly dismissive manner in which Monty treated him and his team was immediately to open fresh wounds and create new foes where he least needed them. By 9 a.m. on 3 January, the morning after his arrival from Marrakech, Monty at his first meeting in St Paul's School had destroyed the COSSAC blueprint, replacing it with a five-, instead of a three-, division assault. This would involve extending the US component westwards to what was to become UTAH beach at the base of the Cherbourg Peninsula. Remarking on the lessons of Sicily, Monty declared that what was needed was not a town so much as a bridgehead – and a port. The extra landing craft would have to be found; otherwise there would be 'no show'. Eisenhower immediately gave Monty his unquestioning support.

By 6 January there was a plan; as early as the 7th, at a meeting of the army commanders, Monty made it plain that the capture of Caen was a number-one priority and that his strategy would be to use the British Second Army to the east to protect the US flank, to 'attract and contain' the powerful Panzer forces likely to arrive from the Pas de Calais. But he also added an important caution, which was perhaps insufficiently heeded at the time, namely that 'the British had reached the limits of their manpower' and would be unable to form an extra army group. Although not foreseen at the time this, coupled with the shortage of landing craft, would seriously curtail what might have been achieved at the eastern, British end of the invasion. Finally, as commander of the land forces, Monty declared that he would need to control the administration of both US and British armies. Omar Bradley, the US First Army commander, agreed to this last 'in principle'. Nevertheless there was some resentment in the American camp at the way it was put, and – after the break-out in August – it was to become the major source of strife between Americans and British.

Meanwhile, an early, and critical, disagreement took place over American insistence on pressing ahead with ANVIL, the secondary landings projected for the South of France. In his Prelude to the Alanbrooke war diaries, published fifteen years after D-Day, Arthur Bryant declared that between America's entry into the war in the 'calamitous winter of 1941–42', when Brooke first became CIGS, and the summer of 1944 the Western Allies 'made no major strategic mistake', but 'From the time when the landing in the South of France was agreed, they made several – nearly all at Washington's or Eisenhower's instance – which not only delayed victory and exacted a heavy toll of human life, but threw away part of its ultimate fruits.'* Though history may judge Bryant to have been harsh, this certainly represented the view of Brooke – and of Monty. The argument over ANVIL was to rage long after the war. The main objection of Churchill (who came close to resigning over it) was that he had always wanted the force earmarked for it to be despatched eastwards, across the Adriatic and up through the so-called Ljubljana Gap to liberate Eastern Europe ahead of the Soviets. Stalin had proposed ANVIL at the Teheran Conference and, for the most obvious geopolitical reasons, was keen to see Allied strength deployed in the west. Roosevelt went along. Originally ANVIL was intended to be synchronized with D-Day, when it might have been of some small use in distracting German divisions from the north. As it was, about all it did was to pin down precious Allied landing craft which could otherwise have been employed to strengthen and expand the OVERLORD landings eastwards. Eventually ANVIL (renamed DRAGOON) went in, as per plan, on 15 August, but by this date the Battle of Normandy was won.

Monty fought incessantly against ANVIL as representing an unnecessary diversion of precious landing craft: 'One of the great strategic mistakes of the war', he wrote in his memoirs. It further persuaded him that Ike had no proper sense of strategic priorities. But the overall shortage of landing craft reflected most badly on President Roosevelt and his advisers, and on some of their early decisions after Pearl Harbor. With the need to replace US warship losses uppermost in his mind, in early 1942 FDR was on record as

* Bryant, *Triumph in the West*, p. 24.

saying that he thought construction of landing craft was 'a mistake'. By November he had permitted it to slide down to twelfth place on the US Navy's Shipbuilding Precedence List.* It was not on his 'must' list of programmes for 1943; in March of that year the British were pointing out to the US Joint Chiefs of Staff that invasion in 1944 was being jeopardized by shortage of LSTs and LCTs (Landing Ship Tanks and Landing Craft Tanks) and that British production could not make up the shortfall. This was greeted with the suspicion that Britain was deploying deficiencies as an excuse for shuffling her feet over the invasion plans, while the British in their turn believed (not without reason) that Admiral King was surreptitiously diverting landing craft to the Pacific for his own purposes. The shortage of landing craft seems to have been relative rather than absolute. Out of a massive total of 31,123 of all categories held by the US, by 1 May 1944 King had allocated to OVERLORD only a paltry 2493 – and these with reluctance. As a result, according to the Australian, Chester Wilmot, of the 6000 landing craft available to Ike, less than half were provided from US Navy resources. Admittedly, landing craft were indispensable to the island-hopping war in the Pacific; but, in Wilmot's view, King's tightfistedness here could well have spelled disaster on 6 June.†

It was altogether an unhappy story. In February forty-one of the precious landing craft were ordered diverted from OVERLORD to the Mediterranean and ANVIL, even though only a few weeks previously Ike had himself warned Marshall that ANVIL could 'cost us a month of good campaigning weather'. At the same time, from Italy Alexander was refusing to release to OVERLORD thirteen LSTs, on the ground that they were essential for supplying the mismanaged Anzio bridgehead; nor was it easy to make any swift redisposition between Mediterranean and Channel of these lighter vessels. The truth was that, here, Monty was largely right, and the shortage of landing craft left the OVERLORD planners with limited options.

*

* Aircraft carriers, vital in the Pacific, but of absolutely no use for D-Day, were first: Eric Larrabee, *Commander in Chief*, p. 445.

† Wilmot, *The Struggle for Europe*, p. 179.

With D-Day now fixed for just five months away, from January onwards the vast staffs – British and American – set to work with a new, feverish energy. As Bill Williams observed, 'the difference which Monty's arrival made was the incredible decisiveness which followed'. Noteworthy also was the tremendous self-confidence which now swept over 21 Army Group. The question poses itself: would Alexander, who had also been considered for the command of the invasion land forces, have been able to act with the necessary decision and ruthlessness? Would he have scrapped the COSSAC plan to begin with? Otherwise D-Day must surely have failed.

Says Monty in his memoirs, '. . . I left the details to de Guingand and his staff and devoted my main efforts to ensuring that the weapon we were to use would be fit for battle.' Much as his natural instinct might have dictated, there was little now that Monty, the supreme trainer of men, could do to whip into a shape conforming to his standards the vast, conglomerate force that he was to command. It was too large, too disparate, and from his new elevation he was too far removed from unit commanders to achieve much; and time was too short. Only three divisions and two armoured brigades in England had actually served under him in the desert or Italy and knew his ways.* It was not easy to achieve his aim of 'spreading battle experience over the widest possible area'. Thus, concentrating on priorities, Monty devoted his time and his furious energy to 'bingeing up' the troops. On reaching England he had swiftly recognized, as he confided to his diary, that 'the great mass of the people are getting war weary'. Among soldiers as well as civilians, 'Enthusiasm is lacking.'

He started at Aldershot on his very first day home. As in the desert, his principal objective was as much for the men to see him as the other way round. His technique was simple. He would arrive in a jeep, without formality, and summon the troops around him with a loudspeaker. This would be accompanied by a measured walk down the ranks, with piercing stares into the men's eyes. He would thus address some 30,000 men a day: 'they came running in thousands towards him, would sit at his feet and listen to the thin, religious voice,' recalled Alan Moorehead; ' "Finish the thing off. You and I

* But all subsequently failed to some extent, as will be seen.

are together . . . with God's help we will see the job through to the end." It was the same with each meeting, the same brand of faith and conviction, and he talked with the same assurance to Americans and Canadians, even to the Norwegians and Poles.' One line which made the greatest impact with infantrymen would go as follows:

'You. What's your most valuable possession?'

'My rifle, Sir.'

'No, it isn't; it's your life, and I'm going to save it for you. Now listen to me . . .'*

He would then go on to explain how he would never make the infantry attack without full artillery and air support. Such visits were, as Richard Lamb records, almost invariably:

> successful beyond expectation. He had, after all, spent a lifetime with soldiers, and he loved and understood them, especially young men; he could mesmerize them by his speeches, and he revelled in his popularity. Now he found that the average young soldier expected to die in the coming assault, and he sought to dispel their gloom by instilling a revivalist fervour. In this he was right, for morale in Britain was low.†

Starting on 14 January, his first tour took him round Omar Bradley's US First Army. As his Canadian Personal Assistant, Lieutenant-Colonel Trumbull Warren, recalls,‡ he 'was very nervous. He didn't really know the Americans.' Some of them sniggered, finding his English accent affected and irritating. Diplomatically, he praised 'my good friend Ike', declared how proud he was to serve under him and said Ike had invited him to visit the States, but he didn't know 'whether to start in the North or South'. At which point, recalls Warren, 'some black soldier at the back said: "What the hell are you trying to do? Start another war?!" ' Subsequently Monty dropped the subject from his repertoire, gradually learning how to reach the hearts of the American soldiers – most of them frankly amazed that he, commander of two million men, should take time off to come and see them personally. Bradley himself admitted

* Sir Richard Powell, quoted in Chalfont, *Montgomery of Alamein*, p. 228.

† *Montgomery in Europe*, p. 71.

‡ Quoted in Hamilton, *Monty*, vol. II, p. 509.

that among the British 'the legend of Monty had become an imperishable fact'. He added, 'Even Eisenhower with all his engaging ease could never stir American troops to the rapture with which Monty was welcomed by his.'*

After the Americans, from February onwards Monty made a point of visiting every single unit of the British and Canadians that would serve under his command. His pocket Smythson's Featherweight Diary† often records visits to a division a day, seven divisions a week. The immense amount of travel involved was facilitated by a special train, codenamed 'Rapier', which comprised four coaches converted into kitchens, messrooms, sleeping accommodation and a self-contained headquarters, plus a flatcar on to which the Commander-in-Chief's Rolls-Royce was loaded, prepared for embarkation as speedily as any D-Day landing craft. David Montgomery vividly recalls travelling around with his father on Rapier during the spring holidays of 1944:

> As it was a train only staffed by soldiers, I had to be added to the strength as a supernumerary. At that time I think I was probably a lance-corporal [in the Winchester Officer Training Corps], so I duly put on my Corps uniform and joined the train. This trip the train went to Glasgow, where we visited factories and I remember we went to see an international football match at Hampden Park. On all occasions, of course, my father was treated as a great hero. Coming out of factories he was virtually mobbed by people and indeed when we went to Hampden Park there was a roar from the crowd for him as he entered the Royal Box. He was treated everywhere with great respect and great affection. The reason for these visits was . . . to explain that he was going to win the war for them quickly, and that they must trust him as he trusted them, and prepare for the great adventure.

He also visited the women who were working in the munitions factories:

> for the same reason and to get them involved in the war, and to

* Bradley, *A Soldier's Story*, p. 209.

† Monty's pocket diary contained only a list of engagements. For his personal diary, he dictated a record of the day's events; in the desert this was done every day, but in Europe he was often three or four days late and thus tempted to be wise after the event.

> give them the feeling that they were part of a team, and that he was going to look after their husbands, etc., and so generate morale at all levels. This, of course, was an extremely good idea – but didn't find favour with politicians.

After Monty had given a pep talk in February to 500 railway trades unionists at Euston Station (unprecedented for any soldier, but – because of his unassailable popularity – well received), there were broad hints that he should 'lay off' these visits ('I paid no attention'). Jealous minds accused him of 'politicking', of harbouring political ambitions – quite unfairly. David Montgomery recalls an 'apocryphal story' going the rounds at the time, 'of Churchill and the King having a conversation; Churchill saying to the King, "I'm very worried, I think Monty is after my job." And the King replied, "Gosh! I'm very relieved to hear that; I thought he was after mine!" '

At a 'Salute the Soldier' lunch in the Mansion House in March, at which Monty and Sir James ('P. J.') Grigg, Churchill's Secretary of State for War, were the main speakers, he gave full throat to his messianic self-assurance:

> Can you imagine this conversation in after years? 'What did you do in the world war?' 'I pulled hard to start with; but after a time I began to lose interest and let go the rope. I thought I needed a rest, and more pay . . .' 'And did you win?' 'No. We lost. I let go of the rope and we lost the match. God forgive me, we lost the match.' Is it possible that such a conversation could apply to us British? No, it is impossible. Thank God it is impossible.

'Then let us stand to and get on the rope,' he continued. 'How long will the pull last? No one can say for certain; it may last years, it may take longer, but it will be a magnificent party and we shall win.'

'The Church Militant', remarked Moorhead of this extraordinary *tour de force*, 'had found her champion. The Bishop himself could not have done better than his faithful son.' But at the Mansion House Monty also came dangerously close to criticizing the political leadership when he declared forthrightly, 'it must forever redound to our shame that we sent our soldiers into this most modern war with weapons and equipment that were quite inadequate; we have only ourselves to blame for the disasters that early overtook us in the field'. Given that his immediate political chief, Grigg, was on the same platform, it was particularly audacious. Given, equally, that his main function in these months before D-Day was to boost the confidence of the troops, he would have had to tread most warily over what he *really* thought about the current adequacy of the equipment (notably tanks) that would be taken to France. There were more growls of disapproval from an uneasy government. The BBC was pressured into cutting down his invitations to speak. All of this may help explain why Monty's views on British armour were uncharacteristically muted.*

Nor was every visit to the troops an unqualified success. When he inspected a unit of the new and untried Guards Armoured Division (his relations with the Brigade of Guards always being somewhat uncertain), Rapier was late and the men were cold and stiff from having been kept standing on parade for hours. 'Tell the men to stand at ease,' ordered Monty. 'They are, Sir,' the commanding officer replied frostily. Inevitably more enemies were made. Monty himself recognized the problem in his diary: 'The public, and the Army, are firmly behind me and would support me to the end. But not so the Generals; my own Generals in the field armies are my firm supporters, but outside the field armies is much jealousy.' Shortly after Monty's takeover and following his initial purges, one of the outgoing non-Monty generals remarked caustically, 'The Gentlemen are out. The Players are coming in.' The jealousy, to which Monty referred, among the injured 'Gentlemen' and in high places would, in the longer run, come to afflict him mightily.

Already in his dedication to building up contact with the rank and file he was perhaps neglecting relations with his peers, which would only store up trouble for the future. Says Max Hastings:

> there was an abundance of staff officers at Eisenhower's headquarters ready to poison the ear of the Supreme Commander towards Montgomery. As long as the Englishman remained victorious, he was invulnerable. But should the ground campaign falter under his direction, he had provided many powerful hostages to fortune.†

* See p. 44.
† *Overlord*, p. 58.

And many, possibly even a majority, of the said staff officers were British, not American. But for the immediate and crucial days ahead, by any standard Monty's achievements in terms of morale-boosting were astonishing and unprecedented. Only he and he alone could have effected this miracle of transformation in 1944. It was thus with justifiable pride that he claimed, 'By the middle of May, I had visited every formation in the United Kingdom.' Over a million troops had seen and recognized him in the famous black beret – which he said was 'worth at least an army corps'.

Meanwhile, not unnaturally, apart from the trip aboard Rapier – enthralling for a young boy – David saw little of his father during these weeks. In March Monty came to Winchester to deliver a lecture to the college, one of five he gave between Alamein and VE-Day – occasions which, in the opinion of Bill Williams, were as often as not sources of some embarrassment to his son. On 5 May Monty was writing, apologetically, in a letter complaining about the Augustus John portrait, '. . . I am sorry I have not been able to see more of you these holidays, but April has been a particularly busy month for me; just at present I have very little spare time – if any.'

Since his return to England, the breach between Monty and his mother had widened still further, and on two separate occasions when his sisters Una and Winsome made special efforts to come to see him in the course of his pre-OVERLORD expeditions round England, he had snubbed them with a cavalier brutality that shocked his staff. When visiting a division at Guildford, near where Una lived, Trumbull Warren had suggested that she join them. Monty had been unenthusiastic; by mishap, Una went to the wrong camp and reached her brother's retinue just as it was leaving. Dick Carver, who was with him, shouted, 'Stop the car! There's Una – she'll be upset if you don't say hello!' But Monty ordered, 'Drive on!' Una was furious, and deeply hurt. Trumbull Warren recalled an almost identical rebuff handed out to the unfortunate Winsome. When Monty later received the Freedom of Maidenhead, her local town, Jocelyn Carver would find herself explicitly not invited; she got a ticket, and came and sat at the back – anonymously. 'I think I understand him,' said Bill Williams after the war. 'He had a fear of his family taking the spin off. . . . I think his family knew him too well, he couldn't quite project his image in the way he wished to.' On the other hand, his deep sense of indebtedness to Betty came through when he declared, repeatedly, 'I have got to get John and Dick alive through this war.'

Monty's last tour on Rapier, within a month of D-Day, took him to Scotland. He was very tired, and was persuaded to take a few days' holiday, walking and fishing from Dalwhinnie in the Highlands. But it was not all holiday. Amid utmost secrecy, Monty's 'double', Lieutenant M. E. Clifton James, a peacetime actor serving in the Army Pay Corps, came aboard Rapier with the commission of 'watching his every movement and trying to catch his fleeting expression'.* Clifton James was one important cog in the remarkably successful deception plan to delude the Germans about the Allies' real intentions. He was then despatched to parade openly in Monty's uniform in Gibraltar and North Africa – to persuade Hitler's spies that the main Allied landings were going to come in the South of France, led of course by Monty. The notion of the 'double' tickled Monty's vanity; he liked Clifton James, respecting his courage, and, enjoying the War Office's discomfiture, insisted that the actor–subaltern be paid a full general's pay while he actually wore the uniform.

In his diary for 30 May, Monty's ADC, Johnny Henderson, noted:

> Fellow who is pretending to be General Monty for cover plan, left for Gibraltar. He is dressed in General M.'s beret and battledress and is to have breakfast with the Governor of Malta and then go on to Algiers. The object is to make the Germans think Gen. M. has gone out there to review the forces which will attack in the South of France. It is a risky one, but a lot to lose and not so very much to gain.

On the contrary! He continued his diary two days later, with what seems like a notable breach of security, given all that was at stake:

> Gen. Monty's double has had immediate reaction. The Germans think Gen. Monty to have been in Gibraltar for talks. They put their best spy in England into finding out if he had left the country. The spy has been caught, and his wireless used to send a signal to the Germans to say that Gen. Monty does seem to have disappeared.

* M. E. C. James, *I Was Monty's Double.*

Monty himself, no less indiscreet, recorded this information in his own personal diary, and added, 'I am now going about without flying a flag on my car, and I do not wear my black beret when out.' Even more successful a ploy was Operation FORTITUDE, the 'invention' of a fantasy invasion force directed at the Pas de Calais. Notionally under the larger-than-life Patton, a fantasy '1 US Army Group' was created in south-east England. Through cunning use of a massive array of dummy landing craft, vehicles and signals networks it established a phoney order-of-battle bigger even than the real 21 Army Group. Coupled with this went an output of false intelligence plants to the effect that the main invasion would not be ready for several weeks yet. Very much a British initiative strongly backed by Monty (the Americans were curiously sceptical about this kind of intelligence operation), FORTITUDE was to prove an ace card in the success of OVERLORD. With his extraordinary sixth sense, Hitler remained certain that the main Allied landings would be in Normandy, but – fortunately – failed to pursue his hunches. Rundstedt and the German General Staff (OKW) were completely taken in. If they had granted Rommel's request to move a second Panzer division from the Pas de Calais to St Lô in Normandy, as Max Hastings remarks, 'the consequences for the American landings on D-Day would have been incalculable, conceivably decisive'. If Operation FORTITUDE, with all its attendant success, had been Monty's only contribution to the planning of OVERLORD, this alone should have ensured him a secure place in history.

On 20 May, Peter Earle, a young major currently serving in the key post of military assistant to Brooke's right hand, General Nye, the VCIGS, recorded in his diary, 'The PM had said of Monty, "No good will come of the General if there should be any mishap in the planning." . . . He had been advised to travel less. He has now just returned from leave, as also has Brookie.' Though it was perhaps unusual that so junior an officer should become privy to the innermost fears of Winston Churchill, it was indicative of the deep apprehension at the top, on both sides of the Atlantic, as the relentless clock ticked forward. But, assured that his 'bingeing up' tours had raised morale to the highest possible pitch, Monty was equally confident that there would be absolutely no possibility of 'any mishap in the planning' – certainly as far as he was concerned. In the Smythson pocket diary for 7 April there is just the laconic entry, 'War Game, Thunderclap', and again, on 15 May, THUNDERCLAP, followed by 'Dine CIGS'. Exercise THUNDERCLAP was in fact Monty's grand rehearsal of his master blueprint, run up in the three months since that first meeting at St Paul's. In a comfortless lecture room, in front of two huge maps, on 7 April, Good Friday, Monty held forth to the entire cadre of generals, admirals and air marshals who would take part in D-Day. Also present were Brooke and Eisenhower (and, later, Churchill). Had Göring's Luftwaffe dropped a bomb on the school that day, OVERLORD would have been defeated as surely as if the invasion force were hurled into the sea.

Monty began by putting himself in the boots of his old adversary, Rommel. The enemy would, he reckoned (and events were to show his hunch to have been correct), do roughly what he, Monty, would have done to meet an enemy invasion of Britain in 1940–1: hold his armour 'back from the coast until he is certain where our main effort is being made'. He would then concentrate it 'and strike a hard blow'. Equally accurate was his estimate that the Germans' Panzer divisions, with their capacity to exert a decisive influence on the battle, would be kept directly under Rundstedt's control, and there might be delays before they were released to Rommel.* Correctly he predicted, 'This fact may help us, and quarrels may arise between the two of them.'

Defining the roles of the various armies under his command, Monty explained how Dempsey's British on the eastern flank would seize the key centre of Caen 'as early as Second Army can manage', pivoting on it to form a powerful shield while Bradley's First Army broke out from their beachheads to cut off the Cherbourg Peninsula and capture the vital port of Cherbourg. Landing after elbow room

* Rundstedt, a granite-faced Junker of the old school who never questioned either the authority or content of orders, was already over sixty when the Second World War began, but proved himself one of Hitler's most successful commanders. He had commanded Army Group 'A', the great phalanx of forty-four divisions that broke through the French defences in the *Blitzkrieg* of May 1940. After that had followed intermittent periods of command and retirement. In 1944 he was roughly Eisenhower's opposite number, as C-in-C West, commanding the whole of France and the Low Countries. Under him, Rommel (who had first risen to world fame as his most spectacular Panzer division commander in 1940) commanded Army Group 'B', covering the whole invasion area from Brittany to the Pas de Calais. This consisted of two armies, the Fifteenth in the Calais area, and the Seventh in Normandy.

had been secured, Patton's US Third Army would then push through Bradley's front, clearing Brittany and covering Bradley's southern flank while he broke out south-eastwards towards Paris.

There was, with hindsight, what seems now like a serious deficiency in the role laid down for Dempsey's British Second Army in the D-Day plans, and which was to have a baneful consequence on all Monty's efforts to seize Caen: inadequate provisions were made to secure for the eastern flank the small quadrilateral of land lying between the Rivers Orne and Dives, eastwards towards Marcel Proust's watering-hole of Cabourg. In his original plan delivered on 7 January, Monty had foreseen that the landings would reach that far and that 'the marshy area [east of the Orne] in conjunction with the River Orne would assist to protect the left flank'. In fact, the River Dives, backed by the 'marshy area' (which the Germans would themselves inundate shortly before D-Day, to their own disadvantage), might have made a much better line than the Orne on which to hold off Rommel intervening with forces from the Pas de Calais. The land between would have provided Monty with essential room in which to manoeuvre on Caen. But this extension of the bridgehead was not pursued – partly because of that critical shortage of landing craft, siphoned off by ANVIL and by Alexander, partly because of the coming crisis in the reserves of British infantry (at which Monty had himself hinted that day), and partly because of pressing American needs. Last-minute intelligence of German reinforcements in the UTAH area had made Bradley insist on having the crack 82nd US Airborne Division transferred back to him; otherwise he was threatening to cancel his entire landing. Originally, the 82nd had been earmarked for the Caen area. Monty, however, readily agreed to its being deployed in the operation on Ste-Mère-Église instead. Had it – or another infantry division – been available to back up the British east of the Orne, it might have saved him many thousands of men, weeks of fighting and, possibly, also his reputation.

Nevertheless, it was 'A wonderful day that Monty ran', Brooke recorded with relief in his diary that night. He overlooked what at the time might have passed for a minor error of judgement by Monty, but which was to grow into a major Anglo-American rift and fuel a deadly historical controversy unresolved to this day. When the US commanders entered the St Paul's lecture room that April morning, they found themselves confronted with a map on which Monty had, apparently with little forethought, asked Lieutenant-Colonel Kit Dawnay (now promoted to be his Military Assistant, or senior staff officer, at TAC HQ) to mark in coloured 'phase lines', on the basis of his presentation notes. They showed various lines in north-west France which Monty expected the Allied armies to have reached between D-Day and D + 90. The last, black line stopped just short of Paris. But where the storm burst and where Monty gave every hostage to the mounting ranks of his enemies and critics was Dawnay's marking in of the first two, green lines on the map: D + 17 showed the British firmly in possession of Caen (immediately prior to D-Day, Monty rashly committed himself to getting into Caen by the afternoon of the 6th), while D + 20 put them at Falaise and the Americans at Avranches, holding the strategic hinge of the Brittany peninsula.

It is abundantly clear that Monty did not expect to be pinned to these phase lines – except, possibly, in his intention that Caen would be taken in the first days after the landings. As Dawnay observed to Hamilton in 1978:

> In his [Monty's] opinion it was not of any importance where he would be groundwise between D plus 1 and D plus 90, because he felt sure he could capture the line D plus 90 by the end of three months,* and he was not going to capture ground, he was going to destroy enemy forces.†

Dawnay, adds Hamilton, never dreamed that his arbitrary lines 'would be used in evidence against Monty when the campaign did not go "according to plan" '. Monty himself, in his book *Normandy to the Baltic*, written in 1946 before memories had become seriously ossified, claims that he was 'not altogether happy' at the time about the phase lines, 'because the imponderable factors in an operation of the magnitude of Overlord make such forecasting so very academic'. This is reinforced by the eminent (and critical) British military historian Ronald Lewin, who cautions, 'The danger of such maps is that they are essentially professional tools which, if misused, can do damage. . . . [Such a map] represents a rational estimation

* Which, in fact, he did.

† Hamilton, *Monty*, vol. II, pp. 559–60.

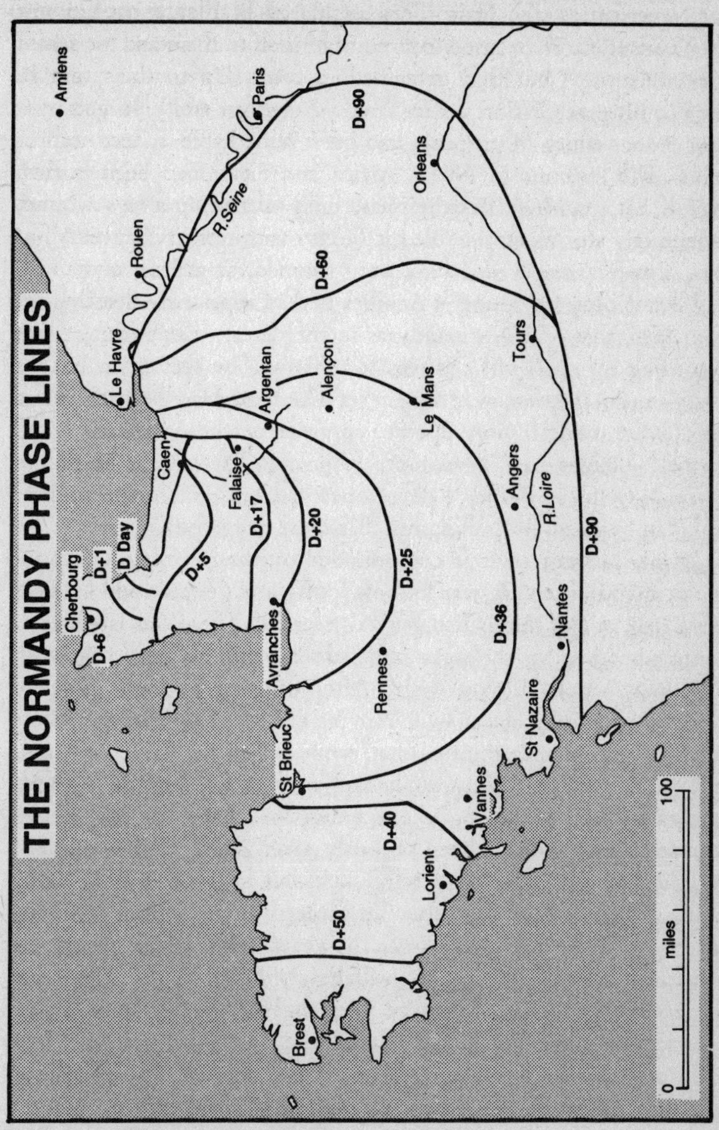

The Normandy Phase Lines

of a possibility, rather than a committal of a cast-iron guarantee.'*

Nevertheless, the phase lines infuriated Bradley, who had not been consulted. He refused to commit himself to them and requested their deletion – but they remained in place. Up to this point in the planning of OVERLORD, Anglo-American amity, forged by a tremendous unity of purpose, had been remarkable, indeed impeccable. The tensions of North Africa and Sicily had been buried, even if not forgotten. But the phase lines opened up a new wound, indefinitely storing up trouble for Monty within the Alliance. All of this, however, might well have been avoided, or at least contained, had it not been for Monty's Achilles heel of repeatedly insisting, *ex post facto*, that – in Normandy as in the desert – 'everything went according to plan'. His motives for this will be seen later, but, as every corporal knew, war was never like that. Had he been just a grain more modest, more open to admit error, the Americans – and history – might have been more forgiving. To write as he did in *Normandy to the Baltic*, 'I never once had cause or reason to alter my plan,' was surely trailing his coat most dangerously.

American distress was compounded by the arrival, after tea, of the Prime Minister. He was looking 'puffy and dejected and his eyes were red', one of the British generals recalled. There was laughter as Monty, bending for the cigar-addicted Churchill his rigid rule, said, 'You may smoke if you wish!' After listening to some gung-ho remarks by Monty about swift-moving armoured thrusts, the Prime Minister got up and admitted that, while he had not been convinced in 1942, or 1943, that a cross-Channel invasion was feasible, 'Gentlemen, I am *now* hardening to this enterprise.' After the war, Eisenhower claimed to have been seriously taken aback: 'I then realized for the first time that Mr Churchill hadn't believed in it all along and had had no faith that it would succeed. It was quite a shocking discovery.' Like the phase lines, however, what seems clearly an American overreaction might well be attributed to the Allies not understanding the same language. Churchill did, though, leave Monty worried that night that he had looked 'tired and worn out, and I fear did not create the inspiring influence I had wanted'. He speculated gloomily, 'If he cracks up now we shall be in a bad way.'

* *Montgomery as Military Commander*, p. 183.

During the latter stages of THUNDERCLAP, disputes with the 'air barons' had been mounting up. Deplorably, a lot of personal jealousies were involved. At the beginning of March, Monty was noting in his diary:

> I can see trouble ahead. . . . Harris (Bomber Command) and Spaatz (American Heavy Bombers) will not take orders from Leigh-Mallory.* I am not surprised. L.M. is a very nice chap indeed and is easy to work with [which, in fact, later proved to be far from the case]; but he is definitely above his ceiling.

Ideally Tedder, Monty's air-force commander from Alamein days, should have had the job; but he coveted the post of Deputy Supreme Commander to Eisenhower – which, under pressure from Churchill, he got. Inter-service communications were not improved by the fact that, though army and navy HQs were at Portsmouth, Allied Tactical Air Forces had their HQ at Uxbridge, on the other side of London. Harris of Bomber Command reigned, remote and unapproachable, from High Wycombe. Occasionally he would emerge to growl, unhelpfully – as he did at Monty's final THUNDERCLAP briefing just three weeks before D-Day – that his bombers were beating Germany into the ground and what, therefore, was the point of a land invasion at all?

On their side, the airmen had had much to contend with. As late as February, Marshall in Washington was urging Eisenhower to consider dropping an airborne division on Evreux, forty-five miles west of Paris – a disastrous concept, as Arnhem was to prove. After much unhappy soul-searching on humanitarian grounds, the Cabinet had finally agreed to Monty's Transportation Plan, whereby the whole rail and road network in northern France would be steadily blasted from the air, night and day. It was recognized that this would inevitably result in heavy French civilian casualties,† but the losses

* Air Chief Marshal Sir Trafford Leigh-Mallory, Air C-in-C of OVERLORD.

† The strategic bomber commanders, Spaatz and Harris, had fought strongly to maintain the maximum effort against German oil targets, in opposition to the Transportation Plan. In the event (though a painful consideration), French civilian casualties – 3000 dead over a period of only two days at the end of May – actually aided the Allies in that, by the time the invasion began, almost all the beds in the emergency hospitals available to the Germans were filled with French civilian victims. The Transportation Plan was vindicated in the tremendous disruption it caused to Rommel's reinforcements on their way to Normandy. The Oil Plan had a less obvious impact on the course of the war.

to the bomber forces had been appallingly heavy. In the two months prior to D-Day, these amounted to 2000 aircraft destroyed and 12,000 men killed. It was therefore perhaps hardly surprising that Leigh-Mallory and Tedder should, consistently, show themselves strongly resistant to any demands from Monty that might seem to risk further losses unnecessarily. In fact, the air barons' declaration that attacks on the Seine bridges would be 'suicide' proved to have been a gross overreaction, possibly influenced by memories of the dreadful casualties inflicted by the Germans in May 1940 on the RAF's vulnerable Fairey Battle bombers when attacking, ineffectually, the Meuse bridges at Sedan. As D-Day approached, Leigh-Mallory was deeply (and, as it turned out, excessively) nervous about the losses that might be suffered by the airborne armadas on both flanks of the landings at the hands of the heavy ack-ack defences in the occupied Channel Islands, Cherbourg and Le Havre – not to mention the danger from Allied ships in the confusion of battle.

As he had proved from the desert onwards, few Allied generals were more acutely tuned in to the capabilities of the tactical air weapon, and its problems, than Monty. In the event 171 Allied squadrons took part in the softening-up phases, and a staggering total of 11,000 sorties were flown on D-Day alone. But, to pacify the air barons, in May he was rashly pushed into promising that the airfields beyond Caen, for which they were clamouring, would be safely in their hands within a few days after the landings. (In his *Operation Victory*, published in 1947, de Guingand insists that no such promises were ever made; but the air barons were quite certain that they were, as were subsequent generations of military historians.)

On 15 May Monty held his Final Presentation of Plans at St Paul's. Apart from all the generals, the King, the Prime Minister and the Chiefs of Staff were in attendance. A calculatedly late arrival was George S. Patton. As the conference was about to begin there was 'an enormous hammering at the door', recalled Goronwy Rees. 'Monty looked around angrily . . . and again there was an enormous hammering.'* Finally the doors were opened, and in marched an unabashed

* Thames Television recorded interview, *The World at War, 1939–45*, in IWM.

Patton – as if to declare that nothing would keep him out, that he would do exactly as he pleased and that he would treat his British superior with total disdain.

As Leigh-Mallory recorded, Monty was wearing 'a very well-cut battle-dress with a knife-like edge to the trouser creases. He looked trim and businesslike.' His manner was 'very quiet and deliberate', speaking for only ten minutes, and 'making use of what is evidently a verbal trick of his, to repeat the most important word or phrase in a sentence more than once'. Churchill's Military Secretary, General Ismay, was reminded of Henry V before Agincourt. Beneath all that unassailable optimism, the little General struck a grave note.

To the Americans, especially, the seriousness of what he had to say was underscored by a tragedy that had overtaken their invasion forces during landing exercises called Operation TIGER a couple of weeks earlier. At Slapton Sands, German E-boats had sneaked through the Royal Navy screen to sink two LSTs. Six hundred US assault troops of the 4th Division had been drowned – more casualties than would be suffered by the whole VII Corps on D-Day itself, as Bradley later noted.

The situation, Monty told his grim-faced audience, was formidable. Latest intelligence reports showed that there were now no fewer than sixty German divisions in France, ten of them Panzer, of which four of high quality were in or near NEPTUNE, the designated British beachhead area. If all went well, by D + 2 the Allies would have twelve divisions ashore, but they would be confronted by the same number of Germans, some of them elite units. By D + 6 he would expect Rommel to launch his 'full-blooded counter-attack' to 'push us back into the sea'. And by D + 8 the balance would have shifted to eighteen against a possible twenty-four German divisions.

It was a sober picture he painted – and not one that Monty would have willingly confided to the men waiting by their tanks and assault craft, all 'binged up' from his fire-and-brimstone pep-talks of the previous weeks. At the end of it, Bradley acknowledged that the British and Canadian armies on the east were to play a 'sacrificial' mission as a decoy to draw Rommel's reserves – historically, a most significant recognition.

On the 21st, Monty took his leave of David, attending – as his diary reveals – 'evening chapel' at Winchester. He would not, he explained to the Reynoldses, make any attempt to bid him farewell nearer D-Day, because the boys would have realized just how close the invasion then was. (Phyllis Reynolds, however, was not fooled, because he had taken the last of his plain clothes – including his winter woollies, evidently not expecting a prolonged campaign – to deposit them in Amesbury School.) He and David would not see each other again for six months.

CHAPTER FOUR

A GALLANT BAND OF KNIGHTS

May–8 June 1944

There is no mistake; there has been no mistake; and there shall be no mistake.

(Duke of Wellington)

the effect was always the same, the same breathless interest that had nothing to do with discipline. Just for a moment here in the orchard or on the beach the General and the soldiers were completely at ease with one another, and all the frightening chances of war were reduced to a simple and sane community of friendship.

(Alan Moorehead, *Montgomery*, p. 169)

BY THE END of May, the whole of southern England had become one immense armed camp, densely packed with pullulating troops, armour and ammunition dumps. A heavy blanket of security gripped civilian life. Historical parallels are always dangerous, but the high nervous tension on both sides of the Channel in these last days before battle prompts thoughts of the Greek camp before the walls of Troy. Perhaps even more appropriate than the obvious parallel often drawn between Monty and Henry V before Agincourt would be one between Monty and Achilles, the dreaded, vengeful Greek warrior, an awkward (if not impossible) but indispensable commander, opposed in single combat to Hector – like Monty's old antagonist, Rommel, a noble general of unlimited resourcefulness, but committed to fight for a bad cause. Certainly on Monty's side there were some elements of personal revenge – Dunkirk chief among them – such as had finally provoked Homer's Achilles into irresistible action.

At the end of April, in preparation for the great adventure the

British Achilles had entered his battle tent, at his first TAC HQ, in a corner of Southwick Park just outside Portsmouth. Moving no less than twenty-seven times over the next twelve months, these consecutive TAC HQs – close to the battle front, but remote from the higher echelons of Allied war councils – would be his home until the Germans came to him to sign the final surrender of May 1945. Paul Odgers, an infantry major and peacetime schoolteacher, found himself (as the Senior Admin Officer) in charge of setting up the first camp at Southwick Park – and all the rest thereafter. Suddenly summoned back from Eighth Army Headquarters in Italy, he discovered to his alarm that there was no establishment laid down for the TAC HQ of an army, let alone an entire army group. He had to invent one. It all had to be done in ten days: 'I then went off and got married, and had three or four days' honeymoon. And I came back, drove down to Southwick Park, and there it was. . . . The whole outfit was in tents . . . with a marquee for Monty's dining room.' Southwick Park had previously been the home of HMS *Dryad*, the Royal Navy's Navigation School.* It now housed the whole of Monty's Main HQ, under the aegis of the hard-worked Freddie de Guingand; Eisenhower also had a forward headquarters there. As a result, so Odgers notes in his TAC HQ Chronicle (written up from his notes shortly after the war), the site:

> was a cramped one, in a quadrilateral of great trees for concealment, and was further straitened by the intrusion of a naval party, but it was convenient for the purpose of control and initial training. . . . there were strange bouts of arms drills and [the inevitable!] runs before breakfast. . . .
>
> . . . Few will forget the sense of a great wind blowing and the place suddenly crammed with Jeeps, trailers, 2½ ton trucks and steel-helmeted Americans.

The main feature inside the house at Southwick was the immense wall map, provided by a toy firm in the Midlands, showing the invasion area and the whole of northern Europe. Once the map had been set up, the two workmen and the naval officer responsible for its erection were locked in, Turkish fashion, until after the landings

* It returned there after the war, where it remains.

had taken place; in another age and another civilization they would probably have been strangled. Staffed initially by 20 officers and 200 other ranks, the tents and caravans of Monty's first TAC HQ were actually located in the grounds of nearby Broomfield House, a modest country residence.* Sergeant Kirby, in charge of Field Security, recalled that there was a 'reverential gap between our camp and the hallowed ground' of Monty's enclosure, where he kept his already famous caravans.

Of the three caravans,† one (captured in the desert from an Italian general nicknamed 'Electric Whiskers') was where Monty had slept during Alamein but which now served as his office; the second (also captured from the Italians) was to be his bedroom for most of the remainder of the war; the third, specially designed on an articulated chassis by the British Trailer Company Ltd of Manchester and presented to him as a gift just a few weeks ahead of D-Day, became his map room, and the nerve centre of TAC HQ. This was where he was briefed every evening by his young liaison officers, and in it a telephone kept him in direct contact with his subordinate commanders. The caravan where he slept, with headroom just adequate for a general of five foot seven inches, was fitted up austerely in varnished teak, much like a ship's cabin. It had a reading light at the head of the built-in bunk, a small table with a lamp, a minute hanging cupboard, an electric fan and heater – plus the supreme luxury of a basin with running water. 'I would turn out of this caravan for only two people,' claimed Monty. 'The King and Winston Churchill.' In Electric Whiskers' caravan he kept photographs of enemy generals, like Rommel, to 'try and decide what sort of person he was, and how he was likely to react to any moves I might make against him. In some curious way,' claimed Monty, 'this helped me in the battle.'

While at this first TAC HQ in England, Monty, de Guingand

* At Broomfield House today, now a family home owned by a Mr and Mrs R. E. Gale, in its rustic, Hampshire tranquillity it is hard to imagine the hubbub of 200 men, drivers and support troops, the hum of the mobile generators and the roar of arriving and departing motorcycle despatch riders. Yet traces of the protective slit trenches and barbed wire still remain, as does the hole where Monty's lock secured his study in the house. Only the great cedar tree, under which Monty posed with the King and Winston Churchill, has gone – felled by the 1987 hurricane.

† All today kept on exhibition, in their original condition, at the Imperial War Museum's Duxford Airfield out-station.

and the inner circle of aides constituting 'A' Mess actually slept and dined at Broomfield House. 'A' Mess, which all through the ensuing year was to remain Monty's holy-of-holies, was a small and intimate affair, where he dined, surrounded by his 'young men', occasionally (and unwillingly) augmented by VIPs, such as the King, the Prime Minister, P. J. Grigg and CIGS Brooke – but rarely by any other senior officer. The leading lights in the larger 'B' Mess consisted notably of his liaison officers, or LOs, who provided his 'eyes and ears', a peculiarly Monty innovation borrowed from the Duke of Wellington (who had employed eight LOs and ADCs at Waterloo) ever since his days as a brigade commander. It was to provide a most essential part of his generalship throughout the rest of the war, and set him apart totally from the way the American commanders ran their show. These LOs were, in the words used by Monty in his memoirs, 'a gallant band of knights':

> young officers of character, initiative and courage; they had seen much fighting and were able to report accurately on battle situations. I selected each personally, and my standard was high. It was dangerous work and some were wounded, and some killed.

They all had to be 'awfully nice lads who would be welcomed by any general', and they became well known throughout the armies, Monty went on to note; '. . . Churchill knew them intimately and one of his greatest delights was to sit in my map caravan after dinner at night and hear these young officers tell me the story of what was happening on the battle front.'

As of June 1944, principal among them were John Poston (formerly his ADC in the desert), Carol Mather and Dick Harden. Poston and Mather had both been with him at Alamein, Harden a tank officer in the 'Desert Rats'. Most had come with him from the Eighth Army; all were in their twenties. As long as they executed their duties efficiently, he treated them like members of an elite sixth form, or even like surrogate sons, always with courtesy and unfailing consideration, encouraging them to express provocative views in the mess of an evening. But woe betide any of Monty's young men who failed to come up to scratch, or who overstepped the mark with personal misdemeanours, such as drunkenness (though casualness of dress was very low in the order of venial sin).

Next there were the personal ADCs, like the barely twenty-four-year-old wartime 12th Lancer Johnny Henderson, Noël Chavasse – members of his original staff in the desert – and the American Ray BonDurant. An ADC was a personal dogsbody, rather like an equerry to a royal, who would accompany Monty on all trips, keeping out undesirable characters, ensuring that the timetable was adhered to and so on. BonDurant also acted as his Chief's eyes and ears vis-à-vis the Americans. Then there was Trumbull Warren, Monty's Canadian Personal Assistant (a superior ADC, one rank higher), who also advised on the Canadian troops in 21 Army Group.

Trumbull Warren, a wartime soldier from Ontario, had served on Monty's staff in England in 1942. On returning to Canada to attend staff college, he received a letter (which he has always regarded as 'one of my treasures'), in which Monty announced, 'I am off to Egypt to fight Rommel':

> and I write to say 'good-bye, my friend'; and I hope we will meet again on the field of battle, some day. I should like you to know that I am very fond of you. If anything should happen to me, against Rommel, I would like you to know that I often wish you were my own son.

After Alamein, Warren joined Monty in the desert, despite being warned by his corps commander, General Crerar, not to take the job on the grounds that every general sent to Africa had failed, that Monty would be no exception and that Warren would fail with him. Warren had replied, 'I am not a regular officer, have nothing to lose, and I worship the guy.' He was somewhat taken aback by his interview with Monty, who asked, not about his military experience, but about his family and his wife. Rejoining his regiment in Italy, he was called back a third time, at Christmas 1943, when Monty told him, 'I have got something very secret – we are going to invade Normandy, Eisenhower is going to be the Commander-in-Chief and I am going to be the Land Commander.' He told Warren that he was allowed to take a few people back with him, and he would like him to come back as his Personal Assistant. 'But if you come, you must stay with me until the end of the war; would you like that?'* Trumbull Warren did just that.

* Warren unpublished tapes.

Captain Ray BonDurant, a former mining engineer from Roanoke, Virginia, had been wounded fighting under Patton in Sicily, then – on being posted to Britain – had been amazed to find himself one of twelve officers picked by Ike's fearsome Chief of Staff, Walter Bedell Smith ('the Beetle'), for an 'elimination contest' to select one ADC for Monty. Bedell Smith had told Monty he could have one American ADC, but when the choice had been narrowed down to two, Bill Culver and BonDurant, Monty had declared arbitrarily, 'I'll take both of you. Bill, you will go with my Main HQ; and Ray, you will stay with me at TAC.' Both stayed till the end of the war. During the preparatory months BonDurant had accompanied Monty on his visits to US units and had been impressed to find him:

> truly very understanding of the American way of fighting wars. . . . he described the British soldier as one who would fight a setpiece battle; he would be told to move so many yards and that was it, and stop and dig in. He said, 'Now you Americans – very much like the Canadians – go cracking about the countryside and just keep going until you get stopped, or run out of gasoline.'*

This made a deep impression on the young American as the fighting in Normandy evolved.

Monty and his young men formed a closely knit team, almost like the family he had never had. The atmosphere was strongly paternalistic, with deep bonds of loyalty in both directions. In a sex-obsessed England of the post-war era, suggestions have been made that Monty might even have had homosexual tendencies. This was largely predicated on the number of unusual friendships he formed in his later years with very young men and boys – including the Swiss, Lucien Trueb. But all those who served in the close proximity of his TAC HQ ridicule the charges. Johnny Henderson for one, who reckons to have shared almost every meal with him from El Alamein to Lüneburger Heide, declared to an interviewer, 'I'd never even thought about it.'† In the eyes of David, his own son, reflecting on the atmosphere at TAC many years later, it possibly resembled more a 'godfather-like relationship, perhaps like a schoolmaster with his best prefects'.

* BonDurant unpublished notes.

† Lucia Santa Cruz for Alun Chalfont's *Montgomery of Alamein* in 1976.

At the higher end of the TAC HQ hierarchy came Lieutenant-Colonel Kit Dawnay, the Military Assistant, responsible for liaison on all military matters with de Guingand, Monty's Chief of Staff at Main HQ. He was also in charge of Monty's personal diary, which constituted his history of the campaign.

Senior to the Military Assistant was Colonel Leo Russell as G-1, Monty's chief staff officer at TAC HQ. Russell was not one of his young men; though a highly competent staff officer, he had had no field experience, and he had an abrasive personality. De Guingand, apprehensive (rightly, as it turned out) about the communications gulf that was bound to be created between Main and TAC, with the Channel between them, had pressed Russell's appointment as his own man close to Monty's side. But the headquarters had hardly hit France before the unfortunate Russell was proved to have been an ill-conceived appointment. Meanwhile, back at Main but always welcome and frequent visitors to TAC, Monty had brought in old favourites from the Eighth Army: the endlessly long-suffering, diplomatic Freddie de Guingand as chief of staff, with the job of carrying out Monty's wishes and picking up the pieces in case of trouble, notably with Brooke and Ike; Bill Williams as head of Intelligence; Miles Graham in charge of Admin; and Charles Richardson as head of Plans.

For all his puritanism in other directions, Monty was a keen gambler, and as an integral part of encouraging high spirits (equally, though always the teetotaller, he never objected to drinking, in moderation, by his young men) he opened a betting book* in 'A' Mess. As de Guingand noted, Monty 'never *laid* a bet himself, but he was always prepared to *accept* one'.† The book's entries show moments of relief, often hilarity, in the tense days before the invasion. On 26 January 1944: 'Admiral Ramsay‡ bets General Montgomery an even £5 that the war with Germany will be over before January 1st 1945.'

* Property of David Montgomery, but on indefinite loan to the IWM.
† *Operation Victory*, p. 369.
‡ Naval commander of OVERLORD.

Underneath was entered 'Paid BLM'.* Not all bets were on such global issues:

> Capt. Henderson bets Capt. Chavasse an even £5 that he will have entered into the state of Holy Matrimony before he reaches the age of 45 years....
>
> Capt. Henderson bets Capt. Chavasse £2.10s that he will defeat him in a race on motor-cycles from Buckingham Palace to the steps of St Paul's School. [Won by Chavasse, bet paid.]

On 2 May, de Guingand was betting Monty that 'the Monarchy will have ceased to exist in England in 50 years' time. General Montgomery bets it will not.' Neither was alive for Monty to collect his fiver in May 1994. Colonel Russell bet Lieutenant-Colonel Dawnay £5 that 'Princess Elizabeth will marry an American subject within the next five years.' More seriously, reflecting concerns about Stalin's reliability even at that late stage in the war, that same day two visiting generals (Richards and Dennis) are recorded as having bet £1 that 'the Russians will make a separate peace with Germany before the year is out, and will leave the remainder of the United Nations to continue the war with Germany without Russian assistance'.

In mid-May Churchill came down to TAC HQ, precipitating a first confrontation, and a serious one. He was tired, nervous and – justifiably – anxious; and with Churchill anxiety usually led to interference. He complained to Monty that there were too many non-fighting men, too many vehicles in the invasion order of battle: 'Where was the bayonet in all this?' He wanted to address the 21 Army Group staff about it. Together with Brooke and Sir James ('P.J.') Grigg,† Churchill was one of only three people in the entire world whom Monty admired and regarded as having a right to intervene. 'With Churchill, Montgomery was intrigued,' wrote Moorehead. 'The broad, sweeping gestures, the ardour, the warrior

* On such bets, Monty almost always took a conservative line – and usually cleaned up.

† Grigg had made his way from humble origins. His language was forthright, often with a barrackroom flavour, but Monty greatly respected his penetrating intellect. He remained a dedicated supporter of Monty throughout.

approach, the Elizabethan colour and enthusiasm – it was fascinating....'* But the unwarranted interference, after all the meticulous planning that had gone before, put him in a cold fury. He replied acidly in the same vein, refusing the Prime Minister access to his staff: 'I cannot allow you to do so. My staff advise me and I give the final decision; they then do what I tell them.'

After haranguing Monty, who threatened to make it an issue of confidence, Churchill backed off. (According to Moorehead, Churchill then broke down and wept; when his biography of Monty was published, however, he was forced to remove this reference under threat of libel proceedings from Churchill.) Monty had won an important victory. Churchill remarked to his staff simply, and somewhat peevishly, 'I wasn't allowed to talk to you,' then left – after writing a eulogistic entry, amounting to a complete climb-down, in Monty's 'Ten Chapters' book:†

Chapter V
On the verge of the greatest Adventure
with which these pages have dealt
I record my confidence that
all will be well
& that
the organizations and equipment of the army
will be worthy of the valour
of the soldier
& the genius of their chief

19.v.44 Winston S. Churchill

Three nights later King George VI came to dinner, to be given a copy of Monty's 'Notes on High Command in War' and of his final message to his senior officers. Together they were photographed under the great cedar tree on the lawn of Broomfield

* *Montgomery*, pp. 197–8.

† Between August 1942 and 1945, as Monty journeyed from Alamein to the Baltic Sea, 'At various stages ... Mr. Churchill wrote a page in my autograph book and recorded his impressions: in his own handwriting.' A facsimile edition of this autograph book was published immediately after the war.

House.* On 1 June, after a final conference, Monty dined his four army commanders – Dempsey, Crerar, Bradley and Patton. The evening, almost reminiscent of the famous scene from *Antony and Cleopatra* (except that no one was carried out like Lepidus), passed with a conviviality that Monty never experienced again with his American allies, for the next three months his subordinates. Always a gambler, Patton entered into the spirit of things by placing two bets with Monty: 'a level £100 [an astronomic sum by TAC HQ standards] that the armed forces of Great Britain will be involved in another war in Europe within ten years of the cessation of the present hostilities,' and £10 'that the first Grand National run after the present war will be won by an American-owned horse'. The affluent Californian did not survive to pay out on either bet. Dempsey retaliated by betting Bradley £5 that the war with Germany would have ended by 1 November. Bradley collected. Before they parted, Monty toasted his guests; Patton as the oldest present replied with a toast declaring 'our satisfaction in serving under him'. He confided to his diary, 'The lightning did not strike me', despite the manifest lie. But he also confessed to coming away with 'a better impression of Monty than I had'. It was an occasion never to be repeated.

The following night Monty recorded in his diary that Ike had 'dined quietly' with him at Broomfield House. Glowingly he wrote in his personal diary:

> Eisenhower is just the man for the job; he is a really 'big' man and is in every way an allied commander – holding the balance between the allied contingents. I like him immensely; he has a generous and lovable character and I would trust him to the last gasp.

Halcyon days! Alas, this happy opinion would not endure very long after D-Day. After dinner the two commanders went to Southwick Park for a conference to discuss the weather with the meteorological experts. In his memoirs Monty wrote that it 'looked reasonable, but the experts were worried about a depression over Iceland . . .'. Now began the agonizing count-down to D-Day.

* In the TAC HQ visitors' book, Churchill added after his name in the address column '10 Downing Street'; Brooke, 'War Office'; while the King signed simply 'George RI' with no address.

It was not Churchill alone who was manifesting last-minute nerves. Back in the War Office, General Nye's Military Assistant, Peter Earle, on 30 May recorded in his diary the arrival, in great secrecy, of two American generals with a message for Brooke: 'It occurred to us that the US Chief might be getting cold feet.... It looks as if Marshall wanted Brookie's private off-the-record opinion of the chances of success.... Americans have never contributed to such a hazardous operation before.' Earle then mentioned in his diary a concern little voiced before, but which was to play a significant role in Monty's subsequent handling of the campaign:

> Perhaps the biggest form of doubt I have not yet mentioned – this is MANPOWER.
>
> In the second half of this year we will be approximately 90,000 men short in 21 Army Group. This means a reduction of some five divisions will have to be effected to provide reinforcements. Further, we are about to enter on this vast project with only three weeks' reserves, which is unheard of in the annals of history.

This would be one good reason why Normandy was to be a so much closer-run thing than has perhaps been appreciated. Four days later, on 3 June, Earle was writing on a note of bitter regret shared by many a regular soldier left behind on the 'great adventure': 'This sunny June day as I sit writing in our flat, in civilian clothes, it seems quite impossible to imagine that once again most of my friends will be embarking on a big battle, and I will stay behind....'

He went on to voice a second concern that may seem extraordinary to modern ears, accustomed to communications of the speed of light within the NATO alliance: 'It is interesting to note that at D minus 2 we know not one thing of Russian intentions, where and when and in how great a strength their offensive will take place....' (It had been agreed at the Teheran Conference that the Soviet Union would launch a co-ordinated offensive.) Earle added the piece of disquieting intelligence that Hitler's staff:

> had given absolute priority to the West and are prepared to lose ground in the East, in order to throw us into the sea in the West. Hitler told the Japanese Ambassador this....
>
> It will be a long grim battle leading, I think, to the disintegration of German forces next February....

The following day, 4 June, the eve of invasion itself, Earle was expressing yet another worry which was plaguing the thoughtful back at base – as it would indeed in the months to come:

> It is astonishing, or history will deem it astonishing, that there are no plans beyond D plus 90 which the COS [Chiefs of Staff] have seen. . . . Not surprising, as it is impossible to calculate what the enemy will do.
>
> The frightening thing still remains that Germans have there now more troops than we will have got in by October.*

All these were indeed considerations that might have caused a leader less resolute than Monty, or Eisenhower, to quake in their boots. Worse still, there was one factor over which the best-prepared operation would be totally powerless, as impotent as Homer's Greeks in the face of the uncertain whims of Poseidon: the weather in the unpredictable English Channel. After endless discussion with the experts, Monday, 5 June had been decided upon for D-Day. Because of the tides and the state of the moon, the margins were extremely close. As Monty noted:

> The 6th June was quite acceptable.
>
> The 7th June was not good because it gave two hours of daylight before touch-down on the beaches; but it could be managed.
>
> After that date, the next possible period would not occur for a fortnight. The prospect of having to disembark all the troops after they had been fully briefed, and to wait for two weeks, was full of terrors.†

Full of terrors indeed: On 3 June, Monty recorded the bad news: 'The depression over Iceland began to spread southwards.' It was, he wrote, 'the worst weather forecast we have had since we began to consider the weather six weeks ago.' Kay Summersby recalled Ike being 'bleakly depressed', consulting incessantly with the meteorologists, and grumbling that the weather was 'always partisan and on

* Peter Earle diary.

† Two weeks later, the Normandy beaches were ravaged by storms of almost hurricane force.

the side of the Germans'. It was a fear that would never be far from Allied minds over the coming weeks.

At 4 a.m. on the 4th, the most anxious men in England met at Southwick House, biting their nails. The man in the hottest of hot seats – momentarily become the most important player in the whole orchestra – was Eisenhower's meteorologist, Group Captain J. M. Stagg, a dour Scot from the RAF. The success or failure of the whole operation rested on the accuracy of his forecasting. It required little historical knowledge to recall the fate of the Spanish Armada. But Poseidon remained inscrutable, if not implacable. By the 4th, some of the invasion convoys had already sailed. Alone, and isolated, Monty was for going on, regardless. Tedder, the airman, was furious – deeply shocked at Monty's 'amazingly asserted willingness'* to attack with air support seriously curtailed by the weather. Always with his finger on the fighting quality of his troops, Monty had a point: he argued that 'a postponement would not only have been most harmful to the morale of the troops, but might well have prejudiced secrecy and the possibility of gaining tactical surprise.'

At least one historian, however, remains fiercely critical, regarding Monty's stand as one of his 'few undoubted errors of judgement': 'Given the trouble much less severe weather caused on the 6th, there is little doubt that a landing on the previous day would have found itself in deep trouble.'† Monty himself subsequently admitted that if they had persisted with the original D-Day of 5 June 'we might have had a disaster'. Ike reminded the assemblage that OVERLORD was being launched with ground forces that were *not* overwhelmingly powerful, and that the operation was feasible only because of Allied air superiority. With his casting vote as supreme commander, he decided to wait twenty-four hours. Ironically, as the tense leaders left Southwick House there was a 'beautiful dawn glow', instead of the low cloud that had caused Tedder to oppose the landings. Had the unfortunate Stagg got it wrong? But later that day the winds got up again. Back in London Peter Earle continued in his diary:

> Today is perhaps the most important day in the history of the world, the winds at hurricane force and clouds 10/10th. 'Overlord' has therefore been postponed 24 hours – i.e. Tuesday morning, the

* Tedder, *With Prejudice*, p. 545.
† Hastings, *Overlord*, p. 70.

> weather looks like further postponement – what shall we tell the Russians? Let us tell them quick.

Meanwhile, there was one small consoling piece of news: Rome had just fallen.

That evening the commanders met again; the weather reports were still bad. As Eisenhower dined with Monty, the wind and rain rattled the windows. The decision was taken to assemble again at Southwick House at 4 a.m. on Monday the 5th. At the eleventh hour, Stagg was able to predict a favourable break in the terrible weather. According to Eisenhower's British intelligence chief, Kenneth Strong, 'a cheer went up. You have never heard middle-aged men cheer like that!' All the officers present at that crucial 4 a.m. meeting on 5 June were in immaculate battledress – except for Monty, clad in his 'high-necked fawn-coloured pullover and light corduroy trousers'. Tedder, 'his pipe clenched between his teeth' according to Eisenhower's biographer, Stephen Ambrose, agreed that the operations of heavy bombers were going to be 'chancy'. Ike 'shot his chin out' and asked Monty, 'Do you see any reason why we should not go on Tuesday?' Monty immediately replied, 'No, I would say – Go!' As Ambrose eloquently remarks, upon Eisenhower's word now:

> the fate of thousands of men depended, and the future of great nations. The moment he uttered the word, however, he was powerless . . . a platoon sergeant at Utah would for the immediate future play a greater role than Eisenhower. He could now only sit and wait. . . .

In Monty's recollection, that meeting at which the final decision was taken lasted no more than fifteen minutes. As the commanders departed, the rain still seemed to be coming down in horizontal streaks, driven by a wind of almost hurricane proportions. What if Stagg had got it wrong? During those next dreadful waiting hours, Ike, chain-smoking and drinking one cup of black coffee after another, sat and read westerns in his trailer with his glamorous driver, Kay Summersby, and his naval aide, Harry C. Butcher. He thought about his son John, just about to graduate from West Point. In utmost secrecy he drafted a black, worst-scenario despatch, to be broadcast in the event of catastrophe, ending with the words, 'If any blame or fault attaches to the attempt it is mine alone.' To the historian John Keegan, their simplicity comes across the years as 'the words of a great man and a great soldier', whose greatness has 'yet to be portrayed fully'.*

Though the ultimate responsibility rested with Eisenhower, Monty shared in full measure his lonely impotence. Once the die was cast, there was nothing more that either could do. He sat down to write a review of all that had happened over the previous five months, and a farewell note to David: 'When you get this, the second front will be well on its way. I am sending you a copy of my message, and some photos. Goodbye and God bless you. . . .' In a rousing proclamation to the troops, he declared, 'The time has come to deal the enemy a terrific blow in Western Europe', and, quoting the words of Montrose three centuries earlier,

> He either fears his fate too much,
> Or his deserts are small,
> That puts it not unto the touch
> To win or lose it all.

> Good luck to each one of you. And good hunting on the mainland.

True to his unshakeable principles, Monty retired early and slept well, probably far better than the chain-smoking, coffee-drinking Ike, 'supremely confident' (in the words of Kit Dawnay) that everything possible had been done to ensure success of the landings. The earliest reports, so Monty recorded in his personal diary for D-Day, were that 'all objectives of the airborne troops were secured . . . which was excellent'. As the first fragments of news came through that first, 'longest day', de Guingand recalled how Monty had 'kept to his office most of that day waiting to see when he should move to Normandy'. Johnny Henderson takes up the story in his own, unpublished diaries:

> D-Day has arrived. I got up at 6.30 and went down to the naval and army HQ at Southwick House to find out the form. The

* Keegan, *Six Armies in Normandy*, p. 66.

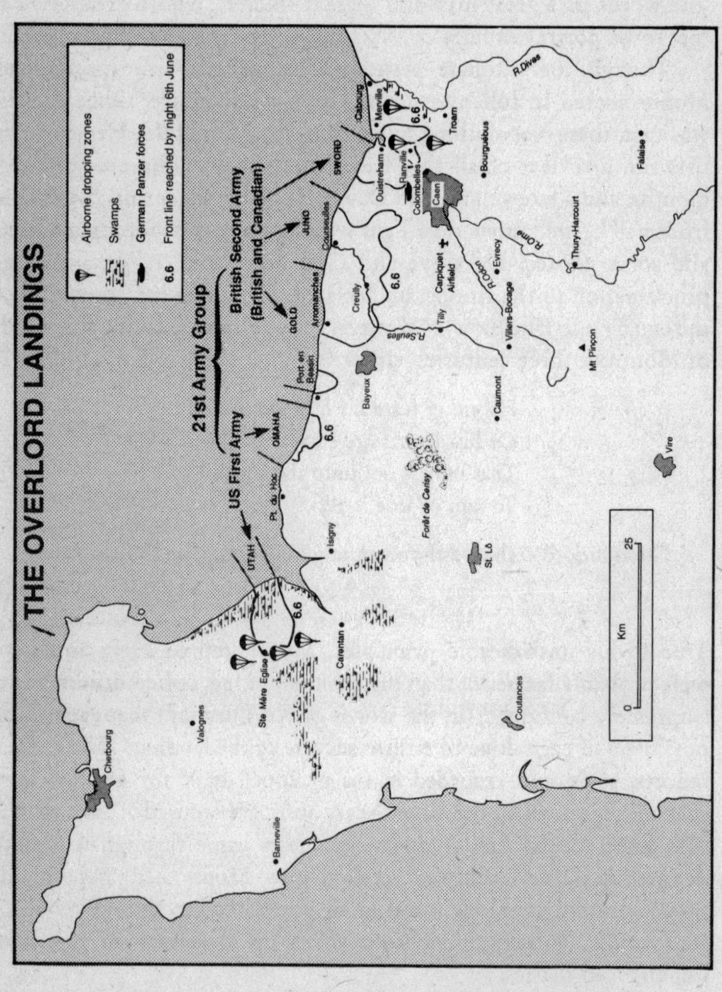

The OVERLORD Landings

Ceremonial March of 47 (London) Division at Lille in September 1918. Monty can be seen on left with Churchill, then Minister of Munitions, in centre.

Left: David with his Mother in Lenk, Switzerland, at Christmas 1936. *Right:* Monty leaves the City Chambers in Glasgow on 22 April 1944 during one of the pre-D-Day tours to weapons manufacturers and industry. Johnny Henderson (ADC) is behind on right, and behind him is David in his school OTC uniform.

Planning for the invasion in London, 1 February 1944. Round the table with Monty (left to right) are Bradley, Ramsay, Tedder, Eisenhower, Leigh-Mallory, Bedell Smith.

Monty addressing US infantry troops in April 1944 during one of his pre-D-Day tours to all soldiers under his command.

Monty accompanied by Kit Dawnay, his Military Assistant, examining a local terrain map during his tour of US forces in southern England during April 1944.

The actor Clifton James (Monty's double in the pre-D-Day decoy plan) inspects the Guard of Honour at Gibraltar.

Field Marshal Rommel inspecting the Atlantic Wall.

Royal Marine Commandos leaving the landing craft to go ashore at St-Aubin-sur-Mer.

The second wave of 9 Canadian Brigade coming ashore late morning on 6 June at Bernières-sur-Mer on Juno Beach.

Men of the 2nd Battalion Royal Warwickshire (Monty's old regiment) advancing through a wheatfield during the final assault on Caen, 8 July 1944.

British troops and vehicles passing inland through a village in Normandy which had just been liberated during the first week following the invasion.

The Prime Minister arrives in Normandy on 12 June 1944 (photograph signed by Churchill for Monty).

Watching an air battle near HQ 8 Corps on 12 June 1944. Left to right General O'Connor, Winston Churchill, Smuts, Monty and Brooke (CIGS).

Left: The King arrives in Normandy and is greeted on the beach by the C-in-C, 16 June 1944 (photograph signed by the King and inscribed by Monty). *Right:* Sir James Grigg, Secretary of State for War, at the Château de Creullet, 18 June 1944.

Monty with his puppies, Rommel (spaniel) and Hitler (terrier), at TAC Headquarters at Blay. The canary cage is outside his personal caravan.

Crossing the Seine at Vernon on 1 September 1944 on the Goliath-class pontoon bridge.

> airborne landings at 0100 hours had gone extremely well and smoothly. Out of 1300 planes carrying parachutists and towing gliders, only 30 had failed to return to base. 6 Airborne Div. reported themselves to be in the correct position. And yet there had been no enemy reaction, either in the air or on the sea. Only one LCT had been sunk by mines.... 0730 was zero hour for the US army to touch shore; by ten o'clock there was still no news of them, but the five brigades of the British army were known to have got ashore successfully. The German radio announced that at 0730 the invasion had started and parachutists had been landed in the mouth of the Seine. It therefore appears that the dummy parachutists had been successful, as a number of these, with banging gadgets, had been dropped in that area.... No news of the American landings came through until 1530 when a flash came that the beaches were clear of enemy.

The brief reference to the Americans in fact cloaked a day of desperate fighting, brilliantly recounted in Cornelius Ryan's *The Longest Day*, that had come appallingly close to the disaster all had dreaded: the invasion stopped on the beaches and pushed back into the sea. But the 6th Airborne landing at Bénouville/Ranville (the famous Pegasus Bridge at the mouth of the River Orne north-east of Caen) had been one of the war's unqualified successes. The gliders dropped within yards of the objectives, taking the German defenders completely by surprise.* Further inland, a tragically large number of paras – many Canadian – were drowned dropping into the marsh areas of the River Dives which the Germans had (unbeknown to Allied intelligence) flooded. The key bridge at Troarn was blown up, with considerable heroism, but the British airborne units were then forced to fall back on Bénouville when no seaborne back-up materialized. This was to prove an incalculable setback to Monty's plans.

Less impressive, overall, was the performance of the Dakota transport pilots, US as well as British. Some – in the face of heavy enemy flak – had had to be forced at pistol point not to drop the Paras short. Leigh-Mallory, who, full of pessimism in the run-up to

* It was nearly jeopardized only by the tardy arrival of the seaborne infantry (in fact, Monty's own 3rd Division).

the invasion, had been predicting casualties as high as 80 per cent, said that afternoon, on receiving reports that only a score of planes out of the many hundreds had been lost, that 'it was sometimes difficult to admit that one was wrong, but he had never had a greater pleasure in doing so than on this occasion'.* Likewise at the other extremity of the landings, the US landings on UTAH beach had been immeasurably aided by the daring descent on Ste-Mère-Église by the elite 101st and 82nd Airborne Divisions.

Meanwhile, the air superiority which Ike had declared to be the all-important factor during those last hours at Southwick (and over which Tedder and the air barons had made such heavy weather) had been wrested from the Luftwaffe almost as if by default. Flying a Spitfire to cover the American landings at OMAHA, a New Zealand pilot, Flying Officer Johnnie Houlton, destroyed a Junkers 88 bomber – the first Allied 'kill' on D-Day – and shared in the shooting down of a second.† But Houlton was one of the few pilots to find 'good hunting' that day. Apart from a couple of brave Messerschmitts that strafed the British beaches, the Luftwaffe was hardly seen. So much for the heavy fears of the air barons. On the other hand, 300 Liberator heavy bombers of the US Eighth Air Force dropped their bombs, which had been intended to soften up the coastal defences, sometimes as far as three miles inland.

To any pilot flying over the Channel that day, the arrayed might of the invasion forces presented the spectacle of a lifetime: 8000 bombers and fighters; 284 warships, including 7 great battleships and 23 cruisers; 4000 landing craft and assorted ships, containing a total of 156,115 British, Canadian and American troops, were deployed under Ike's and Monty's orders.‡ It seemed inconceivable that even the fearsome Germans, bled white by three years' campaigning in Russia and with virtually no air cover, could possibly stand up to

* Ambrose (1), p. 141.

† The plane, ML-407, converted into a two-seater for the Irish Air Force in the 1950s, still flies today.

‡ A fact, too often ignored in the American 50th Anniversary accounts of D-Day, was that American troops were marginally in the minority; 73,000 to 83,115 British and Canadians; 5 British and Canadian assault brigades to 3 American; of the naval forces, only 16.5 per cent were American and 79 per cent British and Canadian. The landing craft were fairly evenly divided; but of the planes deployed on D-Day, 6,080 were American and 5,510 from the RAF or other allied contingents.

such an imposing concentration of force. On the British and Canadian sectors at the eastern end, SWORD, JUNO and GOLD beaches, it looked as if Monty, like Leigh-Mallory, had possibly overestimated opposition. Overall, FORTITUDE, perhaps the most elaborate and ambitious deception plan ever undertaken, had worked – and continued to work almost miraculously better than could possibly have been expected. General von Salmuth's powerful German Fifteenth Army, whose fifteen divisions might well have tipped the balance against the Allies that day, remained pinned down in the Pas de Calais, treating OVERLORD as simply a feint and waiting for the main invasion that was never to come. In Normandy General Dollmann considered the sea to be so rough that he did not trouble to place his Seventh Army on alert; while the promise of bad weather had persuaded Rommel himself, the Hector of the defending armies, to take the risk of driving off for a few days at his home in Swabia.

It was Lucie Rommel's fiftieth birthday, for which her husband bought her a pair of Parisian shoes. Rommel also hoped to make use of his presence in southern Germany to arrange a special interview with Hitler at his mountain retreat at Berchtesgaden. He intended to press Hitler to intervene in the as yet unresolved dispute over the strategic handling of the Panzer forces in northern France. These were being held back by Panzer Group West, commanded by General Geyr von Schweppenburg, whose view it was that they should be kept in reserve far back from the coast and deployed only in a massive, concentrated counter-attack once the Allies were established ashore. In this he was supported by Rundstedt. Rommel held – correctly as it turned out – that if the Allies could not be defeated on the coast and immediately thrown back into the sea, the battle would be lost irretrievably. So, on 8 June, he would ask Hitler for extra Panzer reinforcements and for direct control over the divisions being held back by Rundstedt. At 6.30 a.m. on Tuesday the 6th, while he was arranging Lucie's presents in the drawing room before she was up, Rommel was telephoned by his Chief of Staff, General Hans Speidel, with the news of the airborne landings in Normandy, though it was not yet clear whether this was the real thing or not. Another four hours went by before Speidel could confirm that it was, and Rommel hastened back to France. But through a series of inconceivable blunders the local Wehrmacht command had even failed to react promptly to the airborne landings the preceding night, and it was not till the evening of the 6th that – in Rommel's absence – the high-quality 21st Panzer Division, which was the nearest to the British beaches, began seriously to riposte. It was an extraordinary act of fate, performing now on behalf of the Allies, that both the bad weather and Frau Rommel's birthday should have combined to ensure that Rommel's vigorous hand was off the tiller during those first critical twenty-four hours. It was equally fortunate that he had not received the extra Panzer division he had been demanding from Rundstedt, let alone the two extra that he had intended requesting at Berchtesgaden. Their presence, even without the additional reinforcement from the Fifteenth Army pinned down by FORTITUDE, could so easily have made the difference between success and catastrophe on D-Day. The balance was that fine.

So the British were able to effect almost complete surprise, surging nine miles inland to capture the exquisite medieval gem of Bayeux virtually undamaged. It was to be Monty's coup of the day. But elsewhere some British units repeated, too often, the terrible mistakes of Gallipoli in 1915; instead of thrusting with all speed inland, they had milled around in the beachheads, preparing to be attacked by a ferocious enemy, and 'regrouping' – that popular British army expression so often to be found masking fatal inactivity. They (one of the culprits evidently being Monty's old 3rd Division) failed to advance on the vital objective of Caen until the afternoon, by which time the Germans, with their genius – acquired from so many years of fighting off overwhelming hordes of attacking Russians – for swiftly organizing *ad hoc* defences, had dug in. The failure of these British units to link up with the beleaguered and exhausted 6th Airborne provoked considerable anger.

At the other extremity of the fifty-mile stretch of beaches, the Americans too had succeeded in getting off UTAH beach and consolidating their grip inland. Recalling the Operation TIGER disaster at Slapton Sands only a few weeks previously, many officers of General Lawton Collins' US VII Corps had embarked with dread. In the event the 197 casualties securing UTAH on D-Day turned out to be a fraction of those lost on TIGER. But it was otherwise on OMAHA, where two-thirds of Bradley's troops were directed. Despite their reputation for inventive genius, the Americans had been curiously unreceptive to the 'special tanks' – the flail mine-clearers, the flame-throwers, the bridging tanks with their bundles of 'fascines', and the amphibians – pioneered by Monty's brother-in-law, Major-General Percy ('Hobo') Hobart. These 'gadgets' were to prove vital to the success of the British landings, clearing a way through the minefields and obstacles. Monty had ordered one-third of the British total to be offered to the Americans, but they were refused. Through a combination of high seas and bad handling, one US tank battalion lost all but five of its Shermans, which dropped with their crews like stones into the water.* Many of the beach obstacles erected by the Germans were found intact despite air and naval bombardment. Unlike the flat British beaches, OMAHA was overlooked by high sand-dunes, affording defenders devastating fields of fire, and flanked by imposing, almost unassailable positions atop the high Point du Hoc cliff. Worst of all, by chance (and undetected by Allied intelligence) a veteran German infantry division, the 352nd, had moved from the South of France into the OMAHA sector only three months earlier for defensive exercises.

As the American landing craft hit the beach, they were met by a storm of fire. Many died where they lay, pinned down by invisible German machine-gunners, while lack of those specialist tanks offered by Monty made it almost impossible for the infantry to fight their way to the vital exits in the high beach wall. General Gerow, commanding V Corps with many green troops in it, has been accused of showing a lack of tactical subtlety, but, on that terrible beach totally devoid of any cover, it is hard to see how anything but a brutal, frontal assault could have succeeded. By mid-morning OMAHA was beginning to resemble one of the nightmare battlefields of the Somme, so appalling to Monty. With huge daring, and suffering cruel losses, the US Rangers scaled the Point du Hoc – only to find that the German gun batteries had been withdrawn. Deprived of many of its officers, the US 29th Division became dangerously paralysed, though its Deputy Commander, Brigadier-General Norman Cota,

* Some of these tanks can now be seen in a grimly fascinating French museum at Port en Bessin, the Musée des Épaves, recovered from the sea by French initiative. From letters found in the forty-year-old wrecks, survivors in the States have been tracked down.

who succeeded in getting the demoralized survivors of his division off the beach, was the true hero of OMAHA that day. But without the 1st Division, the 'Big Red One', battle-hardened from North Africa, most Americans agreed the day would have been lost. Many of the US troops had never before come under German fire; the country as a whole was unacclimatized to this kind of First World War massacre. As seen through American eyes, 'for the whole of June 6, the Germans had an excellent opportunity to defeat OVERLORD'.* At OMAHA they failed to grasp it. Nevertheless, it was a sober and anxious Eisenhower who appeared at a press conference to warn America that it was still a 'hazardous operation'.

By midday, Bradley himself had gained the alarming impression 'that our forces have suffered an irreversible catastrophe'. In utmost secrecy, Monty passed to Dempsey a signal asking if Gerow's US V Corps could be transferred to one of the British beaches. Dempsey replied that it would be impossible; it would simply be 'too crowded'. Out of the total casualties of 4649 from the 55,000 Americans put ashore on D-Day, 2000 alone died on that narrow strip of sand called OMAHA. Bradley was to remain haunted for the rest of his life by the horrors of what had happened there. The misfortune of running into a crack German division, deployed for action, affords a terrible indication of what might have happened to OVERLORD as a whole if the deception plan, FORTITUDE, had not worked so brilliantly – or if Rommel had had overall control of the available Panzers, placing as he had wished a second division near St Lô.

The lessons would be conveniently forgotten three months later, with Arnhem.

Probably kept unaware of the full extent of the setback suffered by Bradley, back at Main HQ at Southwick House de Guingand recorded that by the evening of the 6th he 'felt considerably excited. . . . Reports were now coming in. The airborne operations had been outstandingly successful. . . . The landings were going well. . . .' Led by the redoubtable Canadian, Trumbull Warren,

* Ambrose (1), p. 420.

Monty's TAC HQ was now 'on its way across and he was champing at the bit to get going himself'. Johnny Henderson continues the story: 'At 1800 hours we heard that HQ 21 AG had not yet landed, but the C-in-C was determined to go over. We therefore boarded destroyer HMS *Faulknor* at 2200 hours at Portsmouth. 2215 we set sail for France.' In Monty's own pocket diary for the 6th, there is the terse, historic entry: 'Invaded Normandy; left Portsmouth 10.30. . . .'

Monty promptly retired to his bunk, giving Henderson the instruction 'Wake me up at 6 a.m. – report on the battle.' Early the next morning an extremely anxious destroyer captain called Churchill, described by Ray BonDurant as a 'red-bearded young man who looked pretty rugged', confessed to Henderson that in the huge mêlée of ships he was lost, and drifting. The dreadful thought briefly crossed Henderson's mind: what would happen if the frail craft with the Land Commander aboard were to drift on to an uncleared German minefield? Suddenly an American battleship loomed up: the *Faulknor* had 'floated down right off Cherbourg Peninsula!' Once the Captain had brought his destroyer to its proper destination, Courseulles, and while his TAC teams were struggling to get ashore, Monty spent 7 June, D + 1, bustling from ship to ship, almost as if on a peacetime review of the fleet. 'The wind and sea had now dropped, the sun was shining,' he wrote in cheerful recollection:

> and the 'round the Fleet' trips in the destroyer were delightful; there was plenty to look at, ships everywhere, and blockships and artificial harbours starting to arrive. There was no enemy action and few signs of battle on sea or land. It was difficult to imagine that on shore a battle was being fought which was deciding the fate of Europe.

He located Bradley aboard his command ship, the cruiser USS *Augusta*. 'He gave me his situation, which was good at UTAH but very bad at OMAHA,' wrote Monty. With immense heroism, the Americans had got off the blood-soaked beach at OMAHA, but their tenuous lodgement there was at best only a vulnerable two miles deep. Monty instructed Bradley to turn VII Corps, now safely installed on UTAH, inwards to help Gerow's hard-pressed V Corps instead of striking north-westwards for Cherbourg, as had originally been planned. At the same time, Dempsey was ordered to push his western flank as far inland as possible to take the pressure off OMAHA. According to Monty's American ADC, Captain BonDurant, Bradley announced that he was just 'going ashore to find out what is going on':

> General Montgomery said, 'Right, you go with him.' Would you believe, I was there even without a steel helmet! This sounds rather strange, but I didn't have my helmet with me; so they found one big enough for my head and off we went in one of the small boats to Omaha Beach. We went ashore there, and General Bradley – of course he was a tall man – when they let the ramp down he had water up to his knees and I had it up to my waist. Finally we arrived ashore and found that General Collins, who was then about 200–300 yards away, had set up a small headquarters there and after a short visit with him, General Bradley and his party then came back to the Headquarters ship. Going up the side on the ladders, I twisted my left ankle and was incapacitated for about an hour or so until they shot some sodium pentathol in and that got me going.

Monty expressed himself well satisfied with Bradley's report. On tracking down Ike aboard his command ship, and perhaps underrating the weight of the titanic responsibilities on the Supreme Commander's shoulders, he found him manifesting signs of acute anxiety. It did not conform to Monty's idea of the *sang froid* and self-confidence that a commander should display once battle was engaged. For himself, he would never admit to anyone that things were not going exactly 'according to plan', an approach which, carried to excess, was to get him into serious trouble over the next weeks. As far as the British Second Army front was concerned, his principal worry that evening was stated with extreme brevity: 'Caen was not captured and it was clear that the enemy intended to hold it strongly and to try to drive in my eastern flank.'

Meanwhile, back at RAF headquarters, cloud moving in again was seen to be 'seriously upsetting', recorded Leigh-Mallory:

> The German army is being reinforced and I cannot bomb the reinforcements in daylight. . . . I have a feeling we are losing precious time at a moment when the main movements of the enemy

> are beginning. . . . Generally speaking, Allied Air Forces are not doing as well against the German army as I had hoped. . . . most unfortunate.

Nevertheless, returning to the *Faulknor*, a serene Monty once again bunked down at 9.30 p.m., giving orders that he intended landing early next morning.

His TAC HQ teams, however, divided – for obvious safety reasons – between three American-manned landing craft, under the orders of Colonel Russell, Trumbull Warren and Paul Odgers respectively, had been having no easy time of landing and setting up the first camp for the Chief. Warren, the Canadian, was the only one who had actually taken part in a landing – in Sicily:

> The others had only read it in the book and didn't know what it was really going to be like. I told them that it would be utter confusion – and indeed it was. We were supposed to land at 0700 hours, and in fact it was very late afternoon and almost getting dark when we made it.

Odgers recorded that the 'special flotilla' of LSTs, heavily laden with vehicles and equipment – including the three caravans – had dropped anchor off JUNO beach on the 6th: 'vain efforts were made to attract the attention of the Rhino ferries.* These useless efforts continued all night to the accompaniment of heavy bombardment by the battle cruisers and an occasional scurry of Messerschmitts.' In frustration, the commander of Odgers' LST, who 'had no charts and no knowledge of where he was supposed to land, drove boldly on to a sandbank and there stuck until two o'clock in the morning'.† In the rough seas, with the American ship's tannoy alternately announcing battle news and playing 'Cow, Cow Boogie', a grave minor tragedy now occurred: the three-ton truck carrying the officers' and sergeants' mess kit, together with all the Scotch, slid off the ramp and disappeared into the sea.

Otherwise, the various components of TAC all reached shore safely. Russell, first ashore, set up a site at Ste-Croix-sur-Mer, a crossroads between fields interspersed with German trenches, where

* Flat ferries towed by tugs.
† Odgers, 'A TAC Chronicle'.

(according to Odgers) they 'passed an uneasy night in armed conflict with some neighbouring Royal Engineers'. It was, thought Odgers with his experienced eye, 'an exceedingly moderate location' such as only a staff officer innocent of battle experience, like Russell, would have established. Nevertheless, they now sent off to fetch Monty ashore.

Today, approaching the British landings aboard the brand-new 27,000-ton *Normandie* ferry, almost as large as the battleship *Warspite* which had bombarded the German positions of fifty years before, after a comfortable five-and-a-half-hour passage compared with the two days and nights many troops had spent on the crowded landing craft, the first sight that greets a visitor and visible half an hour out, is a thin ribbon of coast, grey with a slash of ochre suggestive of sand. Wreathed with the smoke of battle, this was the first glimpse of the British sector that Monty, awoken at 6.30 a.m. on the 8th, on board the *Faulknor* and well within range of the German batteries, would have had. Suddenly, 'there was a slight shudder', Monty recalled. Just like Odgers' LST, the *Faulknor* had run aground on a sandbank. The navy's story was that Monty had sent a message up to the bridge urging the Captain to go in still closer. The Commander-in-Chief was, said Henderson, 'most anxious to get ashore and got a little irritable when no boat came to fetch him', while the unfortunate Captain Churchill, having now committed two solecisms, doubtless feared for his future.* Johnny Henderson continues the story on the 8th:

> Trum and Noël arrived and we went ashore, and were transferred to a DUKW [amphibious trucks] to get out of the sea. Went straight off inland to TAC HQ which had been set up at Ste-Croix-sur-Mer. There were still small pockets of enemy about and a large number of snipers. We were concerned about the Chief flying his flag but he was determined to do so and it was a stirring sight to see how delighted the soldiers were to see him. Tired and weary faces lighted up. Soldiers waved from all directions. He had break-

* Given the long-rehearsed details of D-Day, it seems extraordinary that both these ships with their vital cargoes should have been grounded in apparently so amateurish a fashion, so close to enemy guns. But this is how the best of plans often turn out in the confusion of war. According to Odgers' account, the three components of TAC HQ were 'capable of functioning together though not singly'. Thus the loss of any one of the LSTs could have been a major disaster.

> fast and immediately went out to see General Dempsey at Second Army HQ nearby.

Colonel Russell's choice of the first TAC HQ in north-west Europe at Ste-Croix at once proved an unsuitable if not disastrous one. It was too close to the enemy lines, and under regular shellfire, while the chaos as more and more troops poured into the cramped confines of the bridgehead made its operation almost impossible. As one of his first tasks, BonDurant was sent off:

> to locate the present American headquarters. Of course, I thought I had done a good job on this, noted all the signs. But everything was in a state of upheaval; the next day, when his driver and General Montgomery plus myself started up to the headquarters, along the way many of the signs had been moved and I found that I was lost. Hated to admit that; did not have to; General Montgomery sensed it and said, 'You're lost. We might as well ask these people here where it is.' So we asked somebody, found the headquarters and everything came off all right; but I was very embarrassed at that and I must say a little more careful thereafter.

Monty decided to move as soon as possible. Fortunately, Trumbull Warren had located 'the grounds of a lovely château',* where he:

> found fifteen Germans . . . all of which he took prisoner. We moved early afternoon. Progress was satisfactory, but no more and the Chief was obviously worried about an enemy counter-attack to the west of Caen, against the Canadians who had already taken a knock. He was tired and rather on edge; nothing was right – yet when Howard Marshall, the BBC rep, called to see him, he showed no sign of tiredness. Only confidence. . . .

In view of the immense importance that the failure to take Caen was to assume, in terms of both the campaign and Monty's reputation, this is a most revealing account. It shows Monty clearly concerned about this first setback to his blueprint, but at the same time refusing

* Henderson diary, 8 June 1944.

– as a matter of principle – to allow to any outsider that anything had gone wrong.

What had gone wrong? In the damning words of one of the 6th Airborne Brigade commanders, General Sir Nigel Poett:

> It was well on the cards that Monty could have taken Caen on the first day, but 3rd Division were late in joining up with us from Sword Beach. At first light one of my companies could have taken Caen; in the afternoon it would have needed a whole battalion, and by night a division.*

Poett may well have been indulging in wishful thinking; opinions about Caen, of which there are hundreds, vary radically. Max Hastings, who regards the failure to take Caen as planned on D-Day as 'an immense strategic misfortune', reckons that 'it was never realistic to imagine that the British infantry battalions could march through Caen on their feet on the same day they had landed. The only possibility of dramatic success lay in a concentrated, racing armour thrust by 27th Brigade.' It was, he argues, 'chiefly the fault of over-optimism and sloppy thinking by the planners, together with the enormous difficulty of organizing a major all-arms attack in the wake of an amphibious landing'.† As will be seen later, however, one reason for the failure was the British infantry's lack of any armoured troop carriers capable of moving up closely behind the tanks, such as the Germans had long possessed.

Writing after the war, Bradley expressed himself 'keenly disappointed'. The failure of the British tank formations that first day was to characterize, and plague, all Monty's subsequent efforts to wrest Caen from the Germans; more will be said of it. Meanwhile, with their accustomed speed and vigour, Rommel's 21st Panzer Division of I SS Panzer Corps had arrived and taken up position around the city. Further west, the Canadian 3rd Division was forced to withdraw in the face of a major counter-attack at Authie. Thrown prematurely into the battle, by the evening of the 8th half of 21st Panzer Division had in fact been destroyed. Monty was delighted. Nevertheless Caen

* Quoted in Lamb, *Montgomery in Europe*, p. 93. Poett later became C-in-C Far East.
† Hastings, *Overlord*, pp. 116–17.

remained secure in German hands. An opportunity had been lost. Clearly it would have been far better if he could have taken Caen, like Bayeux, in the shock of those first two days, and let the Germans batter at what Hitler insisted was considered a key nodal point; and it would have saved many, many Allied lives. This returns us to one of the mysteries of the OVERLORD plan: why a far greater effort was not made on D-Day to extend the bridgehead so efficiently seized by 6th Airborne over the Orne and Caen Canal at Bénouville, thereby outflanking the city from the east, while at the same time interdicting the arrival of Rommel's reinforcements from the Pas de Calais. Had the additional landing craft only been available, the beaches from the Orne eastwards to Cabourg, half a mile wide at low tide, would have offered as good landing as anywhere else. The hinterland was flat and open, criss-crossed with narrow ditches a little like Holland, but none of them serious enough to impede armour. Given the immense Allied air and naval superiority, the argument that the approaching craft would have come under fire from the Le Havre heavy coastal guns hardly holds water. On D-Day Canadian paratroopers briefly took the key town of Troarn, astride the Caen–Le Havre highway, but had to abandon it in the absence of any serious follow-up.

Henceforth Rommel recognized the Orne–Dives quadrilateral as an area to be defended at all costs. Consequently, through many weeks and costly attacks to come, all Monty's efforts to break the Caen log-jam would founder because of the lack of space on his eastern flank.

For all his attempts to play it down, here was a first serious setback to the campaign with many repercussions to come. Nevertheless, he wrote in his first despatch to de Guingand that day, 'I am well satisfied,' and in a letter to 'Simbo' Simpson he explained, 'The Germans are doing everything they can to hold on to Caen. I have decided not to have a lot of casualties by butting up against the place.' He would now endeavour to take it from the right flank, south-eastwards from the village of Villers-Bocage – duly conscious of his promise to Leigh-Mallory and the air barons to gain them the coveted airfields inland from Caen. Despite his determination not to 'butt up against the place', Dempsey was ordered to mount 'a strong thrust' on the 9th – ambitiously, towards Falaise and Argentan far to the south of Caen.

In London, Monty's optimism was reflected in the news broadcasts, and in Peter Earle's diary entry for the 7th: 'Yesterday's messages were quite incredibly optimistic. . . . CIGS summary 0705 hrs. 6th June 1944 – General Montgomery says that on this army front he "could hardly want the situation to be better".' Meanwhile, at about this time Monty received a brief postcard from Ireland, addressed to 'HQ 21st Division, Normandy, France'. It was from his mother Maud, with a note of family history:

> I believe you landed at the same spot from which William the Conqueror sailed in 1066. Our ancestor Roger Montgomery was his 2nd in Command – like you. The old Montgomery Castle was near Lisieux.
>
> Please send autographs.

CHAPTER FIVE

STALEMATE?

8–23 June 1944

> All very well here in France and the battle is going according to plan. I have my TAC HQ over here now, with all my caravans, and am comfortably installed and living the open air life. It really pays.
>
> (Montgomery, letter to his son, 12 June 1944)

> A commander must have time to think.
>
> (Montgomery, quoted in Antony Brett-James, *Conversations with Montgomery*, p. 146)

As MONTY had declared to 'Simbo' Simpson, it was not his intention to suffer casualties 'by butting up against the place.' Yet, between D-Day and the end of June Monty would make three attempts, each costly and unsuccessful, to wrest the focal point of Caen from Rommel. In July he would try again, with Operation GOODWOOD, and then with BLUECOAT. One is tempted, once again, to think of ancient Troy, with Hector and Priam anxiously patrolling its thick walls as the Greek forces, arriving by ever more ships, massed beneath them. Instead of those protective walls, Rommel's defenders – small packets of veteran, resolute SS men – had dug themselves into 'hedgehogs', small strongpoints with all-round fire such as had proved so cost-effective against the massive onslaughts of Soviet manpower on the Eastern Front, deploying their tanks like mobile pillboxes. But there was to be no Ulysses with a Wooden Horse – unless it be FORTITUDE, with Patton's fake army group pinning down the German Fifteenth Army across the Pas de Calais and deceiving Rommel into making that ill-timed visit home for his wife's birthday. Henceforth Monty before Caen would have no more scope in which to outmanoeuvre his foe (as he had done in the wide-open desert spaces) than did Agamemnon and Achilles around Troy. It would be a long, slogging battle. In the eyes of the British press – and more so of the American, ever impatient for results – Caen would come to seem like a Troy, barring the way to Paris.

This was not, however, how Monty saw it.

Monty and his 'young men' were digging themselves in within the pleasant park of the Château de Creullet, which Monty described as 'a very pleasant spot', lying midway between Bayeux and Courseulles, where Monty had landed, and opposite the weakest part of the German line. A Louis XIII château, Creullet* belonged to the Druval family. As of June 1944, the incumbent was the seventy-five-year-old Marquis, described by Major Paul Odgers in his account as 'a dubious ex-cavalry aristocrat', who came under instant suspicion as a pro-German *collabo*. A colonel in the First World War, pro-German insofar as he was very anti-Russian, his story was not atypical of the tragedy of Occupied France. A few days after Monty arrived, asked by a French-speaking British officer 'Who do you want after the war?', the Marquis had replied unashamedly, 'Pétain!' As it happened to be the day that de Gaulle landed in France and arrived at Creullet, it did not exactly enhance his image. The following day, the Luftwaffe bombed the château, blowing out the windows. Taking no chances with security, Monty arbitrarily ordered that all the shutters in the dubious Marquis' château which faced the TAC encampment be permanently closed. So when Churchill, George VI – and de Gaulle – stayed at TAC HQ, all the village knew – except Monsieur le Marquis, who, behind closed shutters, was kept literally in the dark.

In his own diary† the Marquis recorded how at lunchtime on D-Day the occupying Germans had left 'in a hurry, and some disorder'. One hour later the 'Tommies' arrived, in the shape of Trumbull Warren, who promptly flushed out the fifteen Germans he found asleep in the Marquis' garage. The Marquis then bicycled leisurely down to the village, to find out what was going on, discovered the Germans had flooded the nearby Seulles river, and returned to

* Confusingly enough, half a mile away stands the medieval château of Creully, later inhabited (with unfortunate consequences for Monty) by the BBC.

† Unpublished papers at Château de Creullet.

encounter a hundred vehicles of a 'mysterious HQ' taking possession of his park. Sequestered behind closed shutters, he never knew the identity of his uninvited guest until after Monty had moved on two weeks later.

Had he been a German general – or an American – Monty would almost certainly have set himself up in comfort inside the château itself, expelling the Marquis. A hundred miles away, his old rival Erwin Rommel, returning hastily after a hazardous all-day drive to take control of the battle (which was, in effect, already as good as lost by the time he arrived), had returned to his headquarters at La Roche Guyon on the Seine. Belonging to the ancient Rochefoucauld family, the château was a typical site for a German general to choose: it backed on to a steep cliff, making it a hard target for bombers, while a labyrinth of caves burrowed out of the cliff (in both world wars, the Germans showed a remarkable mole-like predilection for 'digging deep') were crammed with defending weaponry.

Meanwhile, still back in England, Eisenhower was bustling anxiously between Southwick Park and Bushey, where – unlike many of his subordinate US generals who tended to select far more ostentatious billets – he spent as much time as he could at the rented Telegraph Cottage. In sharpest contrast, Monty lived – as he had in the desert, and would almost throughout the rest of the campaign (with the exception of the winter lull) – outside in his caravans. These were grouped closely together, superbly camouflaged as haystacks or trees (but – incongruously – always with a small portable flagpole flying the Union Jack), and well removed from the château.

It was certainly to prove safer that way. For days the headquarters of the commander of the whole invasion lay only three miles from the most powerful concentration of Panzer forces he had ever faced. Remarkable even by Second World War standards (quite unheard of in 1914–18) was the concept of so senior a commander, in effect the Commander-in-Chief of half a million men, situating himself so close to a far from static front line. But this was Monty – and a superb display of self-confidence. Sporadically Creullet was shelled and bombed, causing casualties (one shell fell close to the tent where his ADC Johnny Henderson was sleeping). When that old South African wizard, General Smuts, visited with Churchill four days after

Monty's arrival, he pronounced mysteriously 'I smell Boche,' and a very frightened sixteen-year-old German deserter was led in, having been found, half-starved, cowering under a stone bench in the woods – 'within fifty yards' of Churchill and Smuts, recalled Henderson. After that there was a thorough 'beating of the bushes', and the single defence platoon was reinforced by commandos and tanks. Odgers records the camp being 'cramped' while 'the perpetually wet weather made it gloomy under the trees'. But, in his simple tastes, Monty himself found little to complain about. Sensing his needs, Madame Druval had even supplied him tactfully with a range of most unlikely flower vases as *pots de chambre*.

To David on 12 June he wrote, '... I have my TAC HQ over here now, with all my caravans, and am comfortably installed and living the open-air life. It really pays.' To Phyllis Reynolds he described his surroundings cheerfully: 'The French civilians in Normandy do not look in the least depressed; there is plenty of food, plenty of vegetables, cows, milk, cheeses, and very good crops.' Perhaps thinking of his Pétainist host, he even wondered whether they really 'wanted to be liberated!!', and in that same ebullient tone he was writing to de Guingand at Main HQ, 'I am enjoying life greatly and it is great fun fighting battles again after five months in England.' Given the grim casualties that these 'enjoyable' battles were then causing, such comments have been picked upon by later critics as indications of callousness. Much more, however, they reflected Monty's determination to keep up 'binge', in the rear areas as well as up at the front. It combined with a sense that for Monty real contentment came only when he was out in the field, employing that dedicated professionalism to the full. But not least it revealed Monty, like Henry V, at his happiest in a campaigning environment, at TAC surrounded by his young men.

It was at Creullet that Monty established the style and rhythm for his TAC HQ. Borrowed from his adversary, Rommel, in the desert, its great essence was mobility: the whole headquarters could 'move into a field and be completely operational in forty-five minutes'. The largest single component was the Signals Service. With highly sophisticated gear, capable of receiving top-secret ULTRA and

PHANTOM messages,* each time TAC made one of its twenty-seven moves it left behind a vast spaghetti of wires and cables, to be exploited by local farmers for years to come for patching their fences. But, as we have noted, the real nucleus of Monty's communication system was his team of young liaison officers, or LOs, his eyes and ears. Major Dick Harden of the Royal Tanks describes being rushed home, mysteriously, from Cairo and finding himself interviewed at Southwick by Monty, 'wearing one of his old grey sweaters'. 'What are my duties?' he enquired:

> 'Haven't you read of Wellington at Waterloo? There's a copy here if you haven't.' I replied 'Yes, I have, because I passed out in Military History on Wellington!' There were no orders given at all. I asked, 'Can I have leave? I haven't seen my parents since going to Egypt in 1940.' 'No, no telephone allowed. . . .'

Nevertheless, like most of the others, Harden stayed through to the end of the war.

In action, however, the LOs' duties were much more clearly defined. Late in the evening, they would each receive from Monty their orders for the next day. Typically, Johnny Henderson records in his diary for 17 June 1944:

> Gen. Monty sent me off to see General Bucknall, commanding XXX Corps, to find out his plan for the part XXX Corps was going to play in the breakthrough. I then went on to visit 49th and 50th Divs. XXX Corps' plan was to strike south to Aunay with 49th Div. and then do a wide right hook with the 7th Armoured directed on the same place.

That day ended: 'Sent off after dinner to 11th Armoured Div. to fix Monty's visit for tomorrow. . . . Whiskey, and plenty of it.' Later, towards the end of the campaign deep into Germany, another LO described how:

> Monty would say, 'Look, such and such a division is going to cross

* ULTRA was the codename for the top-secret intercepts of Germany's Enigma crytography, probably the most battle-winning contribution of British intelligence during the whole war. The PHANTOM service listened in to the Allied networks, thereby providing Monty with swift confirmation of his liaison officers' reports on exactly where formations were and what they were doing.

> the Elbe tomorrow – I want to know exactly what the form is, how far they have got, what their morale is like, have they got any problems, and so forth.' . . . And he [the LO] would go right down to the Battalion and find out from the CO [commanding officer] how things were going. And the LO would come back in the evening and brief Monty exactly where everyone was. So he had as full a picture as anyone else – a far fuller picture than the Army Commander! . . . A marvellous source of intelligence for Monty.

On their return in the evening, covered with dust and exhausted from shuttling about the front in an open jeep, often under shellfire, the LOs would be debriefed by Paul Odgers, who described himself as 'the home chap' ('I didn't go out on missions'), dictating their notes straight 'to very fast typists'. They were never allowed a meal or a bath 'until they had unburdened themselves, and we got it straight from the horse's mouth'. After they had got scrubbed up, they would then deliver their report orally (using the typed notes) to Monty in person, standing in the map caravan – usually hunched because there was comfortable headroom only for one small general. Mounted on the inside walls, the maps showed every forward position and the location of every command post in 21 Army Group. Monty would listen raptly to these young officers, seldom interrupting except to say 'Good', 'I see.'

Thus the LOs had immense powers to make or break senior officers. Though usually well received, they were not universally popular, being sometimes regarded as 'sneaks' – particularly by commanders who had cause to worry. One of the later LOs, Terence Coverdale, reckoned that 'this reporting over the heads of everybody else, down to seeing platoon commanders', sometimes upset even the impeccable 'Bimbo' Dempsey, commander of Monty's British Second Army. On the other hand, it made junior commanders feel that they were constantly in touch with the Commander-in-Chief; there would be none of that terrible sense of isolation experienced in the trenches of the First World War. Undeniably the LO system kept Monty supremely in touch with hourly developments at the front, and, whatever the criticisms, it was his own special way of fighting the war.

It was, however, emphatically not the American way, and this provided one of the many contributory factors to the misunderstandings that were to ensue. Considering the breezy informality between ranks that existed, to all outside appearances, in the US forces, command structures tended to be rigidly hierarchical. Peppery generals did not take kindly to having twenty-five-year-old junior officers arriving in the midst of battle to ask them what they were up to. The American Captain Ray BonDurant, surprised at the slender numbers of Monty's personal staff and commenting, with mild understatement, on the separation of TAC and Main HQs, noted that it was all 'a little different from our American way of doing things'. (He had observed, with detached amusement, the landing, only a few days after D-Day, of Monty's two Rolls-Royces – one of them a glossy black: 'That would never have happened on the American side of the fence . . . !')* For these reasons, Monty's US liaison officers did not prove a great success – through no fault of their own.

Monty's young staff, most of whom stayed with him right on through to the end of the war, found the atmosphere of TAC inspiriting and exciting. Kept acutely on their toes during hours of duty, off duty the atmosphere – as well as the dress – was extremely relaxed. 'It was really fun, very jolly,' recalled Carol Mather.† 'Contrary to belief about Monty's "austerity", he had a very good sense of humour. Being with him was always a great adventure. He encouraged teasing.'

Paul Odgers agreed: 'He valued the family atmosphere of TAC HQ. . . . there was an intense family atmosphere – high jinks – and Monty liked it.'‡ It is easy to see how the tightly bonded little group at TAC gradually grew into the 'family' which, apart from David, the lonely leader had never had. Johnny Henderson remembered how he 'liked holding court; he didn't want anyone too clever,'§ while a latecomer to the family, Hereward Wake,|| was mindful of how 'he never frightened one – in his relations with the LOs, young officers, he was always relaxed, lighthearted. But as soon as a senior

* BonDurant unpublished notes.

† Later Sir Carol Mather, Conservative MP. Interview 24 November 1992.

‡ Interview 20 November 1992.

§ Interview 29 November 1992.

|| Later Sir Hereward Wake, Bart. Interview 25 November 1992.

officer came in, everything changed – he froze up. It was rather unattractive.'

In this remark (and it was an opinion shared by many of the TAC team), Wake pinpointed what was one of Monty's major failings, a real Achilles heel, already noted from pre-war days: idolized by the rank and file and by junior officers, he was unable to get on with, or communicate with, those nearer his own status. From this stemmed a multitude of evils. Remembering the post D-Day visits of Winston Churchill and the King, BonDurant was amazed that 'we never had – normally – the major-generals of the staff. This was strange to me; I was not familiar with that organization.'

The worst aspect was, as the harassed de Guingand feared it would be, the physical division between TAC and the vast back-up staff machinery at Main HQ, whose job it was to organize the logistics of implementing Monty's orders. It had worked all right in the desert, when the two headquarters were separated by only a few miles of sand, with roads and adjacent airfields readily available, and de Guingand would go forward to TAC daily. But in Normandy for the many weeks before the bridgehead had expanded sufficiently, with Main still at Southwick, the Channel acted as a most unwelcome barrier between the two. Later, when the swift-moving advance began, Main would find itself left far behind again, sometimes even out of wireless touch. Dick Harden claimed, 'I only saw the Chief of Staff [de Guingand] two or three times in the whole war!'* This was confirmed by Monty's former Chief of Plans, Charles Richardson, who claimed that 'Monty for a large part of the time was running the battle without a chief of staff.'† In the opinion of Paul Odgers, one of the longest-serving TAC officers,

> there was very real isolation from Main. The awkwardness became apparent and was dangerous at Blay [the third and longest stop in Normandy], from the Allied point of view. Monty had very bad links backwards. SHAEF was terribly ill informed. . . . If you want to criticize Monty, he had *no political sense*. At army-group level this was absolutely necessary.‡

* Interview 23 November 1992.
† Interview 26 November 1992.
‡ Interview 20 November 1992.

Richardson added, 'Things would have been different with Ike if Freddie had been on the right side of the Channel, but Freddie couldn't be spared from Main.'

Here then lay perhaps the greatest disadvantage of Monty's TAC HQ system. As Johnny Henderson, and many others, reckoned, the affable and congenial Freddie was the one man on Monty's staff who could 'nudge Monty with Ike, and he wasn't there'. All too often geography dictated that he was simply out of touch with what 'Master' was really thinking. Even though, as soon as an airfield was opened, Monty's intelligence chief, Brigadier Bill Williams, and Brigadier Belchem, the BGS Ops, flew out every day in a Dakota to see him, this peculiar isolation 'from other senior officers and from people of his own age' definitely contributed, in Richard Lamb's view, 'to Montgomery's failure to understand the criticism and jealousy which his conduct was arousing amongst the British and American chiefs at SHAEF, and at Bradley's US First Army'.*

At least, however, this sweet isolation preserved for Monty the peace and tranquillity he deemed essential for a leader. As he was wont to say, 'a commander must have time to think' and 'Somebody's got to go mad, but it won't be me!' That 'somebody' was often, very nearly, the unfortunate Freddie – at various moments on the brink of physical if not mental breakdown. 'I will *not* get bogged down in details,' Monty had told his staff shortly after taking over 21 Army Group back in January. 'I never read any papers. Half of all papers are not read and the other half are not worth reading.'†

Within this haven of peace and reason that Monty insisted upon, his staff came to appreciate the meticulous care he took over his health, mindful of the lung trouble which, derived from his First World War wound, had come so close to dismissing him from the army on the brink of war. 'He looked after himself very carefully, not only from the point of view of medicine, not having a smoke or a drink and that sort of thing, but if it was cold, "I want my woolly, you know." He was very careful never to get himself into any draughts . . . very conscious of his teeth,' recalled Terry Coverdale.‡ No less solicitous for his good health, the army had attached to TAC

* *Montgomery in Europe*, p. 97.
† D'Este, *Decision in Normandy*, p. 163.
‡ Montgomery Collection.

a twenty-eight-year-old medical officer, Bob Hunter,* who had just qualified as a GP on the eve of war in 1939. When it was learned that Monty wanted to go ashore immediately after D-Day, the Royal Army Medical Corps told him they could not guarantee medical services – 'as a compromise it was agreed to send a doctor to TAC HQ for three weeks – a major'. In fact, Hunter was to remain till the end of the war and beyond, becoming Monty's personal physician. His duties, he claimed, were not arduous. Monty was never ill, except for the occasional cold. Hunter's worst problem turned out to be Monty's predilection for being photographed chewing on an iron-like army ration biscuit when visiting the front. After flying back to London to fetch two new sets of dentures, broken on the hard-tack, Hunter ordered 'No more biscuits'. Under-employed, he found himself charged with looking after Monty's growing household of dogs and other pets.

Meanwhile, the health-giving recipe of bed at 9.30 p.m. was most rigorously adhered to; not even an army commander was allowed to breach it. There was only one exception, Trumbull Warren recalled. A young signals officer, claiming to be 'from J-branch', arrived at Creullet late one night and insisted on seeing the General. When told it was quite out of the question, he persisted several times, declaring ominously that if he wasn't admitted Monty would be furious. Warren finally gave way and woke up Monty. Instead of being reproved, he was warmly thanked, and told that if ever any officer ever arrived from 'J-Signals' he must be brought in at once, whatever time of night or day. Warren was mystified, but many years later when the secret of ULTRA came out,† decided that this must have been the matter brought by the young signals officer, for which Monty was alone prepared to break his routine.

Rather more threatening to Monty's good health (though he paid minimal attention to the risks) was of course the danger of enemy action during those first days in Normandy. Apart from the incidental shelling, as Monty wrote to 'Simbo' Simpson on the day of his arrival, sniping in the back areas had been 'very troublesome': 'The

* Later Lord Hunter of Newington, and Vice-Chancellor of Birmingham University.

† ULTRA remained a tight secret until the 1970s. The 'J-Signals' referred to by Trumbull Warren might, however, also have come from the equally secret PHANTOM service.

roads have been far from safe and we have lost some good officers.* I have been alright myself, though I have toured the area all day. There have been women snipers, presumably wives of German soldiers; the Canadians shot four women snipers.' Two days later, recording a 'very near miss' at TAC from a nocturnal bomb, Monty noted that the number of women snipers shot had risen to eight. Little more was ever said about this small incident of war, as to who these mysterious maenads really were, or whether perhaps the Canadians ('a bit jumpy') had been somewhat trigger-happy. But it prompted Monty to direct in the same letter (to de Guingand): 'Do not let any VIPs visit me. . . . I have two Army Commanders who have never commanded Armies in battle before, and a large number of inexperienced Divisions and Generals, and my time is very fully occupied; I have no time to spare for visitors.'

Nevertheless, Monty was under heaviest pressures, from directions he could ill resist. On the 13th, he wrote to P. J. Grigg, the outspoken Secretary for War, and increasingly his friend and ally, 'It is not a good time for important people to go sight-seeing. . . . I do not want to take my eyes off the battle. Have lunch with me and depart in the afternoon.' Infinitely harder to put off was an impatient Winston Churchill, barred from having a grandstand seat on a bombarding battleship on D-Day, but eager for the sound and smell of battle. Much as he might venerate the great warlord, according to Bill Williams, Monty habitually found it 'an intolerable disturbance' to have 'Winston's podgy finger poking its way into an enterprise he clearly did not understand'. Recalling Churchill's last-minute interference on the eve of D-Day, to have him around asking questions when the situation at Caen remained so tricky was particularly undesirable. Nevertheless, on the 12th, accompanied by Brooke and Smuts, he descended, regardless of the perils, and causing Monty – vexedly – to cancel a conference with Bradley scheduled for that morning, thus offending American sensibilities. At Creullet, the Prime Minister recorded:

> We lunched in a tent looking towards the enemy. The General was in the highest spirits. I asked him how far away was the actual front. He said about three miles. I asked him if he had a continuous

* These included the commanding officer of his old regiment, the Royal Warwicks, Lieutenant-Colonel Herdon – killed at the head of its 2nd Battalion.

> line. He said, 'No.' 'What is there then to prevent an incursion of German armour breaking up our luncheon?' He said he did not think they would come.*

Such bland confidence may well have been designed to discourage Winston from overstaying his leave. But Monty clearly overdid it: Churchill returned to London, in a state of high excitement, promptly to inform Stalin, 'We hope to encircle Caen, and perhaps make a capture there of prisoners.' With parallel self-assurance, Monty confided to his diary that the Prime Minister had been 'in very good form, and he was quite prepared to take orders and do what he was told – which was a great change!!'

Next arrived de Gaulle, on the 14th – not, however, inspiring any entry in Monty's pocket diary. Four days later, Monty wrote to David, 'I have had a great many visitors recently: the Prime Minister, General de Gaulle, the King, the Secretary of State for War . . . and many others. I had never seen de Gaulle before; he speaks English, but not very well.' On the 14th, always to remain a red-letter day in French history, amid much fanfare and with a substantial retinue, the leader of the Free French landed at Courseulles, on the Canadians' JUNO beach,† almost four years to the day since he had left his beloved France.

Almost immediately trouble began. To the surprise of the British, instead of thanking Monty for liberating *la Patrie*, de Gaulle began to lay down the law, declaring that, since he was now in France, he was in charge – a claim he abandoned only with considerable ill grace. After arriving virtually unannounced at TAC for lunch,‡ in the afternoon he suddenly disappeared. A short while later, a report came through that he was causing a major traffic block in Bayeux – making a speech to the locals, his first 'walkabout' on French terri-

* *The Second World War*, vol. VI, p. 11

† Although it was the conveniently sheltered inlet where TAC had also landed, in view of de Gaulle's subsequent career one almost wonders whether his footsteps were heaven-directed, or whether he particularly chose to make his first landfall in France on a Canadian – rather than British or American – beach. Today the tiny hamlet of Courseulles-sur-Mer lies on the boundary of two communes, and remains the source of lively argument as to which had the honour of receiving de Gaulle on that historic day.

‡ In the address column of Monty's TAC HQ visitors' book de Gaulle wrote with simple grandeur, 'France.'

tory, with military traffic unable to get through. 'Monty', recalls Johnny Henderson, 'was furious, and gave orders for him to be stopped and sent back to England.' Then followed, curiously, an order from Churchill, direct, counter-ordering Monty's instructions and telling him 'to leave de Gaulle in peace'. But the proud Frenchman never forgave Monty, or the British, for this insult to France – through his person. Monty's unflattering commentary on the visit in his personal diary was:

> a poor fish and gives out no inspiration. I gave him every facility to go where he liked, but asked him to leave the lodgement area before dark – which he did. His general reception in Bayeux and other places was lukewarm; his staff had to keep shouting, 'General de Gaulle,' and pointing to him.

When Ike was told that de Gaulle in his Bayeux speech had declared that the Free French were now reconquering France 'with the aid of the Allies', he all but had a seizure. Meanwhile, in the wake of de Gaulle's visit members of TAC noted a steady increase in the flow of French 'patriots' to Creullet, denouncing neighbours as suspected *collabos*. The simple British, far removed from the passions of French wartime politics, were shocked by the spectacle of local women being dragged off to have their heads shaven.

'The PM is very anxious the King should come over here; just to land for two hours, have lunch with me, and go away,' Monty told 'Simbo' Simpson:

> I said I would agree to that. The date may be Friday this week, or Saturday. . . . Whatever date is settled, keep anyone else away on that day, i.e. warn Eisenhower off if he proposes to come the same day. I cannot deal with more than one VIP – and have told the PM today he must not come again just yet.

Some might find this something of an insight into the almost godlike posture that Monty was already beginning to assume, prescribing whom among the great in the land he would have and whom he would not have. The ancient Greeks might have found there an element of hubris, the pride provoking to the gods that rides before a fall. On the 16th, there duly arrived King George VI. Johnny Henderson (who had had no time to write anything in his diary for the past week) had been unloading the Commander-in-Chief's two Rolls-Royces. He recalled arriving 'at TAC for breakfast where great preparations were being made for the King's arrival at 1200'. It reminded him of preparations for an earlier visit from the sovereign, in North Africa, when a new 'thunder-box' had been painted, the paint not drying before the royal posterior arrived. With a youthfully critical eye he recorded of the Normandy visit:

> HM was a little short and sharp on arrival, having had a rough journey, but soon warmed up. After lunch a small investiture was held in front of the Chief's caravan. John Poston was given his MC. . . . He wasn't allowed to go anywhere else as there were still snipers about. It is a pity he is not more forthcoming with the troops – never waves to them or shows much sign of interest. His Equerries seem to be a collection of old poops. After he arrived back in England that night, it was announced on the wireless that he had seen Monty at his HQ in the grounds of a château – in fact did its best to tell the enemy where our HQ was.

The consequences of the extraordinary indiscretion of the BBC, housed as they were in another château at the other end of the village (the London press was no less indiscreet), were to be swift and potentially disastrous.

Two days after the King, P. J. Grigg arrived on a landing craft – as requested, for lunch only. Henderson recalled him returning:

> that evening, takes with him some Camembert cheeses, of which there are plenty. He is a really genuine man and obviously all out to help. Very much to the point and not afraid to say what he thinks of other people; consequently, his unpopularity in the political world; he was most interested in the lack of enthusiasm on the part of the French people – said de Gaulle is not the man to give France a lead.*

Caen remained tantalizingly outside Monty's reach. On the 9th, the day Dempsey had been due to launch his 'strong thrust towards Villers-Bocage', Henderson found Monty, after two nights of 'little sleep', tensely 'unapproachable':

* Henderson diary, 18 June 1944.

> said someone must get up at five each morning to get him the news by seven, and see that the caravan is cleaned out. Gen. Dempsey came to see him and it was decided to hold north and west of Caen, where the enemy were counter-attacking, and push 7th Armoured Div. south of Bayeux, and then swing round left-handed, so taking the enemy and Caen from the rear. Gen. Monty wrote this out in a letter for me to take back to the Chief of Staff. After much difficulty, I caught an ML [motor launch] returning to Portsmouth, 2100 hours; when about thirty miles out to sea, both engines broke down. The situation was not improved by a report that six enemy E-boats were approaching at thirty miles. Thank goodness the engines soon mended and we made a detour.

But somehow, through an inexplicable piece of incompetence back at SHAEF, Eisenhower never received Monty's personal signal explaining his intentions. 'He had awakened in a snit,' recorded his aide, Harry C. Butcher: 'no information from Monty, who had agreed to cable every night'.* Here was an instance of isolation between the headquarters – leaving Ike frustrated and angry – where the blame appears in no way to have attached to Monty.

The British and Canadian units that had landed on D-Day were clearly tired and had lost much of their cutting edge. Having been blocked frontally before Caen, and rejecting the costly prospect of 'butting up against the place', Monty ordered Dempsey now to outflank it from both sides. For this he employed 51st Highland Division to move eastwards through the exhausted 6th Airborne Division and across the Orne, to swing round on Caen from the left flank, while 7th Armoured (the famous Desert Rats, under Bucknall's XXX Corps) would spearhead the attack on 10 June by seizing Villers-Bocage, the gateway to Caen from the west. These were two of Monty's most tried and experienced divisions, which had fought under him at Alamein. At the same time, he intended dropping 1st Airborne Division at Evrecy, south of Caen, to complete the trap. But the plan started at once to go wrong when Leigh-Mallory vetoed the air-drop, on the grounds – yet again – that RAF losses would be too high, not least through being shot at by the navy over the

* Butcher diary, 11 June 1944.

Channel. Furious, Monty denounced Leigh-Mallory, 'sitting in his office' in England, to de Guingand as 'a gutless bugger, who refuses to take a chance and plays for safety on all occasions. I have no use for him.'

Much more serious, however, was the bloody nose administered to the Desert Rats at Villers-Bocage. Reacting with great speed on his return, Rommel had already begun to move up elements of three Panzer divisions – 21st, 12th SS and Panzer Lehr – all of them first rate. A fourth, the 2nd – the elite Vienna Division, which in 1940 had been the first to reach the Normandy coast, slicing in two the Allied armies – was also moving up from Amiens, undetected by Allied intelligence and despite constant attacks by Allied fighter-bombers along its route. But what happened to Monty's 7th Armoured on the morning of 13 June was more of the order of the isolated battlefield incident that reverses a trend, the 'rider lost for want of a nail', than a powerful riposte by weighty forces. Because it illuminated more than just this one local setback, it may be worth recounting in some detail.

Despite the loss of few tanks, 7th Armoured had made surprisingly little progress on the 10th and 11th. Greeted with a tremendous welcome by cheering French civilians in Villers-Bocage, the tank crews dismounted while Lord Cranley's 'A' Squadron of Cromwells of the 4th City of London Yeomanry pushed on beyond the town, in what appears to have been a fairly leisurely manner. Lying in wait on a well-sited rise just outside the town, however, were five of the dread Tiger tanks of a company of I SS Panzer Corps, mounting 88mm guns. They were commanded by a much decorated young *Obersturmführer*, or captain, Michael Wittmann, who had already made a name for himself as one of the Panzer aces on the Russian front.* Moving largely by night, under constant Allied air attack, Wittmann had been on the road from Beauvais ever since Rommel had begun to organize his armoured ripostes on D + 1. He planned to spend the 13th carrying out urgent maintenance, then observed

* By the time Wittmann was killed, in the Falaise Gap in early August, he could claim destruction of no less than 138 tanks and self-propelled guns, and 132 anti-tank guns, and was looked upon as perhaps the most successful tank commander of the entire war. It was exceptionally bad luck that the vanguard of the Desert Rats should have come up against him that day.

with amazement the British column halted only a few hundred yards downhill from him at Point 213. 'They're acting as if they've won the war already,' remarked his gunner, Corporal Woll.* Without waiting for his other Tigers to join him, Wittmann set off down the hill to embark upon what Carlo D'Este rightly describes as 'One of the most amazing engagements in the history of armoured warfare'.† Destroying the leading tank at almost point-blank range, thereby blocking deployment of the British force, Wittmann roared down the length of the helpless column, slamming one 88mm shell after another into the thin-skinned Cromwells and half-tracks. He then trundled on, still single-handed, into Villers-Bocage, surprising the 4th CLY Regimental Headquarters and knocking out the commanding officer's tank and most of the rest. One solitary Firefly Sherman‡ commanded by a sergeant managed to hit Wittmann with his 17pdr, but caused only superficial damage.

Within five minutes this single Tiger had shattered the lead element of 7th Armoured Division. Refuelling and rearming, Wittmann then joined his four other Tigers to shoot up what remained of Lord Cranley's 'A' Squadron at Point 213, from which – apparently – only one survivor managed to escape. By the end of the day, Wittmann had destroyed twenty-five British tanks and twenty-eight other armoured vehicles, and killed some eighty infantrymen – including three officers – from the supporting battalion of the Rifle Brigade. His own tank was eventually disabled, but he and the crew escaped to fight another day. A 7th Armoured intelligence report exaggerated Wittmann's handful of Tigers into 'up to forty'. The accompanying infantry of 50th Division had got pinned down by the expert troops of Panzer Lehr on the right, using a new weapon that was to prove deadly in the close fighting in the bocage, the *Panzerfaust*,§ and were thus unable to help. So by nightfall, instead of attempting to reinforce the battered spearhead, the commander of XXX Corps, Lieutenant-General G. C. Bucknall (who

* From Paul Carell, *Invasion: They're Coming*, p. 155.

† D'Este, *Decision in Normandy*, p. 179.

‡ Specially adapted by Monty to mount a 17pdr gun; it was the most effective Allied anti-tank weapon, but was still not equal to the German 88, and seldom a match for a Tiger. (See Chapter 6.)

§ A rocket-propelled anti-tank weapon carried by infantrymen, far deadlier than either its American equivalent, the bazooka, or the cumbersome British PIAT.

had had both of his escort tanks knocked out when visiting 7th Armoured that day), decided it was too dangerous to remain in Villers-Bocage and withdrew westwards – to the fury of Dempsey, the Army Commander, who later claimed he had never been consulted.*

This crucial key to Caen from the west was to remain firmly in German hands until August. Damned for their timidity, both Bucknall and the 7th Armoured commander, Major-General G. W. E. J. Erskine, were henceforth marked men with Monty and would lose their heads over the next weeks.† In the words of Carlo D'Este, 'Almost single-handedly this one audacious and brilliant German tank commander had crushed the British advance around Villers-Bocage and forced the 7th Armoured Division on to the defensive.' Perhaps even more important from the defenders' point of view, it did wonders in restoring morale – and in showing how the vast material advantages of the Allies could still be checked by German technical superiority and tactical skill. D'Este goes so far as to reckon that the failure of Bucknall's right hook was 'to prove one of the costliest Allied mistakes in the liberation of France',‡ sacrificing as it did a great opportunity to break through Rommel's 'still unsettled defences' round Caen.

On the left flank of Dempsey's pincer movement, short of supporting armour and with too little space to deploy within the hemmed-in confines of the Bénouville bridgehead, the veteran 51st Highland Division had also been stopped in its tracks by the 21st Panzer Division and pushed back to the Orne. 'Thereafter,' wrote Monty, 'any attempt to enlarge the Orne bridgehead met very determined resistance.'§ It was an indication of just how seriously Rommel took the possibility of a British break-out eastwards from the Orne – and, equally, how regrettable for the success of OVERLORD it was that greater efforts had not been made to seize that vital open land between Orne and Dives on D-Day. In an unusually

* Even though a new main road has been built, from a vantage up on point 213 it is still extraordinarily easy to trace the exact course of this disastrous action.

† Bucknall was – perhaps mistakenly, as he had forfeited Monty's confidence at Villers-Bocage – permitted to stay on till August.

‡ D'Este, *Decision in Normandy*, pp. 183, 198.

§ *Normandy to the Baltic*, p. 59.

revealing commentary that was to have important bearings on the forthcoming EPSOM attack to seize Caen, fixed for 22 June (but postponed by the weather), Monty wrote reflectively in his personal diary for the 18th:

> I have been thinking a lot on the problem now in front of us. I am not altogether convinced that I was right about launching VIII Corps from the bridgehead east of the Orne. . . .
>
> There is very little room there; and before undertaking any large-scale operations in that area, I feel we have first got to push the enemy back eastwards, and establish our own flank on the R. Dives.
>
> This will take time and would require another division of infantry, and at the moment we have not got one.

The commander of the veteran 51st Highlanders, Bullen-Smith, would also soon accompany Bucknall and Erskine into limbo. Thus three of Monty's veteran divisions from the old Eighth Army were seen to have performed before Caen very poorly. Coming on top of the disappointing performance on D-Day of his own 3rd Division, this must have been a most unpleasant shock to Monty. It was in his character, motivated by loyalty to the 'home team', to conceal such painful disenchantments manfully from his superiors – and particularly, on top of his normal reticence in that direction, from the leader of the 'away team', Ike. This was to be an important factor in the forthcoming July crisis of confidence between himself and the Americans

So what had gone wrong? Even the normally mild-mannered and reticent 'Bimbo' Dempsey was furious with the two commanders Bucknall and Erskine. Speaking to the trustworthy Australian war correspondent, Chester Wilmot, shortly after the event he declared forthrightly that the 7th Armoured attack 'should have succeeded . . . but by this time 7th Armoured was living on its reputation, and the whole handling of the battle was a disgrace'.* In the unfortunate

* From Wilmot's 'Notes on Conversation with General Dempsey', unpublished, in Liddell Hart Archives. Broken by his dismissal in Normandy, Bucknall ended his career as GOC Northern Ireland, prior to his early retirement in 1947. He died in 1981.

Bucknall, very much a 'Monty man', Monty seems to have made one of his rare misjudgements of character. On the basis of his handling a division in Sicily and Italy, Monty had brought him back to command a corps for OVERLORD. Brooke, however, had nurtured misgivings from the start. At the THUNDERCLAP briefing back in April and May, given seven minutes to speak Bucknall had rambled on for seventeen, and had then unceremoniously been told to sit down. 'Very weak', commented Brooke in his diary at the time, and 'unfit to command a Corps'.*

As regards the performance of 7th Armoured, it would be unfair to suggest there were no moments when it had shone at Villers-Bocage. Michael Carver,† then commanding the 1st Royal Tank Regiment, recalled having 'a good little battle', taking advantage of the slowness of the ponderous Panthers and Tigers to traverse their turrets to knock out several at 200 yards' range with the outmatched 75mm guns of his Cromwells (he disputes their inferiority to this day). But the record strongly suggests that this may have been a one-off action. Shortly before D-Day, a brigadier on Monty's planning staff had made some damning observations about indiscipline in the division:

> They were not under control – they were forcing people off the road, assing about generally – in a way that experienced troops going into battle would not behave. I mean, they were the Desert Rats, the most famous division in the British Army, and they were fed up and irresponsible.‡

Somehow the Desert Rats seemed to have lost that spirit and determination which had made them so formidable in the early years in the

* Cited in D'Este, *Decision in Normandy*, p. 193.

† Later Field Marshal Lord Carver and Chief of the Defence Staff 1973–6. Interview February 1992.

‡ General Sir Otway Herbert, quoted in Hamilton, *Monty*, vol. II, p. 616. Lord Carver, in 1994, strongly rejected Herbert's criticisms as 'based on second-hand information' by 'an unpleasant, bad-tempered man who always seemed prejudiced against the division'. He insists that the 'Desert Rats' – as of June 1944 – were 'definitely *not* fed up and irresponsible.' Equally he found no supporting archival evidence for General Dempsey's claim [p. 145] that 'the withdrawal of 7 Armd Div was made without his knowledge or approval;' nor that he had any reason to be 'furious'. (Letters to the author 8 June and 14 September 1994.)

desert. One may also recall Monty's dissatisfaction with its corps commander, General Lumsden, at Alamein. Says Max Hastings, 'they had become wary and cunning in the reduction of risk'.* After so many years of non-stop fighting in the desert, they had just had too much, a condition aggravated by their rooted lack of confidence in the weapons they were asked to do battle in.†

On the American side, there was considerable anger about the retreat from Villers-Bocage. The crack 'Big Red One' 1st Infantry Division had given strong flank support to the 50th Division during the attack, and afterwards had found itself left exposed in front of the Caumont Gap. Monty was held responsible. To the Americans it seemed that neither he nor Dempsey had displayed sufficient 'grip' on the battle, and they regarded it as Monty's first real failure in Normandy. Temperatures were further raised by his display of conceit and optimism, followed by his insistence, both in private and in public, that 'everything had gone according to plan'. As will be seen, there were reasons for this insistence, but it was undoubtedly Villers-Bocage that began the serious American criticism of Monty's 'lack of drive' and excess of caution. Possibly he had underestimated, as had most of the Allied commanders, the problems presented to attackers in the terrible bocage country. Its 'clinging misery', as Max Hastings aptly described it, provided a common denominator of horror which British and Americans, infantry and tankmen alike, would forever associate with the Normandy campaign. Created by the passage of farm carts over the centuries, its sunken lanes – sometimes twenty feet deep and bordered on either side by dense hedgerows – provided the defender with superb natural defence lines, almost resembling the trenches of 1914–18. It was heaven-sent terrain for a fanatical Hitler-Jugend with his lethal, short-range *Panzerfaust*. Tanks could not climb out of its deep banks, and if one were knocked out it could seize up an entire column, leaving it easy prey to a prowling Panther.

*

* *Overlord*, p. 135.

† At Sandhurst Armoured OCTU at the time, one of the authors (AH) well remembers his troop officer, a Captain Russell, who had won the MC in the desert, returning from Normandy to say of some of the Desert Rats' commanders: 'They're "bobbing", I'm afraid. Every time they approach a hedgerow they imagine there's a Tiger behind it.'

By 14 June, D + 8, it looked disquietingly as if the Allied front had congealed. To the west, the Americans had failed – after most bitter fighting – to take St-Lô, which with Caen was one of the two key pivots of the front. More disturbingly, they had been pushed out of Carentan, which posed a distinct threat to the hard-won link-up between UTAH and OMAHA beaches. Monty pressed Bradley to recapture it and push westwards to sever the Cotentin Peninsula at Coutances. It was thus all the more urgent for the British and Canadians to keep up the pressure towards Caen, so as to prevent Rommel moving his armour to attack Bradley at Carentan. Already four Panzer divisions had been identified around the Caen sector, and Monty realized that it could only be a matter of days, if not hours, before Rommel felt strong enough to mount his first co-ordinated counter-offensive – which would be a massive blow, instead of the piecemeal efforts made to date. Meanwhile, his own troops, after eight days' hard fighting, were showing signs of exhaustion, and no further serious offensive could be launched until the arrival of the fresh, back-up VIII Corps. Commanded by Lieutenant-General Sir Richard O'Connor – one of the early desert generals, who had been captured by Rommel in 1941, but escaped daringly from a POW camp in 1943, and a colleague Monty admired from his days at Staff College in the 1920s – VIII Corps began to arrive on the 15th. But, to Monty's fury, loading delays in England meant that its leading formation, 'Pip' Roberts' crack 11th Armoured Division, was landing two days behind schedule. This was, he claimed, 'to have unfortunate repercussions on the subsequent development of my plans'.

It was becoming a serious race against time – just how serious no one could know better than Monty, with his long-standing knowledge of Rommel and of the force and speed with which he was capable of reacting. Meanwhile, there was always the frightening factor of Normandy's uncertain weather, the capricious Poseidon of modern times. At a stroke it could deprive the attackers of their one ace card, air superiority – or, more dangerously, cut the lifelines across the Channel upon which everything depended. Whatever his increasingly vocal critics at SHAEF might say, it was essential – Monty knew – to maintain his forces 'well balanced' in the face of almost certain counter-attack. This meant a period of apparent inaction, infuriating to an out-of-touch Ike, always espousing a principle of *l'attaque, toujours l'attaque* across the board. Though Monty could write, after the war in his memoirs, that at Caen 'the acquisition of land was not so pressing', from his despatches to Brooke it was quite clear that he still intended to take Caen at the earliest opportunity. On the other hand, he could with equal justice claim that his overall basic strategy, 'to pull the Germans on to Second British Army, and fight them there, so that First US Army can carry out its task the easier', which he reiterated to Brooke, and which he had delineated so clearly back at St Paul's during THUNDERCLAP, remained quite unchanged and unshaken.

The essential tragedy of Monty's relations with the Americans was that he could not, and never would be able to, bring himself to admit to Eisenhower (or even to Churchill, for that matter) that there had been a setback, however temporary, to his plans. To explore the reasons for this curious debility, one has perhaps to go right back to his earliest childhood, to his wretched relations with his mother, to his ensuing lifelong inability to 'open up' to contemporaries, to the additional self-imposed isolation that set in after the numbing death of Betty. One might add his intrinsic loyalty to the 'home team' which made it intolerable for him to admit that failure might in part be due to a flawed instrument – his beloved British Army, in the training and rehabilitation of which he had been so intimately involved. There was also his recognition that it had to be constantly 'binged up'.

One of his sternest critics, Carlo D'Este, allows that, after Villers-Bocage, 'there was nothing wrong with Montgomery's new strategy; the problem was that he never admitted it was any such thing'.* But D'Este quite misses the point about it being 'new', given all that Monty had told his command audiences at various times well before D-Day. What it in fact showed was Monty, as at Alamein, reacting to a tactical setback with considerable strategic flexibility. Regrettably, however, this was not how things looked to Ike, isolated back at SHAEF in England, nor to the US press and politicians back in Washington, already plunged into the fervour of a presidential election year. Aided by a British press growing only marginally less impatient (the first of Hitler's secret V-weapons, the doodlebugs,

* D'Este, *Decision in Normandy*, p. 202.

had landed on London on 13 June) and by the generalissimo's own rash boastfulness in advance of battle, the public image was indubitably a confusing one. On the one hand, he wanted to take Caen, but couldn't; on the other, he didn't want to, but went on regardless.

To those few, like Brooke, who understood Monty and what he was really saying, the question was: when the moment came, would Monty be able to muster the strength necessary to defeat, decisively, the divisions that Rommel was daily piling up in the Caen sector? This was something about which Monty at least, in his invincible self-confidence, had no doubts whatsoever. But whether or not Ike ever properly understood Monty's strategy remains one of the unresolved, and incessantly argued, mysteries of history.

On 15 June, Monty went to see Bradley, who had only recently moved his headquarters ashore from USS *Augusta* (because of the shallowness of the OMAHA bridgehead). Paradoxically, the Army Group Commander now found himself located *ahead* of his subordinate Army Commander. By a misfortune, or misunderstanding, that same day Ike – accompanied by his deputy, Tedder, his newly commissioned son, Second Lieutenant John Eisenhower, and an escort of no less than thirteen fighters – had gone to Creullet, only to find (to Ike's considerable irritation) that Monty had already left. With Bradley that day, Monty had shown high good humour: the GIs they passed had welcomed him with acclaim, and Bradley had treated him with the respect, and admiration, which he genuinely felt at that time. The meeting passed off with total accord. Monty wanted to see St-Lô captured, but accepted Bradley's resistance to risking heavy casualties simply 'to take a place-name' – which echoed his own feelings about Caen. Top priority was to be given to capturing the key Channel port of Cherbourg. Accordingly, Bradley unleashed 'Lightning Joe' Collins and his VII Corps. Aged forty-eight, a fighting Irishman from Louisiana, Collins – who had already commanded a division with distinction on Guadalcanal – was, and remained, one of Monty's favourite American generals. He was as ruthless with his subordinates, and with himself, as Monty was.* By the 18th, Lightning Joe had broken out across the Cotentin Peninsula to the little seaside resort of Barneville on its west coast, and then swung swiftly

* Collins shone brilliantly during the Battle of the Bulge, and became US Army Chief of Staff in succession to his old chief, Bradley, in 1949.

northwards towards Cherbourg, sealing off four German divisions. It was the first tangible success of the campaign – at least that the armchair critics, poring over their maps in Grub Street, could comprehend – and it showed US mobility at its very best.

In TAC HQ's betting book at Creullet, John Poston bet his American colleague Ray BonDurant £3 that 'US troops will not have entered Cherbourg by midnight on 20 June.' Poston won; invested on the 21st, Cherbourg was not actually captured – after a bitter battle – until the 29th. When told that Monty had declared Caen to be 'really the key to Cherbourg', Collins had exploded, 'Brad, let's wire him to send us the key!' Nevertheless, the early investment and capture of Cherbourg was a distinct feather in Monty's cap – as well as Lightning Joe's. The only trouble was that, on Hitler's explicit orders, German demolition crews had done the most thorough job imaginable, reducing the port to such a shambles that it would not be fully operational until late September – with serious consequences for the campaign beyond Normandy. This was a serious disappointment to Eisenhower and Monty.

In the meantime, O'Connor's fresh British VIII Corps had arrived, and Monty was planning his next effort to roll up Caen from the west. The attack would be codenamed EPSOM and was planned for 22 June. It would not attempt a pincer attack from east of the Orne, where the Germans were now established in great strength, but instead would strike on a narrow, concentrated front only four miles wide between Carpiquet airfield (so coveted by the air barons) and Villers-Bocage.

But Poseidon struck first.

Writing to David on 20 June in his usual breezily uninformative manner, Monty disclosed simply, 'All goes well here except that the weather is very bad and it is extremely rough on the beaches. I myself am very fit and the open-air caravan life suits me.' He was in fact referring to the worst storm recorded in nearly forty years, of almost hurricane strength, which struck Normandy out of the blue. Johnny Henderson tells the story in his diaries:

> 19 June: The plan for the breakthrough has been altered. The Chief took the whole morning rearranging the plan, and then telling

Dempsey the D-Day for the start has had to be put back again. Weather is bad and the unloading of ships getting badly behind. There is a slight shortage of ammunition. The enemy are sending over a lot of leaflets to our soldiers, saying how London is being destroyed by Hitler's new weapons. Some leaflets we were dropping over the Germans blew back into our lines, saying 'surrender now'!

20 June: Coningham [commander of Allied Tactical Air Forces] tries to fly over to see Monty, has to turn back owing to bad weather. Monty goes to XXX Corps to choose 'new COs for five regiments who have lost their colonels'. While doing so, three ME-109s came over the hedge at zero height, scraping the camp, missing the caravan Monty was in by inches.

21 June: Foul day. Not one of the vehicles could be unloaded. This has put the attack back another twenty-four hours. . . . The Americans are now all round Cherbourg. . . .

22 June: Weather still foul. . . . The Chief sent me out to 49th/50th Div. – with 90,000 cigarettes for each. He buys these out of his Comfort Fund money and hands them out. They certainly pay a very big dividend. The Chief of Staff (Freddie de Guingand) flew over with Bill Williams (G-1) to see the Chief – a pity he is not here to liven the party a little more. Kit, Trum, Noël and myself, the Chief's personal staff, were told by the Chief that we were to talk more at dinner!!!!

On the 23rd Henderson was at last able to write, 'The weather has been perfect and they are off-loading as fast as possible. The big push is now to be next Monday, 26th.'

In the course of those three days of storm, however, untold damage had been wreaked. The submarine cable had been severed, 'and we cannot talk to England', noted Monty on the 21st in his personal diary. But even being cut off from contact with Main HQ was a lesser problem. One of the most brilliant innovations of OVERLORD had been the Mulberry artificial harbour, partly a brainchild of the restless genius of Churchill himself, whereby in greatest secrecy great pontoons and blockships had been assembled on the south coast of England, then anchored off the British beach-head at Arromanches. It was also the terminus of that other great invention, Pluto, the undersea pipe which fuelled Monty's great army.

Both were regarded as essentially temporary measures, until the port facilities of Cherbourg became available. Under the OVERLORD logistics plan, Cherbourg had been counted on to discharge 150,000 tons of supplies by 25 July; in fact the total achieved would be less than 18,000. Never in his wildest nightmares had Monty anticipated that this first great port captured by the Allies would be largely out of business until the end of September, by which time most of the other ports of France and Belgium short of Antwerp would be operating. So all supplies, food, fuel and ammunition for a force now approaching a total of half a million continued to funnel through Arromanches and up the beaches. With vigour the Americans had begun to replicate their own Mulberry on hard-won OMAHA beach, but this was totally destroyed during the three days the storm raged, never to be replaced. Altogether some 800 ships of all sizes were beached or lost – far more than were sunk by German action during the whole campaign – while immediate losses in supplies amounted to 140,000 tons. By any reckoning, it was a major catastrophe. Fortunately the original British Mulberry, though damaged, remained intact.

What would have happened had it been destroyed – or, worse still, if the terrible storm had suddenly arisen during the critical period following D-Day – hardly bears thinking about. In its aftermath, Group Captain Stagg wrote tactfully to Ike, reminding him that, if on 5 June he had decided to delay OVERLORD until the 19th, it would have run into this devastating storm. The story of the Spanish Armada would have been repeated. Eisenhower scribbled at the bottom of the message, 'Thanks, and thank the gods of war we went when we did!'* History has reason to be grateful for the accuracy of Group Captain Stagg and his experts.

With the air forces grounded, the Mulberry harbours paralysed, no supplies or fresh troops getting through and Rommel poised to strike, it was for Monty the most anxious moment since D-Day. It was also one of the moments that makes historians appreciate how much more of a close-run thing OVERLORD was than is generally – and smugly – accepted. Not for the first or last time, one is drawn

* Ambrose (1), p. 424.

to contemplate, and perhaps marvel upon, what a weight of destiny rested on Montgomery. Based, almost certainly, on the self-confidence that Monty was continuing to radiate backwards via 'Simbo' Simpson, at the War Office in London Peter Earle recorded on the 22nd, 'Now we are absolutely safe; under no conditions can we be pushed into the sea, unless we make some frightful mistake, which we shall not do.'

In the shorter term, by the 23rd, when the storm abated, the British Second Army build-up found itself still three divisions behind schedule. Air support was suspended, Allied heavy artillerymen were rationed to twenty-five rounds a day or less – all this at a time when the Germans were stepping up their shelling of the Allied forces in advance of Rommel's anticipated counter-offensive. Weather had prevented Eisenhower from visiting Bradley on the 20th, and altogether links between Monty and the rear were at their most tenuous. Prospects for EPSOM, now already delayed several days, were far from auspicious. As Monty himself admitted to 'Simbo' on 23 June, 'The enemy has had a great stroke of luck in the bad weather. It has saved him.'

Nevertheless, the previous evening Monty summoned together all his commanders at the Château de Creullet to discuss the forthcoming operation, now scheduled to start on the evening of the 25th. It would be his last day there. In a long letter to his successor at Eighth Army, Oliver Leese, then slogging his way up through Italy, he explained:

> The Press that came with the King gave away the area of my HQ. . . . A nearby château was destroyed by bombing two nights later; and heavy gunfire was opened on my HQ two days after that, and I had one killed and two wounded. I then decided to move my HQ, and am having no more visitors!!!

Uncharacteristically, Monty admitted to David on 18 June, 'A great deal of bombing and shooting goes on by night, so I have now got my bed put in a hole in the ground and I sleep quite safely below ground level.' Johnny Henderson was more precise in pinpointing the blame:

> Yesterday [22 June] we got shelled after the King's visit. The *Daily Mail* has practically given the route, therefore leaving little doubt

> in the enemy's mind as to where we were. We therefore moved today to Blay (six miles west of Bayeux) so as to be more in the middle. We are now just in the American sector.

With Rommel on the move, Creullet might conceivably find itself just too near the front line for that tranquillity Monty deemed essential for a commander if he was to think.

CHAPTER SIX

'A Straightforward Infantry Bash'

23 June–10 July 1944

For if the trumpet give an uncertain sound, who shall prepare himself to the battle?

(I Corinthians xiv: 8 – one of Montgomery's favourite quotations)

A man's courage is his capital, and he is always spending. The call on the bank may be only the daily drain of the front line or it may be a sudden draft which threatens to close the account.

(Lord Moran, *The Anatomy of Courage*, p. x)

On the eve of the next great push, EPSOM, the TAC betting book reveals a moment of passing optimism within its new quarters at Blay: 'Gen. Crerar bets Gen. Montgomery an even £1 that the war with Germany will be over by 1–9–44, i.e. that Germany will have asked for an armistice by that date.' Trumbull Warren raised the bet to £10; both had to pay up. On the 26th, Johnny Henderson duly noted in his diary, 'The attack started early this morning. XXX Corps will move forward to secure the east flank for VIII Corps attack. A foul day, raining most of the time so the vehicles could not operate. Good progress was made however.' He added:

> Cherbourg has almost fallen; Ray BonDurant went up there today. The Americans are right in the town and the German commander has been captured. Ray went down to some of their concrete fortifications and came back with five cases of Hennessy 3 Star Brandy – damned good too!

The following day, the weather still 'foul', Henderson observed the tell-tale signs of anxiety in Monty: 'The Chief has been in wonderful form the last fortnight – now again he gets worried and it is advisable to keep well away – let others get the rockets. He gets irritable, doesn't concentrate, fusses over little things.'

Monty had every cause to be irritable: first, the 'foul' weather had seriously limited the use of the air weapon to soften up the defence; secondly, ULTRA revealed that a new SS corps of two further Panzer divisions, the 9th and 10th, despatched from Russia, had now reached the sector exactly where O'Connor's VIII Corps was due to strike. This might be presumed helpful to Stalin, long crying for a second front to remove pressure from the east, but, as noted by Peter Earle back with General Nye at the War Office, this 'realizes Monty's worst fears – a delay of five days may cause a great, extravagant armoured battle in the Caen area, with the enemy driving towards Bayeux'.

Originally the plan for EPSOM that Monty had agreed with Dempsey called for a 'demonstration' by Bucknall's XXX Corps on the British right flank near Caumont – close to where the Desert Rats had ground to a halt two weeks previously – while the main blow by O'Connor's fresh VIII Corps would attempt to outflank Caen from the north-east, across the Orne, yet again. But, following the earlier failure of the 51st Highlanders to elbow more room eastwards from the Orne, Monty had allowed himself to be persuaded by Dempsey to cancel this fresh pincer attempt, reaching:

> the conclusion that an attack by VIII Corps from the bridgehead east of the two rivers is too risky. The bridgehead is too small to form up satisfactorily; there is no room to deploy artillery east of the rivers; the L of C [lines of communication] would be dependent on the bridges, and there is always the risk that the enemy, who is very active in this sector, might upset our arrangement just before the start of the attack.

Once again, this seems like a significant admission of that fundamental flaw in the planning of OVERLORD, that the attack on the eastern flank had not been made strong enough – for which the deficiencies in landing craft and of British infantry were jointly responsible. With hindsight, given that Dempsey's revised plan failed utterly, perhaps Monty should have granted him more time to create the necessary elbow room on the left.

Meanwhile Dempsey placed all his eggs in one basket, aligning with XXX Corps on the right, attacking southwards across the River Odon in a straightforward punch through the centre of the line. If successful, it would then curl around – as 7th Armoured had been intended to do previously at Villers-Bocage – to envelope Caen from the west. But, apart from the mounting pressure being imposed on him by Eisenhower, and Churchill, to attack, Monty had his own most pressing tactical reason for striking without delay: to spoil the powerful counter-attack which ULTRA had warned him Rommel was planning. At his disposal Rommel now had seven Panzer divisions. At least on paper, this represented the largest concentration of German armour seen in France since Dunkirk. Only four miles wide, O'Connor's attack frontage was extremely narrow, facing positions which the Germans had had three weeks in which to strengthen, and held by the tough Hitler Youth 12th SS Panzer Division. There was about the scale of the operation something grimly reminiscent of the First World War push – and the results would be depressingly similar.

Without air support, the infantry went in with that same dogged courage that personified the Tommy slogging forward on the Somme, never questioning his orders and seldom losing confidence in the wisdom of his officers. Wearing the identical flat, unprotective steel helmets, carrying only slightly less cumbersome packs, the Scots battalions sometimes advancing behind a piper, attacking British infantry looked little different from their fathers a generation previously. But the men seemed smaller after five years of warfare and rationing, their faces more strained than the well-fed Americans; their badly designed and ill-fitting battledress made them seem somehow less martial than the Germans. To a young subaltern with the 2nd King's Royal Rifle Corps, Edwin Bramall,* who would become the last British Chief of the Defence Staff actually to have fought in the Second World War, the advance moved forward in classic infantry formation that was 'pretty unimaginative, all the things that we had learned to do at battle school. A straightforward infantry bash.'

What, then and later, British troops as well as GIs particularly recalled was the deadliness of the German mortar crews, the terrifying shriek of the 'Moaning Minnies', the multiple-barrelled rocket

* Later Field Marshal Lord Bramall (quoted in Hastings, *Overlord*, pp. 138–9).

projectiles copied from the Russian army. In the chaos and smoke of battle, there were many 'own goals' – men killed by accidental discharge of light weapons, shot up by their own aircraft, shelled by their own short-firing artillery or (perhaps worst) run over by their own tanks in the confusion. To all this, the soggy Norman summer added its own dimension of horror: men hit and falling in the waist-high wheatfields would often remain hidden from sight of stretcher-bearers, until too late. The dead would be marked, hastily, by a rifle with helmet perched on top, 'looking like strange fungi sprouting haphazardly through cornfields'. The very long days (with daylight from 4.45 a.m. to 11.15 p.m.) in themselves simply meant an extra few hours of combat, of the risk of being blown apart by a well-aimed mortar.

Monty had assured Eisenhower at the start of EPSOM, 'I will continue battling on the eastern front until one of us cracks; it will not be us. If we can pull the enemy on to the Second Army it will make it easier for First Army when they attack southwards.' In vicious hand-to-hand fighting, casualties on both sides were appalling. By the last day of June, the River Odon was dammed up by the bodies of both sides. At one point, men of 'Panzer' Meyer's 12th SS were reported to have thrown themselves fanatically on to British tanks with explosives tied around their waists.* What made the casualties at EPSOM particularly shocking to troops fresh to battle was perhaps the very compression of the battlefield – just like those of Flanders, where British manhood had bled so appallingly in the First World War. Though it was the kind of fighting of which the Germans had had prolonged experience in the east, it was not what Allied troops had been trained for at their battle-schools in Britain. Nor were the losses tolerable to Monty, with all his aversion to what he had seen in Flanders in that earlier war.

In his diary for the 27th, Johnny Henderson recorded, 'The weather is still foul, but VIII Corps doing well and 11th Armoured are well over the Odon and approaching the high ground. Two SS Divs have been identified on the other front.' There then followed

* It was also Meyer's 12th SS which, in mid-June, committed one of the worst atrocities of the Normandy campaign, shooting nearly forty British and Canadian prisoners against a stone wall of the Château d'Ardrieu. After the war, Meyer was sentenced to death by a Canadian war crimes court, the sentence later commuted.

three days of silence. In the meantime, after 'Pip' Roberts' highly rated 11th Armoured had come to a standstill in front of the well-defended 'high ground' (Hill 112), Dempsey had decided to call off EPSOM. Like those pushes of 1914–18, the gain in territory had been negligible – not much over five miles – and in no way had the British threat to Caen been enhanced. Casualties on both sides had been appalling – to Monty, quite unacceptable. Overall, O'Connor's fresh VIII Corps had suffered 4020 casualties in the five-day campaign; over half of these had come from the 15th (Scottish) Division, and they were valuable – if not irreplaceable – trained infantrymen. After this, its first battle, a major of the King's Own Scottish Borderers was overcome with horror at seeing his battalion lose 150 men: 'We were one big family. I knew every man.' A platoon commander of the same battalion evoked the 'dull weight of depression' as the casualties began: 'It seemed there was no hope or sanity left, but only this appalling unknown and unseen, in which life was so precious . . . and where all was loneliness and rain.'*

On the German side, however, losses from this slogging battle – out of sight from Monty and details of which even ULTRA could not penetrate – were far more serious.† Once again, Rommel had been absent from his post at the critical moment, summoned with Rundstedt to Berchtesgaden to explain the situation to Hitler. In his absence, his Seventh Army Commander, General Dollmann, poisoned himself after hearing that Roberts' 11th Armoured had got across the Odon. At this point, as a direct result of EPSOM, both Rundstedt and Rommel now favoured abandoning Caen. There followed, on 1 July, the famous telephone exchange between Rundstedt and Field Marshal Keitel, Chief of Staff of the OKW, 'What shall we do?' 'Make peace, you idiots,' replied Rundstedt, for once in breach of military discipline, 'what else can you do?' One of the most competent of the Wehrmacht's generals, Rundstedt, was now sacked and replaced by Field Marshal von Kluge, who had commanded the irresistible Panzer force that had burst into France in May 1940.

But none of this could be seen, immediately, by either Dempsey or Monty. In calling off EPSOM, Dempsey was motivated by the threat of Rommel's anticipated counter-offensive. When the newly

* Quoted in Hastings, *Overlord*, pp. 139, 141; Robert Woollcombe, *Lion Rampant*, p. 49.
† Up to EPSOM, from D-Day German losses had totalled 43,070, including six generals.

arrived SS Panzer corps from Russia attacked with 200 tanks, Dempsey made a grave miscalculation, not accepting it to be the main German effort. For some reason, an important message had failed to reach him from 15th Division – to the effect that it had not only triumphantly beaten off the Panzer attack, but turned it into a rout. To some extent it was a repeat of Villers-Bocage, compounding the alarm caused by the appearance of the German heavy tanks. It was perhaps not appreciated at the time just how under-strength each Panzer unit in fact was, formidable formations as they might seem on paper. Following their arduous approach marches under incessant attack from the air, dogged too by the brave men of the French Resistance, they had arrived at the front considerably reduced both in numbers and in striking power. Had Dempsey only had the determination to persist, so the latter-day historians now tell us, EPSOM might well have brought the success that both Monty and the home front demanded.

'In fact, "Epsom" *was* a success', insists one of Monty's sterner critics, Richard Lamb, 'for it compelled Rommel to switch the bulk of his tanks from the American (western) sector to halt the British threat to Caen'.* Following EPSOM, Monty noted himself on the 29th the appearance of three more Panzer divisions on the Odon, making 'a total of eight PZ divisions all involved in trying to stem my advance west and south-west of Caen; this is excellent.' This was, after all, precisely the nub of Monty's whole strategy. But, as Lamb adds, 'the newspapers in London and the USA were clamouring for Caen to fall; they could not know that by 29 June there were only 140 German tanks facing the Americans in the western sector, against 725 facing the British and with virtually none in reserve'. What was particularly hard for public opinion, let alone the ever-impatient Churchill, to take was the news that Bradley's Americans had seized Cherbourg, while at Caen Monty seemed completely stuck. Why? Eisenhower was manifestly disappointed.

Where most of Monty's critics agree is in recognizing the disservice, both to the Allied cause and to his own reputation, he did in persisting on every occasion with the claim that everything had gone 'according to plan', and that he was adhering to his original scheme.

* *Montgomery in Europe*, p. 116.

Had he not maintained this façade of half-truths, posterity (if not Eisenhower at the time) would have been better able to appreciate the true genius of his flexibility in Normandy. At no point in the Normandy campaign did he allow himself to be caught off-balance by the massive array of Panzers facing him, let alone 'embarrassed' by the enemy, to the extent of losing the initiative. But after EPSOM, as a result of his inability to admit to setbacks or explain his strategy (and, as regards the latter, there were obviously the best of security reasons for not revealing his hand to the enemy), back in England his critics, and that dangerous accumulation of foes from the snubs and sackings of the past, were beginning to come out of their holes.

July 1944 was a month of immense pressure on Monty, comparable to the days of October 1942, the anxious wait in the desert before Alamein. (But how much more so was July a time of anxiety on the other side, for Rommel – and Hitler.) At his new TAC HQ near the village of Blay, the casual visitor, however, would detect little if anything of this strain. Paul Odgers, who set it up in a series of big meadows a few miles west of Bayeux, on the hinge of the American and British armies, regarded the new camp as one of TAC's 'best sites'.* It 'seemed far removed from the war'. But Odgers also recalled it as a time of 'almost continuous rain, the few days of misty heat, the Camembert cheese, the Tiger and the Panther tanks† and the sight of the Lancaster bombers moving upon Aunay-sur-Odon and Caen . . . every Sunday "Tiger" Poston led the officers' football team.' He also remembered it as a time of subterranean stresses, during the 'long July wait' as the protracted battles for Caen were fought out. Unexpectedly, Monty would stay on that tranquil, open hillside at Blay for six weeks, the longest of any of his sojourns during the French campaign.

To David on 2 July he wrote:

> 'Here are (a) some eggs from Normandy; (b) some chocolate and (c) some boiled sweets. I now have two dogs – (a) a fox terrier called Snicky [later rechristened Hitler]; (b) a golden cocker span-

* Odgers, 'A TAC Chronicle', 30 July 1945.

† Two captured tanks which Monty had had placed at the TAC gates, for morale purposes.

> iel called Rommel. Both eight weeks old. Also a cage of two canaries.
>
> I hope all goes well with you.

To Phyllis Reynolds, five days later, he was rather more expansive:

> All goes well here – except the weather which is completely foul; it seems to be quite impossible to get a whole fine day – actually today *has* been fine and I have been collecting livestock.
>
> I now have six canaries, one love bird, two dogs.
>
> The dogs are puppies, about ten weeks old. One is a fox terrier, given me by the BBC men in France; I have named him Hitler. The other is a gold cocker spaniel, brought back by Col. Dawnay – who bought it from some girl in a girls' school!! I have named him Rommel – as his coat is the colour of golden sand from the desert.
>
> Hitler and Rommel both get beaten when necessary . . . both coming 'to heel well'.

These new acquisitions seemed to reveal a curiously sentimental side to Monty, even a certain residual tenderness for his old adversary, of Achilles for Hector. Not everybody at TAC shared Monty's enthusiasm for his pets. Chalfont records one of the dogs as being 'unlovable'; his 'main interest in life was leaving souvenirs of his presence in the most inconvenient places'. But the growing menagerie was, of course, as immune to criticism as was its owner's conduct of the war. It was looked after by the under-employed medical officer, Bob Hunter. He drew the line, however, at a cow presented at Blay by the local mayor. Monty was delighted by the idea of fresh milk, but Hunter found himself entangled reluctantly in the rigmarole of having it checked by the veterinary service for tuberculosis. 'Almost immediately we moved, and I said "no more cows!" '*

However, it was over another domestic animal, a looted pig, that a much more serious matter, a real storm in a teacup with deeper undertones, blew up at Blay. There had been ugly rumours filtering back to de Gaulle's headquarters in London of looting by Allied personnel in what the French regarded as liberated, sacred France,

* Interview 16 December 1992.

but what many of the liberators held to be simply occupied territory. Towards the end of July rumours had even reached the ears of the Foreign Secretary, that lifelong Francophile Anthony Eden. He asked the Permanent Under-Secretary, Sir Alexander Cadogan, to take it up with the army at the highest level, with Brooke personally. On 4 August, Brooke passed on the complaint to Monty, then in the midst of the break-out battle, with the exhortation:

> do all you can to prevent looting and scrounging. The latter is probably the most dangerous as it has a false air of respectability about it and rapidly degenerates into looting!
>
> It is an important matter which might well affect our relations with the French.

Three days later Monty wrote a frigid letter to Major François Coulet,* de Gaulle's aide in Normandy:

> Dear M. Coulet,
>
> There are some rumours going round that the troops are looting. Have you any evidence to give me on this subject, as if it is true I will see it is stopped. On the other hand it may *not* be true; in which case I would be glad to hear so from you.

The letter must be regarded, however, as somewhat disingenuous in the light of what had occurred in the meantime much closer to home. At the beginning of July, the senior staff officer whom de Guingand had had attached to TAC, Colonel the Hon. Leo Russell, OBE, had been shocked to observe – amid the rural tranquillity of TAC – a bloodied pig running through the camp. It transpired that an abortive attempt to kill it had been made by Noël Chavasse. When pork was served up at dinner that night, Russell declared angrily to Monty (according to Dr Bob Hunter), 'I'm not going to eat *that*. It's loot!' Apparently a French farmer on whose land TAC was encamped had tracked down his missing sow, dismembered, in

* One of de Gaulle's favourites, Major Coulet – a rather dashing figure – had an eventful life. While on the General's staff in London, he had fallen in love with the wife of Quintin Hogg (later Lord Hailsham; she, Natalie, was the sister-in-law of Basil Liddell Hart), whom he later married. After the war he became an ambassador, and on de Gaulle's return to power in 1958, frustrated with never having seen actual battle during the Second World War, during the Algerian War was permitted to form his own parachute regiment, with which he gallantly dropped when in his fifties.

the cook-house of the Commander-in-Chief's personal mess. Noël Chavasse attempted to hush up the affair by offering the farmer £2 (about two days' pay for a captain in 1944), but the Norman had refused, claiming that the animal was a valuable sow in pig, and threatening to report the matter to Civil Affairs Branch in Bayeux. Russell, carrying out an investigation as the senior staff officer at TAC, was told 'that the incident had caused considerable feeling among the local inhabitants who were comparing us unfavourably with the Germans'.* Next he was shocked to discover, right behind Monty's own mess, a wire-netting enclosure full of looted pigs, ducks and chickens. A 'liberated' piano was also found. Russell then carpeted the recently decorated Major John Poston, who appeared to be the principal culprit. To his fury, instead of showing any kind of remorse, 'He implied that the Commander-in-Chief not only did not disapprove of these activities but at times even incited his staff to take part in them.'

Among these battle-hardened young officers (who were clearly much amused by the whole saga), the respectable but unworldly staff officer with no field experience was rapidly making a fool of himself. Instead of handling the matter with a light touch, he rashly allowed it to escalate by making a personal complaint to Monty himself – on 14 July, a time when Monty was somewhat preoccupied with sending the whole Second Army into the great GOODWOOD battle. Monty (mischievously, and evidently sharing the amusement of his young men) at first pooh-poohed Russell's allegation, giving the bristling Colonel the impression that he did not regard looting as 'a serious offence'.† Not entirely to his credit, Monty also did nothing to defuse the situation, icily losing his temper with a 'So you accuse my personal staff of looting?' 'I replied', said Russell, 'that this was exactly what I had intended to convey and that I had sufficient evidence to institute Court-Martial proceedings.'

A brave but foolish man, Russell had now truly thrown the fat in the fire. Twenty-four hours later he was telephoned by de Guingand, who told him that he was being recalled to Main HQ. De

* Russell report to VCIGS.

† One may recall the episode of the looting of the wine cellar of the Prince de Merode in Belgium in 1940, when occupied by HQ of the 3rd Division, then under Monty's command, to which he had in all probability also turned a blind eye.

Guingand wrote off the incident as a regrettable 'clash of personalities'. Russell replied that a 'more serious matter' of principle was involved. De Guingand flew over two days later, the very eve of GOODWOOD, and in his most gently diplomatic way tried to persuade the upset Colonel that, deplorable as it may seem, looting was a fact of life with armies in the field: 'If I am campaigning and I see a duck that I want, I take it; I may give the man ten francs or so if he complains, but I take the duck all the same.' Bent on hanging himself, Russell insisted that he intended to go ahead and institute court-martial proceedings, to which de Guingand retorted, 'You can do what you damned well please – nobody will pay the slightest attention to you. . . . You certainly can't stay in 21 Army Group after this. I will ring up MS* and say that you are willing to throw up your job for a couple of pigs.' Russell interjected, 'For a principle.'

The story ended with a six-page report by Russell, duly itemizing the looted items – 'Plates, soup 11, Plates, meat 46. . . . Chickens 6, Rabbits 2, Pig 1, Sheep 1' – which found its way to the desk of the VCIGS, General Nye, absurdly wrapped up in a folder marked 'MOST SECRET: TO BE KEPT UNDER LOCK AND KEY'. Only Nye's good sense prevented it from going on upwards, to Brooke himself. Had it done so, coming on top of all the other much more serious criticisms that had been piling up about Monty's command defects, together with Eden's intervention about looting, it might easily have placed him in a dangerous position. Recalling, as he would have done, the reproof he had administered to Major-General Montgomery over the VD lapse at the beginning of the war, Brooke would have had to act, at a time when Monty was more vulnerable than at any other time in his career. The whole episode, in itself hilariously evocative of Gilbert and Sullivan, showed the British Army establishment – about to plunge into its biggest test of the war – at its very worst, echoing the kind of foolishness against which Monty himself had fought so hard in the 1920s and 1930s.

The high-principled Colonel passed into outer darkness, but his departure had a wider significance. Officers at TAC at the time felt, in retrospect, that the pig was 'secondary'. 'Already the problem was there,' explains Johnny Henderson:

* Military Secretary branch in the War Office.

> Monty did not want to have Russell in his mess. It was quite apparent, in two to three days of landing, if it hadn't been the pig, it would have been something else. . . . He just didn't fit – or rather Monty determined that he didn't! He liked holding court – he didn't want anyone too clever, hence Leo Russell was out. . . . A very narrow-minded, clever fellow, his nose was thoroughly out of joint.*

A more far-reaching implication was that Monty seems to have regarded Russell, not as one of his 'team', but as de Guingand's man, almost as something of a spy, reporting back to Main and conversely attempting to impose Main's view upon him. With the sacking of Russell, the injurious isolation of Monty, surrounded by his puppies and canaries, increased by yet another notch, not least because there was now no one to tell him what was going on at Main, or vice versa. (It was 'unfortunate', reckoned Kit Dawnay, 'for he wouldn't have anyone in his place'.) This peculiar isolation 'from other senior officers and from people of his own age' Richard Lamb thought definitely 'contributed to Montgomery's failure to understand the criticism and jealousy which his conduct was arousing amongst the British and American chiefs at SHAEF, and at Bradley's US First Army'.†

The new surroundings at Blay proved, however, a happy choice. Monty was to remain there for the next six weeks, all through the bad days of stalemate and fierce criticism from outside, and the planning of the great break-out. During all this time, extraordinary as it may sound, not even the local farmers were aware of the Allied Ground Commander being in their midst.

Though symptomatic of Monty's relations with senior officers who were not of his own 'team', as an enemy Russell was a flea compared to the air barons and the members of Ike's staff at SHAEF now increasingly arrayed against him. In his relations with the senior airmen Monty was not well served, with the possible exception of

* Interview 29 November 1992.

† Lamb, *Montgomery in Europe*, p. 97.

Air Vice-Marshal Harry Broadhurst, 83 Group Commander AEAF* (which contained the RAF close-support fighter-bombers). Monty's reputation as the one British general who truly understood air–ground cooperation should have been pretty secure, from the desert and earlier. Typical was his pre-D-Day instruction to Dempsey of 4 May: 'Army HQ must never plan a move of HQ without first consulting Air HQ. The deciding factor in the location of Main Army will be whether it will suit Air HQ.'

To the innocent mind, therefore, it might seem astonishing that the most virulent critics of Monty were to be found in air force blue – and British to boot.

To be sure, the airmen could point with anguish to the casualty figures: between D-Day and the end of June, losses from this much smaller service exceeded those of the ground forces. By May 1945 the RAF could claim that, in terms of a post-war elite, British Empire losses† roughly equalled the sacrifice of that generation of officers, the 'brightest and the best', in Flanders in 1914–18, so often held to be the cause of British decline in the inter-war years. Although, as in his relations with the Americans, Monty himself had much to answer for, there is an ugly story of inter-service rivalry and personal jealousy from which the air barons emerge badly. We have already seen the unedifying row with Harris (and Spaatz) over the 'Transportation' versus 'Oil' strategies. We have noted, too, the hopelessly over-cautious estimates of D-Day losses by Sir Trafford Leigh-Mallory, who had huge responsibility as overall commander of the AEAF. A thick-set, stolid man with jowls and a small, artificial-looking moustache, Leigh-Mallory's reputation had already caused

* Allied Expeditionary Air Forces.

† By the end of the war, overall aircrew losses, by far the largest in Bomber Command and all of them officers or NCOs, were to total 55,750 out of the RAF total dead of 72,794 in the Second World War; while British Empire officers killed in the trenches of 1914–18 totalled 38,834. One is entitled to ask, however (as Max Hastings does so effectively in *Bomber Command*), whose wrong-headed strategy of putting almost all the eggs in the one basket of long-range bombers had led to these deadly losses, for so little relative gain. The apostles of strategic bombing can elicit the figures of Luftwaffe fighters destroyed over Germany in the campaign of '44, and the number of the deadly dual-purpose 88mm guns deployed to defend German cities; both of which in consequence helped the Allies in Normandy. The question remains as to whether this was worth the dreadful cost in Allied airmen, not to mention the destruction of German – and French – cities. The argument will continue.

controversy from the time of the Battle of Britain, when he had commanded 12 Group. In 1944, many of his RAF contemporaries thought that he had been promoted well above his ceiling. His early conception of the Transportation Plan proved totally ineffectual, until extensively redrafted by Solly Zuckerman, a brilliant zoologist, and throughout OVERLORD his influence was more apparent than real. What there was of it was seldom helpful to Monty. By the time of GOODWOOD, Monty was to come round to Leigh-Mallory, as the 'least worst' alternative, but the baneful effect of the airman's excessive caution and pessimism was to be felt again, at the time of the fateful mistakes of Antwerp and Arnhem.*

At the very top of the air tree sat the bomber chieftains, Harris and Spaatz, still believing that Germany was on the verge of collapse from strategic bombing† and constantly resentful of any diversion of their 'heavies' for Normandy. Even an American expert like Carlo D'Este admits that the resolutely obstinate Harris proved 'far the more co-operative' of the two. Sandwiching the unfortunate Leigh-Mallory were, from above, Air Chief Marshal Tedder, the air architect of Desert Victory, who – though now Ike's deputy – still maintained tight control of the strategic air forces, and, from below, the New Zealander commander of the Allied Tactical Air Forces, Air Marshal Sir Arthur 'Maori' Coningham. Neither got on with Leigh-Mallory, but both hated Monty with a passion, largely it seems stemming from real or imagined slights from the desert, when Monty had tactlessly walked off with all the laurels of victory. Interviewing him shortly after the war, the distinguished American military historian Dr Forrest C. Pogue found Coningham 'the bitterest critic of Montgomery I have heard speak'. To Brigadier Charles Richardson, Monty's loyal BGS Plans, whom he sent to RAF Headquarters Stanmore specifically to ensure closest relations with the airmen, Coningham was 'a bad man, a prima donna . . . frightfully affected,

* Leigh-Mallory died tragically in an air crash with his wife on his way to take up a new command in South-East Asia in November 1944. His naval opposite number on the OVERLORD planning staff, the greatly respected Admiral Sir Bertram Ramsay, died similarly; so did Coningham shortly after the war. After Leigh-Mallory's departure, Coningham now came directly under Tedder; in theory this streamlining of command should have eased the army-air relationship – it did not.

† Post-war evidence showed that German arms production actually reached its peak during 1944, the year the bombing was at its height.

hot on choosing his next château! . . . We distrusted him completely and when I was with him with the air barons at Stanmore, I recognized him as a bastard. . . .' Harsh words! During the crucial days in Normandy, 'Maori' Coningham steadfastly refused to have his headquarters anywhere near Monty, while to officers at TAC HQ like Johnny Henderson he was always 'the snake in the grass and plays dirty games behind the army's back. He will not co-operate. This is not helped by the fact that Leigh-Mallory and Coningham do not get on.'*

Much more damaging, however, because more powerful and – as Eisenhower's deputy – constantly at the ear of the Supreme Commander, was the pipe-smoking and brittle intellectual Tedder, who nourished a low opinion of the British Army (in which he had served back in 1915) in general and of Monty in particular.† Charles Richardson found him 'misguided, academic, vain and conceited – therefore he was upset by Monty's personality'. Tedder's 'attitude and behaviour were very strange', Richardson considered, and almost amounted 'to conspiring against Monty the very moment total victory was only days away [at Caen]'.‡ Undoubtedly Monty had given hostages to fortune in his rash and boastful promise to Tedder before D-Day of speedy seizure of the Caen–Falaise airfields, for which Tedder never forgave him. De Guingand in his memoirs, however, insists that on more than one occasion he warned the RAF 'against relying upon acquiring airfields'.§ Moreover, the fighter-bomber leaders most dependent on close-in fields, Harry Broadhurst and the forty-year-old General Pete Quesada, both independently admitted that they could manage without. 'I never felt myself short of any airplanes,' Broadhurst told Carlo D'Este; 'we could call on enormous reinforcements if we wanted them.' For once, as far as Tedder was concerned in 1944, Monty seems to have been fairly blameless; 'nothing could be further from the truth,' stresses D'Este, than the idea 'that he was at fault in the dissension with the air chiefs'.||

* Henderson diary, 6 July 1944.

† Tedder once described Monty as 'a little fellow of average ability who has had such a build-up that he thinks of himself as Napoleon. He is not.'

‡ Montgomery Collection. Interview 26 November 1992.

§ *Operation Victory*, p. 393.

|| D'Este, *Decision in Normandy*, p. 223.

Reviewing Tedder's memoirs* two decades later, the judicious Bill Williams remarks damningly, 'it still seems unlikely that he fully understands even today what the Field Marshal was really up to'.†

Tedder's behaviour towards Monty at SHAEF, consistently disloyal and thoroughly conspiratorial as it was, reflects no credit on him – and little on the RAF. At Stanmore, Richardson found the atmosphere 'very strange indeed . . . not congenial'. With the stiffening of enemy resistance around Caen by mid-June and the abandoning of a joint Monty–Leigh-Mallory airborne scheme, a mood of 'near panic' prevailed, with Tedder talking openly about a 'dangerous crisis'.‡ How, one sometimes asks, was the war ever won?

In almost every campaign since 1939 – Korea and Vietnam being particular cases in point, the hi-tech brilliance of the Gulf War of 1990–1 providing possibly the first exception to the rule – the claims of Western airmen have, with depressing consistency, far exceeded actual performance. With 12,000 aircraft available, giving a ratio of some twenty to one over the Luftwaffe, far in excess of the air superiority which had enabled Hitler to defeat France so swiftly in 1940, even allowing for the dread novelty of the Stuka dive-bomber, Allied preponderance in the air was staggering. In the long run, it would prove decisive – and so it should have done. Harris' boast that he would give the ground forces 'a walkover' proved an exaggeration, however. Enemy units might have been delayed reaching the front, and have been depleted *en route*, but they were never prevented *in toto*. The terrible flying weather in Normandy – eliminating on average one day in three throughout the summer – was one factor; straightforward inaccuracy, particularly of the heavy bombers (as Allied troops were shortly to discover to their dreadful cost), was another. In any case, the appalling devastation caused to the terrain by heavy bombs often proved highly counter-productive to the attackers, as had been discovered in Italy at Monte Cassino.§

In all this sky-blue firmament, there were two conspicuous stars: the commanders of the two fighter-bomber units, Quesada and

* Appropriately entitled *With Prejudice*.

† *Times Literary Supplement*, 27 April 1967.

‡ General Sir Charles Richardson, *Flashback*, pp. 175–9.

§ The ancient monastery had been reduced to rubble by Allied bombers the previous year, to virtually no advantage. In fact the rubble slowed the Allied advance.

Broadhurst. An outstanding fighter commander and one of the youngest American senior generals, Major-General Elwood R. 'Pete' Quesada was a Californian of Spanish extraction, a bachelor of quick intelligence, charm, enthusiasm and great ability, improbably a cabinet-maker in his spare time. Landing on D-Day + 1 in a P-38 Lightning fighter, he commanded IX Tactical Air Command, which was responsible to Bradley (who rated him 'a jewel') for close air support. His opposite number with Monty, AOC (Air Officer Commanding) 83 Group, was Air Vice-Marshal Harry ('Broadie') Broadhurst, at thirty-nine a rugged and much decorated (DSO and Bar, DFC and Bar, AFC) Hurricane fighter ace from the Battle of Britain who had established an unusually happy rapport with Monty in the desert. A hater of office routine, considered by his contemporaries (affectionately) as just too rough-and-tough to make it to Chief of the Air Staff, in contrast to Coningham 'Broadie' at the very earliest opportunity set up his headquarters in Normandy. At some peril, he flew himself regularly to and fro in a captured German Storch light plane, painted bright yellow, an almost daily and popular visitor to TAC HQ. ('But', he admitted, 'Monty got more and more isolated, and if it hadn't been for the Storch I would never have seen him.' Coningham and Leigh-Mallory seldom did.) Years after the war Broadhurst still could not understand why, while the Germans had their army–air co-operation 'all wrapped up' in 1940, 'we never did. Perhaps it was because the old sweats in the RAF, from the First World War, didn't trust the old sweats in the army!'* That said a lot. Whenever Dempsey's ground forces needed close air support, however, they got it from Broadhurst and his rocket-firing Typhoons, which were to prove probably the most potent weapon against the heavy German Tigers and Panthers.

Under mounting pressure from Churchill, Eisenhower and now even Brooke, on 30 June Monty decided to launch CHARNWOOD, a 'direct assault from the north' to capture at the least the main part of Caen west of the Orne, including Carpiquet airfield. In comparison with EPSOM (and later GOODWOOD) it would be a limited

* Interview 26 May 1993.

attack of only one corps, in which the Canadian 3rd Division (whose commander, Major General Keller, had not so far distinguished himself) would play a lead role, and was designed simply to give Monty more breathing space for the 'big push' to come. What was new about CHARNWOOD, however, was the massive use of the heavy, strategic bombers to soften up the defenders. After Tedder had intervened to veto use of this weapon in June, Monty's relations at least with Leigh-Mallory had improved to the point where a reluctant Harris agreed to release the required Lancasters. (Tedder appears to have washed his hands of the whole operation, remarking that 'it would encourage the Army to ask on every occasion for heavy bomber support, and . . . the strategic bombers would thus be unduly diverted from their proper tasks', while to Solly Zuckerman, the inspired architect of the Transportation Plan, he declared acidly that 'he was not interested as "he was neither concerned with Cassinos nor with agriculture" '.)

So on the night of 7/8 July, 460 four-engined Lancasters, each carrying five tons of bombs, carried out what Monty described as 'a remarkably accurate operation'. The area struck was a small rectangle at the north of Caen 4000 yards wide and 1500 deep. To avoid any possibility of hitting the attacking infantry with 'friendly fire', a last-minute adjustment moved the 'bomb line' appreciably southwards. A French nun taking shelter in the cellars of the Hôpital du Bon Sauveur monastery, one of Caen's many exquisite medieval jewels, felt the earth 'shake with the storm of falling bombs. . . . Evidently the complete destruction of Caen – or what was left of it – had been decided upon.'

Within an hour, Caen had received the same intensity of bombing as Hamburg in the great fire-raids of the previous year. But the Lancasters did little more than destroy what remained of an ancient and beautiful medieval city (though, miraculously, the great Abbaye in its centre survived). The British infantry saw scant sign of destroyed German gun positions, tanks or German dead, and still met fierce resistance. On moving into Caen itself two days later, they found 'just a waste of brick and stone, like a field of corn that has been ploughed. The people gazed at us without emotion of any kind; one could hardly look at them in the face, knowing who had done this.' One heroic French doctor who had remained at his hospital all through June described the bombardment as 'absolutely futile'; all it did was 'to choke the streets and hinder the Allies in their advance through the city'. It was tragically clear that nothing whatever had been learned by either the army or the air barons from the pulverizing of Monte Cassino. Even Monty admitted that 'difficulties' 'arose from the cratering and the obstruction from masonry and debris caused by the bombing, and it will be seen that in our next operation of this nature it was decided to employ small bombs'.

He could at least claim, with some justification, that the capture of most of Caen (trumpeted by the British press, eager for a success story, as a major triumph) 'greatly simplified our problems on the eastern flank'. In effect, this meant that it had partly rectified the gross error at the initial landings, the failure to secure the land between the Orne and the Dives. It sounded horribly like another communiqué from the Somme. Had it been worth it? Despite the devastating barrage from the air, Allied casualties had been appalling, especially among the infantrymen, whom Monty could ill spare. Within the infantry battalions 'losses of 25 per cent were the rule rather than the exception'. It was shocking of Tedder to belittle the battle, as he did, to Eisenhower on 8 July as merely 'Company exercises'.* At least, according to the latest ULTRA reports, Monty's renewed, costly pressure on Caen had achieved his main objective: all eight of the German Panzer divisions, save one battered unit, were now still pinned down on the British front, away from Bradley.

What would have happened on the crucial American front if those Panzer divisions had reached it, with Bradley desperately pushing for space and a launching-pad for the ultimate break-out, is suggested by the fighting there. After six days of hard fighting in the deadly bocage country, striking for St-Lô, the Americans had been able to advance no more than five miles, sometimes only a hundred yards in a day, and at painfully heavy cost. By 10 July both Bradley and Dempsey were forced to pause for rest.

During CHARNWOOD, trigger-happy ground forces came close to scoring a devastating 'own goal', when Broadhurst flew up in his Storch to watch the bombing of Caen. Dempsey, the Army Commander, asked to go along. The fighter-bomber leader was

* Tedder, *Without Prejudice*, p. 559.

delighted, because 'we'd been having a lot of trouble with suppressing the [friendly] ground ack-ack. Shooting at everything with these new divisions coming in.' He wanted to make a point as forcefully as possible to Dempsey, but it was soon apparent that these two important commanders were taking the most enormous and irresponsible risk, especially given that they were in a German plane:

> Suddenly Dempsey said to me, 'Harry, Harry! For crissake put her down, we're being fired at!' I looked back and even though we were doing eighty miles per hour, the guns were all behind, and puff-puff. . . . So I dived for the ground and . . . there were all these chaps machine-gunning us as well. Everybody was shooting at us.

A Canadian captain came up and demanded Dempsey's identity card: ' "Don't be a bloody fool, I'm your commanding officer." We had been hit eleven times.' After this harrowing experience, Dempsey rang up Broadie to say that henceforth 'I can assure you no ack-ack is going to fire a *bloody gun* other than horizontally in *my* sector.'* As much as anything else, it may well perhaps also have been a small token of what the ground forces, victims all too often of friendly fire, felt about the airmen.

Why then, given the results, and with the experience of Cassino in mind, did Monty resort to the heavy bombers, both at CHARNWOOD and two weeks later again, on an even bigger scale, at GOODWOOD? It is one of the most important issues to emerge from the Normandy campaign, and the answers are to be found in the failure of the Desert Rats at Villers-Bocage, earlier in the hesitant performance of Lumsden's *corps de chasse* at El Alamein, in the accumulated losses suffered by British manpower (mostly through capture) in all those defeats and surrenders from 1940 onwards, and even further back in the terrible bloodletting of the First World War – all of them aspects intimately experienced by Monty personally.

At the gates of TAC outside Blay, visitors were taken aback to see two battle-stained, knocked-out German tanks – a formidable Tiger and a Panther. Monty had had them towed there for much the same

* Quoted in D'Este, *Decision in Normandy*, p. 314.

reason as some oriental warlord, a Tamburlaine, might keep his defeated enemy captive in a cage – to prove that he was neither immortal nor invulnerable. But when Eisenhower and Bradley visited Blay on 2 July, Bradley's ADC, Major Chester B. Hansen, was arrested by the discordant contrast they made with the peaceful tableau of Monty's puppies gambolling in the grass: 'Huge tank. Panther had been hit by 75 which simply glanced off it. Tankers are concerned about it. Need a heavier gun.' The VIPs were then given a lecture by a British tank general on the two tanks, following which the main discussion was 'on the best method of dealing with the Panther'.

Hansen's diary says it all. Seeing the tanks of 1944 at the Imperial War Museum, a casual tourist with no specialist eye whatsoever will immediately be struck by the puniness, antiquated aspects and fragility of the British tanks of 1944, against the heavy, workmanlike and threatening lines of the German – and the Russian – machines. Among the self-propelled anti-tank guns, the brilliance of German improvisation is also readily detectable: a tank chassis with a few bits of armoured plate slapped on and mounting a high-velocity 88mm or long-barrelled 75mm, with a squatly effective profile appropriately dubbed the 'Rhinoceros', rushed out (often by cottage industries just behind the front) in great quantities to meet the flood tides of Soviet T-34s on the Eastern Front. Meanwhile British weaponry experts were still arguing about the *perfect* weapon. In the eighteen months that had gone by, pathetically little advance had been achieved on the inadequate tank designs of the desert.* Even the new mainstay of the British armoured regiments in Normandy, the Cromwell, looks like the thinly armoured tin box that it was; the heavy, slow Churchill infantry tank (its specifications had been issued in 1940, but its defects had not been cured until 1943 – and then by no means all of them) suggests a lumbering, primitive behemoth from 1916. Worst of all, each still mounted either the 6pdr or the low-velocity 75mm, compared with the massive German high-velocity 88s and 75 longs – and despite all the bad experiences of North Africa now nearly two years back.

A leading British military historian, Correlli Barnett, damns Brit-

* See pp. 44–6.

ish Second World War tanks (with few exceptions) as 'mechanical abortions that foreshadowed the disastrous car models launched into world markets by the British automobile industry in the postwar era . . .'. He castigates 'over-hasty, botched, piecemeal development instead of thoroughgoing preliminary design and testing; exactly the same calamitous pattern as with the new models of British cars after the war'.* As a result, in terms of production of armoured fighting vehicles (AFVs), whereas in 1942 Britain produced 8611, Germany (despite Harris' and Spaatz's devastating strategic bombing of her industry) peaked in 1944, to turn out 19,002 AFVs – equal to two-and-a-half times the total British tonnage. 'Only a minority' of the British products, notes Barnett, 'could be said to be battleworthy', while in contrast 'Virtually all the German production consisted of first-class combat vehicles, even if the Tiger did present some maintenance and transporting problems because of its size and complexity.' One of the notable German advantages was that engines were based on proven, first-class civilian design, which was rugged and easily serviceable, lending itself to mass production between manufacturers.

Who, in Britain then, was to blame for one of the war's great scandals? Who sent so many thousands of young men to a horrible death in second-rate death-traps? Who were the 'guilty men'? Correlli Barnett claims that 'the mechanical failings of British tanks were largely the fault of commercial firms incompetent at design, development and manufacture'. He singled out 'batch production virtually by hand, utter want of standardization of parts and components' as a British industrial disease certainly not cured after 1939. None of this, however, could absolve from responsibility the politicians or the War Office, held responsible for 'the failure to evolve clear design specifications to fit clearly conceived battle doctrine; a failure every bit as damaging and time-wasting as those which critical historians attribute to Nazi munitions administration'.

Given all the bad experiences of North Africa (suffered not least by the Desert Rats), it does seem quite extraordinary that, in the nearly two years between Alamein and D-Day, better tanks could not have been evolved by the Allies – in the expeditious way in

* *The Audit of War*, pp. 161–4.

which the Wehrmacht had responded to the threat of the Soviet T-34 by producing the Panther and the Tiger. Here Brooke, and even Monty himself, cannot escape blame – though, as will be seen, it was Monty who, late in the day, managed to combine the best British gun (the 17pdr) with the best American tank (the Sherman).

It is a truism that, in a peace-orientated democracy, the panoply of war generally reflects the civilian industrial base rather than that which it requires ideally to win a war. But, as Correlli Barnett acidly notes, the pre-war British motor-vehicle industry 'had concentrated on small family cars and light vans, suitable for a sedate Sunday outing to the seaside and deliveries of groceries . . .'. Detroit was perhaps equally open to blame. The thirty-ton M-4 Sherman, whose surprise advent on the battlefield had helped turn the tide in the desert in 1942, had all the merits and defects of the US automobile industry such as Ralph Nader in the 1960s had savaged as 'Unsafe At Any Price'. It could be mass-produced in vast numbers;* it was fast (30 m.p.h.) and spaciously comfortable (until it 'brewed up') for crews, compared with the British Cromwells; but it had an uncomfortably high profile in battle. It had inadequate armour, easily caught fire and mounted a 75mm gun descended with little modification from the famous piece that had been the mainstay of the French Army in 1914 – though too light even then. Excellent in 1942, by 1944 it was totally outclassed, capable of penetrating only 68mm of armour; the German Panther, star of Normandy, boasted 100mm of well-sloped frontal armour, while its long 75mm KwK 42 could penetrate 118mm of armour at 1000 yards – and the Sherman had only 68mm of frontal protection. The main fault of the Panther, and even more of the heavier (58 ton) Tiger, lay in the slow traverse of its turrets, so the best chance the Allied Shermans and Cromwells had in Normandy was when three or four could each take on one of the superior German Panzers – much as the three little British cruisers – *Ajax*, *Achilles* and *Exeter* – had worried to death the mighty *Graf Spee* in the Battle of the River Plate.

When one considers the quite staggering performance of the US war industry after Pearl Harbor, and the native instinct for innovation, it is just as deplorable as Britain's delinquency that – after

* So much so that, in Normandy, two-thirds of all the tanks used by the Allies were Shermans, despite the advent of the Cromwell and the Churchill.

the bloody nose received at Kasserine Pass – America could not have produced a better tank for Normandy and, worse, had made only feeble efforts to produce a more powerful gun than the obsolete 75mm. By 1944, Britain had at least done just that by introducing (very late in the day) the best Allied anti-tank gun of the war, the 17pdr. It was lighter (and therefore more manoeuvrable) than the German 88, heavier than the Panther's 75 KwK 42, but with a velocity sufficient to penetrate most Panzer armour. The trouble was, typically, that no British tank turret had been designed big enough to mount it; secondly, unlike the German 'Rhinoceros' self-propelled guns, it was generally mounted to be trailed, muzzle pointing backwards. This was fine for fighting a defensive action, as had been all too many of the battles fought by the British Army since 1940, but not – as in all the battles since Alamein – on the attack. The Germans, with their superlative adaptability, used their tanks and self-propelled guns like mobile pill-boxes, in the way the hard school of experience had taught them over the years of defensive retreat in Russia, keeping them constantly repaired by excellent workshops concealed in the forests of Normandy (like the Forêt de Cinglais south of Caen). But the British 17pdrs were constantly handicapped for want of mobility.

It was on Monty's personal insistence that as many British-operated Shermans as possible had had the 17pdr mounted in their more capacious turrets – but only a short while before D-Day. These, as we have seen, were called Fireflies and were progressively distributed on a ratio of first one, then two, to a troop of five tanks. At last, for the first time in the whole war, in the Firefly the British had a tank almost equal to the Panzers. Late in the day, the Americans produced a 76mm gun, but it was ineffectual and had an appalling muzzle flash which made observation of hits almost impossible. Monty offered the Firefly to the US forces but (perhaps on grounds of national pride) this was refused until August when the battle in the bocage against the Tigers and Panzers was almost won. Then, when the Americans later that summer asked the War Office to convert 700 of their own Shermans into Fireflies, this was refused 'on technical grounds' (= lack of facilities).

It was, whichever way you looked at it, a sad story. No less debilitating for the British Army was the lack of an armoured personnel carrier. Until American half-tracks arrived, British infantrymen had to depend on their feet, on 'soft-skinned' lorries incapable of cross-country deployment or on the toy-like Bren-gun carrier. Dating back to the BEF in 1939, under-powered, under-protected and carrying only two or three men, the latter typified the 'family car or delivery van' mentality castigated by Correlli Barnett.* What this meant in practice in Normandy was exemplified by the critical failure of Monty's old 3rd Infantry Division to seize Caen and move on across the Orne on D-Day. Had they been equipped with a suitable personnel carrier, such as had long carried the German Panzer Grenadiers into battle, or even with more American half-tracks, they might have pushed forward a great deal more aggressively. It took, finally, a Canadian general, the inspired Guy Simonds,† to solve, with utmost simplicity, the eternal problem of infantry unable to keep up with the tanks – by creating (as the Germans would have done) an improvised armoured troop carrier out of a Priest self-propelled gun, minus its ordnance.‡ But this was only to arrive in time for GOODWOOD, by which date many lives and much ground had been lost.

With this constant, costly inferiority in fighting machines and the resulting dread that a Tiger was lying in wait behind every bocage hedgerow, was it any wonder that heroic veterans like the Desert Rats worsted in so many encounters should have flinched at Villers-Bocage, and again on several subsequent occasions? Perhaps Monty, for old times' sake of the desert, placed too high expectations on 7th Armoured. In the opinion of the commander of rival 11th Armoured Division, 'Pip' Roberts, they had 'been in battle too much and done too much fighting. . . . their tanks would reach a corner and then not go round it'. Monty, he thought, should have 'disbanded 7th Armoured', but this would have been almost as dangerous a blow to British *amour propre* as Monty himself being 'disbanded' by Churchill. 'I used to find', continued Roberts, 'when I was given an Armoured Brigade who had little battle experience it was like getting

* Both its gun, the Bren LMG, and the Sten submachine gun, standard automatics of the British infantry, were inferior to their German counterparts, the Spandau MG-42 and the Schmeisser.

† Whom Monty deemed far and away the best of the Canadian commanders, if not one of the best of all.

‡ This was to be the forerunner of the basic armoured infantry carrier employed by NATO armies for many years after the war.

a fresh second horse.'* The trouble was that, as someone remarked, too many tankmen had been made to cross the starting-line once too often. To answer the question why it was that German Panzer crews, veterans of all those gruelling battles in Russia, did not suffer from the same inhibitions, one comes back to the same old story – confidence in their equipment.

By the first days of August, Monty himself, writing to Simpson about the belated sacking of Erskine, commander of 7th Armoured, had reluctantly come to similar conclusions: 'The old desert divisions are apt to look over their shoulder and wonder if it's OK behind or their flanks are secure and so on.'

To Monty, all this was a most bitter personal disappointment, which he was prepared to go to some lengths to conceal from the world at large – particularly (and mistakenly) from his American allies. Details of the tank regiments' distress at the casualties they were suffering because of the inadequacy of their equipment were, however, certainly not concealed from him. Only a week after D-Day, on 14 June, Monty was writing to Freddie de Guingand, expressing himself 'very disturbed at some of the reports which compare British armour unfavourably with Germans'. This was echoed ten days later by de Guingand cautioning him from Main:

> If we are not careful, there will be a danger of the troops developing a Tiger and Panther complex. . . . P. J. Grigg rang me up last night and said he thought there might be trouble in the Guards Armoured Division as regards 'the inadequacy of our tanks compared with the Germans'. . . . Naturally the reports are not being circulated.'†

On 6 July, Monty was coming back with a more sombre assessment, telling the War Office that the thin-skinned 'Cromwell tanks must eventually go', but recognizing that there was a nasty morale problem. On the 25th, presumably appreciating that there was little that could immediately be done about it, he issued a stern edict, ordering

* Quoted in Lamb, *Montgomery in Europe*, p. 161.

† PRO WO 205/5b. The Guards Armoured Division was a recently formed unit from the Brigade's elite infantry regiments. It had not yet seen action, was often regarded by Monty with misgivings, but was to acquit itself well, with characteristic dash and *élan*, in the later Normandy battles, in the sweep to liberate Brussels, at Nijmegen Bridge and in the bloody clearing of the approaches to the Rhine.

that there be 'no more reports for the present. . . . Alarmist reports written by officers with no responsibility and little battle experience could do a great deal of harm.'

In the meantime, rumours of the tank crisis had reached the House of Commons, where some awkward questions were asked. The Labour MP Richard Stokes, who had a gallant record from the First World War, made a point of informing himself in detail about tanks and pursuing Churchill relentlessly. In March he had suggested that a captured Panther be brought to the House and put on display, for MPs to make the necessary comparisons. The Prime Minister refused coldly, on the ground that the 'trouble and expense' would not be justified 'to satisfy the spiteful curiosity of my Honourable friend'. In reply to Conservative questions on 20 July, Churchill took cover behind a statement he had made back in March: 'The next time that the British Army takes the field in country suitable for the use of armour, they will be found to be equipped in a manner at least equal to the forces of any other country in the world.' He, better than anyone, must have known that this was being most economical with the truth. Five days later, Stokes was on his feet again, demanding from the Secretary of State for War an asssurance that Allied tanks in Normandy were 'at least the equal of both the German Tiger and Panther'. Grigg evaded the issue, declaring that open discussion was not in the public interest. On 2 August, Stokes savaged the government, declaring, 'we are just as far behind the Germans as we were in 1940 . . . a disgraceful state of affairs'. The debate ended with the Speaker reproaching Stokes for using bad language when he had quoted a letter from a Churchill tank man, suggesting that Grigg should go and fight in 'one of those ruddy things'. Stokes was then laughed at for his lack of patriotism. In Normandy, however, it remained no laughing matter.

Echoes were also reaching the American press. In the *New York Times* C. L. Sulzberger exposed the Sherman 'scandal'. A GI was quoted as stating that the 'people who built the tanks I don't think know the power of the Jerry gun. I have seen a Jerry gun fire through two buildings, penetrate an M-4 tank and go through another building.' US infantrymen were reported to be using captured German

Panzerfausts rather than their own much less effective bazookas.* At last Ike was urged into sending a long telegram to Bedell Smith, de Guingand's opposite number, calling for a thorough investigation. On both British and American fronts the disquieting reports about the tanks continued: 'Only our superior numbers and our magnificent artillery support keeps them in the field at all,' or, during a shoot-out between massed Shermans and Cromwells and some outnumbered Tigers and Panthers during GOODWOOD, 'had it not been for repeated attacks by rocket-firing RAF Typhoons, matters would have gone far worse for the British than they did'.

If it had only been lack of dash or over-caution on the part of some veteran tank units like the Desert Rats, coupled with the inferiority of their weapons, that might have been acceptable to Monty. But by the beginning of July much more fundamental, and disturbing, flaws were beginning to emerge among the British infantry regiments as well, and some of the most battle-tested at that. It suggested that the trouble was more than just a matter of equipment. Perhaps symptomatic was this disturbing confidential report written on 30 June by the commanding officer of a line regiment, the 6th Duke of Wellington's, which had been in action for only four days with 49th Division near Tilly-sur-Seulles:

> (1) I arrived at 6 DWR on the evening of 26th June. From am 27 Jun until am 30 Jun we have been in contact with enemy and under moderately heavy mortar and shell fire.
>
> (2) The following facts make it clear that this report makes no reflection on the state of 6 DWR when they left UK:
>
> (a) In 14 days there have been some 23 officer and 350 OR casualties.
>
> (b) Only 12 of the original officers remain and they are all junior. The CO and every rank above Cpl (except for 2 Lts) in Bn Hq

* Even less popular in the British Army was the dreadful spring-loaded PIAT, which tended to break the collar-bone of its operator when fired, had a range of less than fifty yards, and carried a feeble punch.

have gone, all coy comdrs have gone. One coy has lost every officer, another has only one left.
(c) Since I took over I have lost two 2 i/c's in successive days and a coy comdr the third day.
(d) Majority of transport, all documents, records and a large amount of equipment was lost.

(3) *State of Men.*

(a) 75% of the men react adversely to enemy shelling and are 'jumpy'.
(b) 5 cases in 3 days of self-inflicted wounds – more possible cases.
(c) Each time men are killed or wounded a number of men become casualties through shell shock or hysteria. . . .

(4) *Discipline and Leadership* . . .

(c) NCO leadership is weak in most cases and the newly drafted officers are in consequence having to expose themselves unduly to try and get anything done. It is difficult for the new officers (60%) to lead the men under fire as they do not know them. . . .

Conclusion . . .

(a) 6 DWR is not fit to take its place in the line.
(b) . . . There is naturally no esprit de corps for those who are frightened (as we all are to one degree or another) to fall back on. I have twice had to stand at the end of a track and draw my revolver on retreating men.

The CO recommended that the battalion be withdrawn to the UK for reorganizing, and that he should be relieved – regardless of the effect on his career: '. . . I have the lives of the new officer personnel (which is excellent) to consider. 3 days running a Major has been killed or seriously wounded because I have ordered him to help me to "in effect" stop them running during mortar concentrations.'

In quoting this report in his book, Max Hastings remarks that 'it is seldom that the plight of a moderate unit under pressure on the battlefield is so precisely chronicled'.* Under any circumstances, the story of the 6 DWR was a terrible one, especially painful for a commander as dedicated to the high level of training and morale of

* *Overlord*, pp. 148–9. See also Lamb, *Montgomery in Europe*, p. 110.

his troops as was Monty. He was merciless with the unfortunate CO, writing to Grigg that he displayed 'a defeatist mentality and is not a "proper chap" '.* The battalion was withdrawn from the 49th Division and disbanded seven days later. But it was, regrettably, no isolated example, and there were other episodes in Normandy of company commanders drawing their revolvers to stop men running away. Some divisions (like the 15th Scottish) fought all through with conspicuous courage and skill; but others (such as the 53rd Welsh) were, as Hastings notes, found to be 'too unreliable to be entrusted with a vital role'. As a sop to Monty's reputation, Hastings concludes that the British failure before Caen in June 1944 revealed 'a weakness of fighting power and tactics within the British Army much more than a failure of generalship by Sir Bernard Montgomery'. It is a view depressingly well supported by other military historians such as Richard Lamb and the American Carlo D'Este. Another factor sprang from the closeness in time between the two world wars. In 1939 many volunteers rejoining the colours at relatively junior levels had fought in the Great War. They often brought with them the essential gloom and lethargy that was the heritage of that appalling experience.

None of this could have afforded Monty much comfort at the time. After all that he had done to raise standards of training and morale in the army to the pitch where it could meet the supreme test of Normandy, such reports must have been profoundly dispiriting to him. They were certainly not something which simple pride would permit him to discuss with Ike and his US allies – or even, for that matter, with Winston Churchill.

These accounts of British Army shortcomings in Normandy are in no way intended to lessen the repute of the many men and units that fought with so much conspicuous skill and gallantry in an intensely bitter campaign. Nor were the shortcomings restricted only to the British. At various times Bradley recognized how much his divisions lacked determined and thoroughly trained infantrymen. All too often unnecessary casualties had been suffered, especially from deadly German mortar fire, because of his troops' reluctance to 'dig in'. Many American lives could have been saved, particularly in the

* Grigg Papers, Churchill College, Cambridge. Hastings, *Overlord*, p. 150.

savage fighting round St-Lô in July, if only the infantry had been better instructed on what to expect in the bocage; and yet, that part of the English countryside where so many Americans had been stationed during the pre-OVERLORD months, in the steeply cut lanes of Devonshire, was closely similar to that of Normandy. Some of the green American troops were particularly raw and sluggish. An American major, veteran of Sicily, observed the dismal action of the 79th Infantry Division:

> They were almost a cruel laugh. They had one regiment attacking through our assembly area whose commander could not read a map, and they lost more men than I've seen through damn recruit tricks. It is quite evident that they are not prepared for combat – a shameful waste of good American lives.*

Very often, under similar battle conditions, American losses would be substantially in excess of what the British would have suffered, and always depressingly higher than those of the Germans.† Much of the trouble stemmed from faulty priorities back home, which, in the vast expansion of US forces after Pearl Harbor, had put too low a premium on infantry recruitment, leaving their rifle companies to become a receptacle for the substandard recruit.

Where the Americans, at least in the judicious opinion of an expert like Colonel Carlo d'Este, had the edge was as follows: 'Whereas American employment of experienced divisions paid handsome dividends throughout the entire campaign in Northwest Europe, the British experience was not always happy.' He was thinking of the Desert Rats and the 51st Highland Division (which, by mid-July, Monty was reporting to Brooke as being 'not battle worthy'), noting how they contained 'too many men who had again and again been ordered to put their lives on the line'. It was very much a question of battle fatigue, not least the consequences of five

* Hastings, *Overlord*, p. 161.

† Such unnecessarily high losses were almost certainly a factor in the criticism by US commanders, levelled at Monty, that the British and Canadians were 'standing still'. Monty's response to this was this acrid entry in his diary for 19 July: 'The bigger American casualties are due to their lack of skill in fighting.' Worth noting are the comparative casualty figures by the end of June: 34,034 American to 24,698 British and Canadian – when much of the hardest fighting was taking place on the British–Canadian end of the line.

gruelling, often disheartening years of warfare – something of which the fresh, young Americans were often unaware. As Lord Moran observed in his *Anatomy of Courage*, 'A man's courage is his capital, and he is always spending it until, unrelieved, he goes bankrupt.'

On 20 July, a day of great import in the German history of the Second World War, Dempsey's intelligence officers passed back to Monty a German document, captured from the crack Panzer Lehr Division, which contained some disturbing remarks about the performance of British infantry: 'a successful break-in by the enemy is almost never exploited to pursuit. If our own troops are ready near the front for a local counter-attack, the ground is immediately regained.' It continued: 'it is best to attack the English, who are very sensitive to close combat and flank attack, at their weakest moment – that is when they have to fight without their artillery'. It went on to describe the morale of the British infantry as 'not very great. . . . the enemy is extraordinarily nervous of close combat. Whenever the enemy infantry is energetically engaged they mostly retreat or surrender. . . .' The report claimed that 'the Germans could generally tell exactly where a British attack was coming because artillery fire was concentrated on the target usually for three hours beforehand'.*

This was a viewpoint endorsed to a depressing extent by an acute New Zealander, Brigadier James Hargest, attached to 50th Division.† Of the fighting in the Normandy bocage, he noted, 'The English soldier . . . differs from the soldier in the Dominions. I notice that as soon as men lose their officers in the thick growth they lose heart.' Meanwhile, critical of some of the company officers of 50th Division, he observed during a battalion attack in June that, from a distance of about 600–800 yards, he could pick out almost every officer by the sun glinting off the talc of his map board. It was hardly surprising that, in that day's fighting, 'all four coy comdrs were hit'. Common to both American and British armies, as the losses in Normandy mounted like this (but emphatically not shared with the Wehrmacht), was an acute deficiency in the combat quality of junior leaders, notably NCOs. Many had been commissioned to fill the gaps in platoon commanders. Because of this deficiency, Hargest observed how men of 50th Division, whenever German Spandaus or mortars

* PRO WO 171/221.

† Where he was tragically killed on his farewell visit to the division.

opened up, would 'go to earth and stay there'. Thereby both men and morale would be lost: 'It's all wrong. Had we young officers of spirit and training* to *push* these patrols we might achieve something.' Had they reached his eyes at the time, Hargest's conclusions would have been distinctly worrying to Monty: 'The troops have not that spirit essential to Victory. It appears to me that the Higher Comd will do well to depend on air, artillery and tanks [which was, in fact, precisely what Monty would be forced to do in the forthcoming GOODWOOD offensive]. I realize that the enemy's morale is lower but ours frightens me.'

Over the past year, the Canadians had been persuaded to transfer 673 young officers to the British Army; though Monty had asked for twice as many, they won forty MCs and suffered 75 per cent casualties. But the transfers highlighted a serious defect within the British Army, well in advance of Normandy: a critical shortage of trained infantry, soldiers and leaders. Even the gloomy estimates made in 1943 were proved to be far out by the losses round Caen in June and July. In May, Grigg had warned the War Cabinet that by the end of September it might find a shortfall 'as high as 35,000' men. But this presupposed that losses, from all causes, would be spread fairly equally across all arms. In fact, the infantry were suffering something like 80 per cent of all the losses. How were they to be replaced? Britain no longer had any ready pools of manpower; the same was true of Canada, which had so bravely and loyally sent large reserves of its limited manpower to help the mother country. More serious, because of the errors in US recruitment policy already mentioned, it would shortly become a problem even for America with her huge population. Illustrative of the British manpower crisis, of which no one was better aware than Monty himself, is the fact that by 17 July, the eve of GOODWOOD, 21 Army Group casualties had risen to 37,563, an increase of 60 per cent over the figures at the end of June. Most of these were infantry. A total of 6654, all ranks, represented the available reinforcements.† By 14 August, the date of

* Something of a blow at Monty here, given that 50th Division had been trained by him in England, then fought under him both in the desert and in Italy.

† On the same calculations, following GOODWOOD casualties were to soar to 52,165. Immediately available replacements had fallen to 2387.

the break-out, Monty was cabling to Brooke, in great secrecy and with considerable alarm:

> Regret time has come when I must break up one infantry division. My infantry divisions are so low in effective rifle strength that they can no – repeat NO – longer fight effectively. . . . The need for this action has been present for some time but urgency of the present battle operations forced me to delay decision.

By the end of the month, the 59th Division had disappeared – under greatest secrecy.

It was with similar secrecy that Monty had failed to lay out fully before Ike his problems at the beginning of July, which would have helped explain to the Americans the apparent British reluctance to go on sacrificing infantry battalions in attacking Caen. This was a major error. Moreover, this realization of how crucial it was to preserve British manpower, superimposed on his innate dislike of losing men and combined with painful appreciation of just how badly flawed were some of his most experienced divisions (not to mention their weapons), was to act as a major factor in all Monty's unhappier dealings with Ike between Normandy and VE-Day. Certainly it goes a long way to explain the excessive caution of which subsequent historians have accused him.

When all the post-mortems are totted up, however, there remains one salient factor on which most veterans of any of the six Allied armies in Normandy would agree: in the vernacular of the times, the Germans were just 'bloody good'. Max Hastings observes how by and large both British and American armies 'had found it difficult to work up the driving power, the killing force, necessary to break through well-positioned German forces on the battlefield'.* Why? Given the odds against them, in Normandy, in the east, at home, all uttering the same very clear message – that Germany was going to lose the war she had started – it remains one of the miracles of military history that Rommel's 'Trojans' in Normandy should have fought so hard and so well.

* *Overlord*, p. 169.

A great deal of analysis has already been made, in post-war Germany as well as in the US and Britain,* and much more space than is essential to this book could profitably be devoted to it. Allied views on the man-for-man superiority of the German Army, not only in Normandy but going back to the First World War and even to the Franco-Prussian War of 1870–1, are depressingly consistent. In his learned study America's Colonel Dupuy concludes that the German Army's superiority of 'score effectiveness' was comparable in both wars, while on every Second World War battlefield, including Normandy, and despite the staggering Allied air superiority, 'the German ground soldiers consistently inflicted casualties at about a 50% higher rate than they incurred from the opposing British and American troops under all circumstances . . .'.†

This ratio continued as late as December 1944, right up to Hitler's last-gasp Ardennes offensive. In Normandy, when weather removed the air factor, engagements were regularly won by the Germans. Between 1943 and 1944, despite the constant reverses on all fronts, plus the effects of strategic bombing – both physical and moral – this German superiority had declined only marginally.

What were the reasons for it? There was all that combat experience in Russia, battling incessantly against a numerically superior enemy, for which no amount of training on Salisbury Plain could substitute. Combined with this went an extraordinary instinct for fieldcraft, providing an ability to melt into fields and hedgerows, turning every square yard into a well-concealed strongpoint – which was what made of the dense Normandy bocage such an unforgettable nightmare for the Allied troops attacking there. By 1944, the Wehrmacht had developed a highly developed capacity for fighting, and moving, without air cover. And there was, perhaps, a willingness to take casualties unacceptable to an Anglo-Saxon democracy. In his book, Colonel Dupuy advances five additional theories. They are:

1. Genetics, viz. Hitlerian notions of a super-race.

* Notable, in the former, are the various studies made by the German Militärgeschichtliches Forschungsamt of Freiburg im Breisgau.

† Colonel Trevor Dupuy, *A Genius for War*, p. 253. In Russia, German 'score effectiveness' over the Soviet forces was of the order of six to one, reflecting, says Colonel Dupuy, Stalin's penchant 'for mass attacks without regard to casualties'.

2. An inherent capacity for militarism.
3. Fear of defeat and invasion of the homeland.
4. A society which encourages efficiency.
5. The creation of more effective military institutions than were found in other countries.

In his arguments, Dupuy virtually discards the first four hypotheses in favour of the fifth – possibly to the extent of over-simplification. Certainly in Normandy, as elsewhere, there was evidence of brilliant organization, and of the all-pervasive German General Staff system – but it was not the whole story. We have seen the relative flaws both in Allied tank production and in infantry performance; on the German side, in Normandy it is recorded at 44.9 per cent of the Wehrmacht were organized into combat units, as opposed to only 20.8 per cent of the Americans, with the British just marginally better.

In terms of use of manpower, perhaps the biggest German advantage over the British and Americans lay in their training of junior leaders, particularly of NCOs; which in turn harked back to the *Auftragssystem** incorporated by the elder Moltke in the Prussian military machine in the nineteenth century, and in which resided the great strength of the German fighting machine in three consecutive European wars. The superb fighting reputation of the British Brigade of Guards was to a large extent based on the excellence of its NCOs, but they were never trained to take over a company in the event of all the officers being knocked out. Of course, in the exigencies of battle, it happened from time to time. But they were not *educated* for what was basically contrary to the whole hierarchic and class system within the British Army – against which even the iconoclastic Monty never set himself. In contrast, the *Feldwebel* and *Unteroffizier* of the German Army *were* educated to this responsibility. In the latter stages of the First World War, an infantry battalion would often be led by only ten officers, with platoons commanded by a *Feldwebel*, or senior NCO, instead of a subaltern. These accomplished NCOs would become dedicated Nazi leaders during the Freikorps era of the 1920s, providing the key cadres for the

* Literally, 'mission system'.

Second World War, and training on their succession as losses whittled away their ranks.

The very essence of the *Auftragssystem* was that a subordinate commander would be accountable for carrying out the 'mission concept' of his superior, with or without orders. This presupposed the instillation of a considerable sense of initiative into the junior cadres. Far from being a horde of rigid and inflexible robots (which was always one of the most insidious of all Allied misconceptions about the Germans), the Wehrmacht thus had a far greater ability to react or to regain the initiative – especially in a moment of reverse – than was possessed particularly by the British Army of 1944. Coupled with this was the deeply ingrained principle of 'When in doubt, attack!' (whereas, in the British Army, all too often the conditioned reflex would be 'When in doubt, dig in!'). Again and again in Normandy, as on the Russian front, a hole opened in the front would be sealed by the desperate initiative of a small detachment of men, often without an officer, equipped with a solitary 88, a *Panzerfaust* or a Spandau – or, like Obersturmführer Wittmann at Villers-Bocage, with a solitary Tiger. Another example of this capacity for improvisation and swift opportunism inherent within the *Auftragssystem* was shown by Colonel Kurt 'Panzer' Meyer, the thirty-three-year-old commander of 12th SS Panzer, on its arrival near Caen just after D-Day. Its supply train disrupted by Allied air attacks, Meyer organized his teenage Hitler Youth into shuttling fuel to the tanks in jerrycans loaded into Volkswagen staff cars. The Canadian advance was halted.

What the *Auftragssystem* meant is encapsulated by a remark by a twenty-two-year-old corporal serving with a second-echelon infantry division: 'We felt that they [American troops] always overestimated us. We could not understand why they did not break through. The Allied soldier never seemed to be trained as we were, always to try to do more than had been asked of us.' This was an echo of Frederick the Great's famous motto 'Mehr Sein Als Schein' ('Be More Than You Seem'), but it had a correlation, too, with a German national phenomenon which historians like Dupuy perhaps wrongly ascribe to purely military organization. Within the Wehrmacht, certainly, there existed an almost unique tradition of shared responsibility, of true *Kameradschaft*, the sense that any German soldier was 'his brother's keeper' ('If something went wrong,' notes

Dupuy, 'a German officer or soldier would feel the responsibility to do something about it, regardless of personal risk or physical danger'), something akin to the American 'buddy system', but far stronger. Yet anyone, however, who lived in the peacetime, anti-militarist West Germany of post-45 would also recognize this quality of mutual concern and supportiveness as one of the nation's great social strengths, which *inter alia* for several decades lay at the foundation of the industrial peace which gave the Bundesrepublik its *Wirtschaftswunder.*

One of the true miracles of the Wehrmacht's performance in Normandy must lie in the extraordinarily high morale maintained in the teeth of appalling adversity. Shortly before his death in 1944, Rommel told his young son Manfred,* in despair:

> All the courage didn't help . . . sometimes we had as many casualties on one day as during the whole of the summer fighting in Africa in 1942. My nerves are pretty good, but sometimes I was near collapse. It was casualty reports, casualty reports, casualty reports, wherever you went. I could never have fought with such losses. If I hadn't gone to the front nearly every day, I couldn't have stood it, having to write off literally one more regiment every day.†

The consistent will to fight on in Normandy can of course be in part explained by the Nazi system, by the fear of failure it imposed or by the personal devotion to Hitler – the repeated exhortation of 'No retreat: it's a Führer order.' Many of the units sent to Normandy were composed of young fanatics of the SS. 'We no longer expected total victory,' said one SS sergeant, 'but we still felt an absolute sense of loyalty. In Russia we had fought men against men. We knew that in Normandy it would be men against machines.'‡ Symptomatic of the SS ethos was the attitude of their hard-hitting, ruthless leader, 'Panzer' Meyer, quite unashamedly 'unreconstructed' even after 1945 and telling his interrogators, 'You will hear a lot against Adolf Hitler

* Almost exactly the same age as David Montgomery, only son of a professional soldier, Manfred Rommel had a curiously parallel life to the son of his father's adversary. He had a distinguished career as *Oberbürgermeister* (lord mayor) of Stuttgart, while David was carving his own career in Latin America and as a vigorous member of the House of Lords. Over the years they became close friends.

† Liddell Hart (ed.), *The Rommel Papers*, p. 496.

‡ Quoted in Hastings, *Overlord*, p. 65.

in this camp, but you will never hear it from me. As far as I am concerned he was, and still is, the greatest thing that ever happened to Germany.'* This is, however, far too simple to represent the whole truth; many non-Nazi German soldiers simply fought on out of motives of national pride, of that sense of responsibility to one another – to the platoon, the company, the regiment. But perhaps most of all they fought on out of fear of what was going to happen to the *Vaterland*. 'Let's enjoy the war,' said a member of 'Panzer' Meyer's 12th SS, 'because the peace will be terrible.'

Here the sense of how 'terrible' the peace was going to be was ardently fanned by the Allied formula of 'unconditional surrender', the slogan so unwisely imposed by Roosevelt on a reluctant Winston Churchill at the Casablanca Conference of 1943, almost off the cuff as it were. It is probable that no other single factor so stiffened German resistance in the West as this misguided war aim declared by the Allies. Later, when German morale was at an all-time low after the crushing defeat of Normandy, it would be rekindled by the helpful Allies with the revelation in September 1944 of the ill-considered Morgenthau Plan, whereby German industry would be razed to the ground, the country perpetually pastoralized. A German NCO claimed that he and others were motivated above all by those principles of '. . . "Unconditional Surrender". If for the rest of my life I was to chop wood in Canada or Siberia, then I would sooner die in Normandy.'†

The fact remains, whatever one may think of its moral philosophy, that even in 1944 the German Wehrmacht retained many of the qualities with which it had started the war as the most efficient military machine ever known. Many of its weapons were, as has been seen, simpler, more reliable and deadlier than those of the Allies. Defeats and retreats in Russia had given it superb training for fighting on the defensive, denied to the mass of British or American units; and they had not worn down the soldierly virtues of courage and loyalty. On top of it, as possibly the greatest adjunct to morale of all, there was superimposed the Allies' gift of 'unconditional surrender', comparable to the kind of 'backs to the wall' stimulus that had saved Britain in the lonely summer of 1940.

* Brett-Smith, *Hitler's Generals*, p. 162.
† Hastings, *Overlord*, p. 185.

CHAPTER SEVEN

BREAK-OUT

2 July–10 August 1944

The good general must not only win his battles; he must win them with a minimum of casualties and loss of life.

(Montgomery, *Memoirs*)

As Bradley said, 'We must grin and bear it.' It became increasingly difficult to grin.

(Montgomery, *Memoirs*, p. 257: on the press, after GOODWOOD)

Why the American army has to go with Monty I do not see, except to save the face of the little monkey.

(General Patton, the day before departing for France)

JULY 1944 was the time in Monty's life when all the accrued hostilities and jealousies of the past threatened to erupt and engulf him. For the first time his relations with the long-suffering Ike showed signs of deteriorating, under dual pressure both from the relentless US press corps and from the steady drip of poison from the powerful anti-Monty faction back at SHAEF. During the first few weeks of July, a series of top-level meetings took place at Monty's TAC HQ at Blay which were crucial, not only to the further prosecution of the campaign, but to Monty's own future as well. The pressures were immense. In Britain, since the first of Hitler's much vaunted 'secret weapons' had struck the week after D-Day, the V-1s had been raining down, the blasts of their huge explosive warheads causing appalling, indiscriminate destruction. Over the next three months, out of a total of 8000 launched, 2419 actually struck the London area.* During that first month of June–July they caused 2500 deaths; after civilian casualties of 2000 during the previous year,

* A total of 30,000 V-1 and V-2 rockets were fired at Britain by the end of the war.

the total for 1944 soared to 53,000 in the London area alone, while 2000 airmen were lost in efforts to combat them. With 23,000 houses destroyed the damage to property was colossal, transportation was seriously disrupted, and war production fell off. But disproportionately far greater was the V-1s' effect on British morale, wearing down frayed nerves to a worse extent than ever the manned bombers of the Blitz had done. One tends to forget just how considerable was the initial impact of the V-1s, coming at this late stage in the war. At one point, Churchill seriously contemplated resorting to poison gas in reprisal.

For the battered German defenders in Normandy, Goebbels' adroit propaganda building on exaggerated reports of what the 'terror weapons' were doing to the British produced a remarkable lift in morale. Yet, ironically, in the long run the success of the V-1s may have aided the strategic success of Monty's plan, by persuading the German High Command that his number-one priority would now *have* to be the occupation of the Pas de Calais, whence the missiles were launched. Thus the faulty appreciation that the break-out would, inevitably, come from the British end of the line received a further boost, distracting German eyes from Bradley and Patton.

The impact of the 'buzz-bombs', as they called them, was perhaps particularly marked on the nerves of Eisenhower and his SHAEF staff back at Bushey Park, unaccustomed as Americans were to this kind of promiscuous warfare against civilians. 'Most of the people I know', wrote Ike's aide, Captain Butcher, 'are semi-dazed from loss of sleep and have the jitters, which they show when doors bang or the sounds of motors from motorcycles to aircraft are heard.'* In one week Butcher reported a total of '500 dead and more than 1500 seriously wounded'. By a bizarre success of British intelligence, which duped the Germans into aiming the V-1s short of London, a heavy concentration kept falling close to Bushey Park – and Ike's retreat at Telegraph Cottage.† On one night alone, 19 June (the worst, when 305 death were recorded), no less than twenty-five shattering explosions were counted. At the beginning of July, Ike sent a note to Kay Summersby reporting that 'Buzz-bombs chased

* Captain Harry C. Butcher, USN, *Three Years with Eisenhower*, p. 504.
† Irving, *The War between the Generals*, p. 171.

us to cover about six times during the afternoon and three or four going home.' One exploded so close as to bring down the ceiling and break the windows in Ike's office. Everybody at SHAEF was becoming red-eyed with fatigue, and highly irritable. 'Dad is tired,' Second Lieutenant John Eisenhower admitted to one of Ike's aides.

On top of all this stress, Eisenhower found himself under all the mounting pressures from home of an election year, which compounded the instinctive impatience of the US press. As far as Monty was concerned, as the whispers at SHAEF grew louder that something had gone badly wrong with his strategy before Caen, suddenly the reservoir of all the bad relations, the rebuffs and the sackings which he had been storing up against himself over the past two decades began to overflow in a torrent of resentments and jealousies. From Tedder downwards at SHAEF, his foes among the senior British officers there had become at least as damaging as his American critics. Most dangerous of all, even Churchill's instinctive suspicions of generals who failed to produce swift results were at last beginning to take over. By the third week in July, Monty had reached the most dangerous moment of his entire career, his head within inches of the chopping block. Isolated at TAC, in the verdant fields of Blay, with his dogs, his canaries and his young men, to an ominous extent he was all too unaware of what was afoot.

On 2 July, accompanied by Bradley, Ike arrived at Blay. It was one of only nine times that he and Monty were to meet during the whole campaign,* and, in line with Monty's own rigid principle that commanders should always 'go forward', it was Mahomet who came to the mountain. Accompanied by a vast retinue of newsmen and photographers, and delighted to find a respite from the 'buzz-bombs', or 'doodlebugs', Ike had arrived in Normandy on a five-day tour – harried from Washington by Marshall and Stimson, the Secretary of War – with the specific brief to get things moving, to break the apparent stalemate. It was a purpose similar to Churchill's when he descended on the desert in 1942. Eisenhower was immediately frustrated to discover that, in the bocage country near St-Lô,

* An extraordinary state of affairs when one considers that, during the brief Gulf War of 1990–1, the coalition generalissimo, General Schwarzkopf, and his British subordinate, General de la Billière, conferred almost every day, even though de la Billière wielded much less influence in terms of numbers of troops deployed.

Bradley's forces were as bogged down as Dempsey was at Caen – despite a three-to-one superiority in infantry, and eight-to-one in armour.* The conversations were less warm than on previous occasions. Monty had been warned by Brooke to keep off the controversial issue of ANVIL, constantly postponed and now scheduled for August. (ANVIL, as we have seen, was the US-inspired scheme for a subsidiary landing in the South of France, near Toulon, hotly disputed by Churchill since its very inception.)

As the Americans broke out by the end of July and began to spread rapidly westwards into Brittany, Churchill (to the despair of Brooke) began urging that the landings be transferred to the Brittany ports. 'Why should we bash in the back door,' he put it to Roosevelt in a telegram on 1 August after a three-hour tussle with Ike, 'when we have the latch key to the front door?' Eventually ANVIL (renamed DRAGOON) went in, as planned, on 15 August. But by this date the Battle of Normandy was virtually won. Most of the enemy casualties turned out to be wretched Russians who had opted to fight for the Germans against Stalin; it did not divert a single enemy division from the north, though it is argued by protagonists that, by liberating intact the vast port of Marseilles, more men and supplies eventually reached the front than through all the Channel ports put together. However, had Antwerp and its approaches been cleared – as they should have been in early September – this would have been largely academic. But this belongs to a later part of the story.

Monty also challenged ANVIL on the ground that it represented an irrelevant dispersal of effort. As the campaign progressed, he came to recognize it as typical of Eisenhower's philosophy of war, of wearing the enemy down by attacking on all fronts more or less simultaneously – a General Grant to Monty's Sherman – whereas Monty consistently spoke up for the maximum concentration of force. Moreover, as he declared in his personal diary and made abundantly plain to the Americans, his highest priority remained 'to have no reverses or setbacks'.

With unusual docility, Monty did what Brooke asked; he acquiesced over ANVIL. According to his memoirs, he regretted it ever after, holding it to be 'one of the great strategic mistakes of the war'.

* To this date the Allies had already landed 2920 tanks: 1744 British to 1176 US.

He added, 'But I wanted to show willing to Ike; I had been showing unwilling in other matters, and I sensed then that there were more of these "other matters" to come.' These were key words indeed. The 'other matters' on which Monty wanted Ike to 'show willing' were considerably more far-reaching, and Monty's views on them even more unacceptable to Ike than anything he could possibly say about ANVIL. It all hinged on the question of command. When Monty had been placed in command of OVERLORD land forces, under Ike, it had been a temporary appointment pending the arrival of Patton's Third Army in Normandy. This would then give the Americans, for the first time, the anticipated preponderance on the battlefield. Even without the mounting discontent back home over Monty's apparently sluggish conduct of the battle, it was inevitable that the Americans – according to tradition – would want their troops to fight under overall US command. Thus it was presaged that Omar Bradley, uniquely respected by Americans and British alike as the best of all the US fighting generals, would be promoted to command a new army group of the two US armies, *pari passu* with Monty retaining control only over the British and Canadian armies in 21 Army Group. Meanwhile, both army groups would come under Ike's direct control as field commander. In an ideal world, there were a variety of reasons why it would have been more sensible for Monty to have retained total control over the Allied ground forces, but Monty's prickly character, combined with the new American position of dominance, rendered this quite unworkable. Monty would never see that; what he could see, with more than a little justification on his side, was that it would be out of the question for Ike himself to take over conduct of operations from an office in southern England.

The meeting of 2 July at Blay was a brief one, Ike spending most of his time in Normandy with Bradley, with whom he felt infinitely more at ease. The next day, Monty's ADC Johnny Henderson wrote in his diary:

> The American advance south started this morning. The Chief's big plan is to get all the enemy strength against the British sector and then to swing down the western edge of the Cherbourg Peninsula, and then spread out from there. This is what has started. Progress was, however, slow. . . .

That a twenty-five-year-old British captain should have comprehended this confirms that Monty's 'plan' must have been perfectly plain – at least to his immediate entourage. If it was not plain to Ike, as the post-war battle of the memoirs suggests, something must have been fundamentally wrong between the two generals – but who was not speaking clearly? Who was not hearing what was said? It was the age-old problem of communication between the great and powerful. The question remains, and will continue to remain, unresolved.

On 7 July, Monty wrote to Brooke to give his view of the meeting with Ike:

> SYSTEM OF COMMAND IN FRANCE
>
> There is great pressure at SHAEF to get the US Army Group in operation, commanding the two US armies; the pressure comes chiefly from the younger element.
>
> I am keeping right clear of all discussion.*

He added that he had gone on to explain:

> that if he [Ike] forms a US army group, and SHAEF wants to take direct charge of the battle, he himself must come over here and *devote his whole and undivided attention to the battle*. Any idea that he could run the land battle from England, or could do it in his spare time, would be playing with fire.
>
> Eisenhower himself has, I fancy, no delusions on the subject.

Here Ike would shortly prove him mistaken. Monty went on to explain to Brooke that Ike had agreed to 'form the US Army Group, with Bradley in command, to put it under me'. He would thenceforth command '1 US Army Group. Second British Army. First Canadian Army. And I see no difficulty in this.'

There were, however, quite clearly Americans (and British) at SHAEF who did see difficulties, and on his return they soon got to work on Ike, not notably reassured from his visit to Blay. It was equally clear that Ike too intended that the new 'command system' should be transitory. Given the often confused (and rather unmilitary) syntax to which Ike resorted when President as well as in his profession, his directives in 1944 seldom read like the com-

* Not strictly accurate; but, if he did 'keep clear' as he thought, this might have been one more instance of his self-imposed isolation from SHAEF, and from Ike.

mands of a generalissimo.* On 6 July, after a talk with the increasingly critical Tedder, 'it was agreed', so Tedder records, 'that the Supreme Commander should draft a letter which would tell Monty tactfully to get moving'.† But the resulting letter was indeed excessively tactful:

> I am familiar with your plan for generally holding firmly with your left, attracting thereto all of the enemy armour, while your right pushes down the peninsula and threatens the rear and flank of the forces facing the Second British Army.

This of itself suggests that Ike *was* unquestionably 'familiar' with Monty's overall strategy at that point, and that all the post-war wrangle between the generals and their partisans may have been largely unnecessary. Ike then promised that he would 'back you up to the limit in any effort you may decide upon to prevent a deadlock'. Couched in his rather woolly way, determined never to offend the susceptibilities of any of those prickly prima donnas under his authority, always the cheerleader, rarely the authoritarian team-captain, this letter would have been read by Monty more as an exhortation than as a direct order to 'get moving' – and certainly not as an instruction to reverse the strategy with which Ike claimed to be 'familiar'.

It was at this point that Tedder passed his deplorably scornful remark about Monty conducting 'Company exercises', also exchanging moans with his senior airman, Chief of the Air Staff Portal, just returned from his trip to Normandy: 'The problem was Montgomery, who could be "neither removed nor moved" to action,' wrote Tedder two decades later, still unrepentantly deaf to Monty's own problems with his ground forces, his 'flawed instrument'.

To Ike's letter, Monty replied calmly with a Nelsonic blind eye:

> My dear Ike,
>
> Thank you for your letter of 7 July.
>
> I am, myself, quite happy with the situation. I have been working throughout on a very definite plan, and I now begin to see daylight. . . . I think we must be quite clear as to what is vital

* He always tended to be much clearer on paper; the Anglo-American fiasco of Suez may well have reflected something of the imprecision of the spoken Ike.

† Tedder, *Without Prejudice*, pp. 557–8.

> and what is not; if we get our sense of values wrong we may go astray.

This was a clear refutation of Ike's Grantian philosophy of 'bulling ahead on all fronts'. Monty declined Ike's perhaps rather indelicate offer of the loan of an American armoured division on the British front:

> we really have all the armour we need. The great thing is to get First and Third US Armies up to a good strength, and to get them cracking on the southward thrust on the western flank, and then turn Patton westwards into the Brittany peninsula.
>
> To sum up.
>
> I think the battle is going very well.

Meanwhile, on the 6th, Churchill, affected as he so often was by external voices like those of the press, clamouring for results, or by the rumbles within SHAEF (where Monty had now been christened 'Chief Big Wind') or from Washington, attacked Monty with unprecedented ferocity before a meeting of the Chiefs of Staff. 'Apparently Ike had said that he was over-cautious,' Brooke recorded: '... I flared up and asked him if he could not trust his generals for five minutes instead of belittling them.' He described the confrontation as 'one of the heaviest thunderstorms that we had'.*

That same day, heralding a new turn in the war, but also bringing fresh thunderstorms for both Ike and Monty, there arrived in Normandy, in secrecy and in advance of his fresh Third Army, the swashbuckling George S. Patton Jr, the most unpredictable prima donna of them all.

In Homeric terms of Greeks and Trojans, Patton the affluent cavalryman with his pair of pearl-handled .45s might perhaps be rated with 'Diomede the Horsebreaker', ruthless, irresistible to women and not giving a damn for anyone. After champing at the bit in England all those months, for a while not even sure whether his old buddy Ike was going to give him a command at all, on arriving in Normandy he was like a Rottweiler unleashed. To his much tried wife Beatrice, he announced – in perfect truth – 'When I eventually emerge

* Bryant, *Triumph in the West*, pp. 229–30.

it will be quite an explosion,' and the blast would by no means hit only the Germans. The months in purdah had done little to reform his views on the British, let alone Bernard Law Montgomery. The day before embarking from England, he wrote in his diary, 'Why the American army has to go with Monty I do not see, except to save the face of the little monkey.'* The following day, after lunching with Monty, he added, 'Monty went to great length explaining why the British had done nothing.'

Nevertheless, it would have been difficult for Patton, for all his dislike of Monty, not to be excited by the grand design of his Normandy strategy, and particularly the role that was to be allotted to him and his Third Army. When the break-out came, the bulk of his Third Army, renowned for its mobility and dash, was to wheel eastwards on Bradley's outer flank and head for the River Loire. What was remarkable (and a testament to the crass stupidity of German intelligence, never on a par with German tanks) was that, even after the arrival of Patton, FORTITUDE – the brilliant deception plan – continued to glue the OKW's eyes to the Pas de Calais. This preoccupation was intensified by the allure of the V-1 sites. By the time the OKW began to move further reinforcements from the Fifteenth Army towards Normandy, it would be too late. Yet, according to Monty's BGS Plans, Brigadier Richardson, who presented a gloomy appreciation on 7 July, the day after Patton's arrival, this was seen to be a finely balanced risk, and unless Monty was to 'drive south until we get out of the bocage', there was a danger of the German build-up opposite him reaching dangerous proportions. Here, from within Monty's own team, was yet further pressure upon him to keep up the momentum.

It was in this context that costly CHARNWOOD had taken place. On 5 July Johnny Henderson had recorded in his diary, 'The Chief is now tee-ing up a big party for 8th July to get Caen. He is willing to bet me we will have the western half of it – that is west of the River Orne – by midday on the 10th.' He went on to add, as an aside typical of the unflustered tempo at TAC, and in contrast to the

* Blumenson (ed.), *The Patton Papers*, vol. II, p. 472.

hubbub and intriguing back at SHAEF, 'Interesting conversation at tea about coeducation. Verdict 3 to 2 against it being a good thing.' Monty won his bet with Henderson. Wisely, he had made no suggestion in advance of CHARNWOOD about it being the prelude to a break-out, but less wisely he allowed the capture of the heap of rubble which was what remained of the centre of Caen to be trumpeted as a great victory – which would play dangerously into the hands of his foes.

Just as CHARNWOOD was under way, on 8 July Monty received a rather unwelcome letter from Ike 'expressing concern at our lack of progress. This is the first time he has ever expressed any view on the battle; and it arrived at a rather unfortunate time – just as we were about to capture Caen!'

Of all the Anglo-American conferences that prefaced the great break-out, none was more significant – or more harmonious – than Monty's discussions with Bradley at TAC HQ on 10 July. Monty always rated Bradley, with his quiet, understated manner and above all his supreme professionalism, highest among all the American top commanders.* His manner of operating bore a surprising similarity to Monty's; he too preferred calm detachment around him, even installing his personal map in a caravan like Monty's at TAC, where he would work quietly 'with my coloured crayons, outline various operations and would soon find out that one wouldn't work because of the road net. . . . it wasn't until I had the thing quite well outlined that I brought in a corps commander.' Certainly until this point in the campaign there had never been so much as a whisper of discord between them, all their dealings being sober and workmanlike, with a clear mutual understanding of what they were up against. Bradley arrived in some gloom. Of the big US break-out effort on 3 July, Johnny Henderson recorded, 'The Americans have made only slight headway. They fired every gun on Independence Day.' Even in a second book written twenty-two years after his own memoirs, and long after his relationship with Monty had gone sour, Bradley admitted, 'My own break-out had failed. Despite enormous casualties and loss of equipment, the Germans were slavishly following Hitler's

* According to his biographer, Stephen Ambrose (1), p. 227, Ike himself regarded Bradley as 'capable of almost anything'.

orders to hold every yard of ground.'* He recalled dreading that 'we faced a real danger of a World War I-type stalemate'. On top of the dreadful nightmare of the bocage, the flooding caused by the Germans in Cotentin had given rise to endless headaches. Bradley didn't think he could launch the big American break-out until he had gained a 'good firm start-line along the St Lô–Périers road'. So far this remained out of his reach.†

'Monty was wonderful,' recalled General Dempsey of that meeting: 'There were no recriminations – although Bradley had obviously made his own task the more difficult by trying to buck the whole line right along instead of concentrating and punching a hole in one important sector.' In his most comforting and supportive manner Monty said quietly to his much less battle-experienced American subordinate: ' "... Never mind. Take all the time you need, Brad." Then he went on tactfully to say: "If I were you I think I should concentrate my forces a little more" – putting two fingers on the map in his characteristic way.' Thus, 'without Bradley realizing it', Dempsey continued, Monty 'got across to him the idea that he must concentrate his forces for a solid punch at one point'. Monty instructed Dempsey to 'go on drawing the German strength ... so as to ease the way for Brad' and his new offensive, codenamed COBRA. After the meeting with Bradley, Dempsey offered Monty in private a break-out on the eastern flank, despite what this would mean in terms of losses to Britain's increasingly precious infantrymen; 'but Monty did not favour such a change of aim'.‡

Monty now sent off a new directive of simple clarity, stating (or rather restating), 'My broad policy remains unchanged. It is to draw the main enemy forces in the battle on our eastern flank, and fight them there, so that our affairs on the western flank may proceed the easier.' To ensure that there could be absolutely no misunderstanding, copies were sent to the four army commanders, to Ike and Brooke and the air barons. Behind an infantry shield, Dempsey was to withdraw his armour from battle and regroup it into a powerful offensive corps of three armoured divisions. The mere threat of them breaking through the ever thinner German defence crust should

* *A General's Life*, p. 272.

† These attacks cost the Americans nearly 40,000 casualties.

‡ Interview, 1952, in Liddell Hart Archives.

suffice to commit Rommel, paralysed by Hitler's lunatic *Führerbefehl* (Führer's order) to yield no inch of ground, into a suicidal last-ditch defence behind the Orne. Around Dempsey's tank spearhead would be constructed the new major offensive, GOODWOOD, to start on 17 July – later delayed to the 18th. Although Monty was sometimes accused of treating the delicate-looking Dempsey more like a corps than an army commander, detailed planning of the operation was left to him. Dempsey later recalled that, in addition to the overriding objective of continuing to attract the enemy Panzers on to the British shield, 'another consideration was the need to expand the bridgehead, which was becoming overcrowded as reinforcements and supplies were pouring in all the time'. Here, if needed, was belated recognition yet again of the failure to secure the land eastwards from Caen between the Orne and Dives rivers. It was settled at that meeting of 10 July that Bradley would push the US First Army forward out of the bocage and the marshlands, starting on the 20th – closely, indeed inextricably, linked with the British–Canadian GOODWOOD attack – though Monty himself would have preferred the two attacks to go in simultaneously. Thus, that day, in the words of Carlo D'Este, 'The wheels were now set in motion for the two greatest offensives yet initiated in Normandy, one of which was finally to prove the beginning of the end for the German army of the west.'*

On the 14th, Monty sent his trusted Military Assistant, Lieutenant-Colonel Kit Dawnay, back to England with a seven-page letter for Brooke. In it he told him, with the usual Monty self-assurance, 'The time has come for a real showdown . . . to loose a corps of Armoured Divisions into the open country about the Caen–Falaise road. . . . the

* D'Este, *Decision in Normandy*, p. 334. He adds, however, that the breakthrough 'had little to do with the original concept laid down in Montgomery's masterplan', but had been largely developed by Bradley and Dempsey acting independently. This is not strictly fair, as should be abundantly plain from the extracts from Monty's orders quoted above. Nor is it quite accurate to say as does Martin Blumenson (quoted by D'Este, p. 338) that 'The Germans massed their forces [around Caen] not because Monty drew them there but because they were trying to fulfil a purpose of their own.' Indeed, but what other purpose than to ward off the most dangerous attack which Monty's strategy constantly led them to believe was going to come from the British, and not the American, end of the front?

possibilities are immense with 700 tanks loosed. . . . anything may happen.' This was, however, all carefully toned down by Dawnay in his commentary to Brooke, to avoid any impression that Monty was intending definitively to break out at Caen:

> he has no intention of rushing madly eastwards. . . .
>
> All the activities on the eastern flank are designed to help the force in the west, while ensuring that a firm bastion is kept in the east. At the same time all is ready to take advantage of any situation which gives reason to think that the enemy is disintegrating.

All this should have made perfectly plain the limitations of the GOODWOOD objectives, but Monty was possibly unwise to write to Ike at the same time on a more flamboyantly optimistic note, promising that 'my whole eastern flank will burst into flames on Saturday. The operations on Monday may have far-reaching results.'

The immediate motives behind such optimism will be seen shortly, but was it psychologically prudent to encourage hopes in somebody who was pressing, and in turn being pressed, for results as fiercely as Ike was at the time? It was thus in this same vein that he responded on the 14th: '. . . I would not be at all surprised to see you gaining a victory that will make some of the "Old Classics" look like a skirmish between patrols.' It seems that he had definitely not taken on board the intended scope of GOODWOOD; Bradley had. Nothing, one would have thought, could have been much clearer than Monty's instructions following his meeting with Bradley on the 10th, but Ike's biographer, Ambrose, is probably right when he suggests that Monty erred in not going back to SHAEF in person to explain to Ike precisely what his plan was. Once again, one could see the downside of Monty's whole system of command, of his isolation within the 'family' at TAC HQ.

Though Monty was never one to share his innermost thoughts even to de Guingand (still back at Main, in England), in the excessive optimism deployed on Ike one should read, not so much the old familiar Monty boastfulness, as his deep concern about the shortage of British manpower – coupled with the growing warnings of the 'flawed weapons' outlined in the previous chapter. As always, too, maintaining the morale of his troops was of paramount importance;

by mid-July, it was far from impeccable. Their 'binge' had to be kept up. From the outset Monty had decided that GOODWOOD, which he hoped (and expected) would be the last big British–Canadian effort in Normandy before the break-out, should be a battle of material rather than men. Technically inferior as they might be, he had a numerically superior mass of tanks in his pocket; and, compared with the infantry, their casualties had so far been negligible. With replacements piling up in England, tanks were expendable. Instead of infantry, he would strike with a massed assault of armour, the three divisions withdrawn from the line and mustered under General O'Connor. Once again, they would strike across the Orne, attempting to outflank the Germans still hanging on to what remained of Caen from the south-east, and heading for the dominant Bourguébus Ridge. Instead of the unprecedented artillery barrage that had preceded Alamein, he would use the strategic bombers with a devastating blow such as had never been used before – even at CHARNWOOD – to blast a corridor for the armour.

Thus it was to his old foes, the air barons, more specifically than to the Supreme Commander himself, that Monty's inflated promises were directed. Since CHARNWOOD, Leigh-Mallory, previously a 'gutless bugger', had risen dramatically in his esteem: 'It is very important that Leigh-Mallory should remain as Air C-in-C,' he wrote in his diary on the 19th. 'When planning in England, we did not think very highly of Leigh-Mallory, but we all agree now that he is the only "Air Lord" who will do anything to help the army win the War; and he is completely genuine and sincere.' In marked contrast, Coningham was 'a very jealous person and I am beginning to feel he is anti-army. . . . not a loyal member of the team . . . untrustworthy and no one likes him. I thought Tedder was all right, but from what the CIGS said I have now certain doubts.'

After the anger and scathing remarks that CHARNWOOD had generated, the only way he could have got Tedder, via Leigh-Mallory, to release the strategic and tactical support bombers he needed was to assure him (as he did on the 14th) that, 'if successful, the plan promises to be decisive'. That a ground-force commander should have to deceive his own air-force colleagues was a truly deplorable state of affairs. But it was also 'essential' that the Germans be deceived into thinking that GOODWOOD represented an all-out attempt to break through towards Paris. This, inevitably, meant the sacrifice of the element of surprise.

Thus, before it even started, GOODWOOD had two big strikes against it. First, in a rare piece of good intelligence work, the Germans were able to predict the exact direction of the armoured thrust and its objectives (though, with several thousand tanks and vehicles on the move, it cannot have been all that difficult; General Sepp Dietrich, commander of the 1st SS Panzer Corps, observed in post-war internment that all he had to do was put his ear to the ground). On the 15th, Rommel himself had visited the area east of Caen yet again, in what was to be his last visit to the front, and had predicted with deadly accuracy the place and date of GOODWOOD, instructing 21st Panzer to meet the attack in depth with line after line of 88s. But a second and much more fundamental flaw in the British plan was to be found in the appalling congestion within the area east of Bénouville, where the bridgehead had hardly expanded since it was seized by 6th Airborne on D-Day. This would render deployment of O'Connor's great phalanx of armour almost impossible.

Monty's deception of the air barons worked – but at a cost. At 0400 hours on 18 July, in a rare breach of standing procedure, Johnny Henderson woke 'the Chief up to tell him the air show was on, as he wished to know the final decision of Bomber Command in England. He went straight off to sleep.' From British airfields, 1100 heavy bombers took to the air against this one small corner of Normandy, in perhaps the most awe-inspiring air bombardment ever launched against ground forces. At 0530, some 6000 tons of bombs were dropped on the German positions east of the Orne alone, largely by RAF heavies; at 0700 US medium bombers joined in, but had to return to base without dropping their bombs because of the dense clouds of smoke and dust over the battlefield; at 0830, a third wave of US mediums dropped nearly 90,000 anti-personnel bombs in the Bourguébus area – confirming to German intelligence, if nothing else, what was Dempsey's objective. By the end of the 18th, over 4500 aircraft had been in action, and they were supported by massed artillery and long-range naval guns firing nearly a quarter of a million shells. On this 'perfect opal summer morning', to de Guingand, watching the bombing from the top of a haystack with 'Maori' Coningham, it resembled:

> a swarm of bees homing upon their hive. I thought how terrible it must be to suffer under the Harris technique in a German town. . . . One appreciated the great bravery of those pilots and crews as they flew straight into the most ghastly-looking flak.*

In his diary, Monty wrote, 'nothing could live under it'. But, not for the first or last time in modern warfare, a commander was misjudging the effectiveness of strategic bombing on a battlefield.

At the receiving end, the German tank crews found their Tigers 'literally buried and others turned upside down as if their 58-ton weight had been no more than playing cards'. With bare hands, crews had to dig them out – every aperture, gun muzzles, air filters, exhausts, choked with earth. Some of the men were crazed by the bombardment, describing it – in precisely the same language their fathers had once used about the Battle of Verdun in 1916 – as 'a vision of hell'. Yet, once again, the survivors proved the miraculous capacity of the Germans to continue fighting in the teeth of overwhelming bombardment, proving too the basic failure of massive airpower. The defences, the most formidable ever encountered during the whole campaign, remained unbroken: five concentric lines of dug-in tanks and 88s.

No one at Second Army HQ, TAC or SHAEF seems to have grasped the full strength of the German defences at GOODWOOD. Johnny Henderson wrote in his diary for the 18th:

> At 0745 the 11th Armoured Div. started moving forward, followed by the Guards Armoured, the 7th Armoured. They carried all before them and had soon advanced some six miles. It seemed they had completely broken through when they reached Cagny but there they seemed to halt. In the rear, there was a scene of intense confusion, a tremendous number of vehicles trying to get down this severe bottle-neck. The Armoured, not wishing to go forward without the infantry following up, stopped. This allowed the enemy time to sort himself out.

* De Guingand, *Operation Victory*, p. 403.

It was the first time the Guards Armoured had gone into action, and they handled their tanks with typical dash and courage. But, at the opposite extreme to the excessively wary Desert Rats, they were sitting ducks for Rommel's well-sited 88s. Here the dangers of too little experience proved almost as injurious as too much of it, and their very freshness paid its heavy penalty. The Guards Armoured lost sixty tanks that day alone, while 'Pip' Roberts' 11th Armoured had ninety knocked out. The total British loss was nearly two hundred. 'Ronsons', they nicknamed the Shermans in the Guards Armoured, with little affection: 'One flick and it's alight!' One of the tanks destroyed carried 11th Armoured's Forward Air Controller, which meant that close air support was forfeited.

Back at Dempsey's headquarters there was dissatisfaction, once again, at the sluggishness of the 7th Armoured in closing up. Worse still was the separation that occurred between the armour and the infantry following up; again, it was the lack of any armoured personnel carrier that made itself particularly felt. This provoked a major row between Roberts (at thirty-seven the youngest divisional commander in the British Army, and reckoned to be its ablest tank commander) and O'Connor, whose tactics some felt still lay rooted in the Western Desert of 1941. A future Chief of the Defence Staff, Michael Carver, then commanding an armoured brigade at GOODWOOD, criticized Monty sharply for not having 'learnt the lesson from El Alamein that you cannot in open country move infantry up to support armour in lorries. Soft vehicles are no good.'

Gains on that first day of GOODWOOD could be measured in yards; it is difficult to see what persuaded Monty to signal Brooke, 'Operations this morning a total success.' Had his LOs let him down for once, or was he still playing to Ike and the air barons in the gallery? Charles Richardson could only suggest that 'he probably had a rush of euphoria; he was under great stress, with Winston and Brooke about to arrive at TAC – then, of course, exaggeration is a characteristic of the Ulsterman . . . !'* At a disastrously optimistic press conference held by Monty that day, Bill Williams, Monty's intelligence chief, recalled studying Alan Moorehead's expression of 'wonderful Australian disbelief': 'It was a ghastly performance. . . .

* Interview 26 November 1992.

The fact is you can't tell lies to the press and not expect to pay for it – it was as simple as that!'* As a result, the following day *The Times* proclaimed, 'SECOND ARMY BREAKS THROUGH'. It would not be long before Monty was made to reap the whirlwind.

On the 19th, Dempsey tried again, but his troops were tired and depleted. He claimed that there had been 'a maximum of fifty enemy tanks around Bourguébus', but the British armour proved hard to goad into accepting further losses. It was with his Canadian infantry that Monty now found himself disappointed; as early as the 8th, and again on the 16th, he had been complaining that Major-General Keller, commanding the 3rd Canadian Infantry Division, was 'not fit to command a Canadian division'. He had put this to the Canadian army chief, Crerar. Of Crerar he also had the poorest opinion; he had 'no real qualifications . . . to command an army; he is not a commander and inspires no confidence'. A week later: 'The real trouble is that Crerar wants to show at once that he is a great soldier; he has made a sad mess of the whole business; the truth of the matter is that he is a very poor soldier and has much to learn.' This was Monty at his most acidulous; but Keller had remained. On the 19th, Monty noted that the 3rd Canadians had been 'very slow' and that it would have 'helped to quicken up the whole business' if Crerar had taken his advice and sacked Keller.

On the 20th, another Normandy thunderstorm brought GOODWOOD to an end in a welter of mud, and imposed a further postponement to COBRA. Thus ended the last and biggest British (and Canadian) tank battle in Normandy. One division had lost over half its strength; overall it had cost Monty more than 400 tanks, or 36 per cent of his total strength in Normandy (though a number of them were recoverable), to 120 German. 'I was prepared to lose a couple of hundred tanks,' said Dempsey after the war, 'so long as I didn't lose men. We could afford tanks because they had begun to pile up in the bridgehead.'† Yet it was the nearly 6000 human casualties, comprising over 13 per cent of total British losses since D-Day, that had told Monty it was time to stop. Among the dead, killed with the Welsh Guards by a mortar splinter near Emiéville, was one of the

* Montgomery Collection. Interview 12 November 1992.
† Quoted in D'Este, *Decision in Normandy*, p. 387.

best-loved painters of his generation, a talent with a great future – Rex Whistler.

Recriminations and post-mortems were immediate and ferocious. There was particular rage among Crerar's Canadians, two of whose infantry battalions had lost over 200 men each. Ike was said to be 'blue as indigo' with fury; 'only seven miles were gained – can we afford a thousand tons of bombs per mile?' he exploded in the hearing of his aide, Captain Butcher.* Infantrymen, like Terry Coverdale with 3rd Division, later to become one of Monty's LOs, never understood why three armoured divisions had failed to break through: 'it was wonderful tank country'.† But, as far as armour was concerned, once again it was the inadequate British tanks that had failed in the face of the German 88s and dug-in Panthers.

Sackings followed swiftly. On 26 July, there was Bullen-Smith of 51st Highland Division ('The Division is "down" and will not fight,' Monty wrote in his diary, bitterly disappointed at the failure of the third of 'his' divisions from desert days). Kit Dawnay recalled an emotional scene when Monty told the unfortunate commander:

> 'You must go, the men won't fight for you, and you will go home now. . . .' Charles came out with tears pouring down his face. . . . Monty, deeply moved, said, 'If I don't remove you, Charles, men will be killed unnecessarily. You must go' – that was all.‡

Next came Erskine of 7th Armoured (possibly long overdue: 'he will not fight his division and take risks,' Monty wrote to 'Simbo' Simpson) and Bucknall of XXX Corps, both on 3 August. The Canadian, Keller, retained his command – until Allied bombers intervened.

At first sight, and particularly in the wake of all the expectations that Monty had himself so imprudently aroused, GOODWOOD seemed little short of a disaster. In terms of ground won, as Monty himself admitted after the war, he had still failed to gain that vital space east of the Orne; 'we had not yet pushed the extreme left flank up to the Dives'. Back in the VCIGS's office in Whitehall, Major Peter Earle noted, 'to my mind this has not gone well. With absolute superiority in armour, weapons, men, air, we have been held up by

* Butcher, *Three Years with Eisenhower*, p. 531.
† Interview 16 November 1992.
‡ Montgomery Collection.

the ragged remnants . . . of five PZ divs.' Yet reports seemed to indicate that 'tactically Monty had been successful', and on this basis Earle went on to predict that by September 'the German army will have collapsed. . . . Mark this well. I say that the German army will have collapsed, and the War will be over, with the British army west of the Seine and the US army to the south of it.'

Among the mass of the fighting men at the front, however, even after GOODWOOD and despite all the setbacks and the dreadful casualties, Monty's legendary popularity did not wane. The rank and file continued to trust him in the most remarkable fashion. 'The effect was always the same,' recalled Alan Moorehead:

> the same breathless interest that had nothing to do with discipline. Just for a moment here in the orchard or on the beach the General and the soldiers were completely at ease with one another, and all the frightening chances of war were reduced to a simple and sane community of friendship.*

But within the precincts of SHAEF, Whitehall, Washington and the media, his reputation now seemed impaired beyond recovery. Bradley, in his second book, compiled in extreme old age, claimed that 'Whatever hopes he [Montgomery] had of remaining overall ground commander died with Goodwood.'† In fact, as will be seen later, they would have died anyway once US forces exceeded the British in number.

Yet was all this odium entirely fair? One has to look at the long-term, strategic results of GOODWOOD, which became apparent within a matter of days. Years after the war, Richardson, ever loyal to Monty (though critical), reflected, 'I can't believe that Monty wanted to break out at GOODWOOD, but he *did* intend that the battle should be more successful than it was. . . . He would have been historically greater if he could have admitted that things didn't go according to plan.'‡ But that was Monty. Admitting his own error (in an extraordinarily rare *mea culpa*) Monty in his post-war memoirs

* Moorehead, *Montgomery*, p. 169.
† *A General's Life*, p. 274.
‡ Interview 26 November 1992.

did blame himself – 'partly' – for spreading illusions about the break-out:

> for I was too exultant at the press conference I gave during the GOODWOOD battle. I realize that now – in fact, I realized it pretty quickly afterwards. Basically the trouble was this – both Bradley and I agreed that we could not possibly tell the press the true strategy which formed the basis of all our plans. As Bradley said, 'We must grin and bear it.' It became increasingly difficult to grin.

That most sensible of American critics, Carlo D'Este, rates the series of operations round Caen as one of the 'most untidy' Monty ever conducted. True; but the terrain round Caen was as 'untidy' as any battlefield one could find – it was not the desert. And, as has already been indicated, the German Army had never fought with greater skill or with more desperate tenacity, quite unbroken by the overwhelming might of Allied air supremacy. As the next fortnight would prove, GOODWOOD ought to be regarded as a strategic success because of the way in which it continued to pin down Rommel's armour in the east just as Bradley was squaring up for the COBRA break-out in the west.

The figures are revealing: on 5 July, the number of German tanks facing the US First Army totalled 215, compared with 690 facing Dempsey (sixty-three infantry battalions to sixty-four); by the 10th, the number had sunk to 190 as against 610, and that figure of 190 remained constant right through to 25 July when COBRA was in full swing (comparable infantry figures had risen from eighty-five battalions to ninety-two).* The accepted view has to be that, if the Germans could have shifted one single battered Panzer division towards Bradley at the end of July, it would have made his break-out far more difficult and costly – if not actually impossible.

The fact that the British should have selected codenames from British equestrian terminology, EPSOM and GOODWOOD, may bring smiles to American faces. A much more suitable sport than racing from which to draw, however, would have been the bull-ring, PICADOR instead of GOODWOOD. One could note Liddell

* Montgomery, *Memoirs*, p. 259.

Hart's superb simile of the Matador's Cloak for the Manstein Plan that had conquered France in 1940: of the cloak waved in the north to distract the French from the terminal sword-blow which was going to be thrust home in the south. In Normandy, the parallel should be with the Picador, that grim, unromantic performer, little loved by the spectators of the bull-fight, who sits rocklike on his wretched steed's back* as he rams and twists his lance into the bull's powerful neck muscles. In this cruel sport, only when those neck muscles are destroyed to the extent that the proud bull can no longer raise his head to gore the matador, can the sword be plunged in between the shoulders.

This is, surely, precisely what Monty's strategy was all about, all along.†

Possibly the greatest spin-off of air barons' effort at GOODWOOD had been the fortuitous elimination, on its eve, of Monty's most dangerous and oldest adversary, Field Marshal Erwin Rommel, the Hector of the German camp. On 16 July, after returning from Caen Rommel had sent off what would turn out to be his last despatch to Hitler, warning of 'a grave crisis' and the impending certainty of an Allied breakthrough, ending with words that were ultimately to sign his death warrant: 'It is urgently necessary for the proper conclusion to be drawn from this situation. As C-in-C of the Army Group I feel myself in duty bound to speak plainly on this point.'‡

Meanwhile, in Germany a deadly conspiracy against Hitler was reaching fruition (though unbeknown to Rommel). That same day, at Blay, Johnny Henderson was recording this conversation:

* Usually a broken-down nag; but Dempsey's and Crerar's armies were certainly not that!

† Account should perhaps be taken of what might be called the Terraine Principle. The military historian John Terraine remains one of the few diehard supporters of Field Marshal Earl Haig's strategy on the Western Front of 1914–18, so appallingly costly in British lives. Terraine postulates, quite simply, that you cannot make an omelette without breaking eggs, that there are no short cuts to winning a modern, total war without inflicting massive casualties. In the Second World War, he points out, the breaking down of the German Army was done this time on the Russian front, where the Verduns and Sommes of the 1940s took place – out of sight of Western eyes.

‡ Liddell Hart (ed.), *The Rommel Papers*, pp. 486–7.

> General Browning (Commander of all the airborne divs)* asked General Monty today if he would like to have Rommel bumped off. By dropping the odd parachutist they have found his HQ and know where he goes down to fish and shoot pigeons. General Monty said 'Yes' – so the party is going to be arranged.†

It was unnecessary. The very next day, returning in his staff car to La Roche Guyon, Rommel was strafed by two of Broadhurst's fighter-bombers in the preliminaries to GOODWOOD. Ironically, the village near where it happened was called St Foy de Montgomery, after his adversary's crusader ancestor.

The driver lost his left arm, and Rommel was thrown out of the car with splinter injuries to his face and four fractures of the skull. After recovering in hospital, several weeks later he gave orders that he should be transported back to Germany, so as not to fall into the hands of the advancing Allies. This sealed his fate, and possibly prolonged the war another eight months. Rommel never gave another order in Normandy.

Three days after his wounding, there took place at Hitler's 'Wolf's Lair' in East Prussia the historic Stauffenberg bomb attempt. Rommel, the professional soldier, committed to his *Soldateneid*,‡ was genuinely shocked. His attitude towards Hitler was by now highly complex. On the one hand – deeply pessimistic ever since Montgomery had secured his foothold in Normandy – he was seriously contemplating a 'separate' peace, something along the lines of 1918, in which his armies in the west would have laid down their arms, while (notionally) keeping the Russians at bay in the east. On the other hand, though his Chief of Staff, Speidel, was close to the plotters, Rommel profoundly disapproved of any *attentat* against

* Whose daughter Tessa was by curious dynastic fate later to marry David Montgomery.

† Henderson diary, 16 July 1944. This conversation, hitherto unrevealed, is now confirmed in an excellent study of Rommel, *Knight's Cross*, by General Sir David Fraser, published 1993 (p. 512). It appears that, while Browning was with Monty on the 16th, the head of the SAS in England was applying for approval to parachute a detachment into France to 'kill or kidnap and remove to England Field Marshal Rommel or any senior members of his staff'. Approval was not granted till the 20th, the operation then scheduled to take place on the night of 25/26 July. By this time, however, it was superfluous; Rommel having been eliminated by more orthodox means.

‡ 'The Soldier's Oath', of ancient and almost holy significance in the German military tradition.

the head of state. His first letter since being wounded, from his military hospital in France, admits to his wife that it had 'left me badly shattered. We must thank God that it passed off as well as it did.'* Back at home near Ulm in Württemberg, the convalescent Field Marshal could not sleep; he and his fifteen-year-old son would talk till 3 a.m., the longest that they had been so close together (something not granted his opposite number, David Montgomery: 'an experience I never had'). 'Of course my father knew that the battle for Normandy was lost,'† Manfred told his friend David at a reunion to mark the fiftieth anniversary of the Battle of Alamein:

> he knew this since the first days. But what they‡ tried to do was first to convince Hitler to surrender, but this was not possible. And then they prepared surrendering on their own responsibility, in France, in order to let the Americans and British enter central Europe; but this, of course, was not so easy. It was not possible for all of the German Army to turn their rifles and march against Hitler. And my father delayed because there could be a psychological situation to surrender the very moment of the Allied penetration through the German front. As you know, my father also for the first time in his life had SS troops under his command.
>
> ... Probably my father was wrong, but he never believed that there would really be a plot against Hitler. He believed that the whole responsibility was on the Commander-in-Chief in the West, to end the war in good time.

The bomb plot, Rommel told his son,§ was 'stupid': 'The revolt should not have been started in Berlin, but in the west.' The only hope would have been that:

> the forcible American and British occupation of Germany would have become an unopposed 'march-in', that the air attacks would have ceased, and that the Americans and British would have kept

* Liddell Hart (ed.), *The Rommel Papers*, p. 493.

† It appears that as early as March 1943, Rommel, with a true Scorpio's swings of mood from elation to pessimism (in sharp contrast to Monty's cold balance), had already told his subordinate, Colonel Hans von Luck (later to command a key regiment of the 21st Panzer Division in Normandy) that the war was already lost (Ambrose, *Pegasus Bridge*, p. 57).

‡ That is, Speidel and the other army conspirators.

§ Liddell Hart (ed.), *The Rommel Papers*, p. 486.

> the Russians out of Germany.* As for Hitler, the best thing would have been to have presented him with an accomplished fact.

It was probably this argument, thought Lieutenant-General Fritz Bayerlein,† that 'brought Rommel and Speidel to the decision to open independent peace negotiations with the Western Allies, after they had been finally forced to the realization that the German front in France would collapse within a few weeks'. Everything had been prepared, claimed Bayerlein, when, on 17 July, 'fate intervened'.‡

For three months after learning that Germany's most popular soldier had been advocating a separate peace, Hitler held his hand. On 14 October, two generals arrived at Rommel's house, bringing him the option of taking poison or appearing before a 'people's court'.§ Rommel took the first option. Thus disappeared from the scene Monty's twice-defeated opponent, the Desert Fox, the Hector of the German Army in Normandy. No Briton who had ever fought against him, either in the desert or in Normandy, regarded Rommel as anything other than an honourable soldier. Yet the myth grew in the post-war era, fostered by the story of his death and complemented by the many books and movies deifying Rommel, that he had long been anti-Hitler. In fact he had remained totally loyal to the Nazi war machine until Normandy persuaded him that the war was unwinnable. Nevertheless, while a short-term gain for the Allies, his death may have proved a long-term net loss – insofar as, with his immense reputation, he was the one German military leader who could conceivably have brought about a large-scale military surrender after the Battle of Normandy was lost. However naïve the concept, possibly Rommel saw himself as a latter-day Yorck von Wartenburg, who at Tauroggen in 1812 negotiated the famous separate peace with the invading Russians, thereby enabling them to march against Napoleon unopposed. The ifs of history are always perilous, but what misery might have been saved had Hector survived to surrender

* In view of the demand for 'unconditional surrender', not to mention undertakings given to Stalin, this was an illusory hope.

† Rommel's Chief of Staff in Afrika Korps, who commanded the elite Panzer Lehr Division in Normandy.

‡ Liddell Hart (ed.), *The Rommel Papers*, p. 488.

§ Such as, in mocking trials, had sentenced to death the brave officers tracked down after the failure of 20 July.

to Achilles: hundreds of thousands of young lives, a hecatomb of Jews in the concentration camps, Dresden and possibly Hiroshima?

As far as Monty and the immediate battle were concerned, from the moment he learned of Rommel's removal from command he lost all interest in the man. The picture above his table in the caravan disappeared, to be replaced by that of Rundstedt, his new adversary. There was absolutely no sentimentalism, nor any gesture of triumph; he simply ceased to talk – or even think – about his old foe. Certainly he would make no morbid pilgrimage to St Foy de Montgomery, where Rommel had been struck down.

Immediately in the wake of these great events, on 21 July an explosive Churchill arrived at Monty's TAC HQ at Blay. There was little secret among the young officers of the entourage that he had come for the head of the 'Chief'. Planning to visit Normandy on the 20th, Churchill had been enraged to learn from Ike that he had been asked by Monty to keep all visitors away during GOODWOOD.* This act of tactlessness was so out of character with that supreme diplomat that one can only assume that it reflected both the conspiratorial pressure of Tedder at SHAEF and Ike's own anger at the calling off of GOODWOOD and its apparent failure. On the night of the 19th, Brooke was summoned to the bedside of a furious Churchill, wearing a new blue and gold dressing-gown, but in an unholy rage: 'What was Monty doing dictating to him; he had every right to visit France when he wanted? Who was Monty to stop him?'† After all, Churchill declared, in the last war when he had been Minister of Munitions, Haig had always allowed him to visit. At the War Office, Peter Earle recorded that Churchill 'was furious, like a child. A storm in a teacup of the first magnitude was whipped up.' To Ike, the Prime Minister wrote, in petulance, '. . . I have no intention of visiting General Montgomery's Headquarters, and he should not concern himself about me in any way, except that he should provide a Staff Officer who could show me about,' while to Brooke he declared, ominously,

* It should perhaps be recalled that, as well as GOODWOOD, this was the very time that TAC was embroiled in the looted-pig drama – possibly not the most opportune moment for a visit from the Prime Minister (see Chapter 6).
† Bryant, *Triumph in the West*, p. 234.

'If however General Montgomery disputes about it in any way, the matter will be taken up officially, because I have both a right and a duty to acquaint myself with the facts on the spot.'

After two such onslaughts in a fortnight, Brooke realized that his protégé Monty was in the gravest danger of his whole career and flew off to Normandy on the 20th to warn him. Monty explained that Bradley had just had a visit from the American Secretary of War, Stimson, the fire-eating 'Colonel' (as he was nicknamed). Stimson had stayed 'so long that orders for an attack could not be got out, and the attack had to be postponed for twenty-four hours'. According to his diaries, Brooke led Monty to his caravan and, virtually at the CIGS's dictation, Monty sat down and wrote an emollient (if somewhat disingenuous) letter to the enraged Prime Minister, saying that 'this is the first I have heard of your visit', and continuing with almost an excess of unction:

> I hope that you will come over here whenever you like; I have recently been trying to keep visitors away as we have much on hand.
>
> But you are quite different, and in your capacity as Minister of Defence you naturally are above all these rules.

He hoped that the Prime Minister would stay in one of his caravans, 'which will be held ready for you at any time'. The letter, according to Brooke, 'worked like magic'. Apparently forgetting that the CIGS had just been over in Normandy that day, Churchill rang to tell him, 'I have just had such a nice letter from Monty; he wants me to come to France whenever I like.'

That night Brooke recorded 'a bad night with buzz-bombs, finishing off with one well within the quarter-mile radius of this flat'. Meanwhile, his scientific adviser had come to warn of 'impending rocket attacks' by the German V-2s. Three days later it was his sixty-first birthday, but he 'almost felt like seventy-one'.

Clearly Monty still remained in great peril, however. On the afternoon of the 20th, the day GOODWOOD had been called off, Ike came again to Blay, where the bleakest exchange to date took place. Evidently Monty had stressed his deep concern about British manpower and casualties, and suggested that the Americans were better placed to accept the burden. This was followed the next day by a brusque letter from Ike, reminding him that 'eventually the American ground strength will necessarily be much greater than the British. But while we have equality in size we must go forward shoulder to shoulder, with honors and sacrifices equally shared.' Was the tone perhaps indicative of a grave error on Monty's part, his inability to open up to Ike much earlier on all his concerns about the 'flawed instrument'? Earlier in what must have seemed to Monty a rather governessy letter, Ike had stressed, 'I feel that you should insist that Dempsey keep up the strength of his attack.' This was the nearest to a direct order, indeed a rebuke, that Ike had passed to Monty during the whole campaign so far, though to the ever-hostile Tedder it was 'not strong enough. . . . It contains no *order*.'

When Churchill reached Blay, however, Monty – surrounded by his dogs and canaries (Churchill was always susceptible to canary allure, as he himself had one that sat on his head while in bed, to the eternal discomfort of visiting VIPs) – immediately deployed his most potent charms, exuding self-confidence and optimism. (This latter was, in fact, now quite genuine, in that ULTRA signals showed that GOODWOOD had, as he hoped, left the Germans facing Bradley, where the break-out was shortly to take place, seriously under strength.) 'Setbacks? What setbacks? The battle is going excellently according to plans,' was how Alan Moorehead reconstructed the scene.* The officers at TAC were bursting with curiosity to know what had happened in Germany the previous day, Brigadier Bill Williams having gleaned from 'scraps of ULTRA' that there had been a 'sort of revolution'.† Monty was 'most intrigued and like a schoolboy', and eventually put a direct question. 'Winston', Williams recalled:

> was completely nonplussed. He sat on the only stool in Monty's map caravan and looked at us in silence for a moment. Then I remember very clearly he produced a long chain with keys on it and unlocked two despatch boxes. . . . 'There is something about it in here – see what you can find.'

There now ensued an extraordinary scene as Monty and Williams 'scrabbled' through a jumble of mixed-up papers, including ULTRA

* *Montgomery*, p. 204.
* Quoted in Lamb, *Montgomery in Europe*, pp. 143–4.

signals, the greatest secret of the war. 'I suddenly realized', Williams remembered, 'that Winston had come from London with all this stuff in his despatch case unread, and that he was "naked" in face of the possible sudden end of the war'.* Williams was amazed that the Prime Minister could have been so 'unbriefed' about this colossal piece of news. Monty, however, was 'excited like a schoolboy at the possibility of surrender that morning'.†

Most important was the encouraging news Monty was able to give the Prime Minister about the prospects for COBRA, which, had it not been for the bad weather that had brought GOODWOOD to a close, should have started on the 20th. After his departure, Monty wrote to 'Simbo' Simpson, 'The PM has just been here very friendly.' He sent him off with a bottle of cognac 'as a peace offering'. It was an unusually astute psychological ploy, knowing Churchill's *faiblesse* and that brandy was currently as rare as hens' teeth in London. 'And everything was made clear,' Monty wrote in his campaign diary, 'I told him that whenever he got angry in future he was to send me a telegram and find out the truth. He promised to do so.' Thus Monty was saved to fight another day by that tempestuous volatility of Winston Churchill's which oscillated constantly between love and hate. At TAC, Johnny Henderson clearly recalled being left with the impression that he was 'going to be given another month'.‡ On his return to London, Ike grumbled to Butcher that Monty had 'obviously sold Winston "a bill of goods"', and then criticized Monty's 'slowness' to Churchill – all of which was passed back. Brooke and Monty, in their turn, were both greatly angered. D'Este claims that Monty was 'stung by Ike's remarks and never forgave',§ ultimately taking his revenge in his memoirs. Brooke groaned in his diaries, not for the first or last time, that it was clear 'that Ike knows nothing about strategy'. Tedder fumed, but then was silenced – though it was utter self-delusion to imagine that Britain's most popu-

* Quoted in Lamb, *Montgomery in Europe*, pp. 143–4.

† In fact, hamstrung as it was by the principle of 'unconditional surrender', British official reactions to overtures put out by the brave Germans around Stauffenberg were frigid, to say the least. Not untypical of attitudes was Major Peter Earle's diary entry for 20 July: 'No one need have taken much notice of this incident – it could well have been attributed to a madman – had not Hitler . . . made a series of hysterical and contradictory speeches.'

‡ Montgomery Collection.

§ D'Este, *Decision in Normandy*, p. 398.

lar soldier could have been sacked at that point, on the brink of the greatest triumph, without inflicting a terrible wound upon British *amour propre*. Undoubtedly, had the forthcoming Operation COBRA collapsed in a welter of blood and recrimination (as indeed it looked like doing in its early stages), it would have been questionable whether Monty could have long survived.

Nobody, however, could have foretold that, within a matter of days, the whole situation was to be so dramatically reversed.

'The weather', Monty noted glumly in his diary on the day Churchill left him, repeating a familiar formula, 'has been ghastly; pouring rain all day. The attack of First US Army could not take place.' The anxiety must have been appalling for Monty that day. Everything – not least his own personal survival – now depended on the capricious Normandy weather, just as it had during that other time of extreme strain, 5 June. The same applied the following day, the 23rd, a Sunday. Monty recorded attending 'our usual Sunday service in the local R.C. Church.'* It can be safely assumed that his prayers would have been particularly fervent that day. Still the weather remained 'too bad for air action'. At the other end of the front, Bradley was heard to exclaim grimly, 'I'm going to have to court-martial the Chaplain if we have much more weather like this.' In England, tossing away a soggy cigarette, his nerves at snapping point, Ike declared gloomily that it was 'going to be the death of me yet'.† The one consolation, and a truly remarkable one, was – as recorded by Peter Earle in the War Office on the 20th – 'the almost unbelievable success of our deception plan. It is quite incredible that today, seven weeks after the campaign was started, twenty German divs including two PZ divs are stationed . . . north of the Seine, awaiting the arrival of a notional Army Group "led by General Patton".' But, he continued, 'This ruse cannot hold much beyond the end of July when moon and tide are right for landing. Thus we see that Monty has about a fortnight more to break out.'

* Johnny Henderson noted that there had been a 'first-class ecclesiastical row' when the Roman Catholic chaplains heard that Monty was using the Catholic church.

† Ambrose (1), p. 462.

In every sense time was running short. Even on the now expanded US front there was a crisis of space, with not enough of it yet to bring in the troops waiting in England and back in the US. These included Patton's forces. On 18 July, after the bloodiest of fights, Bradley had registered an important victory (and one up on Monty, still apparently stuck at Caen) by capturing the ruined centre of St Lô, but he had suffered nearly 11,000 casualties in the process. The Americans had now landed 770,000 troops (of which almost 10 per cent had become casualties) to the 591,000 of the combined British and Canadians (who had lost 49,000 men by 23 July) – thus already establishing a significant numerical superiority. But still Bradley had not been able to break out of the wretched labyrinth of the bocage on either side of St-Lô.

On the 24th, COBRA was billed to begin at 1300 hours, but was cancelled yet again because of the weather. Nevertheless, a terrible thing happened. Some 1600 US bombers set off from England. They 'could not see the target because of mist', Monty recorded tersely in his diary, 'and returned to England. But some dropped their bombs before they could be stopped.' As a result, 700 tons of bombs rained down on the US front line, killing twenty-five American soldiers and wounding 131. It was the kind of nightmare every commander dreads – not least Monty, on whom it would make an important impact, with strategic consequences, during the next critical stage of the battle. But it *happens*, in the best-ordered armies; it happened in the Second World War more often than people at home ever realized, with commanders automatically accepting a figure of 5 to 10 per cent of casualties caused by 'friendly fire'. In Normandy, on the British and Canadian sectors, the RAF were sometimes guilty and (less forgivably) the home-team gunners – though never on quite the same scale as during COBRA. Bradley was apoplectic: it seemed like a clear breach of faith by the airmen, who had promised to make their bomb run parallel to the St Lô–Périers road, but had instead made it at right angles. The airmen counter-charged, blaming the brief they had been given.

Yet, the very next day, in the urgency to press ahead with COBRA come what may, with Ike running 'up and down the line like a football coach, exhorting everyone to aggressive action',* and Tedder fussing him with disloyal telephone calls to ask 'why Monty was not doing more and what Eisenhower was doing about it',† it happened again – only worse. The commander of the hapless 30th Division, which was hit for the second day running, described it as:

> horrible. The ground belched, shook and spewed dirt to the sky. Scores of our troops were hit, their bodies flung from the slit trenches. Dazed and frightened ... doughboys were quivering in their holes. ... An old front-line campaigner [another general] said it was the most terrifying thing he had ever seen.‡

Bradley was anguished: ' "Oh Christ," I cried, "not another short drop?" '§ The airmen were unrepentant; in the investigation that ensued, they blamed the smoke and the dust obscuring target identification and insisted that their bombs had fallen 'within the normal expectance of errors'. Years afterward, Bradley declared that they had 'simply lied'.|| Back at SHAEF there was consternation; but the lesson had been learned that 'heavy bombers cannot be used in tactical support', and Ike pledged that this would be 'the last one'. It cost the Americans 111 killed and 490 wounded; among the dead was a lieutenant-general, Lesley McNair, the highest-ranking Allied officer to be killed in north-west Europe. McNair had just been designated commander of the phantom army group in England to replace Patton, 'whose presence in Normandy', says D'Este, 'could not be kept a secret much longer'. As a result, McNair was buried in utmost secrecy, to avoid compromising FORTITUDE. After the war the US War College in Washington DC was named after him.

What, in his deep distress and anger at the 'own goal' disaster, could not be seen by Bradley at the time was that things were infinitely worse on the enemy side. Bayerlein's Panzer Lehr Division was the principal armoured formation facing Bradley. The bombing

* In the words of Bedell Smith (*Saturday Evening Post*, 15 June 1946) as quoted by Chester Wilmot in *The Struggle for Europe*, p. 362. Wilmot noted that Captain Butcher's simile was 'even less flattering ... "Ike is like a blind dog in a meat house – he can smell it, but he can't find it." '

† Ambrose (1), p. 463.

‡ Hansen diary, 25 July 1944.

§ *A Soldier's Story*, p. 348.

|| *A General's Life*, p. 279.

of the 24th, so punishing to the Americans, did little damage; but Bayerlein wrote of the 25th, 'It was hell. . . . My front lines looked like a landscape on the moon, and at least 70 per cent of my personnel were out of action – dead, wounded, crazed or numbed.'

He had only fifteen tanks left in reserve to meet the American attack: 'a new SS tank battalion was coming in with sixty tanks to drive to the Vire River and cut off the Americans. They arrived – five tanks, not sixty.'* There was no option 'but retreat'. Yet still the fragile crust held. By the evening of the 25th, troops of Bradley's 30th Division, doubtless badly shaken by the bombing ('two successive days of bombing took the ginger out of our front-line troops', wrote General Courtney Hodges),† had advanced less than two miles, with the surviving German artillery hitting back hard. The 26th seemed equally indecisive.

Meanwhile, to the east, with superb timing and under the inspired Canadian II Corps Commander, Lieutenant-General Guy Simonds, Monty had unleashed the Canadians to attack towards Falaise. Striking without the usual give-away of a preliminary softening-up bombardment, Simonds suffered 1500 casualties in a single day and gained little territory, but, in the words of Stephen Ambrose, the Canadians 'did effectively screen the major offensives and delayed a German shift of reserves to the United States Front'. Ambrose, so often highly critical of Monty, goes on to make a crucial admission: 'German reinforcements came too late. Montgomery's insistence on drawing the Germans to Second Army's front was about to pay huge dividends.'‡ It came just in time – as in New York the *Herald Tribune* was proclaiming gleefully, 'ALLIES IN FRANCE BOGGED DOWN ON ENTIRE FRONT', and in London *The Times* was criticizing Monty for his 'breakthrough' talk during GOODWOOD.

On the 25th, Ike paid another visit to Monty. He was suffering from high blood pressure, doubtless a consequence of all the nights of lost sleep caused by the buzz-bombs. To Monty he:

> talked a good deal about public opinion in America and hinted that there was a feeling that the US troops were doing more than British

* Liddell Hart Archives. Liddell Hart (ed.), *The Rommel Papers*, pp. 487–91.

† Quoted in Lamb, *Montgomery in Europe*, p. 150.

‡ Ambrose (1), p. 466.

troops. This was proved, to their own satisfaction, by the fact that they had more casualties and captured more prisoners.

Nevertheless, Monty continued, 'He was very pleasant about everything. I assured him that the British troops on the eastern front would not stop but would continue hard.' Beneath the 'pleasantness', one can assume that Monty was seething at Ike's relaying to him the digs of the US press in this manner. The previous week when Brooke, during his visit, had put the same issue to him, Monty had reacted violently, writing savagely in his personal diary, 'This is amazing. The bigger American casualties are due to their lack of skill in fighting.'

This was also the very day when Ike, in despair at what looked like the failure of COBRA and under renewed pressure from his awe-inspiring boss, General Marshall, was finally about to call for Monty's sacking. But by now Churchill had swung solidly behind him.

On the 27th, Bradley's most hard-hitting commander, and Monty's favourite, 'Lightning Joe' Collins, broke through with his VII Corps at St Gilles, just west of St Lô. Collins was employing a 'secret weapon' of amazing simplicity. Called 'Rhino', it consisted of heavy tusk-like prongs, fabricated out of steel salvaged from Rommel's underwater obstacles and welded on the front of the Shermans. Used like a bulldozer, it drove through the deadly hedgerows of the bocage with sheer force, while keeping down the vulnerable nose of the tank. It was a design that might have been borrowed from the despised 'specials' of Monty's brother-in-law, 'Hobo' Hobart; and, like so many simple inventions, it was remarkable that it had not been thought up many weeks – and lives – previously. The 'last pitiful remnants'* of Bayerlein's once proud Panzer Lehr Division were rounded up. Bayerlein, Monty's old opponent in the desert, having had six cars shot up under him during the campaign, made a miraculous escape through the American lines – only to be captured later. 'The Americans', he recorded, 'were now pouring through into the open country with nobody to stop them – just as Rommel had predicted.' On the right of Lightning Joe, Middleton's VIII Corps,

* Liddell Hart (ed.), *The Rommel Papers*, p. 490.

vanguard of Patton's new Third Army, suddenly found its advance virtually unchecked. On 30 July, six days after all had looked so black for the prospects of COBRA, it had reached the key town of Avranches, at the base of the Cotentin Peninsula and on the hinge of Brittany and Normandy. A new sense of exhilaration, not experienced since the taking of Cherbourg, gripped the Americans. This was the kind of warfare God had designed them for – the mantle of Lee, Jeb Stuart and Sherman was upon them, the days of slogging before Fredericksburg and of the murderous 'sunken lanes' of Virginia were over. The breakthrough had been achieved; the most decisive phase of the campaign now began.

Two days later, on 1 August, Patton was unleashed, his Third Army officially operational and all pretence of the now unnecessary FORTITUDE deception discarded. The US 12 Army Group now came into being, under command of a promoted Bradley, who was replaced at the head of US First Army by General Hodges. Monty recorded in his diary for that day, 'I now command: 12 Army Group,* Second British Army, First Canadian Army.' In fact, as becomes clear from the tenor of his diary and the correspondence with the Americans, with the creation of 12 Army Group, formal recognition of US numerical pre-eminence in north-west Europe and the arrival of the unrestrainable Patton, Monty's control over Bradley and his troops was progressively nominal. With all the questionable consequences for the coalition's future prosecution of the war, the individual commanders, prima donnas all, would increasingly do their own thing. Most notable, of course, was George S. Patton Jr, over whom Bradley and Ike himself had singularly little control; about the only person who did was the strong-minded Beatrice – and she was conveniently 7000 miles away. Certainly, in terms of Wellington's famous remark about his generals, he would have 'frightened' the Iron Duke.

By the evening of 1 August, the US 4th Armoured Division under Patton – the commander who (but for Ike, backing him as Brooke had Monty) had several times so narrowly escaped spending the rest of the war under a cloud and in obscurity in the US – had sliced

* Which Monty had originally assumed would be called 1 Army Group (see p. 200).

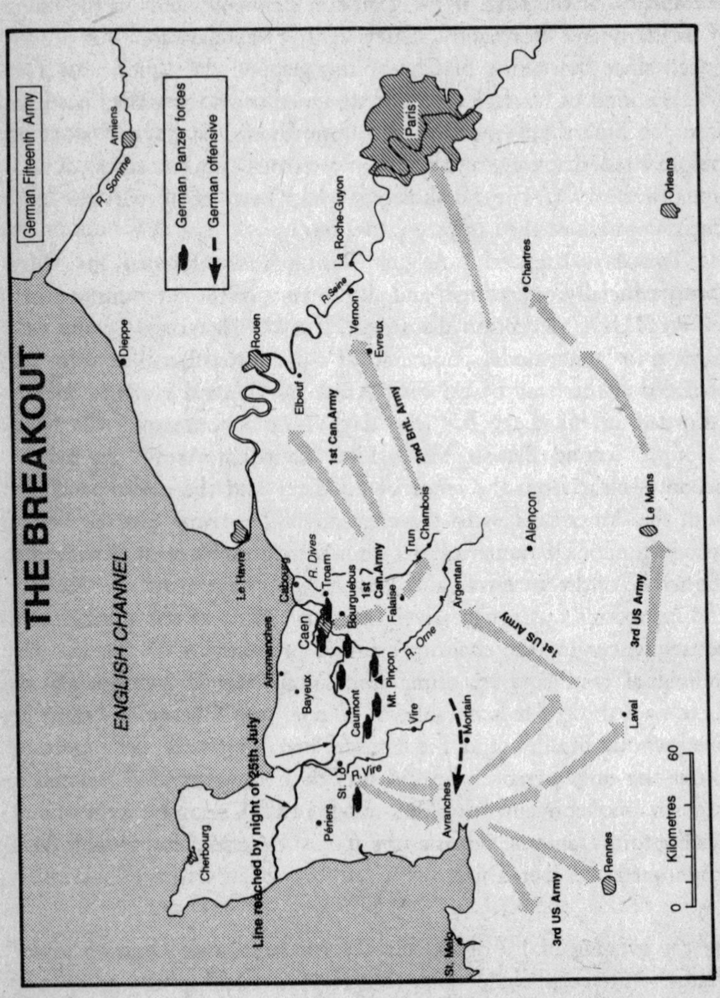

The Break-out

into Brittany, reaching Rennes forty miles away. Patton's mission, assigned by Bradley, was first to isolate Brittany, then to seize the main ports like St Malo, Lorient and Brest, to replace the overloaded beaches of Normandy (with Cherbourg still far from operational). Only then was he to swing eastwards. With the dreadful memories of the bocage and slow infantry slogging in the style of the First World War so recently behind, the Americans assumed that the capture of Brittany would be no pushover. But the astonishing vacuum that suddenly appeared before their eyes was irresistible. In his 'General Operational Situation and Directive' of 6 August, M-517, Monty, noting that Patton had reached the sea at Vannes on the southern coast of Brittany and was rapidly occupying the whole peninsula, gave the order to 'pivot on our left... swing hard with our right along the southern flank and in towards Paris... drive the enemy up against the R. Seine'. Bradley was totally in agreement with this important change of direction. Who actually was progenitor of it has been argued by historians ever since, though (as may be recalled from the hotly disputed phase-lines map of May) the thrust to the Seine was always uppermost among Monty's intentions. There is the barest mention of Brittany in M-517 – except that 'No more troops will be used for this task than are necessary, as the main business lies to the east.'*

Nevertheless, Patton, on the loose, went ahead and committed the whole of Middleton's fast and hard-hitting VIII Corps, with Haislip's XV Corps standing by, to Brittany – then struck off at a tangent due south to seize Nantes. Thereby, with an audacity verging on rashness typical of this Diomede, without waiting for orders or worrying about anything so humdrum as logistics or his flank, he left his umbilical cord with the bulk of Bradley's forces in the Cotentin and Normandy, via the narrow hinge at Avranches, highly vulnerable. Patton's diversion into Brittany has been criticized, variously, as one of the great errors of the campaign. Ambrose argues the merits of the case most judiciously: in the event the Brittany ports were not cleared until too late for the campaign (the fate of Cherbourg should have instructed Ike); if Middleton had been strongly reinforced, possibly he could have taken them sooner; on the other hand Patton

* The words repeat a telegram to Brooke of two days previously.

would not then have been strong enough for the crucial action just ahead at Falaise. Ambrose concludes, pointedly, that it was possible, 'had Eisenhower ignored Brittany altogether and sent Middleton toward Falaise [due east, instead of south and west], he could have achieved a greater success there'.* But, in one of the most damning criticisms of his subject, he goes on to conclude that instead Ike 'failed everywhere. Patton was too weak at Falaise, and Middleton was too weak in Brittany. The policy of scattering forces had nothing to recommend it, especially in view of Eisenhower's insistence on DRAGOON [ANVIL].'† Here is an insight fundamental to Ike's whole philosophy of war, of 'bulling ahead on all fronts', which would return to plague his relations with Monty in the next stage of the campaign, and (as Monty always felt) possibly even delay the ending of the war.

On the 3rd, after six weeks in the pastures of Blay, Monty shifted his TAC HQ to the Forêt de Cerisy – to be close (for the first time in the campaign) to Main, which had at last arrived from England. Two days later he wrote in his personal diary, 'The general situation is now so good that I can issue my orders for the destruction of the German forces south of the Seine.' This was serious talk. Two days later he was recording the launch of a predictable and heavy German riposte against Patton's exposed lines of communication at Mortain: 'up to four Pz. divisions were used'. Because of ULTRA, it did not come as a total surprise, although, as so often with a German initiative, it struck with uncomfortably greater punch than expected. Code-named LÜTTICH (German for Liège) after Ludendorff's great victory which had opened the way to the Kaiser's great encirclement strategy in France, thirty years previously to the day, its aim was clearly to drive through to Avranches, no more than fifteen miles from the German spearhead. This Mortain offensive', the first on this scale since D-Day, was a personal gamble by Hitler, liberating armour from the Fifteenth Army pinned down in the Pas de Calais,

* This was certainly the view of one of Patton's divisional commanders, Major-General John S. Wood of the fast-moving 4th Armoured, who, in despair, protested, 'We're winning this war the wrong way, we ought to be going toward Paris.' Ever afterwards Wood was convinced that Patton's decision was 'one of the colossally stupid decisions of the war', reckoning that he could otherwise have reached Chartres in two days (see Frank Price, *Middleton*, p. 188).

† Ambrose (1), pp. 469–71.

now that FORTITUDE was at last blown. It came far too late to affect the battle, but was unpleasant enough to suggest what might have happened to the Allied invasion forces had FORTITUDE failed to deceive. As it was, Bayerlein reckoned that it might well have 'resulted in a resounding victory' but for Allied air superiority.* Monty gave orders to 'put the whole of 2nd T.A.F. [Tactical Air Force] on to deal with the attacks' – its pilots claimed 120 tanks destroyed – while Ike boldly guaranteed to supply Patton with 2000 tons of supplies daily, if he were to be cut off. Patton was ordered to halt his advance and be ready to take a defensive position. Informed by ULTRA of what Hitler was up to, and the exact scale of his attacking forces, Bradley and his subordinates reacted coolly and professionally, the attacked GIs with stalwart heroism. To some British observers, without intent to patronize, it seemed to be the moment when the American Army had at last come of age.

Still shaken from the effects of the 20 July bomb, Hitler persisted in reinforcing failure, despite the protests of Rommel's successor, Field Marshal von Kluge, and the Seventh Army commander, Hausser, who had replaced Dollmann. This renewal of the attack Hausser described as 'a death blow not only to the Seventh Army but also to the entire Wehrmacht in the west', to which Kluge (himself in fear of implication by the 20 July conspirators, currently under torture) replied simply that it was 'a *Führerbefehl*'. Hausser was shortly to be proved correct in his prediction. At Mortain, Hitler had placed the forces in Normandy in the deadliest of traps. By the night of the 8th, Kluge was forced to disengage – despite Hitler's ranted orders.

The Allies', and Monty's, supreme moment had arrived. On the 7th, in his personal diary, Monty recognized that the enemy Mortain effort westwards was 'a real mistake; if he persists here I will turn the southern wing up northwards to Alençon and Argentan and get in behind him'. By coincidence, it was the day that the Supreme Commander landed to establish his first command post in Normandy, in an orchard near Tournières. Like Monty he had assembled a menagerie of pets: 'the peppiest little black tomcat you can imagine',† given him by Tedder and christened Shaef; then there was

* Liddell Hart (ed.), *The Rommel Papers*, p. 490.

† Quoted in Irving, *The War Between the Generals*, pp. 237–8.

a tan-coloured cocker spaniel – called Monty. 'Shaef has no truck with Monty,' claimed Harry Butcher. 'He chases Monty away.' And there was Ike's Irish driver–mistress, Kay Summersby – with the beloved Scottie, Telek, kept safely in reserve back at Telegraph Cottage.

The day after Ike's arrival, 8 August, Bradley outlined to him a new concept to trap the German Seventh Army with a 'short' left hook, between the Canadians now advancing on Falaise from the north and Patton swinging up from the south to Argentan. To the visiting US Secretary of the Treasury, Henry Morgenthau, Bradley described it as 'an opportunity that comes to a commander not more than once in a century. . . . We're about to destroy an entire hostile army.'* In whose mind the notion of the 'Falaise Trap' first occurred has been obscured in the passage of years by the claims and counter-claims of the principals and their knight-errant historians. Possibly it was a case of great minds thinking alike, for Monty's diary entries for the 8th and 9th suggest that the thinking was entirely shared between Bradley and himself. Monty, however, also had in mind a longer 'hook', a wider enveloping movement concurrently 'to the Seine about Paris' – though de Guingand and Williams here supported Bradley. 'It was obvious that if we could bring off both these movements we could virtually annihilate the enemy in Normandy,' wrote Monty after the war.

The trap was set. Could it be closed?

Meanwhile, to the east, on the British and Canadian front† on 28 July Monty had ordered a further attack by Dempsey – called BLUECOAT and scheduled for the 30th – to lend extra support for Bradley's break-out. Monty in his orders to Dempsey instructed 'all caution to be thrown overboard, every risk to be taken, and all troops to be told to put everything into it'. Instead of trying to batter a way out of that congested area east of the Orne once again, he would attack south from Caumont with the objective of capturing the dominant feature of Mont Pinçon, to disrupt the rear of General Hausser's forces facing Avranches. On the 29th, Monty had visited

* Bradley, *A Soldier's Story*, p. 424.

† By 23 July the Canadian commitment had risen to a whole army, the Canadian First.

Bradley, where he found the Americans 'quite happy'. Ike was there, 'and we had a talk':

> Ike is not an easy person to have 'listening in' when you are having a conference with your subordinates; he cannot stop 'butting in' and talking – always at the top of his voice. He is so keen that you cannot be angry with him; but it is a nuisance. I like him very much but I could never live in the same house as him; he cannot talk calmly and quietly. . . .

At first, the hard-hitting 11th Armoured under 'Pip' Roberts did well, driving a deep wedge between Hausser's Seventh Army and the newly constituted, but battered, Fifth Panzer Army under SS General Sepp Dietrich. At one point on 1 August Roberts' tanks were within reach of the key junction of Vire, through which the German army withdrawing from Mortain would have had to pass. But, as the result of a silly misunderstanding of boundaries which left Vire to the Americans, a great opportunity was lost – for which Monty has often been held responsible. It was, at any rate for Roberts, 'one of the reasons why I consider Monty was much better at setpiece battles than seizing opportunities'.* By the following day, typically, the Germans had swiftly converted Vire into a well-defended strongpoint, and once again grievous losses in tanks were suffered by the Guards Armoured Division, fighting near Bény Bocage.

It was during BLUECOAT that Monty's patience with Generals Erskine (of the Desert Rats, 7th Armoured) and Bucknall finally expired and both, as we have seen, were now sacked – Erskine replaced (perhaps surprisingly, given Monty's reservations about the Guards, especially when in tanks) by a Guardsman, Brigadier Verney, and Bucknall by Horrocks, Monty's old friend from the beaches of Dunkirk, who had been recovering from wounds. Two other brigadiers were also sacked; but it must have been a telling blow to Monty to have to expose, finally, the shortcomings of a division like the Desert Rats in which he had once had so much confidence. A failure in the eyes of the press especially, in the light of Bradley's and Patton's spectacular advances, and however disappointing to Monty personally, BLUECOAT did – once again – block off from the

* Quoted in Lamb, *Montgomery in Europe*, p. 158.

Americans three Panzer divisions and three battalions of heavy tanks that could have done a great deal of damage at Mortain.

On the 8th, Monty opened a fresh drive – codenamed TOTALISE, and led by Monty's favourite Canadian general, Guy Simonds – through that churned-up territory east of the Orne, to clear the Bourguébus Ridge finally and thrust on to Falaise. Simonds was backed by the Polish 1st Armoured Division, which for five years had been bursting for action and was now attacking simultaneously with the desperate Warsaw uprising. Churchill had just visited Monty at his new TAC HQ in the Forêt de Cerisy. He stayed for an hour and was anxious to get Monty's support for switching ANVIL (now renamed DRAGOON), due to be launched in just eight days' time, from the Mediterranean to Brittany, where Patton was sweeping ahead. Even at his most capricious moments, Churchill was seldom more out of touch with logistic realities than here – to the despair of Brooke. Diplomatically, Monty ducked the issue, saying that he was 'not well acquainted as to the political and strategic aspects of such a switch', but feared that it would 'be very unwise to make any changes . . . . such a proposition would probably produce a row with the Americans and the Combined Chiefs of Staff in Washington; we do NOT want any rows at present. Therefore, leave the thing alone.'

That night Simonds' Canadians, taking a leaf out of the German book, attacked without any preliminary bombardment, his infantry riding his converted self-propelled 'Priests' for the first time in the history of warfare. By dawn the Canadians had penetrated three miles, but in the course of the morning another disastrous 'own goal' took place, with B-17 Flying Fortresses of the US 8th Air Force dropping the bulk of their bombs on the Canadians. The headquarters of 3rd Canadian Division was hit, and Keller (the General commanding whom Monty had wanted to sack anyway) badly wounded. The Canadian armour ran on to a line of 88s, flak guns which had been removed from the air defences of Caen. On the 9th, the Hitler Youth of the 12th SS Panzer, so hated by the Canadians for the atrocities committed in the early days of the campaign, battered but still deadly, managed to knock out forty-seven tanks – almost the entire strength – of the British Columbia Regiment. It was a small consolation that, the same day, the Canadians claimed to have accounted for the Tiger ace, Obersturmführer Wittmann, victor of Villers-Bocage in June.* His Tiger was despatched by a concerted salvo from no less than five Shermans – typifying both the odds now existing against the Panzers and what it still took to knock out a Tiger. The Canadians ground to a halt, seventeen miles short of Falaise. Meanwhile the Poles' performance had been disappointing and – uncharacteristically – 'lacking dash', with the division 'still on its start line' on the 9th. Under greatest pressure, Monty ordered Crerar to 'give it a tremendous jerk up, and push it on'. The enemy was 'doomed', he wrote in his personal diary for 10 August, but the Canadians *had* to get to Falaise 'in the next forty-eight hours'.

* Subsequently, however, Wittmann's death was also claimed by the Northamptonshire Yeomanry, who had actually led the Canadian army in the attack through the German lines the previous night, and who, later, found his body beside a destroyed Tiger tank.

CHAPTER EIGHT

'TRIUMPH – AND DISASTER'

29 July–1 September 1944

If I find any Limeys in the way, I shall shoot them down.
(General Patton, on Monty's scheme to drop airborne troops near Orleans)

Monty is my tactical master. He is probably the finest tactical general we have had since Wellington; but . . . on some of his strategy and especially on his relations with the Americans, he is almost a disaster.

(Field Marshal Brooke to General Sir Frank Simpson)

. . . the worst day of my life.

(Hitler, on hearing of Falaise, 15 August 1944)

DURING THE days that Monty was preparing the Falaise Trap, the great Armageddon that would destroy the German forces in Normandy, the culminating, decisive battle of his whole career, he had moved with TAC into the Forêt de Cerisy. A relocation of only a few miles, it was a pleasant, thick wood whose tall hornbeam and beech trees provided the most perfect natural camouflage under which TAC could spread out and organize itself for the long journey which would take it eventually to Lüneburg Heath and the surrender of the Third Reich. For the first time since Monty had left England in June, his Main HQ with Freddie de Guingand had at last caught up, and was now at Le Tronquay less than five miles away – a helpful proximity, which would last no more than ten days before Monty and TAC were on the move again, sweeping fast eastwards with the advance. Meanwhile, Paul Odgers recalls, a special Communication Squadron from TAF was making its invaluable, but 'inconspicuous and somewhat hazardous beginning'. As often as not its twin-engined Dakotas would take off from 'a dusty airstrip on the main road', with the pilot, Captain Russell, astounding all-comers by his feats of landing the Dakota on the shortest run-offs.

In Monty's letters home to David and to Phyllis Reynolds, consistent in their detached calmness, there is little indication of what was afoot. To David the correspondence of July had consisted chiefly of brief notes, reporting that the dogs were well, but that all his canaries except for one had died, and enclosing parcels of sweets and chocolates from Normandy. On the 29th, reacting to David's summer-term report from Winchester, he wrote:

> You seem to have had quite a few beatings last term; I hope your behind stood up to it all right and is not too tender!!
>
> PS. I am sending you some chocolates via Major Attlee, the Deputy Prime Minister.

David himself recalls two incidents of petty unruliness typical of the natural rebelliousness against the system of a boy approaching sixteen. He suspected that he 'wasn't much thinking about the great events of state, but about more mundane matters as to whether the House was going to win the next round of cricket, football or whatever it was'. One incident involved writing an essay mocking a 'very boring' cleric form-master, the other manufacturing in the lab 'a very simple explosive called nitrogen iodide', which exploded under carpets at the slightest touch. Judging from the tone of his letters, Monty was faintly amused by these minor peccadilloes – certainly not reacting to them with anything comparable to his severity when, at the time of Alamein, David had had a glass of sherry too many with the never-to-be-forgiven Jocelyn Carver.

About this time, Major Peter Earle, assistant to General Nye, the VCIGS, and an officer of the smart 60th Rifles, flew out, to form his first impression of a general poised on the brink of triumph. After a depressing detour via Caen Abbey amid the ruins, he wrote to a friend, 'we all felt, I think, most embarrassed by the presence of the French people, some sullen, but withal, friendly, dignified and calm'.* Then he met 'Fantastic General Monty': 'he really is rather terrible; a simple, narrow-minded man. A bad and raucous actor. A wonderfully clear-headed tactician who can expound, leaving no

* Earle diary, 2 August 1944.

possible alternative, his ideas of what should be done,' was Earle's first impression. In his caravan:

> Monty was at his best. Clear, simple understanding, single-minded purpose; without the caravan, at lunch, he was terrible, raucous, loud acting, public house jokes, bawdy. His greatness is his self-confidence, absolute clarity and simplicity, which he can impart to others. His downfall will be his acting, which is bad and bad things never succeed.

Despite all the photographs he had seen, Earle was surprised to find 'Quite a small man, compared with Alex, Jumbo, Ike and minute compared with Brooke.'

On the 5th, Monty wrote cheerfully to David of the move from Blay:

> I now have my caravan headquarters in a large forest, well away from main roads and dust. The dogs love it. And so do our rabbits; we have six of these and they run about in the Mess and play with the dogs, and are very tame; the puppies at first were frightened of them, now they chase them around the Mess tent.

Then, almost as an afterthought, 'All goes very well here and we are gaining large tracts of France every day; and "collecting in" large numbers of prisoners. We took 6000 yesterday....'

Amid it all, on 9 August, Monty now received one of his most unusual visitors, a friend on the margins of Bohemia left over from his marriage to Betty, a man who astonished the army officers at TAC in his crumpled, para-naval uniform. He wrote to David, 'I have A. P. Herbert staying with me at the moment. He is an MP and a Petty Officer in the Navy; he is a most amusing person. . . . he will probably write some amusing stuff about me and my life here when he gets back.' An engagingly eccentric figure, maverick independent MP for one of the two Oxford university seats, author of *The Water Gypsy*, playwright and composer of cheerful musicals, humorist and pioneer in the struggle to ease the divorce laws, 'APH' was the nearest to a purely personal (and most unlikely) friend, and was brought over (in the words of Bill Williams) for 'a little light relief'. At the end of July, APH had been 'astonished and delighted' to receive an invitation, and to learn that Monty was going to send a

Conversation piece painted by James Gunn at the Château Everberg outside Brussels in September 1944. Left to right round the table are Dawnay, MA; Ray BonDurant (standing), American ADC; Johnny Henderson, ADC; Trumbull Warren, Canadian PA; and Noël Chavasse, ADC, with his back to the painter.

Monty examining the remains of a V2 bomb which fell near HQ 79th Armoured Division commanded by Major General Hobart, his brother-in-law, who is on the left of the picture.

Paratroopers in a shellhole at Arnhem.

Ike leaving after a stormy conference on 29 November 1944 at Zonhoven, which was the longest stop of TAC Headquarters during the whole campaign, and the only time that he lived in a house rather than the caravans.

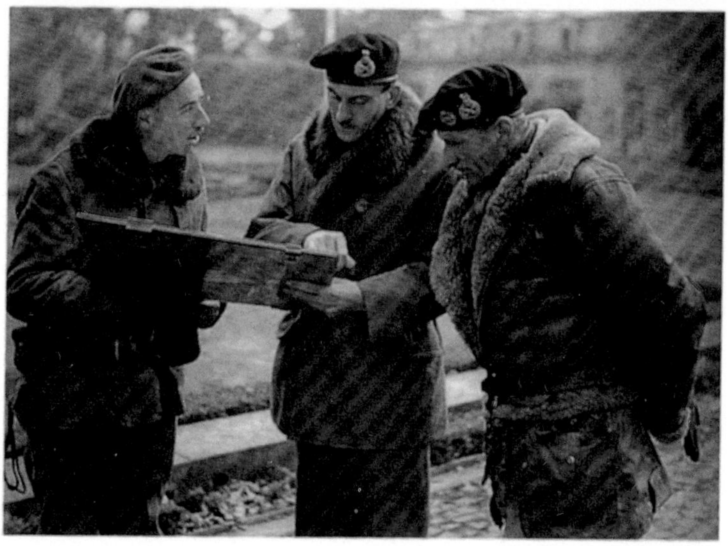

Monty with the much-respected General Guy Simonds of the Canadian Army listening to a report from a liaison officer.

Lieutenant General George S. Patton, commander of US 3rd Army, which became operational in Normandy in July 1944 and spearheaded the break out of the southern end of the sector into the Saar.

Troops of the 83rd US Infantry Division in the northern part of the Ardennes salient.

A shattered German tank, the turret torn off by anti-tank fire, symbolizing the ferocity of the American defence at the end of December 1944.

Soldiers of the US 26th Infantry Division (Yankee) working their way through a town during the Battle of the Ardennes.

Sherman tanks of the US 3rd Army Division in action during the Ardennes offensive.

Monty, Eisenhower and Bradley in Holland on 2 March 1945 on the occasion of an investiture when Ike decorated British officers and Monty decorated American officers.

Churchill, Brooke and Monty have lunch on the banks of the Rhine on 26 March 1945.

Monty briefing his liaison officers at Ostenwalde in April 1945. Left to right are Eddy Prisk, Tom Howarth, Peter Earle, John Poston, John Sharp, Dick Harden, Charles Sweeny and Maurice Franz. Poston and Sweeny were killed a few weeks later.

Monty receives the representatives of Doenitz and Keitel at TAC Headquarters 21 Army Group on Lüneburg Heath on 3 May 1945. Standing at left is Colonel Joe Ewart, the interpreter, who was killed shortly thereafter.

Signing the surrender documents on 4 May 1945. Featured at table are Admiral Wagner, Admiral von Friedeburg, Monty, General Kinzel and Colonel Poleck.

Monty at Ostenwalde to which he returned on 3 June 1945 on an Arab stallion called Rommel (after its previous owner) which had been wounded in the desert.

plane for him. Stopping off at Portsmouth in Monty's new private Dakota from the Communication Squadron – to pick up the General's laundry – he recorded of the Forêt de Cerisy:

> If Sir James Barrie had ever set a scene in a battle headquarters, I thought it would have been like this. It would have been perfect for *A Midsummer's Night's Dream*. Tall, thick trees reached up to the sun. In the luxurious fern a tame rabbit wanders about at the batman's heels. The absurd dogs, Rommel, Hitler, Keitel and company, romped on the camouflage netting; and in the General's caravan a canary sang its head off . . . but for the marquee and the khaki, it might have been a gypsy encampment. After nearly two months of doodlebugs in London river, the battle headquarters was a haven of peace and I had a good night at last.*

Monty was kindness itself, enabling Betty's old friend to become 'the first sailor over the Orne' and allowing him exceptional concessions such as he would never accord Ike: 'Smoke your pipe, Alan, smoke your pipe.' Herbert, bemused, sharply perceived one of Monty's 'secrets':

> One is inclined to imagine the headquarters of a great general in time of war as a scene of feverish activity and even noise; staff officers bustling about, telephones ringing everywhere, despatch riders roaring in and out, pigeons banging into cages, multitudes of clerks and orderlies, and reporters.
>
> For all I know, there may be such goings on elsewhere, but they were not to be found at Monty's TAC HQ, and he considers that the job of supreme leader in the field is to *think*, and he insists on having time and conditions for thinking.

Made a member of the mess with Monty's young men, APH was swiftly caught up in the famous Betting Book, incautiously losing to Noël Chavasse an even ten shillings that 'the war with Germany will be over by 23.59 hrs Oct. 31 1944'. He found it difficult to 'imagine a happier little community. There was youth in the air. Nor did austerity command the meal.' After the nine o'clock news from

* *Independent Member*, p. 320.

England, 'you went to the "map caravan" to hear what the boys had to say'. That first night at TAC, recalled Herbert:

> the 'Chief' (as his followers called him) ordered Falaise, not so far away [and where also he recalled William the Conqueror had been born], to be shelled for the first time, and the famous 'pocket' began to close.... as we stepped out of the caravan into the fairy forest, it would be interesting to see the outcome.

Quite openly Monty revealed to Herbert that he had been rung up and asked to give the Poles pushing on Falaise 'a pat on the back. "I said, 'No, give the Poles a kick in the pants. They will do better next time.' " I believe they did. No one wanted a second kick.'

In response to current American criticism, APH felt that 'no one can be a "showman" unless he has something to show', and Monty in truth 'blew the army's trumpet, not his own'. He returned home, cherishing 'The impression of a single binding, driving, electric force', and publishing a poem (of excruciating doggerel), entitled 'Coeur de Lion': 'I saw Montgomery – tremendous man, loosing the lightning from a caravan. Sitting calmly in his corduroys; the coolest thunderbolt....'

On the 14th, while huge events were developing, Monty was writing to David non-committally, 'The two photos of myself and the PM are a present for Aunt Phyllis. Myself, dogs and birds are all very well.' A letter to Phyllis that same day was, once again, more informative and brimming over with self-confidence: '... I have the bulk of the German army in NW Europe nearly surrounded.... if he escapes me here he can only be driven back on to the Seine – over which river there are now no bridges below Paris, as we have destroyed them all.' It was a terrible glimpse into what 'liberation' was signifying for *la belle France*. 'We will see what happens,' Monty concluded.

This self-confidence may well have been additionally fired by a letter from Brooke that morning, thrilled by the good news of the battle, and radiating rare warmth from one austere man to another:

> You can go on relying on my firm support, my dear old Monty. We have now been working together for a long time, and in some unpleasant places, where we have been able to appreciate each other properly. If I do talk plainly to you at times, it is because I know

> that I can help you by doing so. There are people who don't understand you and I have had some pretty stiff battles at times.

Clearly warning Monty of the conspiracies that had been going on behind his back at SHAEF, Brooke repeated:

> You can go on relying on me to the utmost to watch your rear for you. I have complete confidence in your ability to beat the Boche. Unfortunately there are a lot of jealous, critical, narrow-minded individuals in this world.... Waging war may well be difficult, but waging war under political control becomes at times almost impossible!

Was Brooke, one wonders, trying to warn Monty of some fresh crisis, some new conspiracy, brewing up ahead?

On the 15th, which Adolf Hitler was bemoaning as 'the worst day of my life', Monty was writing to David, whose sixteenth birthday was coming up, 'I enclose £5 for your birthday; you must spend it as you think best. The operations here go very well and we may put a great many Germans "in the bag". It is very hot.' Meanwhile he had moved his TAC HQ, once again, southwards with the axis of the break-out and so as to be still nearer to the Americans. The chosen site, at Campeaux, was one of the prettiest of any, set amid cornfields overlooking the banks of the meandering Vire, bordered with willows and poplars – a typically idyllic Norman scene. By the 19th, after only five days there, he was on the road again, now heading due eastwards, described by Paul Odgers as 'a dusty noisome journey over the battlefield of Mt Pinçon in the midst of an endless column of vehicles'. Just outside the small ruined town of Condé-sur-Noireau, midway to Falaise, they found a 'clean site' on a hillside below the village of Proussy, gazing out eastwards distantly across the long-coveted River Orne – like Moses over the Jordan. 'It was wet here, but the news was exhilarating,' recorded Odgers, 'and we were out of the bocage; the country stretched for miles before us. It became clear that a faster advance than had ever been planned for would now begin and the HQ was scaled down for active movement.' Diaries, like Johnny Henderson's, now began to dwindle in volume, or ceased altogether.

It was at Proussy that Monty received news of the final closing of the Falaise Trap. On the 17th, he had written to Phyllis Reynolds, telling her that 'everything goes well' and claiming that 'I now have troops in Orleans, Chartres and Dreux. And I have some 100,000 Germans almost surrounded in the pocket. The whole prospect of what may lie ahead is fascinating.' The emphasis, as so often with Monty, was on the first person singular; in fact, the troops that had seized the three French cities were Americans from Patton's Third Army, already operating with a questionable degree of independence from Monty's control, its wide-open flank protected by Quesada's vigilant fighter-bombers. That same evening Monty signalled Brooke, warning him that the two US corps at Dreux and Chartres were 'in a very difficult administrative situation and it is doubtful whether they can move very far'. Once more, as in Sicily, he underestimated the mobility of Patton's force, his ability to swing round points of resistance and the skill of the excellent American mechanics at keeping their tanks on the road. Equally, he (and Bradley, too) overestimated the extent of German resistance to Patton in the south. North of the trap, however, there was still the most bitter fighting, with the Germans contesting every yard of the Canadian and Polish advance on Falaise. Monty told Brooke, 'The best news I can give you tonight is that the gap has now been closed and the Polish Armoured Division has reached Trun and is pushing on to Chambois.' This was, however, Monty being unduly optimistic again; the Canadians and the supporting Poles had got seriously stuck, and the German escape route, narrow as it was, remained open for another three days. Herein was to reside some of the fiercest post-war criticism of Monty by the Americans.

That same day of the 17th, Hitler replaced the blemished and pessimistic Kluge with Field Marshal Model, a fanatical Nazi risen from the ranks, who simply did not know the meaning of surrender.* Meanwhile at TAC Monty had staying Leigh-Mallory, now a respected ally. That evening in the Betting Book, possibly fortified by spirits which Monty reserved for his guests, Leigh-Mallory made a bombastic £5 bet with General Kennedy from SHAEF to the effect that the 'long-term bombing policy against railway communications

* Rather than surrender, Model committed suicide in April 1945. Kluge had killed himself immediately after his dismissal.

was the cat's whiskers, and without it the Allies might well have been driven back into the sea'. In his own handwriting, Monty noted that the Speaker of the House of Commons was to be the referee. It would have been a difficult bet to collect, and certain at that time to have infuriated some of Monty's infantrymen – particularly the Canadians. In a matter of days, the destruction of the German Army caught within the Falaise Trap was to prove, at long last, the apotheosis of air power; but for the time being it was the Allied ground forces which were being scourged – yet again – by 'own goals'. On 18 August, 51st Highland filed a complaint detailing forty separate incidents that day, which had cost them twenty-five vehicles and fifty-one casualties. It reported tersely, 'Continual bombing by own forces. Half the petrol being sent to 2nd Armoured destroyed. During a three-day period 72 Polish soldiers were killed and 191 wounded; the Canadians lost 77 killed and 209 wounded from their own bombing.' And, in the sudden spell of hot Norman weather, visibility was infinite. The night bombers of the RAF seem to have aimed with deadly accuracy, but the chief offenders were once more the daylight B-17s of Spaatz's US 8th Air Force. Such was the Canadian rage that they opened up on the Fortresses. When they hit one, there were cheers.

Not unnaturally, Simonds' Canadians lost heart. Within the armed forces, their relations with Americans were always a little prickly. They were fed up with the way the US press claimed all the glory for Patton, when they knew that it was they – not the glamorous US Third Army – who had been doing all the hard fighting of the past few days. And now this! The performance of both the Canadian Army and the Poles in Normandy cannot help but excite admiration – and indeed emotion. Both forces were manned solely by volunteers from faraway countries with no obvious stake in northern France, their losses replenished from very slender resources. It is impossible to experience with dry eyes the great Canadian War Memorial at Vimy Ridge, the most imposing and beautiful of them all, with its names of 60,000 dead from the First World War and more from the Second, all volunteers from a tiny population to fight and die for whatever it was about the 'mother country' that drew them so selflessly to Europe. They had fought bravely from D-Day onwards, suffering heavy losses – as well as having some of their prisoners murdered by 'Panzer' Meyer's Hitler Youth; on occasions they proved better than the British at close-quarters fighting. 'They went at it like hockey players,' remarked one observer. But, to General Dempsey, sometimes they could be 'rather jumpy, highly strung'. They were short on leadership; discipline was never their strong suit and the losses they had suffered among junior leaders in Normandy had been far harder to replace even than British cadres.

From Monty's point of view, there was also the problem that, as a self-governing dominion, Canada's formations came under Ottawa. Therefore, however much he might like to, he was unable to sack the unsatisfactory Crerar, though he had come to perceive him as 'a nit-picking legalist' who would too often let narrow nationalist sympathies interfere with the prosecution of the war. After he had written to Brooke in July, damning him as 'very prosey and stodgy, definitely not a commander', Brooke had replied urging him 'to make the best use of Crerar, he must be retained as a commander of the Canadian Army'. It was a small taste of what Ike had to stomach daily, as coalition leader. Much as he might admire Guy Simonds, the Canadian II Corps commander, his 4th Armoured Division leading the advance lacked battle experience and was slow-moving. Equally inexperienced were the Poles, now fighting their first battles: they were under strength, had a shortage of good leadership and had a serious language problem.

Monty was exasperated by the sluggish progress of the Canadians towards Falaise, realizing that he now had another 'flawed instrument' in his hands. On the 11th, he had told Crerar that he had to have Falaise 'in the next forty-eight hours'. But forty-eight hours later, the Canadians were still some ten miles short. On the 15th, he told them 'it must be done tonight'. The following day, belatedly, he detached 7th Armoured Division to bolster up the Canadian attack. Why he left it so long is one of the mysteries which make Monty vulnerable to criticism over Falaise. And then why did he choose a division which he recognized had let him down several times already because of its lack of thrust? Why did he not employ Roberts' 11th Armoured, proven to be the best tank division in Normandy, for the direct push on Falaise? The question remains unanswered. Meanwhile, thinking in terms of his 'long hook' to the Seine, Monty was planning to drop an airborne division near Orleans to cork up the German retreat. Patton, when informed, exploded in a burst of Anglophobia, 'If I find any Limeys in the way, I shall shoot them down.' The swift course of events, however, was to avert both of these possibilities.

The Canadians at last took Falaise by the 17th, closing the gap to twelve miles. Monty forcefully impressed Crerar of 'the vital need' to get two armoured divisions to the area of Trun–Chambois, astride the German escape route just east of Falaise, that very day: 'If he can do so, the enemy is caught and we may capture over 100,000 Germans; if he does not do so, many Germans may escape.' By this time, elements of Patton's XV US Corps had reached Argentan, the southern jaw of the trap less than fifteen miles from Falaise, with no real fighting and had been there for the best part of five days. Patton enquired in typical vein, 'Shall we continue and drive the British into the sea for another Dunkirk?' In the light of the savage casualties the Canadians and Poles had been suffering in their advance on Falaise, the remark could hardly have been in poorer taste. But Bradley's reply was quite unambiguous: Patton was to halt and consolidate his forces. He was to take no risks. Patton, he commented, was 'not used to having three or four Germans hit him. He doesn't know what it means yet.' It was a fair admission of what an easy time Patton's fast-moving Third Army had had so far. Monty saw Bradley on the 13th, 17th and 19th (with Patton conspicuously absent) and there was no suggestion at the time – or in the immediate aftermath – that there was any disagreement between them. Bradley made his views quite clear. As he wrote in his memoirs, 'I much preferred a solid shoulder at Argentan to the possibility of a broken neck at Falaise.'*

Considering the force, driven on by despair, that the trapped Germans were presenting to the Canadians and the Poles, evidence suggests that Patton – however much he might rage against Monty – might well have risked a 'broken neck' had he attempted to push further north from Argentan. Bradley also admits that he was 'fearful of colliding with Montgomery's forces'. Nothing of this appears in Monty's personal diaries, but it seems reasonable to assume that both commanders would have been deterred by experience of the

* *A Soldier's Story*, p. 377.

devastating (and continuing) spate of 'own goal' air attacks. The day after their second meeting, Monty was noting that his men were suffering 'a good deal as the pilots shot up friend and foe . . . many complaints, especially from Canadian Army.' In the haze, the smoke and the dust of this violent, closely engaged battle, a collision between ground forces would indeed have become a menacing reality with each step that they took towards each other.

Though Patton, followed by various American and Canadian post-war critics, bitterly blamed Monty for the 'halt order', this placing of responsibility is not supported by the historical evidence. Even in his later, much harsher memoir, *A General's Life*, Bradley insisted, 'Montgomery had no part in the decision; it was mine and mine alone,' and he was 'completely supported' by Ike.* Where Bradley did criticize Monty was in his failure to close the gap from the north. Yet between Trun and Chambois, scene of the most desperate fighting, the Canadians still encountered the stubbornest resistance, with many of their tanks steadily being knocked out by the screen of 88s. It was during this bitter fighting that the Royal Canadian Armoured Corps won its only VC of the war, Major David Currie of the South Alberta Regiment, who alone of his squadron survived the battle intact. As for the valiant Poles, they were actually cut off for three days in an isolated pocket on Mont Ormel, unable to receive supplies or evacuate their 300 wounded. The battle was to cost them 352 in dead alone – just as the heroic uprising in Warsaw was collapsing. A makeshift sign was erected by their Canadian comrades: 'A Polish Battlefield'.

Critics of Monty, like the British Richard Lamb and the American Carlo D'Este, now tend to exonerate him for Falaise. Says D'Este, in a key passage:

> To argue in hindsight that Montgomery had missed a spectacular opportunity is to disregard the problem that there was no certainty he could trap and destroy the German army in the pocket. . . . he was taking an enormous gamble, one he could not, realistically, afford to take at that moment.†

Once again, one comes back to the critical issue of the 'flawed

* *A General's Life*, p. 301.

† *Decision in Normandy*, p. 446.

instrument' and Monty's constant nightmare of infantry casualties that could not be replaced. Already by 14 August, as we have seen, Monty had concluded that he would have to break up 59th Division, a task completed by the end of the month. There was also, as the Canadian official history saw, undeniably 'an element of committee in the Allied system of command during this month of August'. It was to get notably worse, Falaise marking the last time when Bradley would readily function under Monty's orders.

The Falaise Trap finally closed on 22 August, with Patton's men from the south linking up with the embattled Canadians and Poles. Thousands of Germans did manage to escape out of it – a miracle considering the state of the country roads and the narrowness of the gap, and a testament to the remarkable powers of organization and sheer will to resist which still existed in Hitler's broken Seventh Army. But those who got across the Seine did so like the BEF at Dunkirk, without their heavy equipment and with little more than their personal weapons. At last the Allied air weapon achieved its apotheosis, displaying in terms unmatched until the Gulf War of 1991 just what overwhelming air superiority could mean. It was, wrote Monty, 'presented with targets probably unparalleled in this war; aircraft formations were engaging endless columns of enemy transport packed bumper to bumper and rendered immobile by the appalling congestion'. To find a wartime parallel, one would have to reach back to the early days of the Russian campaign. Certainly barely anything quite like it had been seen even during the *Blitzkrieg* on French soil, or at Dunkirk, in 1940. The epic of requitement was turning full circle. Within the trap, the carnage wreaked on the retreating enemy by Broadhurst's and Quesada's Typhoon and Mustang fighter-bombers, and by the artillery closing in from either side, was quite horrific. Shortly afterwards, Broadhurst flew Freddie de Guingand over it: 'he was sick in the Storch. We flew along and we landed and had a look at some of them, and he vomited violently. It was terrible. It was the first time I had been in close contact with the results of my activities.'*

On moving to TAC's new headquarters at Avernes, near the devastated town of Chambois several days later, Sergeant Norman

* Montgomery Collection.

Kirby of the Field Security recalled how the flies 'invaded our camp, bringing infection from the massed corpses in the sweltering Falaise pocket'. Many of the men went down with dysentery, so that 'movement of the Headquarters was further delayed at this point, both by the prevailing sickness and by the continuing congestion of traffic in the valley.'* On the 25th, Johnny Henderson flew low over the Gap with Monty, seeing the results for himself for the first time. He recalled that 'there was a terrible smell, even from the air'. What particularly shocked him, as a cavalry man, were the horses – hundreds upon hundreds, many lying dead still in the traces of wrecked guns and wagons, eyes wide open in anguish.† Even Monty, the professional hardened to many battle scenes, was affected, writing simply in his diary for that day, 'I have never seen anything like it before.' He was not one to spend time exulting over a destroyed enemy, yet he would have been inhuman had not some sense of retribution for the humiliation of Dunkirk, and all the succeeding years of defeats, passed through his mind at that moment.

Certainly he could claim without exaggeration, as he wrote in his personal diary, 'It can now be said that the battle in Normandy is over and that it has been decisively won.' Though exaggerated at the time, in the heat of battle, total German losses at Falaise numbered 10,000 killed and 50,000 prisoners. In the northern, Canadian part of the pocket alone, 344 knocked-out tanks were counted, plus 2447 soft vehicles and 252 guns. On 22 August, Model's Army Group B could count less than seventy tanks surviving out of eight Panzer divisions. 'Panzer' Meyer's arrogant young Nazis of the 12th SS, who had arrived in Normandy 20,000 strong with 150 tanks, were reduced to 300 men with ten working tanks and no artillery, while the crack Panzer Lehr had been totally destroyed by the Americans at Mortain. Over the whole campaign, the Germans were reckoned to have lost 450,000 men, including 210,000 POWs, over twenty generals (including Rommel), 1500 tanks and 3500 guns. Forty-three divisions had been destroyed or badly mauled. Only a score of tanks were ferried east across the Seine, where all the bridges had been destroyed. The sole organized fighting force left in the north was

* Kirby, *1100 Miles with Monty*, p. 57.

† Despite the formidable mechanization of the German Panzers, all through the war the bulk of German infantry regiments still depended extensively upon horse transport.

the Fifteenth Army, now in grave danger of being encircled as Monty swept towards Belgium. Allied casualties since D-Day had by no means been light: 209,672, of whom 36,976 had been killed (roughly in a ratio of two British and Canadian casualties to three American). In addition, 28,000 Allied airmen had been lost, either during the battle or in the run-up to OVERLORD, a heavy price to pay for the air supremacy that had finally triumphed at Falaise. Most serious was the fact that his losses of trained infantrymen had forced Monty to break up one-and-a-half divisions, and two armoured brigades to boot. This, and similar warnings from the US Army, provided Monty with a serious caution about attempting to do too much in the campaign ahead.

Nevertheless, in strategic terms, a decisive victory had been won that would rank with Stalingrad or the North African surrender – though casualties inflicted were higher. It seemed now only a matter of marching and of time (but how much?) before the Third Reich collapsed under such losses. Meanwhile Monty stood as undisputed lord of the battlefield. His grinding, unflinchingly persistent principle of the Picador at Caen had – despite all his critics and all the setbacks – been proved fundamentally correct. His strategy from January 1944 onwards was vindicated, his reputation as one of the great captains of history undisputed. Yet he would, *ex post facto*, diminish this reputation by continuing to insist that 'The outstanding point about the Battle of Normandy is that it was fought exactly as planned before the invasion.' Even his most fanatical devotees could not claim that this was so, but where Monty *had* shown his mastery was in his ability to respond to setbacks, and new eventualities, with a remarkably 'flexible response' – to adapt an expression coined many years later. Had he only been able to admit to setbacks and error, his reputation would have been that much more majestic.

Abruptly, after Falaise the whole tenor of the war changed. For a few happy weeks, a large part of the victorious Allied armies found itself caught up in a tearing pursuit like a hunt after the fox on a glorious spring day. There were pockets of bitter resistance, such as that involving – once again – the bruised Canadians, advancing in the north on the Channel ports which were held tenaciously by the

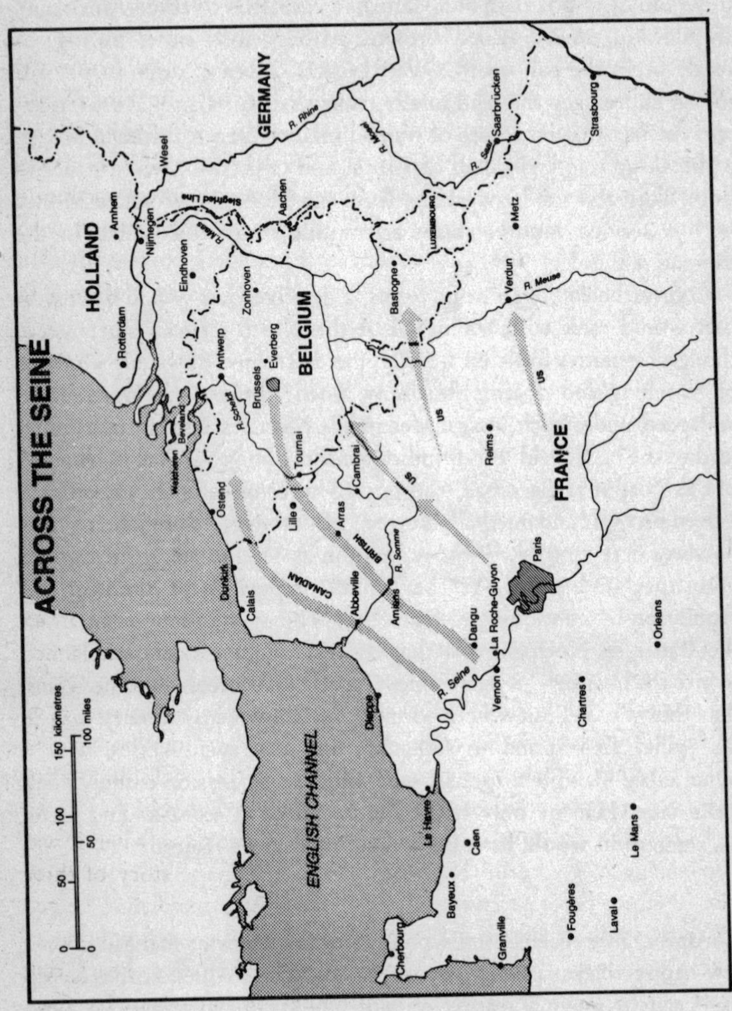

Across the Seine

German Fifteenth Army. (Very properly, they were granted by Monty the distinction of capturing Dieppe, just as the 51st Highlanders were allocated St-Valéry, where much of the division had been rounded up in humiliation in 1940 after Dunkirk.) But otherwise, all of a sudden, the mighty German army in France seemed to be disintegrating. With extraordinary speed, Patton's Third Army was sweeping south and east of Paris, heading for the grim First World War battlefields of Verdun and the German frontier on the Rhine. General Patch's US Seventh Army, the ANVIL/DRAGOON forces moving up from the Côte d'Azur, advanced almost into a vacuum – reaching Lyon and causing Churchill to growl, and Monty to wish that his suggestion back in January to limit them to one division only had been adhered to. Thereby all those landing craft would have been liberated for OVERLORD.

With that sense of diplomacy and fair-mindedness which made him such a great coalition leader, Ike had bowed to Gaullist pressure to hold back Patton and give Leclerc's Free French 2nd Armoured Division the signal honour of liberating Paris. It is questionable whether Monty would have been quite so tactful; 1940 had left him still with deep reservations about French military capacity. On the day that Paris was liberated, 25 August, he reported to Brooke acidly (and with some small element of exaggeration) that when the French armour had entered the outskirts of Paris two days previously, 'they received such a tumultuous welcome from the population that most of the men became very drunk and nothing happened for the rest of the day'. He added that, when they 'became sober' the next day, Patton had to send an American division into Paris to 'lend a hand', while another US formation was required to follow behind – 'for there was a considerable amount of clearing up required'.

Typical of the light-hearted euphoria of those days, when it was good to be still alive in that heady August, was the story of three young Grenadier captains from the Guards Armoured who helped 'liberate' Paris. Ordered after the inferno of the bocage fighting to take a couple of days' leave at the seaside, when they heard that great events were afoot to the south they commandeered a jeep, embellished it with a large Union Jack and headed off in the opposite direction to join the van of the US and French forces entering Paris. They liberated the British Embassy in the Faubourg St Honoré, signing the visitors' book as the first Britons to do so since 1940, then – along with numerous other claimants, like Ernest Hemingway – went on to 'liberate' the Ritz. One of them subsequently made frequent visits to the Embassy – as Foreign Secretary, Peter Carrington MC.* When they regained their regiment at Vernon on the west bank of the Seine:

> 'You nearly missed a great moment,' they said. 'We're about to cross the Seine!'
>
> 'We've been crossing and recrossing it for the last forty-eight hours,' we explained softly, 'by the Pont Alexandre III and the Pont de l'Alma!'

The general euphoria affected all ranks. According to the ever present Kay Summersby, on the way from Chartres Ike 'kept saying with great satisfaction' as they passed mounds of abandoned enemy equipment, 'We certainly caught them with their pants down!' To many officers of Monty's and Brooke's First World War generation, with vivid memories of the amazing swiftness with which the Kaiser had collapsed after the great Allied offensives of August 1918, there was suddenly a strong hope – if not a belief – that history would repeat itself. Soon after the liberation of Paris, the British Second Army was speeding across those Flanders battlefields of Arras and Somme, where so many hundreds of thousands had lost their lives and others spent years in attempts to advance a few miles – and at a far greater pace than even Rommel and his Panzers had sped across them in the opposite direction in 1940. So rapid was the advance that on 31 August, after an all-night rush, 'Pip' Roberts and the 11th Armoured captured Amiens – together with the entire headquarters of the German Seventh Army, including its new commander, General Eberbach. Moving even faster than Patton now, within less than a week Monty's British Second Army vanguard had covered 200 miles. By 3 September, the Guards Armoured had liberated Brussels, while 11th Armoured was standing at the gates of Antwerp. In the east, Bulgaria and Rumania with all her oil had capitulated to the advanc-

* Carrington, *Reflect on Things Past*, p. 53. Another of the three, who knew how to find the Embassy, having lived there when his father was Military Attaché before the war, became a full general – Sir David Fraser, biographer of Alanbrooke and Rommel, and author of other commendable books.

ing Russians, leaving the gateway to Central Europe open; in Poland Soviet forces stood poised on Vistula. How long would, *could*, the Germans go on?

Monty was conspicuous in not taking part in the general euphoria, the back-slapping and the kissing of Paris. At TAC, which had just moved to Avernes in unpleasant propinquity to Falaise when Paris was liberated, Noël Chavasse lost a £1 bet to his chief that he would 'have entered Paris within twenty-one days of that city being captured'. According to Kay Summersby,* Monty in response to an invitation to join Ike in Paris sent back a short, sniffy message declining the honour: 'Ike snorted, then he laughed – "It is just as well," he said, "the less I see of him the better it is for my blood pressure."' It would have been for him 'a pure joyride', Monty wrote austerely in his diary: 'Paris is in the American zone and is no concern of mine.' Alarmed at what it would do to the American liberators, with memories of London before D-Day, Monty was determined not to allow himself, or his armies, to be distracted or debauched by the Capuan delights of Paris. It was premature to celebrate. Certainly no one who had witnessed the Wehrmacht's remarkable ability to recuperate after successive defeats on the Eastern Front would have supposed otherwise. Though not himself immune by any means to the prevailing mood of optimism, Monty better than anyone knew that Hitler was not yet defeated – that there would be some hard fighting ahead. Apart from anything else, from their seemingly indestructible sites in the Pas de Calais the V-1s were continuing to terrorize southern England; and ULTRA was predicting that very shortly the more frightening V-2 rockets would be arriving, without warning, from launchers in Belgium and Holland.

Within the Allied forces, from top to bottom, however, euphoria had taken over. Even the cool-headed Brooke, as early as 2 August, well before Falaise, was writing, 'the Boche is beat on all fronts. It is only a matter now of how many more months he can last. I certainly don't see him lasting another winter.'† That other steadying influence on Monty, de Guingand, felt exactly the same. So was it

* *Past Forgetting*, p. 184.

† To General 'Jumbo' Wilson, Supreme Commander, Mediterranean (Bryant, *Triumph in the West*, p. 260).

any wonder that almost all the senior commanders (and particularly the Americans) now felt the war was as good as won? There was the SHAEF G-2 intelligence summary for 23 August to read: 'the enemy in the West has had it. Two and a half months of bitter fighting have brought the end of the war in Europe within sight, almost within reach.'

There was an understandable urge to go flat out to gain personal laurels. And (for reasons that will be seen shortly), as the tight bonds of Normandy were relaxed, each army commander was almost encouraged to 'do his own thing'. Typically, Patton was the least controllable, though his intelligence chief, Colonel Oscar W. Koch, proved one of the rare realists, warning him that the enemy had 'been able to maintain a sufficiently cohesive front' and that 'it can be expected the German armies will continue to fight until destroyed or captured'. But Patton was not interested in such talk. On the 27th, fast running out of gas, he was faced with ordering a halt to Major-General Eddy's XII Corps. Then – this was the sort of thing that happened to the charmed Patton – he captured 100,000 gallons of Wehrmacht fuel at Sens. Without reporting his windfall, which should then have been distributed according to Monty's requirements, he used it all to continue his own advance – thereby placing an additional burden on the other Allied armies.

As the victorious Allies swept across the line of the Seine, Monty ended the section of his diary for the month of August: 'The Battle of Normandy is over. . . . And they were destroyed. . . . Today, 26 Aug., is D + 81; we are well ahead of our forecast.' In this he was referring back to the notorious phase-lines presentation of April in St Paul's School, which had predicted that the line of the Seine would be reached by D + 90. So, in the event, he was ahead of schedule by a good nine days; the time lost before Caen had been more than made up. The following week he would himself be crossing the Seine, in triumph.

What was missing, however, was that, in all their anxiety to achieve a secure foothold in Normandy and to defeat the German forces there, the OVERLORD planners had formulated absolutely no forward contingency plan after D-Day + 90. Charles Richardson admitted, 'Euphoria took over, and we started planning for a German surrender [as in 1918]. We said, originally, that the Germans would fight to the bitter end, but by the end of August we thought the war could have been over by the end of the year.'* In a way, there was to be a certain alarming similarity, in reverse, to Hitler's masterly blueprint, *Sichelschnitt*, which had defeated France so effectively in the spring of 1940. Unsure of the totality of their success, the Germans then had planned nothing beyond the occupation of the Channel ports. There was no immediate follow-up plan to invade a defenceless Britain, so the BEF was allowed to get away, to fight another day – and ultimately to come back to the continent to defeat Hitler. Now, in 1944, as they crossed the Seine in the opposite direction, each army group was virtually deciding its own strategy. 'The situation is not very clear as regards who is in charge,' Monty wrote to the VCIGS, Sir Archibald Nye, on 26 August.

Meanwhile, standing at the ready to gather the garlands of the greatest success of his career, Monty was about to suffer its most devastating reversal of fortune.

In his personal diary for 19 August, Monty referred at length to 'a very curious incident'. On the 15th, the BBC news had contained a statement to the effect that Eisenhower had taken over personal command in France, with two army groups under him – one, 12 US, under Bradley, and 21 Army Group still under Monty: 'This gave the impression that I had been deposed from command of the land battle under Eisenhower, and a good deal of comment took place.'

The following day, however, the BBC had retracted, stating that Montgomery was 'still in overall charge of the land operations'. Monty went on to note:

> The *Daily Mirror* of 17 August had a leading article demanding that an apology be made to me!† It also had an amusing cartoon.
>
> The whole affair is probably a slip-up by someone; or it may have been done on purpose by someone at SHAEF.
>
> It will NOT do Ike any good; people will say that just as I am about to win a big victory, he tried to step in to scoop the reward.

* Interview 26 November 1992.

† Meanwhile, in Washington the *Times-Herald* was blasting about 'British dominance' of the AEF, while other papers were complaining that Eisenhower was no more than a mere figurehead.

> Actually Ike is far too decent to do anything of the sort; but there are many on his staff who would love to do so.

Of course Ike was 'too decent'; but, with the presidential election campaign now beginning to move into top gear, there were far bigger fish prowling in the sea. It was not just in the run of normal duty that Secretary of War Stimson and his powerful Chief of Staff, George C. Marshall, had of late been paying so much attention to Normandy. One feels that no one but a Monty, outstanding tactician though he had just proven himself to be, but isolated from political realities among his dogs, canaries and young men in that ivory tower of TAC HQ, so totally self-assured, could have been so blind to the writing on the wall. What was about to happen was 'always on the cards', commented Bill Williams, 'only he couldn't ever see it'.* Even without an election year in the US, even if Monty had never put a foot wrong, even if he had been all sweetness and light in his relations with Ike and the Americans, the material, numerical facts of life would have dictated what was to come. A passing acquaintance with American history, with 'Black Jack' Pershing in the First World War, with the national aversion to serving under foreign commanders, would have made it all self-evident. Anybody but a Monty might have seen it all coming and prepared himself to roll with the punches, to get his own way by dexterity and diplomatic manoeuvring. But this was never Monty's way. That was his tragedy. As after Alamein, a change in his character was detectable to those near to him – a certain increase of the head measurement. Symptomatic of it was Monty's commissioning (if not commanding) the eminent portrait painter James Gunn to come out and paint him, almost before Falaise had been mopped up. This was something that neither the modest Ike, nor even perhaps the flamboyant Patton, would have thought of at that moment.

On the 17th, the day after the BBC's retraction, Monty flew to Fougères in the east of Brittany for an important meeting with Omar Bradley at his headquarters. He put six points to the American, beginning, '(a) 12 and 21 Army Groups must operate together as a strong mass, which need fear nothing . . .'. In what was an extremely significant statement, given the strategic error of command that was

* Interview 12 November 1992.

shortly to occur, Monty went on to explain that 21 Army Group, the British and Canadians, would continue on the left flank, clearing the Channel coast with the ultimate objective of securing Antwerp, while Bradley's American 12 Army Group (including Patton) would form its right flank moving north of the Ardennes, aimed at Aachen and Cologne – and then the Ruhr, the industrial heartland of Germany. Here were the origins of Monty's 'narrow thrust' (or 'single thrust') versus the American 'broad front' approach, over which so much passion, and historians' ink, would be spent in the years to come. Monty summarized the discussion by concluding that Bradley had agreed entirely, but added that he had not yet discussed his plan with Ike. He was going to put to him additionally his suggestion that only the US Seventh Army hastening up from the South of France 'be directed to Metz and Nancy, and in to the Saar' – that is, pointing at the centre of Germany.* Monty reckoned that Ike was 'not likely to have any great objections, and he will I think undoubtedly accept what we say'. In this he was totally deluding himself. This was, once again, Monty's wishful thinking at its very worst. If de Guingand had been constantly at his side, as in North Africa, instead of still back at Main HQ close to Bayeux, perhaps he would have been disabused.

It is also worth noting that Monty had just had the outspoken P. J. Grigg visiting him for two nights, undoubtedly fuelling him – as he was wont to do – with the derogatory views of US generalship and professionalism that he shared with CIGS Brooke. Meanwhile that same day, Ike had received – at Bradley's headquarters after Monty had left – a communication from Marshall, the asperity of which had shaken both generals. Clearly reacting to heavy pressure from both the bellicose Stimson† and the US press, Marshall wrote:

* Which is where Patton already had his eyes fixed.

† In 1943, anxious for an invasion to take place that year, Stimson had written to President Roosevelt accusing Churchill of presiding over 'a fatigued and defeatist government which had lost its initiative, blocking the help of a young and vigorous nation' (Hodgson, *The Colonel*, p. 270). It was not often that Churchill was accused of being 'defeatist'. A few months later, in August 1943, the single-minded Stimson had warned the President, 'We cannot now rationally hope to be able to cross the Channel and come to grips with our German enemy under a British commander. . . . The shadows of Passchendaele and Dunkerque still hang too heavily over the leaders of his government . . . their hearts are not in it.' Evidently, the 'shadows' of this gloomy view of British leadership also still hung heavily on 'the Colonel' a year later.

'The Secretary [Stimson] and I and apparently all Americans are strongly of the opinion that the time has come for you to assume direct exercise of command of the American Contingent.' He added that 'The astonishing success of the campaign' had evoked 'emphatic expressions of confidence in you and in Bradley'. Marshall had nothing comparable to say about Montgomery. Both generals were 'somewhat taken aback' at Marshall's tone. Ike for one, grumbling about the influence of the press and public opinion at home, complained that for them 'a resounding victory is not sufficient, the question of "how" is equally important'.* Yet was it surprising that, under such pressures, when he next met him on the 23rd Monty should find to his great annoyance and disappointment that Bradley had 'reneged' on what he had 'agreed entirely' on the 17th at Fougères?

It was on the 20th that Monty made his triumphant diary entry about the Battle of Normandy being 'decisively won'. The following day, in a very different vein he was reacting angrily to Ike's proposals for the change of command – and for future strategy. The previous day, he noted, Eisenhower had convened a meeting 'to draw up plans for the future conduct of the war'. Monty noted laconically, 'My Chief of Staff was present.' But why, one might ask, given the extreme importance of what was afoot, and that the battle for Normandy, now 'decisively won', no longer required his hand constantly on the steering wheel, did Monty not go himself? If it was neither personal pique nor the imperious expectation that Ike should come to him, then it certainly seemed to be one or the other to the hostile anti-Monty faction at SHAEF. De Guingand came to TAC afterwards, bringing with him a draft of the decisions reached, which were then to be sent on to the Combined Chiefs of Staff. 'Eisenhower proposes', Monty recorded coldly, 'to change the system of command on 1st Sept., to separate the two Army Groups and to command them himself, and to send a portion of the land forces eastwards to the Saar. I cannot agree with these proposals.'† He sent 'some notes' for de Guingand to discuss with Ike the following day, during talks that lasted over two hours, then asked the Supreme Commander – in

* Ambrose (1), p. 498.

† It should be noted, however, that to some extent Monty may have seemed to nod assent to the Saar scheme by his remarks of the 17th (see p. 259).

what must have seemed rather high-handed terms – to come to TAC for lunch the next day, the 23rd ('I said it was indicated', were his words, 'that he should come and see me').

The time-frame of this incipient row could hardly have been more unfortunate. Brooke was away from the War Office on a prolonged trip to General Alexander in the Mediterranean (although, all too often, his caustic views on Ike's generalship had precisely the wrong kind of effect on Monty, especially when expressed in person); Churchill had gone to watch the ANVIL/DRAGOON landings from a battleship off his beloved Côte d'Azur;* Brooke's assistant, General Kennedy, was ill; while Monty's confidant, 'Simbo' Simpson, was absent on two weeks' leave. Instead the VCIGS, Nye, flew over on the 21st and stayed the night at Proussy TAC HQ – to try to sweeten the bitter pill for Monty, appreciating full well what a profound shock it would be to him personally, coming so soon after his greatest triumph. But too many hours had been allowed to pass, during which Monty's rage and indignation had built up a formidable head of steam. To Monty, the professional, it was simply both inefficient and dangerous to swap horses in mid-stream; and now, with the main forces of the German Army in the west on the run for the very first time in the war, the moment had in all probability come when they would be unable to withstand one hard, concentrated blow. This was no time to waste talking.

With General Nye came Major Peter Earle of the 60th – by whom Monty was now so favourably impressed as to steal him from Nye and bring him out to his staff in the latter stages of the war. At Proussy, up on a high plateau among apple orchards overlooking the Orne, Earle found TAC trimming itself in readiness for the swift advance which would carry it more than 250 miles and seven more stops over the next two eventful weeks. After a visit to the Mont Pinçon battlefield, redolent with the stench of dead cows and horses, to Earle TAC seemed barely less tranquil than it had to APH less than two weeks previously at Cerisy: 'Archie [Nye] and Monty sat

* Much as he might have disapproved of the operation, this took second place to his desire to observe a real, live landing in progress – which he had been denied by Monty on D-Day. Predictably, it was however a disappointment. 'As far as I could hear,' he wrote, 'not a shot was fired either at the approaching flotillas or on the beaches.... There seemed to be nobody there' (*The Second World War*, vol. VI, p. 85).

on green canvas chairs overlooking the valley north of Condé; guns, shots and mines disturbed the quiet evening. I sat with Kit Dawnay across a few rows of cabbages drinking whisky and water – watching them.' They discussed the five points which Monty had made in his notes that de Guingand was passing to Ike, and which were repeated in a letter Monty had sent to Brooke the previous day. (Owing to his absence in Italy, regrettably the CIGS would not read these until five more days had passed.)

> (1) The quickest way to win this war is for the great mass of the Allied armies to advance northwards, clear the coast as far as Antwerp, establish a powerful air force in Belgium, and advance into the Ruhr.
>
> (2) The force must operate as one whole, with great cohesion, and be so strong that it can do the job quickly.
>
> (3) Single control and direction of the land operations is vital to success. This is a WHOLE-TIME job for one man.

'To change the system of command now,' concluded Monty, 'after having won a great victory, would be to prolong the war.'

That Monty, beneath the composed exterior displayed to Earle as the two generals talked on their green campaign chairs, was seething was suggested in an unusually testy letter written to Phyllis Reynolds, torpedoing any suggestion that his son David might come out to see him: 'quite ridiculous,' he wrote, 'I cannot think who started such an idea. I quite agree with you; he needs to be kept quiet and to mature gradually. . . .' Once again the unfortunate Jocelyn Carver became the target of his disapproval: 'he should not see too much of Jocelyn; the more time he spends quietly at home, the better' – 'home' that summer holidays being, as always, the Reynoldses' school. Two weeks later, on the day of his greatest distinction, he was reinforcing this with: 'I always said that he should never be allowed to go to Jocelyn, or any of her friends, and I still say so.'

Early on the 23rd, Monty flew to Laval to see Bradley at his headquarters before Ike arrived at Proussy for lunch. It was here that he discovered – 'to my amazement' – that Bradley had had a complete change of mind since their meeting of the 17th and was now 'a whole-hearted advocate of the main effort of his Army Group being directed eastwards on Metz and the Saar'. Monty added, 'This was a new one on me, and clearly Ike has been persuading him – or Bedell Smith.' He arrived back at Proussy, in what was unlikely to have been a conspicuously good humour, just in time to receive Ike and his Chief of Staff, Bedell Smith. Monty had not seen Bedell Smith since he had left England for D-Day; he now asked that he go outside and leave Ike and himself to have a private discussion 'on certain vital matters of principle'. This was not how either Ike, or the American system, worked, and – apart from the affront to Smith – it set Eisenhower 'on edge'. According to Stephen Ambrose, Monty then 'tried his best to be tactful,' but in fact made matters worse 'by proceeding to give him a lecture, as if he were patronizing a student at a staff college'.

One can well imagine that Ike, with his notoriously low boiling point, was already bubbling. Producing his own 'single thrust' plan on a map, Monty told him that if instead Ike's 'broad front' plan were followed, 'with the whole line advancing and everybody fighting all the time', the advance would inevitably peter out, the Germans would be permitted to recover their breath – and the war would go on through the winter and into 1945. The consequences would be failure. He also told Ike that, as Supreme Commander, he should 'sit on a very lofty perch' and should *not* 'descend into the land battle and become a ground C-in-C'. Ike tried to explain to him the pressure of public sentiment in the US, to which Monty replied that, if that were the stumbling block, he would be willing to serve under Bradley. Feeling as strongly as he did about the need for unified control of the Allied armies, Monty clearly meant what he said, but 'that horrified him [Ike]!!', Monty wrote in his diary. Once recovered from his surprise, Ike said he could not accept such a suggestion. He still intended to go ahead and take over personal control on 1 September.

Monty then shifted his ground to forward strategy. He wanted an American army of twelve divisions to advance – under his control – on his right flank. Without this he was not now strong enough even to take Antwerp. He also wanted Patton to be stopped where he was, his supplies diverted to Monty's northern thrust. Eisenhower explained that this would leave Bradley with only one army in his 12 Army Group; American public opinion would object. Certainly he could not stop Patton, 'the man with the ball', and current pin-up of the US press. Monty snapped back, demanding to know 'why public opinion should make us want to take military decisions which were definitely unsound'. By this time, tempers on both sides must have come close to explosion. In a moment of rare contrition, Monty in his memoirs published fourteen years later wondered whether he had 'paid sufficient heed to Eisenhower's notions before refuting them'. The answer, given his low and oft-expressed opinion on Eisenhower's professionalism, is almost certainly no. But, he claimed, 'I think I did. Anyhow he listened quietly. . . . I never cease to marvel at his patience and forbearance on that occasion.'* Monty admitted, however, that his arguments 'were of no avail'. From his point of view, the exchange had been about as unsatisfactory as it could be. As one concession in a thoroughly one-sided compromise, however, 21 Army Group would receive priority (particularly in view of the importance of its objectives – the V-weapon launch sites, the Belgian airfields and Antwerp), while Bradley's First Army would provide a 'strong left wing' to be placed under Monty's 'co-ordination and control'. However, under pressure from Marshall the following day and after vigorous protests from the increasingly independent-minded Bradley, Ike's new directive of 29 August withdrew the word 'control'.

Meanwhile Bradley had let Patton off the leash again – on his own, not Ike's, initiative – so that by the 30th he was nearly midway between Paris and the Rhine, aiming for the Saar. If his tanks ran dry, Patton told Eddy (commanding his forward XII Corps) to 'get out and walk', knowing full well that Ike would then be forced to switch fuel to him from the north. 'And so', wrote Monty bitterly in his memoirs,

> we all got ready to cross the Seine and go our different ways. . . . Our strategy was now to become 'unstitched'. . . . All my military training told me we could not get away with it, and then we would be faced with a long winter campaign with all that entailed for the British people.

On the 26th, Monty wrote a long letter to Nye, summarizing developments since his visit to TAC HQ, but clearly intended for Brooke's eyes on his return that day. 'I believe', he wrote, 'that Eisenhower

* *Memoirs*, p. 269.

in his heart of hearts knows he is wrong; I believe he has been pushed into his present decision by Bedell Smith and certain others at SHAEF; I do NOT believe that things in America are really as he says they are.' (But, one may ask, how on earth could Monty, in his isolation, have known what was the prevailing mood in the US, let alone how strong it was?) He then expressed fears, well founded, that Ike would in fact reduce his powers to 'co-ordination' only. He concluded by venting his spleen with an angry blast against the conspiratorial Tedder and the air barons: the air set-up was 'most unsound'; Coningham was 'disliked and despised by all soldiers; he is the world's biggest double-crosser'; and Tedder had done 'nothing' as Deputy Supreme Commander. He feared that all his work establishing friendly relations with the RAF had been 'wasted'.

On the 29th, hardly recovered from his exhausting trip to Italy, Brooke hastened off urgently under appalling conditions to see Monty. Told by de Guingand that the weather was too bad for him to fly on, he had to drive three hours by congested roads from Bayeux, spent an hour and a half with Monty at his new TAC HQ at Avernes, another three hours travelling back to Bayeux, then nearly three hours more on a 'murky fly home', having lost his escort of three fighters in the clouds: 'I hope they returned home.' It was a measure of how much importance he placed on speaking to Monty personally. Brooke told him that he had had to make the journey 'in order to be assured that I was quite happy about the compromise reached with Eisenhower'. He himself was pessimistic, recording on the eve of his departure for France a 'difficult' meeting with the Chiefs of Staff to consider Ike's new plan to take over command on 1 September, which – in total accord with Monty – he felt gloomily was:

> likely to add another three to six months on to the war. He straightaway wants to split his force, sending an American contingent towards Nancy while the British Army Group moves along the coast. If the Germans were not as beat as they are this would be a fatal move; as it is, it may not do too much harm.*

A bare two-and-a-half months later, Hitler's surprise blow in the

* Bryant, *Triumph in the West*, p. 262.

Ardennes would prove even the pessimistic Brooke to be excessively sanguine here. Monty then told him that he was 'satisfied as regards the immediate future', but for the longer term, 'the whole set-up was thoroughly unsound'.

Meanwhile, that same day, having – as part of the 'compromise' – also been given control over all the airborne units that comprised the First Allied Airborne Army, unused since D-Day, he began issuing orders for an air landing in the Tournai area of Belgium, ahead of the speeding British armour.*

Brooke is described as this 'stern and reticent soldier' by Arthur Bryant in his commentary on the Alanbrooke diaries, 'a deeply sensitive and self-repressed man carrying an almost intolerable burden.'† His staccato manner of speaking and sharp tongue, however, did not automatically endear him to Americans; one historian sees him as 'Physically unprepossessing, with narrow shoulders, spindly legs and a seemingly crooked mustache . . . icy and condescending.'‡ But as the superlative war-organizer from the winter of Singapore to the summer of Lüneburg Heath, the architect of Britain's victory in Europe, Brooke's reputation stands on unshakeable ground. He was perhaps the Ulysses of the coalition, the wisest of them all, the only man capable of keeping Winston Churchill on the road and under control, restraining his wilder fancies but, as his complementary *alter ego*, putting into practice his sounder ideas.

He was also the only general whom Monty held in awe, for whom he had total respect. As we have seen,§ that ascendancy of Brooke over Monty dated back to the days of the BEF in 1940, to their relationship as corps to divisional commander. But where perhaps the august Brooke was less than Ulysses-like was in implicitly encouraging Monty in his diatribes against Eisenhower, Supreme Allied Commander and therefore his immediate superior – if not actually adding fuel to the flames whenever the two Irishmen met. When the Alanbrooke diaries were published in the late 1950s, they

* As will be seen, once again the speed of events on the ground pre-empted the increasingly frustrated airborne forces.

† Bryant, *Triumph in the West*, pp. 16–17.

‡ Blumenson, Martin; *The Battle of the Generals, The Untold Story of the Falaise Pocket*, New York 1993, p. 49.

§ Chapter 2.

caused considerable shock, and indeed offence, in the US for the severity of their criticism of Ike in particular and of condescension towards US military leadership in general. Nothing Monty ever said of Ike was sharper than the views freely expressed to him by Brooke – or, for that matter, by the political chief of them both, P. J. Grigg. In today's terminology, all three would have rated as dyed-in-the-wool anti-Americans. One should perhaps recall once more how, to the First World War generation of Monty and Brooke, that lack of any contact with Americans prior to 1942 made them seem as remote as Martians. Monty's former intelligence chief, Bill Williams, probably the most judiciously critical of the survivors on his staff, for one always thought that 'PJ' was at fault: 'Yes, he did hot up Monty. . . . he should have discouraged the Monty link with the War Office, the direct correspondence between himself and the CIGS. . . . It was very irregular: he should have corresponded really only via Ike.'*

Typical of this 'hotting up' was Monty's reply to Brooke's warm letter of 13 August (two days before the BBC's 'curious' leak), in which he had so readily picked up Brooke's refrain, with an unusually sharp attack on his boss: 'Ike is apt to get very excited and to talk wildly – at the top of his voice!!! He is now over here, which is a very great pity. His ignorance as to how to run a war is absolute and complete; he has all the popular cries, but nothing else.' It can safely be assumed that some harsh exchanges about Ike and US professionalism went unrecorded during that visit to Monty by Brooke on the 29th. Brooke came away concluding that it remained to be seen 'what political pressure is put on Eisenhower to move Americans on separate axis from the British'. The following day Monty received from Ike his new directive, telling him that he was to be given 'powers only of co-ordination' over Bradley's forces in the northward thrust. It provoked (in Monty's diary) this reaction of 'hotted up' anger:

> I disagree definitely with Eisenhower's new organization . . . and I disagree definitely with his orders for command (or non-command!) on the left wing. I will, of course, do all I can to make it work; but I shall tell Eisenhower when I next see him that I disagree with it definitely.

* Interview 12 November 1992.

That same day, Monty moved with TAC HQ a long hop eastwards to Fontaine, on a wooded escarpment overlooking the Eure Valley. Just across the Eure, like the Promised Land of Canaan, lay the Seine and beyond the boundless open plain of northern France leading towards Belgium – and the German Ruhr.* It was a day of torrential rain, and Paul Odgers recalled some of the headquarters vehicles getting bogged down in the meadows. Only a few days before, the château had been inhabited by a Luftwaffe headquarters. Two days later TAC was once again on the move, with the sun suddenly coming out as Monty made his historic (and extremely well-photographed) crossing of the Seine at Vernon† on a Goliath pontoon bridge, triumphantly and conspicuously. 'The advance was quickening now,' Odgers noted in his record of TAC, 'and the countryside and villages were less damaged and the population the more enthusiastic'. In smiling sunshine, the TAC cavalcade now swept up 'great tree-lined avenues' to the Château de Dangu, for just another brief halt of two days; but it was to be a memorable one in Monty's life.

Littered with abandoned German equipment, Dangu belonged to a curious nobleman, the Duke of Pozzo di Borgo,‡ of an ancient Corsican family which had successfully managed to back both sides during the Napoleonic Wars. As of 1944, the current incumbent, who had fought against the Germans in the First World War, was described by Odgers rather unsympathetically as having 'a pathetic pride in his grass' and as being 'watched over in a meaning way by the local FFI'.§ According to his son Charlie, the Duke had hidden shot-down Allied flyers before the invasion, 'trying to keep the peace among them – Canadians, British, Americans – all fighting like hell!' But he had also been on manifestly friendly terms with the German

* Today it is an area of prosperous *résidences secondaires* built since the war, while the park at Fontaine where Monty had his last TAC HQ before crossing the Seine now houses a children's holiday home.

† Despite the destruction of all the houses of Vernon along the Seine, and their replacement by unappealing modern council blocks, the exact location of the pontoon bridge, of the Rue de la Boucherie, is easy to find from the church towers in the background. Five miles up the river lies Roche Guyon, site of Rommel's last HQ.

‡ The title, stemming from the Kingdom of the Two Sicilies, was a somewhat spurious one.

§ French Forces of the Interior, i.e. the Resistance.

occupiers. Aged nineteen in 1944, Charlie Pozzo recalled the German infantry retreating, together with White Russians, in horse-drawn carts only days before Monty had arrived. He gave food to Germans hiding in his stables, told them 'I think you've had it,' and left them with their weapons – provided they handed them over and surrendered to the British the following day. Then arrived the British Red Caps* to inform the Duke that they were requisitioning his château for an army headquarters. 'But not on my lawns!' he exclaimed. 'I have always kept the Germans off the lawns.'

'But our General likes grass,' the Military Police evidently replied.

'Then put him in with the cattle!' exclaimed the Duke, unaware of just how grand a general was about to descend on him.

For the first time since leaving Broomfield Park at the beginning of June, Monty installed himself in a house – but only to be painted. For, on the 28th, the new court painter James Gunn (described robustly by Trumbull Warren as 'the most conceited man I ever met') had arrived. Expecting to stay for only a couple of days, Gunn now found himself swept up for over two weeks in the fast-moving, victorious cavalcade, shifting camp repeatedly with TAC HQ. There was a brief moment of repose, as Monty recorded in his diary for 31 August, almost like some eighteenth-century monarch on the field of battle: 'I stayed in all day and gave sittings to Mr Gunn.'†

Meanwhile, back in London, Brooke had called in on the 30th to see Churchill and report on his visit to Monty, and explain 'the difficulties that had been arising with Eisenhower taking control from Monty'. He found the Prime Minister in bed, 'looking ill', with a temperature of 103 after suffering yet another attack of pneumonia. But he rallied to tell Brooke 'that he wanted to make Monty a field marshal, the appointment to coincide (Sept. 1st) with the date of Eisenhower assuming command of Land Forces. He felt that such a move would mark the approval of the British people for Monty's leadership.'‡

* British Military Police.

† Not unnaturally eager for commissions, Gunn in between sittings with his subject also started sketching his ADC Johnny Henderson, but was seen off by Monty declaring 'You're only here to paint me!'

‡ Bryant, *Triumph in the West*, p. 264.

The following day, the King himself – accompanied by his Private Secretary, Sir Alan Lascelles – drove round to the ailing Churchill, who was reclining in bed, 'robed in a sumptuous pale-blue dressing-gown of Oriental design'. Brooke continued, 'The P.M. had the submission ready and he asked the King to sign it then and there – which he did, using the pillow as a table.' 'It would be interesting to know,' Monty added in his memoirs, 'if a British general has ever before been promoted to field marshal in the middle of a battle, that appointment being signed by his Sovereign on the Prime Minister's pillow.'

This staggering news reached Monty shortly before midnight. It was the highest rank in the British Army, a tremendous honour, and at a stroke put him on a par with the great military leaders of the past, with Haig and Kitchener and Wellington – and with Brooke himself. It made him (temporarily) senior to his old chief in the desert, Alexander. The promotion was to be effective from the following day, the very day that Ike was due to take over his job. Thus it could be seen as a neat trick, giving Monty a rank which did not then exist in the American Army and thereby placing him on a rung above Ike, who – until Roosevelt restored the rank of 'general of the armies'* that December – remained only a four-star general. Even for a professional soldier of less vanity and ambition than Monty it would have come as an immeasurable compliment; it was the just reward for a lifetime of achievement, of his struggle against the slings and arrows of family, of the loss of Betty and all the loneliness, and as a vindication of all those hard years of self-discipline, of training, of battles fought in two wars – against both enemy and fellow officers – and now, finally, of his personal conduct of the greatest Allied victory since Stalingrad. As the citation stated, it was 'In recognition of his responsibility for the direction of the campaign in France, which had achieved the decisive defeat of the German Armies in Normandy . . .'. To Phyllis Reynolds he wrote reflecting his surprise in simple words, 'The field-marshal business is rather amazing,'† and evoking the day two years previously when he had left David in

* A rank first created for George Washington. The last to hold it had been General Pershing, leader of the US Expeditionary Force in the First World War.

† No record of any similar letter to David exists.

her care, before travelling out to Egypt as an unknown lieutenant-general.

Ike was among the first to congratulate him, with generous warm-heartedness. From home Brooke's congratulations characteristically contained a wise note of caution:

> You may perhaps have thought during the last five years that I was occasionally unnecessarily rude to you. If I was I can assure you that it was only because I wanted to guard you against the effect of some of your actions which are incorrectly judged by others and lead to criticism which might affect your progress, a matter which has been of *great* concern to me.
>
> I should like at this moment of your triumph to offer you one more word of advice. Don't let success go to your head and remember the value of humility.

He went on to quote Kipling: 'If you can meet with triumph and disaster and treat those two impostors just the same . . .'. Here was a man who knew his Monty.

As Churchill had predicted, the 'field-marshal business' did provide a sop to the feelings of the British public. But not to Monty. In the recollection of a teenage Charlie Pozzo di Borgo (who then went off to join the French 2nd Armoured Division), their uninvited guest was 'mad that day'. What affronted him personally was his simultaneous demotion as commander. Coming so soon after the triumph which had led to the liberation of France and the elimination of nearly half-a-million enemy soldiers, it was an appalling shock, the reality of which he had hardly been able to take on board even after Nye's visit of ten days previously, even after all the earlier indications. A year later, Churchill confided to his doctor, Lord Moran, just how greatly Monty had been hurt by his demotion. In part, perhaps, he was paying the penalty for his inability to communicate with his superiors, but he would have been unlikely to see it that way. Worse, however, than any blow to his self-esteem, Monty's professionalism dictated to him that a deadly mistake was surely about to be made. At the War Office, Peter Earle commented scathingly on the news of Ike's promotion and new accretion of power: 'Colonel Eisenhower of the Operations Divisions, the US War Department, who had never seen a shot fired in his life'.

CHAPTER NINE

AUTUMN BLUES: ARNHEM

September–November 1944

> I feel that Monty's strategy for once is at fault. Instead of carrying out the advance on Arnhem he ought to have made certain of Antwerp in the first place.
>
> (Field Marshal Brooke, Diary, 5 October 1944)

> You will hear no more on the subject of command from me. I have given my views and you have given your answer. That ends the matter. . . . Your very devoted and loyal subordinate Monty.
>
> (Montgomery to Ike, 14 October 1944)

> had the pious, teetotalling Montgomery wobbled into SHAEF with a hangover . . . I could not have been more astonished than I was by the daring adventure he proposed.
>
> (General Bradley, *A Soldier's Story*, p. 416)

BY 1 SEPTEMBER 1944, the main story of this book is completed; events, accelerating, become like an elongated postscript. Though even a visionary like Winston Churchill could not have foreseen it then, 1 September 1944 was a climacteric of Western history which would far transcend the events of the Second World War. It is never easy to set a precise date marking the decline of empires, but the demotion of Montgomery was certainly the moment when – definitively and most palpably – British predominance in the Western Alliance could be seen to pass to the United States, a culmination of the trend which had followed that last moment of British ascendancy at the Casablanca Conference of 1943. From now on, until Roosevelt's untimely death the following year, the 'Grand Design' (the phrase invented by Churchill) would be the design of Roosevelt, not Churchill. It might take the débâcle of Suez in 1956 truly to set the seal on the decline of

British (and French) power, but by September 1944 it was already irreversible.

With that determined grip of the Jack Russell terrier, Monty would not, however, let go of what he was convinced was a terrible error. He would bite away at it all through the autumn and into the winter, with increasing bitterness, until Ike – his mind closed, and exasperated – finally cried, 'Hold, enough!', threatening to make it an issue of confidence, which would almost certainly have spelt the end for Monty. In January 1945, after major disaster had only narrowly been averted in the Ardennes, he would be unable to resist proclaiming 'I told you so,' causing the final alienation from Bradley, Ike and their fellow Americans. Who was right, and who was wrong?

On 3 September, Monty sent a top-secret instruction, Directive M-523, to his (now entirely British and Canadian) 21 Army Group, declaring his intention 'To occupy the Ruhr'. The eastward advance would begin on the 6th. The directive ended by predicting, 'The Armies of the Allies will soon be entering Germany.' From this it was apparent that Monty too had been infected by the general 'victory virus', that euphoria which had accompanied the sweep through France and Belgium, and he was not anticipating heavy resistance. But had swift enough advantage been taken of the German defeat? That same day, talks took place at Second Army Headquarters between Dempsey and Major-General Maxwell Taylor of the US 101st Airborne Division, with a view to seizing bridges across the Rhine in Holland at Arnhem and Nijmegen. A date was fixed, unrealistically close, for 8/9 September.

On 4 September Monty sent Ike an important résumé of his strategic views. It began:

> I would like to put before you certain aspects of future operations and give you my views.
>
> 1. I consider we have now reached a stage where one really powerful and full-blooded thrust towards Berlin is likely to get there and thus end the German war.
>
> 2. We have *not* enough maintenance resources for two full-blooded thrusts.
>
> 3. The selected thrust must have all the maintenance resources it needs without any qualification, and any other operation must do the best it can with what is left over.

4. There are only two possible thrusts: one via the Ruhr and the other via Metz and the Saar.

5. In my opinion the thrust likely to give the best and quickest results is the northern one via the Ruhr.

6. Time is vital and the decision regarding the selected thrust must be made at once and para. 3 above will then apply.

7. If we attempt a compromise solution and split our maintenance resources so that neither thrust is full-blooded we will prolong the war.

8. I consider the problem viewed as above is very simple and clear cut.

The résumé ended with the proposition that Ike drop in to discuss matters for lunch the following day (Ike had meanwhile moved into his Forward HQ at Granville, on the west coast of the Cotentin Peninsula, with a fine view of Mont St Michel – but some 400 miles from Monty's TAC HQ). As ever, there was no suggestion of Monty going back to see Ike. He was, as he explained, too busy with the battle – though, in fact, he had just called a brief pause in the advance, for 'regrouping'. The language of this first key signal to the Allied Supreme Commander since his promotion was typical Monty – clear and forceful. But it was lacking in any kind of deference such as the recently promoted general of another nationality might properly expect from a subordinate, and between the lines could be read all the weight of his – and Brooke's and P. J. Grigg's – accumulated disapprobation of Ike as a strategist and a commander.

In a masterly understatement, Alan Moorehead remarks that the letter 'can hardly have made agreeable reading to the soldiers at SHAEF'.* Ike ignored the luncheon 'summons', not replying until the evening of the 5th. Meanwhile, regardless of Monty's objurgations about 'prolonging the war', that same day Ike had drafted an office memorandum claiming that 'the defeat of the German armies is now complete and the only thing needed to realize the conception is speed'. Accordingly, he deemed it important 'to get Patton moving once again'. Such was the state of Ike's signals facilities at Granville that Monty received only half the message addressed to

* *Montgomery*, p. 213.

him, the second half, on the morning of the 7th, with the first half not arriving until forty-eight hours later. As much as the content, the revelation of the inadequacies of Ike's communications system infuriated Monty, confirming to him all his misgivings about the change in command. How could an active commander-in-chief, with his Forward HQ even facing the wrong way – out towards the Atlantic – possibly take a grip on the big, complex and decisive land battle about to begin on the German frontier? It was all too much like those British generals of the First World War whom Monty had so deplored. But the last two paragraphs of Ike's signal sufficed to tell Monty that his warnings were being ignored, with Ike stating unequivocally 'my intention is initially to occupy the Saar and the Ruhr'. The delayed first paragraph only reinforced this message of what, to Monty, signified the deadliest sin of dispersal – once again: 'While agreeing with your conception of a powerful and full-blooded thrust towards Berlin, I do not agree that it should be initiated at this moment to the exclusion of all other manoeuvres.' It was completely self-contradictory. So Ike was going to compromise, try to please Monty, Bradley and – especially – Patton at the same time, with the consequence, in Monty's view, that he would end up with decisive strength nowhere in the whole line. 'Bulling ahead on all fronts', he would wait for a weak spot to present an opportunity for a breakthrough; but would he then have available reserves to exploit it?

Without waiting for the missing paragraphs to arrive, on the 7th Monty fired off an urgent plea:

> My maintenance is stretched to the limit. I require an airlift of 1000 tons a day at Douai or Brussels and in last two days have had only 750 tons total. My transport is based on operating 150 miles from my ports and at present I am over 300 miles from Bayeux. In order to save transport I have cut down my intake into France to 6000 tons a day which is half what I consume and I cannot go on for long like this. It is clear therefore that based as I am at present on Bayeux I cannot capture the Ruhr.

Once more Monty repeated his request for Ike to 'come and see me' – with, as always, no offer to make the trip himself, or even meet him halfway, on his unbreakable principle that commanders should always 'go forward'. Identical howls about supplies were landing simultaneously on Ike's desk from Bradley and Patton, from which it should have been quite clear (at least so Monty thought) that, unless the Germans really were on their last legs, an early two-pronged attack across the Rhine would be logistically impossible. Predictably, Patton reinforced his requests by getting his Third Army locked into costly and futile attacks (the first time it had suffered significant losses in the campaign) on Metz, so that Ike would be forced to divert more supplies to him. In his memoirs, Monty registers disapproval (it was just as well that he had not known of Patton's actions at the time, he said); yet, at Arnhem, he was in fact shortly about to act in a way that was not all that dissimilar to Patton – albeit with Ike's tentative support.

In his letter to Ike of the 4th, Monty had pressed for an immediate decision, and observed in his memoirs that, 'In point of fact, it was now almost too late.' In those first days of September, events at the front were tumbling over each other with extraordinary speed, even temporarily out of the grip of someone so supremely in touch, and as far forward, as Monty. Under a combination of the pressure of these events, grave problems of logistics, wrangling within the Allied leadership and that mounting euphoria increasingly persuading it that the Germans had 'had it', three terrible errors were about to be committed. They all began with the letter A: Antwerp, Arnhem and the Ardennes.

Communiqués on the astonishingly swift sweep through Belgium at the beginning of September strongly give the impression that Antwerp, then the biggest port in north-west Europe, as well as the one closest to the heart of Germany, now lay firmly in Allied hands. But in fact Antwerp straddles the wide mouth of the River Scheldt, with many of its harbour facilities on the far side of the Albert Canal. Most important, so long as the enemy controlled the tortuous approaches, sixty-five miles long, which commanded its entrance, the island of Walcheren and the semi-island of South Beveland, the great port itself was useless to the Allies. And it was now urgently needed, as Monty had warned Eisenhower in his 'maintenance' plea of 7 September. The failure to seize Antwerp and its approaches at the beginning of September 1944 comes down through the years as one of the greatest errors of the Second World War, greater even than Arnhem – though the two were closely linked. All from Churchill down, but notably Ike and Monty in equal share, were culpable.

Back on 17 August, when efforts were still under way to close the Falaise Gap, his personal diary reveals Monty putting to Bradley at their Fougères meeting the need for 21 Army Group to 'secure Antwerp'. This was followed up, in the self-same words, in a despatch from Monty to Brooke, on 'future plans', the next day. It had noted, as we have seen, that 'Bradley agrees entirely', but that he had 'NOT yet discussed subject with Ike'. On the 28th, Monty was formulating plans for (yet another) air-drop on Tournai, its objective 'to seize the line of the Scheldt'. Once again, events (this time the speed of the advance on Brussels) were to pre-empt this plan. Equally, a proposal by Monty to drop the First Allied Airborne Army on Walcheren Island was vetoed by its commander, US General Brereton, on the ground that it was not suitable for airborne troops.* In the meantime, Monty states that no clear directive was forthcoming from either Ike or Brooke to make the capture of Antwerp and its approaches a top priority. Stephen Ambrose, holding Ike 'ultimately responsible', admits that he was seen to 'waver' here, and 'badly'. This wavering was presumably because euphoria about the impending German collapse momentarily made the port seem superfluous – especially in the light of the destructions wrought by the Germans at Cherbourg and Brest, which suggested that Antwerp could be out of commission months after the Rhine had been crossed, and Germany had collapsed.

On 4 September, the 11th Armoured Division of General 'Pip' Roberts, which had so distinguished itself in Normandy, in a brilliant coup occupied most of Antwerp up to the Albert Canal, saving (with

* Lieutenant-General Lewis H. Brereton, a rather chippy individual whose feathers Monty had tactlessly ruffled when the American had visited him in the desert (see p. 60), and who as C-in-C Allied Airborne Army would be nominally responsible for Arnhem (though he had never before commanded an airborne unit), was one of the least successful US generals. But he may have had a point here about Walcheren. When the Canadians and British finally took Walcheren in November, their lives were made a misery by flooding of the island, where the dykes had been destroyed by Allied heavy bombers.

the aid of the Belgian Resistance) the vital sluice gates and port installations before the Germans could destroy them. But there he stopped. His tanks had just completed one of the fastest advances in history, moving sometimes all through the night. Men and vehicles were fatigued, though not exhausted. Roberts himself, nearly forty years later, insisted that he could have gone on across the Albert Canal that day, resistance being still so feeble:

> Monty's failure at Antwerp is evidence again that he was not a good general at seizing opportunities. My thoughts, like Horrocks' and Monty's, on 4 September were east to the Rhine. We should have looked west towards Walcheren. . . .
>
> . . . Unfortunately, I did not appreciate the significance of the fighting on the Albert Canal, and the Germans did not blow the crucial bridge for another twelve hours. If briefed before, I would have crossed the Albert Canal with tanks to the east of Antwerp and closed the Germans' route into Beveland and Walcheren.
>
> At that time petrol was coming up regularly on lorries, and we saved space on lorries by not using much ammunition. I had enough petrol to continue my advance.*

Comparisons are, of course, invidious but it is a fair assumption that, if a Guderian or a Rommel in the 1940 campaign had been faced with the same problem, under the German *Auftragssystem* they would have seized the advantage and pushed ahead across the Scheldt, without waiting for further orders or supplies. Patton would have done the same. Instead, vital time was lost. What was perhaps even more serious than the failure to secure Antwerp itself was the escape of General von Zangen's Fifteenth Army across the Scheldt Estuary, which was to have a serious effect on the next stage of the battle – Arnhem. As will be recalled, pinned down in the Pas de Calais by Operation FORTITUDE, this army had hardly played a role in Normandy. Its commander (who had taken over from Salmuth) is described by Milton Shulman, who interviewed him in POW camp, as retaining 'the stolid, unimaginative appearance so peculiar to those of his profession', and as 'one of those "reliable" generals'† totally

* Quoted in Lamb, *Montgomery in Europe*, pp. 201–2.
† Shulman, *Defeat in the West*, p. 196.

loyal to National Socialism whom Hitler was now sending to shore up what remained of the Western Front. He would do what he was told, to the last. Largely intact and now being pressed up against the Channel ports by Crerar's Canadians, the Fifteenth Army had been ordered by Hitler to mount a last-ditch defence, and – as the threat to Antwerp materialized – to hold the estuary at all costs. Its only escape route lay east across the estuary, via the semi-island of South Beveland, which is connected to the mainland by a narrow isthmus only 3000 yards wide, with a single road. In an extraordinary feat of improvisation, typical of the Wehrmacht at its best, employing every available small coastal craft and moving by night so as to be out of reach of Allied aircraft, Zangen began moving the main bulk of his army from the Breskens pocket east of Zeebrugge across to South Beveland, in a kind of miniature Dunkirk. 'To my mind,' wrote Brian Horrocks, commander of XXX Corps, '4th September was the key date in the battle for the Rhine. Had we been able to advance that day we could have smashed through this screen and advanced northwards with little or nothing to stop us. We might even have succeeded in bouncing a crossing over the Rhine. But we halted.'* Equally, the job could have been supported by the airborne force which Monty had waiting in the wings to drop on Tournai – and which would later be lost at Arnhem. The Fifteenth Army would have been isolated, Holland left largely denuded of troops. It was far worse than the failure to close the Falaise trap.

Fourteen days later, Brigadier Williams' intelligence summary for 21 Army Group reported that 'probably over 100,000 men had crossed into the Scheldt Peninsula since Antwerp was captured'. Their presence at Arnhem would tilt the balance and turn what might have been a victory into disaster, sacrificing a fine division and the lives of thousands of British, American and Polish airborne troops, while the clearing of the Scheldt Estuary would cost the Canadians and British Commandos some 13,000 in dead and wounded, fighting all through October in the most miserable of conditions, and not clearing until 8 November. By this time any chance of opening Antwerp and ending the war in 1944 had gone. Certainly the local German commander, General Student, was mystified as to why the

* *A Full Life*, p. 205.

British armour did not sever the Beveland Peninsula and then 'rush into Holland'.* Who was to blame? Probably Monty and Eisenhower, in almost equal measure, neither of whom gave the vital order to make Antwerp the number-one priority. Both were guilty of succumbing to that deadly virus, underestimating the German capacity to recuperate. Stephen Ambrose designates it Ike's 'worst error of the war'. Monty thought he could bypass Antwerp and, heading straight for the Rhine, 'bounce a crossing'. But ignoring Antwerp made sense only if the Germans were really defeated; events would very soon prove they were not. He had, Monty claimed in his memoirs, received no orders from Ike about Antwerp, though he had 'agreed about Arnhem'. In fact, Ike in the first instance had specifically placed clearing the Scheldt as second priority, after Arnhem.

Under repeated pressure from Monty, Eisenhower agreed to fly up to Brussels, within a few miles of Monty's present TAC at Everberg, to meet him on the 10th. It was a highly unfortunate encounter. Only a few days previously, while getting out of his plane Ike had most painfully wrenched his leg, so badly that his pilot had had to carry him across the salt marshes. The injury was to give him trouble for months. In private, though never in public, he was often on crutches, or using a cane around the house. 'The pain was so much at times', wrote Kay Summersby, 'that every once in a while he would have to give up and go to bed for three or four days.' When he flew to Brussels, accompanied by his deputy, Tedder, ever hostile to Monty, Ike's discomfort was such that he could not get out of the plane; consequently the discussions had to take place inside it. It seems to have been highly inconsiderate of Monty, who knew of the injury, if not of the pain it was causing, to have forced him to make the flight. The tempers of both men were strained to breaking point. According to the Americans, Monty pulled out of his pocket Ike's directive of the 4th, damning his policy 'in extreme language'. Biting back his rage, Ike is said to have 'leaned forward and put his hand on Montgomery's knee. "Steady, Monty," he said. "You can't speak to me like that. I'm your boss." Montgomery mumbled that he was sorry.'†

* C. Ryan, *A Bridge Too Far*, p. 57.
† Ambrose (1), p. 515.

In his diary account for the 10th, Monty reported that it was his duty:

> to give him my opinion on the situation, and he must know my views; decision as to the action to be taken was then his.
>
> I said that we would do no good by trying to sustain two thrusts; we must put everything into one selected thrust and give it priority; other thrusts must do what they could with what was left over.
>
> He disagreed and said we must get across the Rhine, first on a wide front; i.e. get the Ruhr *and* the Saar, and then concentrate on one thrust.
>
> I pointed out that he had said in para. 4 of part II of his 13889 of 5th September that:
>
> > 'I have always given and still give priority to the Ruhr, rpt. Ruhr, and the northern route of the advance.'
>
> He said that he did not mean this to be at the expense of other operations.
>
> So we really got no further. He is a very nice chap; but he is on the wrong tack, and we shall not now finish off this war this winter.

Monty also revealed to Ike that the first of Hitler's V-2 rockets had hit London the previous day; it had come from Holland and this was bound to affect British views on the direction of the thrust into Germany. (The previous day, reporting the first V-2 strike, Brooke had asked Monty with some urgency 'when I could clean up these places'. He had then reckoned that it might 'take two weeks or more'. In fact the deadly V-2s, with the added terror of their totally unheralded approach, would continue falling all through the winter.

About all that Monty was able to obtain from the meeting on the tarmac at Brussels was Ike's support for his plan to seize the Rhine bridges at Nijmegen and Arnhem, now postponed a week to the 17th. It was that day that Monty agreed with Browning (GOC I Airborne Corps, and deputy commander of First Allied Airborne Army under Brereton) and Dempsey that the whole Airborne Army would now have to be thrown in; 'enemy resistance there is getting stronger', Zangen having already managed to transport a large part of his Fifteenth Army across the Scheldt. But, on the wider issue, it should have been clear to Monty then that Ike could not 'scale down' on Bradley and Patton. And yet, only two days later, with that element of wishful thinking which was Monty's great weakness, he was recording in his personal diary, 'Bedell Smith was sent to see me and promised everything I had been asking for for weeks; the northern thrust against the Ruhr is at last to be given priority.' And on the 16th: 'there is no doubt whatever that my promotion to field marshal on 1st Sept. has played a big part in enabling us to get the business right; it gave me greater weight in all discussion and talks.' This was hardly how Ike saw it. Once he had hobbled back off the plane at Granville, his comment was, 'Monty's suggestion is simple, Give him everything – which is crazy.'

So it would go on through the autumn and winter, and into the spring, with the last damaging wrangles over whether Berlin should, or should not, be the ultimate Allied objective. To Monty, Ike would appear to make concessions, then veer round as soon as Patton or Bradley got at him. It was not all that unlike the portly Lord Derby, Lloyd George's War Minister in the First World War, whom Haig acidly described as 'like the feather pillow, bears the marks of the last person who has sat on him'.*

Illustrative of the extreme coolness which had set in after the unhappy encounter on Brussels airfield, a follow-up letter from Ike on the 15th opened with an icy 'Dear Montgomery'. For the rest of the war their relations would grow progressively remoter, their personal encounters fewer.

The controversy over Ike's 'broad front' versus Monty's 'narrow thrust' on the Ruhr, and later Berlin itself, was to rage right through to the German surrender – and well beyond, to the present day. Simply stated, the pros and cons were as follows. First of all, Monty's strategy never predicated a 'single knife-like' or 'pencil' thrust. The words seem to have been those of his enemy, Tedder, and they provided the rival US and British press fine material for some more mutual chauvinism. Monty's thinking all along was based on a northerly thrust of *forty divisions*, powerful enough to 'sweep all before it'. Even Monty's American critic, Carlo D'Este, finds it 'difficult to understand why

* Blake (ed.), *The Private Papers of Douglas Haig*, p. 279.

Eisenhower refused to acknowledge that Montgomery's proposal was no mere "pencil-like" thrust'.* In his masterly early account,† Chester Wilmot, the Australian war correspondent who accompanied Monty at the Lüneburg Heath surrender, reckoned that in September the prospects for Monty's all-out thrust in the north were 'infinitely stronger' than when he had first advocated it in August. Wilmot argued that in the north the Allies could concentrate their greatest force of armour, and the greatest (and closest) weight of airpower.

Of the motivations behind Monty's persistent pressing of the 'single thrust', he, being Monty, was of course vulnerable to the charge of personal vanity: that he wanted, as he had once remarked before the war, to lead a victorious British army into Berlin. And nobody was more sensitive to the undercurrents of national pride, from which arose a conviction that after five terrible years of war, so much of it fought alone, a British-led British army had a right to play a dominant role in the final victory over Hitler. But all these factors paled by comparison with Monty's deep sense of military professionalism, his belief that Eisenhower's strategy was *wrong*, that he was simply unfit to command this vast Allied force on the ground, that it would all lead to a prolonging of the war, if not to disaster.

Certainly there was a great deal of strategic logic on Monty's side, but was there practicality? Could the heavily bombed German transport system support the vast amount of roadbound traffic, which such a concentrated thrust would involve? Was the strategy diplomatically sound? Regrettably, the argument tended to divide along national lines. Among the British, sole exception was Monty's own Chief of Staff, Freddie de Guingand, who remarks that 'Throughout the war, this was the only major issue over which I did not agree with my Chief.' De Guingand saw it predominantly from a logistical point of view: without the use of Antwerp, with whole armies still supplied off the beaches of Normandy, he feared that it would be impossible to sustain a major attack on the far side of the Rhine. But, close as he was to Ike and the Americans, closer perhaps than any other senior British officer, he feared a major 'crisis between the Allies' if Monty were

* D'Este, *Decision in Normandy*, p. 464.

† *The Struggle for Europe*, pp. 282–3. It was published in 1952, well before the wartime records were released, or the apologias of the principals written. Wilmot was killed in the crash of the ill-fated first British commercial jet, the Comet, the following year.

'given all these resources and yet failed'. He was right. Back in France, as the change in the command structure loomed, Monty had offered to serve under Bradley; but Ike had refused. American public opinion, let alone the now fully-fledged US military, would no longer accept Monty as commander of American troops. Too much personal prejudice was involved. Patton, at his rudest, as of the Battle of the Bulge, saw Monty as 'a tired little fart'. Eisenhower would never have descended to expressing such a view, but Monty was indeed tired – and even more so was the British Army, which inevitably would have had to provide the cutting edge for the 'single thrust'. Even the Monty fan, Chester Wilmot, notes that no less than 1400 British three-tonner trucks, the backbone of Monty's supply system, were now 'useless' because of faulty pistons. Dempsey's tanks were not only short of fuel, but many were simply worn out. There were also more of those endemic 'flaws' we have seen in Normandy, and Churchill himself would shortly be forced to call up the last 250,000 from Britain's pool of manpower. Where then were the fresh forces for the British-led 'single thrust' to come from? One of the only fresh Allied forces was Patton's relatively unscathed Third Army, but he was rapidly wasting it in Metz and the Saar, and anyway would never permit himself now to be any part of a Monty-led operation.

Meanwhile, in the midst of all these debates (themselves inevitably a source of more vital time being lost), the enemy was recuperating at phenomenal speed. Almost as if designed to give this recovery extra impetus, on 15 September an event of some relevance had taken place in the United States. Secretary of the Treasury Morgenthau proclaimed the plan bearing his name, with its declared aim of razing German industry to the ground and turning it back forever into a bucolic economy. At a moment when German morale was at an all-time low, as a reinforcement to the threat of 'unconditional surrender' it could hardly have provided a more heaven-sent gift to Goebbels. A new mood of last-ditch tenacity would now be encountered by the Allies on the battlefield – just at the critical moment when it would be least wanted, or expected: at Arnhem.

Two days after Morgenthau announced his plan, and five days after the conference aboard Ike's plane on the airfield, on a morning of fine flying weather, American and British airborne troops – in fact the whole of the First Allied Airborne Army – landed at Arnhem and Nijmegen, well to the north-east of Antwerp. A short while previously a sixteen-year-old Belgian boy, who was to become ambassador to London many years later, J.-P. van Bellinghem, recalled seeing a British general on a Belgian airfield holding a map with large arrows pointing unmistakably towards Arnhem.* The memory never left him; he knew exactly what it meant, and was astounded by its audacity. (So, indeed, was Omar Bradley. 'Had the pious, teetotalling Montgomery wobbled into SHAEF with a hangover,' wrote Bradley in his memoirs, 'I could not have been more astonished than I was by the daring adventure he proposed.')† Van Bellinghem's recollection illustrates the lamentable lack of security that surrounded the whole operation. So many years later it is all too easy to ignore the quite extraordinary speed, indeed rush, with which MARKET GARDEN was launched. Though delayed a week, it was begun only twenty-three days after the Liberation of Paris. That such a large-scale undertaking – the biggest airborne operation in history – could be prepared in so short a time reveals the efficiency of Monty's planning staff. Yet it was already too late: the bulk of Zangen's escaped forces were in position in Holland. So, too, were two redoubtable SS Panzer divisions, the 9th and 10th, which had fought so ferociously against Monty in Normandy. Now, in the precious days that had been lost since 'Pip' Roberts had reached the Albert Canal, they had been partly re-equipped, and moved to locations where they were not expected.

Strategically, Monty's grand design was to capture the two big bridges at Nijmegen and, further north, at Arnhem, then use them to sweep across the Rhine into the flat northern plain of Germany, around the end of the Siegfried Line, turning the Ruhr in a vast enveloping movement from the north. Initially, Monty had envisaged the air assault being made by only one division, but realization of the

* He thought the General was Browning. According to James Gunn, Browning did fly in, with Dempsey, to see Monty in a Mosquito bomber on 10 September. In his (unpublished) diaries Gunn several times refers to the coming Arnhem operation – further confirmation of the lack of security surrounding it.

† *A Soldier's Story*, p. 416. Bradley did add, however, that though '. . . I never reconciled myself to the venture, I nevertheless freely concede that Monty's plan for Arnhem was one of the most imaginative of the war.'

risks involved persuaded him to drop three, the whole of Brereton's and Browning's First Allied Airborne Army, comprising the British 1st and the US 82nd and 101st Divisions and the Polish 1st Independent Parachute Brigade. The key unit, facing by far the biggest risk in capturing the bridge at Arnhem, was Major-General Robert Urquhart's 1st British Airborne, which – after seventeen cancelled operations (the latest being at Tournai) – had not yet taken part in the war in north-west Europe. Highly trained, keyed-up troops, frustration had brought them almost to the verge of mutiny.* The task of linking up with their lightly armed force devolved upon Horrocks' XXX Corps, which would have to advance sixty-five miles, mostly along a single raised causeway with marsh and dykes on either side. This in effect meant a one-tank front. And the armour had to break through to Arnhem in forty-eight hours, before the Germans could rally forces to crush Urquhart.

On the intelligence available, Bill Williams says he tried to get Monty to 'change his mind' on 10 September. Tragically, the one man who, he felt, might have persuaded Monty that the risks involved were now excessive, de Guingand, was away sick, with stress-induced illness. But, at first, all seemed to go well. The US divisions captured their objectives. In the van of XXX Corps, the Guards Armoured – headed by a famed Grenadier Sergeant Robinson† – rushed the 1200-yard-long bridge at Nijmegen. There they stuck, unable to advance and unable to deploy off the causeway. Some of the Americans accused them of being sluggish.

By the end of the month, the operation had collapsed, with higher casualties than had been suffered during the D-Day landings, and the remnants of Urquhart's heroic division evacuated out of Arnhem.

The tragedy of Arnhem remains all too vividly before us: the airborne divisions, frustrated and unblooded in the war to date, champing at the bit in England; the fact of de Guingand being away sick at the time, his restraining influence removed; the intelligence

* With hindsight, their deployment at Arnhem under the pressure of so many aborted operations strikes one as almost as tragic a misdirection of explosive energy as sending the Canadians to Dieppe in 1942.

† The first officer to get across the bridge was future Foreign Secretary, Captain Lord Carrington.

reports about the newly deployed Panzer units unheeded; the inexpertly chosen dropping grounds, too far from the vital bridge at Arnhem;* the long, hopelessly vulnerable single causeway along which Horrocks' tanks had to travel; the poor wireless communications; the lack of fighter-bomber support; the remarkable fighting power displayed, once again, by the German defenders.† All these were to lead to one of the British Army's most heroic but disastrous actions in war, dealing the worst blow to Monty's reputation.

Why then was the astonishing risk of Arnhem undertaken, by a general reputed never to take an unwarranted risk? Even if it had succeeded, would it have materially advanced the end of the war? It is now generally accepted that the famous catchphrase, 'a bridge too far', was never actually uttered by Lieutenant-General Sir Frederick ('Boy') Browning. Yet it could properly have been, for not only was Arnhem a bridge too far in terms of the relieving ground forces reaching it, but if one studies the map it was too far in the wrong direction – it led the axis of advance due north, into Holland, and away from Monty's prime objective of the Ruhr. Richard Lamb claims, 'If Nijmegen had been the ultimate target, then Montgomery's airborne operation was a tremendous success.'‡ But this is questionable: it was still a bridge too far off the main axis. The logical bridgehead here would have been at Wesel (where, all of six months later, Monty would actually cross the Rhine into Germany). This was where Monty had initially wanted to make his airborne strike. But the air barons had vetoed this, once again, on grounds similar to those they had mustered in Normandy, namely that concentrated flak fire from the Ruhr would make losses in aircraft prohibitively high. On the same grounds, they had refused to make landings on both sides of the Arnhem bridge, or closer to it – either of which

* One has only to walk the ground at Arnhem to realize how hopelessly far removed was the dropping zone at Osterbeek from the vital bridge.

† Despite intelligence leakages caused by faulty security, to some extent the Germans were taken by surprise at Arnhem but – as in Normandy – reacted with extraordinary speed, once more showing their great skill at improvisation. Convalescents and cooks alike were swept up and rushed to the front in *ad hoc* fighting groups under strange officers; gunners were made to fight as infantry, some armed with unfamiliar captured British airborne weapons. Doubtless the recent revelation of the untimely Morgenthau Plan gave morale that little extra fillip.

‡ Lamb, *Montgomery in Europe*, p. 234.

would have substantially enhanced Urquhart's possibilities of success.

Afterwards, Monty claimed – defensively – that Arnhem had been '90 per cent successful'. On no reckoning could it be so considered. Perhaps more to the point was the severe judgement of the intelligence major whose warning of the presence of the unexpected Panzer divisions had gone unheeded, Brian Urquhart: 'The fact was that an unrealistic, foolish plan had been dictated by motives which should have played no part in a military operation that put so many lives and the early ending of the war at risk.'* Despite the pressure of Browning and the airborne commanders 'bouncing' Monty into it, despite the urgency of wiping out the V-2 sites, as pressed on him by Brooke, Monty's action in so uncharacteristically committing himself to a 'foolish plan', so full of risk, has to be seen against the whole background of the dispute with Eisenhower over command and forward strategy. If Arnhem had succeeded – and it might have done if only one or two of the adverse factors had been removed – then it would have been that much harder for the Allied Joint Chiefs of Staff to have continued to reject Monty's 'single thrust'. Monty would have produced a *fait accompli*, a powerful argument which Ike could have resisted only with difficulty.

The long-term consequences of Arnhem were dire, and in good part traceable back to the serial wrangle between Monty and Ike. With hindsight, well may one ask whether – but for that fundamental incompatibility between the two generals – Arnhem, or the Ardennes, would ever have happened. Would Monty have undertaken such a supremely risky operation, were it not that, in despair at the way Ike's strategy was heading, he had to persuade his American critics that he was not just the ultra-cautious commander of Caen, and that he was capable of leading a devastating, single thrust into Germany to end the war? Now, instead of being closer to the Ruhr, Monty found himself extended on a long salient leading nowhere; Holland, starving, remained unliberated; the V-2s continued to terrorize Londoners with impunity. Worst of all, the move northwards had dangerously stretched the Allied front. There was now a gap yawning between Dempsey's Second Army and Hodges' US First

* Sir Brian Urquhart, *A Life in Peace and War*, p. 76. He became Under Secretary General at the United Nations.

Army on his right. This in turn meant that Hodges had to extend his front leftwards to cover the gap. Meanwhile, to the south, Patton was still hammering away, with all his attention directed to Metz and Saar. It was inviting a counter-coup, and disaster.

Full of high hopes and the excitement of pursuing after hounds in full cry, on 3 September (after church parade), TAC HQ had packed up from the grounds of the Pozzo di Borgo Château Dangu and set forth on its longest move. Shortly before leaving Dangu, there had been an alarum when one of the armed Free French patriots had been shot while clearing the woods of Germans. For one night only, TAC paused outside Conty, in a pleasant water meadow amid empty countryside 'with only an occasional abandoned German gun to remind one of the war'. The next day, crossing the old Somme battlefields with their sombre memories for Monty, they stopped for just a further two nights in the grounds of another château, Saulty, on the outskirts of Arras. It was a cramped site with 'the same damp melancholy' as Creullet; but, recorded Paul Odgers, 'news was good here and the LOs brought exciting details of life in Brussels'. Swiftly, concealed from the puritan gaze of 'Master', several of them acquired girlfriends there, eager to bestow their enthusiasm on the liberating British. 'Indeed,' continued Odgers drily, 'Liaison here perhaps reached a pitch of ardency which it was not to reach again till the sterner days of the Ardennes battle.' Meanwhile, still in France, there were frequent encounters with brave Frenchmen who had sheltered Allied airmen and now wanted to join up. With Freddie de Guingand and Main HQ still back at Balleroi near Bayeux, however, communications between the two were never more attenuated.

Crossing into Belgium, the reception was rapturous. In Tournai Sergeant Norman Kirby of the Field Security found his motorcycle 'most cunningly and artistically decorated with red, white and blue flowers'.* At their first stop by a lake-girt château called Houtaing, full of evacuated orphans, ecstatic villagers swarmed into even the most secret of the caravans, making life impossible for the harassed Sergeant Kirby and his men. After another two days, TAC moved

* Kirby, *1100 Miles with Monty*, p. 72.

yet again, into the beautiful grounds of the Château d'Everberg, midway between Louvain and Brussels, amid glorious early September weather. The surroundings were familiar to Monty, since they had been the headquarters of 3rd Division just before the retreat began in May 1940. Up to that very morning, the Princesse de Merode had had quartered on her the Luftwaffe's crack Molders Squadron. 'I have never seen anything like it – they had all come from Paris – at 6 a.m. they all formed up, as if to attention, and mounted in perfect order.' At 9 a.m., TAC HQ arrived to take over their billets – 'just like a hotel!' Recalling what Monty's staff had done to the cellars four years previously, the Princesse was cautiously welcoming. Nevertheless, Norman Kirby recalled a 'general atmosphere of intoxication', in which 'one of our lads married a countess and a few others had "narrow" escapes'. When they gave a 'hop' in the local village of Kortenberg, the whole community arrived with shopping bags, 'and all the refreshments – including free beer and sandwiches – disappeared. Followed by the disappearance of our guests and dancing partners,' noted Kirby, depicting the other side of the Belgian coin.

At Everberg, TAC settled down for one of its longer sojourns – two thoroughly pleasant weeks, disturbed only by the hectic planning for Arnhem. Meanwhile, Main HQ had arrived at the Residence Palace in Brussels; not until the end of the war would the two be so close again. It was from Everberg that Arnhem was planned and launched, from here also that Monty wrote to David, after a long pause, of his entering Brussels to pay his 'respects to the Burgermaster. He received me in great state with officials in brilliant uniforms . . . then I heard the Queen wanted to see me; I was out in my corduroys and grey sweater, so went to the Palace like that!' Five days later, also from Everberg, he was able to report excitedly that Gunn's 'great portrait is finished and is completely the cat's whiskers; it will have to be shown in the Academy next year, and will undoubtedly be "the picture of the year" '. Shortly before the Court Painter, his work completed, departed for England, his name was to be found in the Betting Book wagering glumly, as the struggle for Arnhem seesawed back and forth, £10 that Churchill would die three months after the war with Germany ended. The lost wager was presumably set against the cost of the portrait.

On 21 September, TAC HQ moved from the gentle delights of Everberg to a 'blasted heath' called Hechtel, near Leopoldburg, the 'Aldershot of Belgium'. Here a sinister discovery was made: the wooden stakes and butts riddled with bullet holes of a German execution firing-range, and 200 graves. Anxiously the staff watched as the Dakotas and gliders poured over on their way to Arnhem.* By some curious freak of TAC's wireless reception, Monty found himself more closely in touch with signals from Arnhem than the unfortunate commander, General Urquhart, himself – who for critical periods was totally out of touch with his men, positioned all round him. Odgers recalls that the LOs' trips up the congested causeway to Nijmegen in these desperate days 'were violent missions executed at top speed'. For their part in the battle, several of the LOs were subsequently decorated by the King.

On 25 September, under cover of dark, the tragic remnants – little more than 2000 strong – of Urquhart's brave 1st Airborne Division were withdrawn from Arnhem. Monty had moved his TAC HQ up into Holland, to the great Philips Radio town of Eindhoven, only recently captured in the course of Horrocks' road thrust towards Arnhem. Since the first days in Normandy, the front line had never been closer. One of the LOs' Auster reconnaissance planes was shot up when it 'took a wrong turning' just north of the city. The centre of Eindhoven had been shattered by a savage German air raid a few days previously, but TAC found a site in the city park adjacent to public swimming baths called the Iron Man.† Its members swiftly became aware of the brutal difference in the facts of life between relatively prosperous Belgium, where the affluent Bruxellois lived off a thriving black market, and a semi-starving, bitterly resistant Holland where rich and poor alike ransacked the dustbins. The lack of old people was most marked. 'Many of the old died long ago,' a Dutch friend told Sergeant Kirby. 'You English, you don't know what it means to starve, to have to eat your own pets.' In the grim winter that lay ahead for occupied Holland, the Dutch would

* These would almost certainly have been the unfortunate Poles of General Sosabowski's Polish 1st Independent Parachute Brigade. Not for the first time in the war, the brave Poles drew a short straw. Dropped at Driel south of the Rhine in a desperate attempt to relieve Urquhart, by the time they landed all the crossings over the river were dominated by German guns. Their casualties were the highest of any of the drops.

† Now converted into a civic art centre.

survive on the one national product which was still plentiful – tulip bulbs.

It was at Eindhoven that Monty received an exhausted and deeply downcast Urquhart on his return from Arnhem. Urquhart recalled being greeted by Johnny Henderson, 'who was worried because two of Monty's pets – rabbits or squirrels or canaries – had escaped'. He was given one of the caravans to rest and sleep in, a privilege Monty claimed he set aside only for Winston Churchill and the King. When he had recovered, Monty questioned Urquhart at great length about what had gone wrong at Arnhem. He was most gentle, without any sense of 'you bloody well failed', Urquhart recalled.* Monty followed this up with a moving congratulatory letter to be passed to all survivors, and with letters to the CIGS ensuring that those who had suffered at Arnhem should be 'looked after' with especially sympathetic treatment, and that decorations be set aside for those now in German POW camps. Urquhart never forgot his meeting with Monty, which was in marked contrast to his perfunctory reception by Browning. He noted especially the warmth of understanding Monty had shown, as the fatherly commander profoundly concerned for the welfare of his men. If Ike brought out the worst in Monty, here was the best.

With the failure of Arnhem, the jaunty mood that had tinted TAC in the exciting days of rapid movement from one site to another in September gave way to one of sombre gloom, to which the dank autumn weather of the Low Countries added its own dimension. As October got under way, Monty despatched Kit Dawnay to England with the following, domestic message to Phyllis Reynolds:

> I am sending by him some summer wear to be put away, vests, pants, shirts, etc.
>
> And I want him to bring out my winter wear:
>
> Jaeger dressing gown
> Woollen pyjamas
> Thick vests and short pants. There are some very nice woollen ones I think.
>
> Four of each is enough.†

* Quoted in Hamilton, *Monty*, vol. III, pp. 93–7.
† Montgomery Collection.

Beneath the letter lay the bitter acceptance that the campaign was now inevitably going to drag on into winter, that which Monty had struggled so hard to avoid. In himself he showed signs of deep fatigue. But there were distractions. On 27 October, David received a short note: 'I have had a visit from the King.... "Rommel" is not very well and he has never quite recovered from his attack of pneumonia.' The King's second visit to TAC, this time for a whole six days, was quite an event. Senior officers as well as LOs who had distinguished themselves in the recent battle were decorated. Sergeant Norman Kirby recalled a Dutch friend slashing up her best evening dress to make a cushion and a footstool for the King. It was illustrative of how the Dutch felt about the British, despite the deep disappointment over Arnhem and all it meant for their country, still under Nazi occupation.

During part of this time, Monty was living temporarily in greater comfort back in Brussels at Main HQ. He wrote to David on 3 November, congratulating him on doing cross-country runs:

> I think they are excellent things.... I have, for the moment, left my caravans and am living in a house;* a very palatial residence, full of lovely furniture. I expect the natural repercussions will be that when I return to my caravans I shall catch a colossal cold.

He noted that the dog Rommel was still unwell. Four days later, he set off on a secret visit to London, his first since D-Day, to receive his baton from the King, have his dentures repaired again by his much tried dentist, and participate in a gloomy meeting with Brooke. Major Peter Earle noted how 'he was not allowed in through the front entrance [of the War Office], for security reasons', and there followed this rather engagingly childish exchange between Major and Field Marshal:

> He came into my office and told me the PM had asked him to write something on the battle for Walcheren. 'What shall I write, how do I start? I am going to the country, how do I get it up?'

* For the first time since he had crossed over to Normandy in June. At Creullet and Dangu he had, of course, continued to reside in his caravan. The 'palatial residence' would have been Main HQ in Brussels, rather than the distinctly spartan surroundings, little improved even half a century later, at the Villa Mommen in Zonhoven. Visiting it in 1994, one can see that Monty's hyperboles, reflected – in their very excess – a puritan's delight.

> 'The secret truth', said I, 'is that the PM has asked everybody to write this.' . . . 'Oh well, I needn't write it,' said he. 'Oh yes, you must,' said I; 'I will attach it to the others in your own handwriting; the PM will love it.' 'I will say the British troops are bayoneting Germans up to their armpits. . . .' 'That's it!' I said, 'that will be a Chief of Staff's draft.' 'Rather below their level,' said Montgomery. 'Ha ha, yes, rather below their level!'

Inside the CIGS's office, Monty 'made it very clear that in my opinion we must now accept the fact that the war will go on well into next year. We had gone badly astray in two main fundamentals – (A) we had broken the great principle of concentration; (B) the set-up command control of operations was very faulty.' He continued:

> there are three points, as follows: (a) if we had taken the correct action in early September – as regards concentration and command – we might well have won the war by Christmas; (b) if we take the correct action NOW, we could win the war by the spring of 1945; (c) if we do not take the correct action now, then the war will go on for most of next year.

His pessimism and state of mental fatigue were amply reflected in wagers in the TAC Betting Book at this time – that the war would not be over by the end of June 1945 (he was forced to pay up).

On 8 November, he visited David at Winchester, returning to Brussels two days later accompanied by A. P. Herbert (plus seven London editors), who brought with him once again some badly needed light relief. On their arrival, Monty wrote to tell David, 'a flying-bomb exploded fifty yards away from my house in Brussels, one hour after I got back; all the glass in my windows was broken and I got covered with debris, but no harm was done. I am leaving Brussels tomorrow for the country!!' According to APH, against this background Monty remained 'very gay' and kept urging him to play the piano. Then 'Suddenly the grim martinet came to the piano, and, to the delight and surprise of his staff, burst into song.' The episode occasioned 'Petty Officer A. P. Herbert' to bet Johnny Henderson that 'at least one "doodle-bug" ' would have dropped within half a mile of TAC in Brussels over the next three weeks. He returned home to publish in the *Daily Telegraph* some further cheery patriotic doggerel in praise of his host, entitled 'Field Marshal':

> Who indeed on the land that hails thee,
> Baton in your hand.
> How much they label you a showman.
> They said you were eccentric;
> We could do with several abnormalities like you.

Eindhoven's public gardens becoming, in the words of Paul Odgers, 'exceedingly cold and damp', and Brussels proving to lack tranquillity, the new 'country' retreat Monty's staff found for him was at Zonhoven, in *Flamande* Belgium. Close to Hasselt, and poised facing eastwards to Germany, less than twenty-five miles away across the wide River Maas, Zonhoven was to become Monty's winter headquarters. He would be there for over three months, lodged in a typically Breughelesque home, the Villa Mommen, of simple but appalling taste, with only one bath,* set back a short distance from the main road. Apart from the recent brief interlude in Brussels, it was the first time Monty had slept in a house since leaving Broomfield House. TAC HQ took over surrounding schools and houses for their offices; 'the village is bellyaching still', wrote Odgers a year later. Nothing could have been better designed to dispel the high spirits of Dangu and Everberg in that sunny September than Zonhoven. 'The heating system did not work yet,' recalled A. P. Herbert, 'and Monty's room was always full of the rumble of tanks and guns and lorries. Doodle-bugs roared over now and then from Brussels. But the canaries and the goldfish were on parade as well; the canaries did their best.' 'It was an awful place,' recalls Odgers. 'The flat, dreary, water-logged fields brought depression to the spirit, which the single redbrick village street did nothing to relieve.... The Church frowned on dancing.'† The sojourn at Zonhoven started with bad enough omens; a four-year-old child was run over by an army truck; a nineteen-year-old private died from drinking local wood alcohol; and on 18 December, two days after the beginning of the Ardennes offensive, Monty's beloved cocker spaniel Rommel

* So it remains to this day.
† 'A TAC Chronicle'.

was killed on the main road. He was buried in the Mommen garden, under a simple gravestone inscribed: 'Rommel. Companion of F-M Montgomery from Normandy to Holland. Died 18.12.'44.'*

Winter soon manifested itself as one of the beastliest in living memory, with wartime hazards multiplied by glassy, dangerous roads lethal under nocturnal blackout conditions. The junior members of the headquarters kept themselves warm by secretly brewing (well out of the Field Marshal's range of vision) 'bathtub gin' in what had once been a small family still, and which – through British patronage – grew into a major industry after the war. Every Sunday Monty would lead church parades through the empty, rainy streets. Inside the Mommen Villa, Monty's personal menagerie – though sadly depleted by the decease of Rommel – had been incremented by a bowl of goldfish acquired in Holland and a canary called Herbie, given by a Canadian newspaper. Herbie (according to A. P. Herbert) 'possessed one of the world's undiscovered talents. He sang piercingly and continually; and Montgomery, as if to show his opinion of the way the war was being run, kept him on his desk, making rational conversation virtually impossible.' Eventually even Monty realized that Herbie had to go.

It was during this drab, protracted period of inactivity at Zonhoven that the bonds of reliance, and real affection, were cemented between the Field Marshal and his young men. Mutual loyalties had grown immensely strong. In the prevailing strategic disappointments of the war, more than ever did Monty in his essential loneliness come to depend on his 'family'. Evenings in the mess were always jolly affairs. Monty would discreetly turn a blind eye to the escapades of his officers with mistresses in Brussels. But it was still, largely, a monastic, closed society.

The simple austerity at Zonhoven was in extraordinary contrast to how the various US and Allied headquarters were besporting themselves back in France. SHAEF had moved into the splendours of Versailles, where Ike had set up his ménage with Kay at the Hôtel Trianon Palace. Autumn, Stephen Ambrose notes, was 'never Eisenhower's best season',† but there was no shortage of conviviality, or liquor – which was proving to be the worst problem of the US

* Some unknown souvenir-hunter later made off with the stone.

† Ambrose (1), p. 536.

forces in Paris. The simple midwest farmboy in Ike was infuriated by the excesses he saw in Paris. Following the Liberation, SHAEF's admin chief, General J. C. H. (profanely nicknamed 'Jesus Christ Himself') Lee had moved 8000 officers and 21,000 men into the city, provoking French magazines to refer to SHAEF as Société des Hôteliers Américains en France. At his headquarters in beautiful Nancy, Marlene Dietrich and her troupe would entertain George S. Patton (who celebrated his fifty-ninth birthday on 12 November) and his 'niece', Jean Gordon. Patton would also take Jean on leave to Paris, to the Ritz and the *Folies Bergère*, whenever possible.

It was at gloomy Zonhoven in early December, however, that Colonel Joe Ewart, Monty's German-speaking intelligence officer under the brilliant Bill Williams, first identified a whole new German Panzer army forming up in the western part of Hitler's Reich.

CHAPTER TEN

STRATEGIC DIFFERENCES

December 1944–May 1945

> In Normandy our strategy for the land battle, and the plan to achieve it, was simple and clear-cut. The pieces were closely 'stitched' together. It was never allowed to become unstitched; and it succeeded. After Normandy our strategy became unstitched. There was no plan; and we moved by disconnected jerks.
>
> (Montgomery, *Memoirs*, p. 286)

> I hope the American public will realize that, owing to the handling of the campaign in western Europe from 1 Sept. onwards, the German war will now go on during 1945. And they should realize very clearly that the handling of the campaign is entirely in American hands.
>
> (Montgomery, letter to P. J. Grigg, 7 December 1944)

> I was persuaded to drink some champagne at dinner tonight.
>
> (Montgomery, signal to Field Marshal Brooke, 4 May 1945)

'THE PRESENT situation is that we are completely stuck,' Monty wrote to his friend 'Simbo' Simpson in London on 27 November. 'You would think from the papers that the whole German Army was cracking; in actual fact the Germans have the First and Ninth armies well held.' On the evening of 15 December he signalled Brooke, warning him that he did not 'propose to send any more evening situation reports until the war becomes more exciting'. At the same time he wrote to Ike, with a special request: 'If you have no objection I would like to hop over to England on Saturday 23 December and spend Christmas with my son. I have not seen him since D-Day.' Given the lull in the fighting since Arnhem, the boring tedium at soggy Zonhoven, it all seemed perfectly reasonable. He was looking forward to spending a quiet

Christmas at home with David. It would have been their first together since that grim year of 1937, after David's mother had died. On the 16th, almost the first day that the low-lying countryside had not been entirely water-logged, Monty flew up to Eindhoven for a rare game of golf with Dai Rees, the professional golfer currently serving as Broadhurst's driver. It was there that he heard that the Germans had attacked in force in the Ardennes, against Hodges' US First Army. He immediately flew back to Zonhoven.

That same afternoon, Ike was playing bridge at his headquarters in Versailles with Bradley, Bedell Smith and his close 'buddy' and remarkable purveyor of booze and gossip, Major-General Everett Hughes. Kay Summersby was in close attendance. Earlier Ike had attended a staff wedding, and then cracked a bottle of champagne to celebrate news of his fifth star. It was a day of all-round conviviality. Bradley's aide, Chester B. Hansen, had hastened to join Ernest Hemingway at the Lido, 'where we saw bare-breasted girls do the hootchy-kootchie until it was late'. It was the same sense of 'all quiet' that pervaded the Allied armies from top to bottom, that third week in December. Who could blame them? The only shadow that day had been Bradley warning Ike that his flow of infantry replacements was not keeping pace with casualties – the headache that had begun to plague Monty in Normandy. When the news of the German attack came through, Bradley at first dismissed it as 'a spoiling attack', went on with his bridge, opened another bottle of scotch and did not get back to his forward headquarters in Luxembourg until mid-afternoon on the 17th. Ike seems to have been quicker to spot the danger, but in the absence of news the situation looked uncertain. For several hours it was not clear just how serious it was.

The astonishing and amazingly cheeky thing about what came to be called the Battle of the Bulge (reflecting the dangerous salient it thrust into the Allied lines) was that it had all been done before, over the same terrain, by the same German commander: General von Rundstedt had struck there, with devastating success, in 1940. The reason why it came so close to repeating that success now was also the same – surprise. A certain fatalism about Ike's plans had led Monty to assume that almost anything disagreeable might now happen. Nevertheless he was just as much caught on the hop as were Ike and Bradley; even though, as noted in the previous chapter, his brilliant intelligence team under Bill Williams had identified a whole new Panzer army forming up in western Germany, though they had no idea of its purpose.* It might be assumed that a reasonable enemy commander would be holding this body as a counter-attack force once the Allies began their offensive across the Rhine. Nobody could imagine that, with the Russians hammering closer and closer to Berlin in the east, it would be used for an *offensive* in the west. But Hitler, whose idea the Ardennes offensive was, could hardly be described as a 'reasonable' man. Occasionally, backed by his uncanny intuition, this had proved to be his great strength. Secrecy had been preserved over the massive preparations by the fierce winter weather, which grounded Allied reconnaissance – and by the short days. ULTRA was fooled because, just as in May 1940, all signals went out over secure land lines. And, despite the shock of Arnhem, few still believed that so soon after the crushing defeat of Normandy the Germans could have recovered to the extent of striking as fearsomely as they did. The Germans themselves spoke of the 'Miracle of the West'. As Colonel Dupuy remarks, 'What is amazing is the fact that the Germans had been able to undertake such an offensive at all, and drive 80 kms deep in the lines of an enemy with overwhelmingly superior numerical and material strength.'†

An armchair critic today might well ask, did none of the Allied commanders read history? Or was it just too fanciful to contemplate the Germans trying the same attack, in the same area, twice in the same war – however tempting the thinning of the Allied lines had made that particular area?

Hitler's objective was to crash through the American lines of Hodges' First Army, across the River Meuse, to seize Antwerp. If this succeeded, it would achieve almost exactly what Rundstedt had done in 1940 – splitting the Allied armies in two, the Americans from the British, Bradley from Montgomery. The results would be incalculable. It was a staggering gamble, yet even if Antwerp were reached, could the Germans long hold their gains in the face of Allied air and ground superiority? It was not the French Army of 1940 they were facing. In May 1940, the Panzers had struck two weak

* By the 17th SHAEF's intelligence summary was still dismissing the offensive as 'a diversionary attack on a fair scale'.

† Dupuy, *A Genius for War*, p. 2.

divisions of French reservists, which had promptly caved in, leaving a gaping hole in the line.*

So in December 1944 the full force of two concentrated Panzer armies smashed into two inexperienced American infantry divisions of Hodges' First. By the night of the 18th, German tanks had rent a hole fifty miles wide between Malmédy in the north and Echternach in the south, and were twenty miles over the Belgian frontier, scattering demoralized GIs before them. At one point the Germans reached within a few miles of the gigantic American petrol dump of Stavelot, containing two million gallons, enough to keep an entire Panzer division on the road for a month, with only one company of engineers to defend it. But they then, unaccountably, veered off to the south-west. By the 19th, so Monty wrote, 'I could see little to prevent German armoured cars and reconnaissance elements bouncing the Meuse and advancing on Brussels.'† The threat to the flank and rear of the whole of 21 Army Group was very real. Nevertheless it was precisely the kind of challenge to which Monty rose most superbly. Swiftly he deployed XXX Corps to provide 'stoppers' of armoured units covering each of the Meuse bridges from the west bank, in case the American defence should crack.

Caught on leave in England in a 'pea-souper' fog, Freddie de Guingand returned to find Monty 'looking supremely cheerful and confident. This was of course just his "cup of tea".' De Guingand added that he 'appeared to be at the top of his form and really enjoying himself.... I never admired my Chief more than on occasions like these.'‡ It was also an occasion when Monty's system of LOs now really came into its own. Down in Luxembourg, Bradley was completely cut off from all communication with his First and Ninth Armies north of the Bulge. It fell to Monty's eyes and ears to inform him of what was happening to Bradley's own formations, and he despatched his entire team of LOs fanning out deep into the American sectors to find out. In a matter of hours he had a much clearer view, embarrassingly for the Americans, of what was happening to the US First Army's forces than Hodges himself.

On the morning of the 19th, two of his LOs, Carol Mather and

* See Horne, *To Lose a Battle; France 1940* (London 1990)

† Montgomery, *Normandy to the Baltic*, p. 176.

‡ *Operation Victory*, p. 429.

Dick Harden, went off to Spa, Hodges' forward HQ – which had also been the Kaiser's headquarters in 1914. They were joined by Major (later Lieutenant-Colonel) Tom Bigland, a gunner officer and DSO from the desert, whom Monty had attached to Bradley as his LO. What they found was most disquieting. Hodges had pulled out, and the headquarters was empty, except for 'two Americans', recalled Harden, 'who had just been in bed with two women, and were hanging around'.* 'We found it deserted,' was Carol Mather's recollection, 'with Christmas lunch laid out and every sign of evacuation in a hurry.'† Bigland added, 'the Christmas tree was decorated in the dining room, telephones were in all the offices, papers were all over the place, but there was no one left to tell visitors where they had gone to.'‡ Bigland then returned to Bradley. At the 6 p.m. debriefing that night, the LOs' news that Hodges (who had never impressed Monty as an Army Commander) had abandoned his HQ, without so much as warning anybody, caused him to be 'extremely alarmed'. He was, Mather recalled, 'profoundly worried that his rear communications could easily be severed, all the way back to Antwerp. . . . He was alarmed, but certainly not rattled. In fact he was enjoying himself!' Monty sent Mather out again at midnight – which was 'most unusual'. He was to find Hodges, and 'order' him 'to block the Meuse bridges – even with farm carts! I said, "How can I? He is not under your command!" "Never mind, just tell him . . ." ' Mather located Hodges at 2 a.m., 'mystified as to why he was there'. Ordered to report back to Monty, 'whatever time it was,' Mather found him between 5 and 6 a.m., 'sitting up in bed with a cup of tea'. Bigland later reckoned that Mather's report of First Army HQ having been abandoned was very probably what lay behind Ike next day 'putting Monty in charge of all American troops north of the breakthrough'.

At Ike's, albeit reluctant, insistence, on the 20th Monty temporarily assumed command over both Hodges' First Army and Lieutenant-General William H. Simpson's Ninth, in addition to 21 Army Group – in fact over all the Allied forces north of the Ardennes. As Horrocks of XXX Corps remarked, thanks to his system of liaison

* Interview 24 November 1992.
† Interview 24 November 1992.
‡ *Bigland's War*, p. 81.

officers, at that moment 'Monty was probably the only man who had a completely up-to-date picture of the whole battle front.'* On the face of it, there could hardly have been a more terrible, shaming indictment of how the US chain of command had broken down, and how little effective control Eisenhower, since 1 September the Supreme Land Force Commander, exerted over his forces. It meant that Monty had now got in his hands what he had been pressing for ever since August and Falaise, and what he had failed to get after Arnhem: total command over the Allied northern wing. Predictably, it was a *tactical* triumph, Monty being renownedly at his best when conducting a calculated, aggressive defence, as at Alam Halfa; predictably, it was a *strategic* disaster, in that even the Ardennes would change nothing in Ike's views on the supreme command, and could only lead, once the crisis had passed, to a final showdown between the two leaders.

With a sang-froid that was not considered amusing in Whitehall, Monty in his despatch describing the situation to Brooke observed that 'We cannot come out through Dunkirk this time as the Germans still hold that place.' His immediate impact, galvanizing the badly shaken troops of the US First Army, was magnetic. 'Neither army commander', he reported to Brooke on the night of the 20th, 'had seen Bradley or any of 12 Army Group staff since the battle began. . . . no reserves behind the front . . . morale very low. They seemed delighted to have someone to give them firm orders.' He was also shocked to see how badly cared for were some of Hodges' troops, many of whom had had no hot meal for several days. This was not his way of looking after his men. As at Alamein, he let himself be seen as often as possible up near the front, regardless of the dangers from alleged German killer squads roaming behind the lines dressed in Allied uniforms. Dick Harden recalled Monty visiting the troops of US 7th Armoured Division, where he had found an atmosphere bordering on panic. An officer told him 'We are cut off,' to which Monty replied, 'That's funny, we just drove in!' The division was:

> very shaken but only really because their commander was so shaken. I well remember taking Monty and Johnny Henderson to

* *A Full Life*, p. 240.

> see this Division in the Rolls and I must say the effect of his talk to all ranks had an electric effect. At least they knew what it was all about and that they were on the winning side and not the other.

Monty, Harden recalled, 'gave them a pep talk: "We are going to win – we are going to push the Germans back where they came from." ' Even with troops of another nation, sceptical about Monty's charms, the tonic was unmistakable, no doubt reinforced by the remarkable spectacle of a Rolls suddenly turning up in the middle of the battle. He revealed himself at his very best. 'Those who were with Monty at this time were astonished by the snap and incisiveness of his orders,' recalled Alan Moorehead. His American LO, Ray BonDurant, thought that he 'did much to assuage feelings' at that time of extreme crisis. He deployed 150 British tanks behind the Meuse, to act like 'clothes pins on a clothes line', and asked for Bradley's Major-General 'Lightning Joe' Collins, whose aggressive posture he had admired in Normandy, to form under his command a strategic reserve – supplying one of his own British divisions for it – to prepare a counter-attack.

Further behind the lines, Eisenhower's situation was considerably worse. After conferring on the 18th at Verdun with Patton, who had assured him – to everybody's amazement – that he could counter-attack northwards in three days' time, with three divisions (and did), Ike had returned to Paris to find himself a virtual prisoner in his own headquarters. Warnings that the legendary Otto Skorzeny, the SS major who had rescued Mussolini, was on his way to Paris with a killer squad in American uniforms and jeeps, had thrown Ike's entourage into a panic. As Kay Summersby noted in her diary, 'E. is urged by all his senior staff members to stay in his office and not go home at all'; and on the following day, the 21st, 'He is confined to the office building, which makes him mad.' Briefly, American security went mad, too, as GIs checked out each other with 'Who is Minnie Mouse's husband?' (a password unlikely to have defeated a Skorzeny). Even in February, well after the danger had receded, Ike found himself limited to exercising only within the heavily protected yard of the Trianon. It could hardly have been more humiliating for a commander-in-chief. Most sensitive to the psychological dangers, back in London Brooke was expressing his worries to 'Simbo' Simpson: 'My heart bleeds for poor Ike now because of what Monty will hint at concerning what Eisenhower ought to have done. It will be "I told you so". . . .' With this on his mind, once more playing the role of wise Ulysses, he sent a message to Monty on the 21st, cautioning him:

> It is most important that you should not even in the slightest degree rub this undoubted fact in to anyone at SHAEF or elsewhere. Any remarks you may make are bound to come to Eisenhower's ears sooner or later and that may make it more difficult to ensure that this new set-up for Command remains even after the present emergency has passed.

He added, though it hardly needed saying, 'I myself have thought you were right all along.'

Nevertheless, inevitably, given who he was and given the recent memories of the Normandy controversy, it was only a matter of time before Monty would be offending American sensibilities, raw from the humiliation they had suffered. The weather changed, the sun came out and with it the devastating swarms of Broadhurst's rocket-firing Typhoons, still the most effective weapon against the indestructible Tigers and Panthers which Rundstedt had hurled into the Ardennes in such quantities. By Christmas Eve, the last German offensive in the west had petered out. Just three miles from the Meuse bridge at Dinant an inscription stands near a knocked-out Panther, marking its point of high tide. With immense heroism, the American 101st Airborne, recent veterans of MARKET GARDEN, had hung on determinedly at the key centre of Bastogne, their commander rejecting a German call to surrender with the immortal reply 'Nuts!' As good as his word, Patton, having astonishingly disengaged three divisions and performed a ninety-degree wheel, was driving relentlessly into the Bulge from the south. But there was bitterness in the American camp when Monty held back on his attack with 'Lightning Joe' Collins from the north. It was this that provoked Patton's offensive gibe, 'Monty is a tired little fart. War requires the taking of risks and he won't take them.' But Monty had sound reasons: he was determined not to waste men, British or American, in premature riposte – knowing in any case that, after the heavy losses already sustained, the reserves would be essential for the next stage of the war into Germany.

By the end of the year, after much bitter fighting, the danger had passed. The Americans had lost over 80,000 men, many of them POWs (the Germans some 120,000 men, plus 600 tanks and assault guns) – and all, in Monty's opinion, unnecessarily. On New Year's Eve, Monty wrote to P. J. Grigg, 'All is well and the Germans will now not get what they wanted. But they have given the Americans a colossal "bloody nose" and mucked up all our plans; however, as we had not got a plan I suppose they will say it does not matter.' This renewed tone of bitterness reflected the latest, and nearly terminal, row that had just ensued between Monty and Ike. In a letter to Phyllis Reynolds on Christmas Day, with a terse explanation full of anger about why he had been unable to return for Christmas, the theme 'bloody nose' and 'I am busy sorting out the mess' reappears. So it did in a letter written to Mountbatten (now Supreme Allied Commander in South-East Asia) that same day: 'this thing should never have happened; one ought really to burst into tears. It has prolonged the war by months.' And to his successor at Eighth Army, General Sir Oliver Leese, now Mountbatten's newly appointed Land Force Commander-in-Chief, 'There is no ink that I know would stand up to what I would like to say.' Monty's unseasonal ill-humour was not improved by the fact that, by Boxing Day, in the ten days since the German attack began, he had received only one half-audible telephone call from his superior. He had 'no idea where Ike is'; all Bedell Smith could tell him was that he 'is locked up – whatever that may mean'. Ike was in fact still sealed off in his Hôtel Trianon Palace headquarters at Versailles; 'E. is a bit low in his mind,' Kay Summersby recorded in her diary for Christmas. It was a major understatement: his mood was approaching despair, not aided by regular needling from Monty.

On Christmas Day, Bradley visited Monty at Zonhoven after a rough flight, to find no car to meet him. Contrasts with Christmas at his own headquarters in embattled Luxembourg were noteworthy. Monty's staff officer 'smoked pipes over port' in a leisurely fashion; walls were festooned with Monty's own Christmas cards – as Bradley's ADC noted, the Americans had been too busy to send any that year. Christmas lunch for Bradley that day had consisted of an apple and a pear munched *en route*, following which he received from Monty an earful about American errors, set out with the Field Marshal's inimitably simple, ruthless clarity. Nigel Hamilton in his official biography, generally sympathetic to Monty in his dispute with Eisenhower and the Americans, criticizes him, the perfectionist, here for his failure to comprehend that 'in an alliance of democratic nations, bonded solely for the purpose and the duration of a specific war, muddle and misadventure were inevitable'.* Indeed, in handling American sensibilities, Monty would have done well to have considered his débâcle at Arnhem as a factor contributing to the 'mess' in which the Alliance as a whole now found itself in the Ardennes. Bradley returned from Zonhoven that Christmas Day feeling his national pride deeply wounded – and, quite out of character, was unforgiving.

On the 28th, Monty – now *de facto* commander of thirty-four Allied divisions – finally met Ike, aboard the Supremo's heavily guarded armoured train at Hasselt station, during a lull in the German onslaught. Like Bradley, Ike had had a fatiguing journey and was testy. Once more Monty returned to his old theme of command and the 'single thrust', using his present position of strength as a lever, and finally offering – once again – to serve under Bradley if need be. After he had departed, Monty, assuming that Ike had now swung round to his view, sent off a written confirmation couched in language bordering on the arrogant. On the issue of command, he told Ike that 'any loosely worded statement will be quite useless' (Monty's well-known favourite term of contempt), and that 'if you merely use the word "co-ordination" it will not work'.

Received by Ike back at Versailles, this unfortunately worded letter coincided with news of Monty's holding back on Collins' counter-stroke from the north, which Eisenhower regarded as 'welching'. He had also just received a supportive letter from Marshall, which noted that the British press had been urging appointment of a British commander for all ground forces (that is, precisely the Monty line) and instructed Ike, 'Under no circumstances make any concessions of any kind whatsoever.' In anger, Eisenhower now drafted, with the ready help of Tedder, an 'either–or' letter to Mar-

* Hamilton, *Monty*, vol. III, pp. 241–2.

shall, amounting in effect to a request for Monty's resignation. Coming at this moment of extreme tension on the battlefield, it could only have caused a major crisis within the Allied camp. Fortunately, however, the diplomatic de Guingand was at hand in Versailles. He at once realized the full gravity of the situation and hastened immediately back to Zonhoven to warn Monty that, unless he retracted and apologized formally to Ike, he would be sacked and replaced by Alexander. At first amazed, Monty swiftly grasped the danger, sending back on the 31st a humbled signal: 'Very distressed that my letter may have upset you and I would ask you to tear it up.' It was signed, 'Your very devoted subordinate, Monty.'

A major disaster had narrowly been averted. But it was a dark moment for Monty's personal as well as his professional ambition. On the verge of winning the set, having fought what Nigel Hamilton rates 'the finest defensive battle of the war', he suddenly realized he had lost – possibly the match. With his well-tuned antennae, de Guingand observed, 'I felt terribly sorry for my Chief, for he now looked completely nonplussed. . . . It was as if a cloak of loneliness had descended on him.'

That same day, a not very auspicious New Year's Eve 1944, Monty wrote to David, care of the Reynoldses at Amesbury Preparatory School:

> I haven't really congratulated you half enough on being top of your form; it is quite splendid and I want you to know that I am simply delighted. . . . It was a very great disappointment not to be able to get home for Christmas, but things here would not allow. They are now quite okay and I shall hope to get home for a few days' rest later on.

In effect, Hitler had wagered and lost, forfeiting whatever remote chance he still had of winning the war. For the Allies it would now simply be a matter of time, of marching and dying – and squabbling. There remained two episodes in the story of the Ardennes offensive, as the Bulge was sealed off and the defeated enemy crawled back into Germany. On New Year's Day, while Allied airmen where blearily recovering from the night's revelries, out of the blue several hundred Luftwaffe fighter-bombers, virtually every one that Göring had left, and which were thought to have been long since wiped out, descended on forward Allied airfields in France, Holland and Belgium. Whole squadrons of planes were destroyed on the ground; at Brussels' Zaventem alone they totalled 180, including Monty's own TAC Dakota. (In what was a typical act of generosity, especially considering the recent row, Ike immediately sent him in replacement his own brand-new Dakota, which he had just received. Monty was manifestly touched.)* Coming on the heels of the shock of the German ground offensive, it seemed extraordinary, if not the height of carelessness, that the Allies should still require warning that they had only 'scotch'd the snake, not killed it'. Enjoying their discomfort at being so truly caught with their pants down, Bill Williams' intelligence team at TAC HQ could not resist sending their RAF opposite numbers a pair of braces. Perhaps it was all just one more indicator of battle fatigue. When asked by Monty at the end of the Ardennes battle what he was going to do, Dick Harden answered 'Sleep for two hours,' to which the ever fresh Monty responded acidly, 'If you are tired, someone else will do the job.'

Then, on 7 January, to mark the end of the battle, Monty, in his most disastrous venture in the 'special relationship' to date, held his famous press conference. Getting official clearance for it, he told Churchill that he hoped such a conference would put an end to the anti-American 'slanging match' in the domestic press. In fact, it had quite the opposite result. While conducting the battle before the enemy, Monty had been – as we have noted – at his very best; before the Allied press on the 7th he was at his insufferable worst. It was not so much what he said as the way he said it, and – above all – that it was Monty saying it. He arrived wearing a new red airborne beret (rather tactless, in view of Arnhem), and, recalled Bill Williams, 'was like a cock on a dunghill'.† He praised Ike and the fighting qualities of the American soldier at length and with patent sincerity. But it all came across as regrettably patronizing. When he described 'a fine Allied picture . . . of British troops fighting on both sides of

* He wrote to Ike: 'Such spontaneous kindness touches me deeply and from my heart I send you my grateful thanks. If there is anything I can ever do for you to ease the tremendous burden that you bear you know you have only to command me. And I want you to know that I shall always stand firm behind you in everything you do.' For Monty, this was offering a sop of considerable warmth, following his painful climbdown of the day before.

† Quoted in Lamb, *Montgomery in Europe*, p. 331.

American forces who have suffered a hard blow', this was hardly acceptable to Americans, who had done almost all the fighting and had paid with dreadful casualties. Worst of all, in American eyes, was his remark about it being 'a most interesting little battle', which prompted Alan Moorehead to exclaim to Williams in the shocked aftermath, 'Why didn't you stop him?' Both agreed it was disastrous, with Moorehead later reflecting soberly, 'Looking back on the scene from a world at peace one might marvel that the generals could brawl so cold-bloodedly with one another at a time when so many thousands were exposing themselves to death, and dying.' 'Lightning Joe' Collins for one, whom Monty so greatly admired and who was currently fighting under his command, was outraged: 'Monty got under my skin by downgrading the American troops. . . . only one British division participated in the fighting. It left a sour note.' Eisenhower claimed that it caused him 'more distress and worry' than anything else in the entire war.*

In his memoirs, Monty admitted that the press conference had been 'a mistake', for 'So great was the feeling against me on the part of the American generals, that whatever I said was bound to be wrong.' He went on to claim that the disaster of the Ardennes would never have happened 'if we had fought the campaign properly after the great victory in Normandy', and that it had lost six vital weeks in campaigning time. Most skilfully distorted by Goebbels, the press conference did considerable damage within the Alliance. One early consequence was the removal of Simpson's Ninth Army (signifying the last US troops) from under Monty's command once the battle had moved into Germany. With the Americans licking the wounds inflicted during the Battle of the Bulge, it was clear to Monty that their armies would not be capable of undertaking a major offensive for some little time.

Meanwhile, on 12 January, the long-awaited Russian offensive, four million men strong, began rolling from Warsaw towards the Oder – and Berlin. It was just in time, thought Monty and Ike. By the end of January, chiefly as a consequence of Hitler rashly denud-

* Eisenhower, *Crusade in Europe*, p. 356.

ing the east to launch his attack in the Ardennes, the Russians were only fifty miles from Berlin.

While the Americans were recovering, it devolved on Monty and his 21 Army Group, still supported by Simpson's US Ninth Army, to take over the battle as soon as the grip of an exceptionally harsh winter began to relax. One fact brought home grimly to the Allies by the Battle of the Bulge was that, like Britain, America – despite her vast reserves of manpower – was now in serious deficiency of infantry replacements. Monty had, without discord, agreed with Ike that the next stage would be to break through the Siegfried Line* and close up to the left-bank Rhine. The main objective was Wesel, on the opposite side of the Rhine in the flat country just to the north of the Ruhr. It was here that Monty had originally wanted to seize his bridgehead in September; indeed, common sense still favoured it. Accordingly, starting on 8 February and ending on 11 March, Monty launched two admirably well-knit, almost copybook operations: VERITABLE on the left, and GRENADE on the right flank, adjacent to the boundary with Bradley's convalescent US First Army. There was some of the most bitter fighting of the war in the Reichswald Forest, against defenders who were often schoolchildren of sixteen – 'Werewolves' – driven on with all the ferocity of despair by the menace of 'unconditional surrender' and the terror of Nazi discipline and reprisals (*Sippenhaft*) against families. To Horrocks, it was 'the grimmest battle in which I took part during the last war'. Once again, as in September, it seemed as if Monty had set too low a value on enemy morale. But, with the scent of victory at last in their nostrils, Monty's British and Canadians had never shown themselves to better advantage. Nevertheless, the month's fighting cost the combined armies 15,000 casualties, and Simpson's US Ninth Army 7300, for some 90,000 Germans – over half of them prisoners.

On 5 March, to the south, the Americans began their own operation to close up to the Rhine at all speed. Rivalry between the army commanders, each a prima donna, assumed a new intensity. 'We are in a horse race with Courtney [Hodges],'† Patton wrote to Beatrice,

* Built to protect Hitler's western frontier after the reoccupation of the Rhineland, it had now been swiftly reactivated.

† Hodges was one more general whom, like Monty, Patton despised.

his wife, that day; 'if he beats me, I shall be ashamed.' He was beaten; two days later came the almost unbelievable news that Company A, of the 27th Armoured Infantry Battalion of the US 9th Armoured Division, part of Hodges' First Army, had captured intact the historic bridge at Remagen, midway between the Ruhr and Frankfurt-am-Main. With that capacity for swift reaction which distinguished the American Army at its best, and not only Patton, Ike ordered Bradley to rush six divisions across the bridge. Monty was totally in accord, and, by the time the badly damaged bridge collapsed ten days later, the Americans had a large bridgehead, thirty miles wide and ten miles deep, pointing straight at the heart of Germany.

Uncharacteristically, Patton seemed to be lagging behind. Bradley found him having his hair cut, in an old folks' home in Luxembourg, and told him, 'I want you to take the Rhine on the run.'* On the morning of the 23rd Patton signalled Bradley, 'I'm across!' – jubilantly beating Monty by a matter of hours – and was soon streaking for Frankfurt in the best Patton tradition. This combined success of the US First and Third Armies was bound to affect future grand strategy, as Ike signalled Washington that he would now have across the Rhine around the Remagen bridgehead a force at least as great as Monty's 21 Army Group north of the Ruhr.

By 10 March, Monty was able to fix the date of the 24th for his setpiece crossing of the Rhine at Wesel, an imposingly wide obstacle at that point. Between the ending of the Ardennes and the Rhine crossing he had managed to catch up on some correspondence. To his friend, the Bishop of Rochester, Noël Chavasse's father, with whom he had not communicated for a long time, he wrote on 22 January:

> I am shortly coming over to England for a short rest. Noël goes ahead with my car and, having met me, will spend some leave with you. We have been having a strenuous time lately and I shall be glad of some relaxation!
>
> PS Noël has been forbidden to smoke by me. He says it is not a military order; I say *it is* as he is ever so much better since he stopped smoking, and is a better soldier. I rely on you to see that the order is obeyed during his leave.

* Bradley, *A Soldier's Story*, p. 319.

About the same time he was writing to Loris Mather (father of Bill and Carol) about 'a terrific party here since the middle of December; it is all over now and the German has been seen off!!' He had time to indulge in a note of rare family pride, adding, 'David is *very* well; top of his form at the end of last term and got the form prize. He has become a great cross-country runner and got his "socks" last year.'

Again, there had been a long lapse in his letters to David, to whom he wrote on 9 February, as VERITABLE unfurled, 'I am in the midst of some big battles; you may like to have the enclosed message which I sent out on 7th February. I have been pretty busy since I got back, and I have moved my HQ to a more convenient place.' Then, on 6 March, as he stood poised on the left bank of the Rhine, about to embark on the final and greatest adventure, the climax of his whole life, personal and professional: 'I fear I have not written for some few days; I have had a very big battle on hand and have had very little spare time; but the worst part is over now and I am not so rushed. The next battle will take us over the Rhine!' With it he sent him a watch, bought in Brussels: 'it is a very good one and is guaranteed for five years; so long as you do not drop it! I may say it was very expensive!!'

A week later, on the 14th, he was reporting:

> here I have left my winter house [that is, Zonhoven] and am back again in the woods; we have a very nice site overlooking a river and on dry and sandy soil.
>
> We are now up on the Rhine; it is a pretty large affair – 500 yards wide; but we shall go over it at the right time and place; when we are ready. My canaries find it a bit chilly, living in a caravan; and I fancy the goldfish also notice the change.

Of the enemy Rhineland territory now under his control, he added, 'Every German farm is well stocked with poultry, and I have no doubt many of these will go the way of all poultry!' Continuing this sudden burst of correspondence, he wrote, three days later, 'I was delighted you got into the finals of the rowing; I hope you win. Let me know. I am pretty busy at the moment, getting things across the Rhine, so I see in the papers!!', and on the 20th, 'I now have my HQ in Germany, up near the Rhine. I am beginning to collect a farmyard and now we have: one cow, four geese, ten chickens.' What questions, one wonders, would the law-abiding Colonel Russell, now safely relegated to a staff job back in England, now have been asking about this looting of livestock?

On 7 February TAC HQ had finally departed from its winter quarters in Zonhoven, after three weary months there – the longest stay of the whole campaign. Spring had transformed the village into a sea of mud. Despite the occasional sybaritic allure of leave in nearby Brussels, nobody was sorry to leave this dank Flemish village. As a good ADC should, the ebullient Johnny Henderson had done his best to cheer Monty up over the winter by reading to him from the scores of letters with offers of marriage that had been pouring in since Normandy. But, just from the entries in the famous Betting Book, it was all too evident that a combination of the place and the news had affected even Monty's natural and often excessive optimism. Again and again he is to be seen losing bets about the future of the war. On 17 December (the second day of the Ardennes offensive), he lost £5 to Frank Gillard of the BBC, who wagered that the war would be over by 30 June. By 8 January (the day after the disastrous press conference, by which time the German onslaught had been repelled), he was even gloomier, losing an even £1 to Henderson that Main HQ would not have crossed the Rhine by 1 August; and another bet on the same day that the war with Germany would not be over by 1 October. But everybody's spirits had lifted as the caravanserai squelched out of Zonhoven on 7 February, bound for Geldrop, a small town just over the Dutch frontier, knowing that this meant the war was moving once more. Monty spent what Odgers deemed a 'pleasant month' at 'Golden Geldrop' (as the TAC NCOs called it), supervising VERITABLE and GRENADE, and planning the next stage across the Rhine. There was an exhilarating sense of purpose in the air. Once again, the Dutch townsfolk were wonderfully welcoming. At the beginning of March Churchill came out, patently in better spirits than he had been at Blay during the crisis of July, and pressing a reluctant Monty to permit him to return for the Rhine crossing. In a charming ceremony he awarded the American LOs with MBEs. As Odgers wrote, they now 'became Members of the British Empire in name as long before in fact – so completely was each by now one of ourselves'.

Only one event marred the month at 'Golden Geldrop'. Up to this point, considering the risks taken by Monty's 'gallopers', the LOs, TAC had, remarkably, been spared from serious casualties. Now, tragically, as the war moved towards its end, they began to mount. On 9 February an Auster of Monty's liaison flight was flying Dick Harden and Carol Mather up to Nijmegen. Suddenly they were pounced on by a Focke-Wulf 190. Flight Lieutenant McQueen, the pilot, was killed at once. Miraculously the two LOs managed to land the plane, Harden wrestling with the joystick, Mather in the back – though badly wounded – manipulating the flaps. According to Harden, 'It was a very wet day and we cushioned in a ditch. I got a cut on the forehead, otherwise not injured. Fortunately, as we were just about to land, there was my driver "Tug", who came up in his jeep and managed to carry Carol back to the jeep.' Reporting the episode at length to 'Simbo' Simpson, Monty said that Mather had lost a kidney as a result:

> his left forearm is badly shattered and there is a possibility that some of the nerve has been shot away; if this proves to be so then he might not have the full use of his left arm. In any case he will be over two months in hospital, and then a long period of convalescence will follow.
>
> P.S. I have written full details to Mrs Mather.

In Monty's concern for one of his young men, Nigel Hamilton justly perceived 'the human, compassionate side to Monty which few Americans were willing to see'. On the other side of the coin, to Mather, almost a member of the family, Monty's behaviour on his return from hospital showed the irrationally cruel side of his character: his Chief steadfastly refused to help him pass a fitness test in order to remain in the army. 'He said to me, three times, "You are finished, finished, absolutely finished!"' (In fact, unaided by 'Master', Mather stayed on in the army until 1962.)

McQueen, the dead pilot, the first TAC fatality, was also a great loss. Odgers noted him as a 'quiet scholarly person who seemed to find a real happiness in the life of "B" Mess'. The incident also indicated the considerable danger that Monty faced each time he took off on one of his frequent plane trips

On 10 March, TAC moved on to Venlo, close to the German frontier, where it stayed a week on a heathland site only recently under enemy shellfire, as final details of the Rhine crossing at Wesel were planned. Here, so Odgers recalled, 'the troops had lectures on non-fraternization'. Then, on the 17th, a most memorable day in Monty's life, he set foot in Germany for the first time. Crossing the great Maas (further upstream it becomes the Meuse, which Rundstedt had come so close to reaching just three months previously), in its eighteenth move since landing in Normandy, TAC made 'a short swift move across the German frontier' to set up in a riding stable in a typical German pine forest near the small town of Straelen. It was here that Churchill, much to Monty's annoyance, returned – insisting that he be in on the D-Day of the Rhine crossing, appropriately codenamed PLUNDER. Almost jauntily he wrote after his signature in the TAC visitors' book, '10 Downing Street, London (till further notice!)'. Operation PLUNDER was a typical Monty setpiece operation (and his last), requiring every scrap of his undivided attention. On 23 March, in the typical Monty style, he issued a clarion-call to his troops, concluding with the words:

> Over the Rhine, then let us go. And good hunting to you all on the other side.
>
> May 'The Lord mighty in battle' give us the victory in this our latest undertaking, as He has done in all our battles since we landed in Normandy on D-Day.

To ensure the minimum of casualties in forcing the great water barrier, Monty had assembled an immense force, 250,000 strong, thirty divisions from three armies, with one ton of material and supplies for each man; plus 37,000 British and 22,000 American engineers, with ocean-going assault boats brought up by the two navies. Over 7000 air sorties were flown, dropping 50,000 tons of bombs, which almost totally destroyed the town of Wesel. Monty was leaving absolutely nothing to chance. The Prime Minister, joined by Brooke, had a grandstand seat from the safety of armoured cars for what, in its precision, was almost like the Salisbury Plain exercises Monty had conducted in earlier years. Winston Churchill was allowed to fulfil an infantile, but understandable, ambition of urinating into the German Rhine. Drawing on Churchill's vast sense of history, Monty asked him when it was that British troops had last fought on German soil. Churchill promptly replied that it had been at the Battle of Leipzig in 1813 – as allies against the French. Churchill, the student of Marlborough, was also fascinated by the manner in which Monty conducted the battle through his LOs:

> For nearly two hours a succession of young officers, of about the rank of major, presented themselves. Each had come back from a different sector of the front. . . . As in turn they made their reports and were searchingly questioned by their chief the whole story of the day's battle was unfolded. This gave Monty a complete account of what had happened by highly competent men whom he knew well and whose eyes he trusted. . . . I thought the system admirable, and indeed the only way in which a modern Commander-in-Chief could see as well as read what was going on in every part of the front.*

Before Churchill departed on the 26th, he inscribed grandiloquently in Monty's 'Ten Chapters' autograph book:

> The Rhine and all its fortress lines lie behind the 21st Group of Armies. . . .
>
> A beaten army not long ago master of Europe retreats before its pursuers. The goal is not long to be denied to those who have come so far and fought so well under proud and faithful leadership. Forward on all wings of flame to final Victory.
>
> Winston S. Churchill

The worst news to come in from the far side of the Rhine was that the air drop had resulted in very heavy losses to both the British 6th (30 per cent of their effectives) and US 17th Airborne Divisions. This provided fuel to RAF critics of Monty to proclaim that they had been right all along in vetoing the original scheme to land on Wesel, instead of Arnhem. By the 28th, Monty had secured a large bridgehead menacing the Ruhr from the north, as he had so long

* W. S. Churchill, *The Second World War*, vol. VI, pp. 363–4.

intended, at the small total cost of 5800 Allied casualties – of which over half were from the airborne landings.

To David, Monty now wrote on 26 March, in highest good spirits, 'You will be home by now and I do hope you will have a good holiday. Here, great events are shaping themselves to their final destiny; I have the Prime Minister here; rather a responsibility, but he is enjoying himself greatly, and does what he is told. . . .' On the 29th: 'I sent you a cake via the Prime Minister; it was from New Zealand I think and he took it back in his aeroplane. . . . The battle goes well; I am moving my HQ today close up to the Rhine; my next move of HQ will take me over.'

Now the two great prongs of the Allied armies, Monty's and Bradley's, surged forward, enveloping the Ruhr (without the industrial capacity of which Germany could not conceivably continue the war) from north and south. Monty moved with TAC in short bounds, first to a damp site near Bonninghardt, unpleasantly full of mines left by the retreating Germans, then across the Rhine on the last day of March to Brunen.

It was from Straelen that, as Monty supervised the Rhine crossing in the last week of March, his ultimate and most anguishing row with Ike took place. Exhausted, both physically and emotionally, after the Ardennes, his temper ragged, Ike had been persuaded to take his first real break since D-Day. It was badly needed. Together with Kay Summersby he relaxed for a few days in a villa called Sous le Vent which had been lent him on the Riviera. They were joined there by Bradley and two other WAC girls. Bradley and Ike, without the help (or interference) of their staffs, held long and intimate discussions on the strategy for the last phases of the war. Ike had made it clear he wanted Bradley, his classmate at West Point, close friend and fellow American, to lead the final victorious assault against Hitler. After his brief sojourn in the spring sunshine of the Riviera, it was a reinvigorated and much more decisive Ike that returned. He was now indisputably in command of all Allied land forces for the final show-down with Hitler – and with Monty as well. He was, quite simply, not going to be lectured, or dictated to, by Monty any more. Revealingly, he told Cornelius Ryan long afterwards that by this stage in the war 'Montgomery had become so personal in his efforts to make sure the Americans and me in particular got no credit, that in fact we hardly had anything to do with the war, that I finally stopped talking to him.'*

'Listening', rather than 'talking', might have been more appropriate. But Ike's judgement, made in old age and in the regrettable heat of memoir-writing, was hardly fair.

In one of their few encounters since the takeover in September, Monty went to Simpson's Ninth Army HQ at Rheinberg on 25 March to meet Ike. With him came Churchill. At the meeting Ike was far from frank about what he and Bradley had decided on the Riviera, namely that – now that Monty was across the Rhine – he was about to remove the Ninth Army from his command and shift the main weight of the attack from the north to the centre. Equally, he did not tell the British that he had decided not to capture Berlin, but to leave it entirely to the Russians, and to go for Dresden and Leipzig instead. For this disingenuousness he has been sharply criticized even by his respectful biographer, Stephen Ambrose.† Possibly it was because he knew how passionately Monty (backed ardently by Churchill) wanted to lead the armies into Berlin – as indeed did Patton. It was plainly a duty Ike owed Churchill, as an ally, to disclose this vital change of strategy, especially – insofar as it concerned Berlin – considering all that this would mean to the British people after six terrible years of war and suffering, to national pride and to Churchill and Monty personally. It seems extraordinary that Ike, previously so renowned for his diplomatic skill, should have been so insensitive to British feelings on this crucial issue. Churchill never forgave him, and to explain Ike's silence at Rheinberg in terms of the accrued resentment of Monty's overweening behaviour towards him over the past months seems inadequate – and indeed demeaning of Eisenhower's true greatness of character.

Monty returned to TAC HQ in the riding stable at Straelen, still regarding Berlin as his ultimate objective. Late on the 27th he signalled Ike accordingly, that he was issuing orders for his British Second Army and Simpson's US Ninth to strike out for the line of

* *The Last Battle*, p. 185.
† Ambrose (2), p. 197.

the River Elbe at Magdeburg, that he was moving TAC to Bonninghardt on the 29th, and 'Thereafter my HQ will move to Wesel Münster Wiedenbrück Herford Hanover – thence by autobahn to Berlin I hope.'

Ike was, one last time, infuriated by the tone of this despatch, as well as by Monty's ready assumption that Simpson was to continue under his command. On the night of the 28th, he informed Monty curtly that Bradley was going to aim for the line Erfurt–Leipzig–Dresden, thus swinging well south of Berlin 'to join hands with the Russians', and 'The mission of your army group will be to protect Bradley's northern flank.' On the 31st, Eisenhower spelt it out at the conclusion of a further message, revealing – at last – a new, decisive Ike addressing a refractory subordinate:

> You will note that in none of this do I mention Berlin. That place has become, so far as I am concerned, nothing but a geographical location, and I have never been interested in these.* My purpose is to destroy the enemy's forces and his powers to resist.

'Nothing but a geographical location'! The message could hardly have been clearer – or, given the fixation Monty had had since prewar days about leading a victorious army into the enemy capital, a more brutal blow to his pride.

The final bombshell came with the revelation that Ike was in communication with the Russians – 'my present plans being coordinated with Stalin'. Apparently, so Tedder claimed, Ike neither consulted him nor showed him the signal to Stalin. It was an extraordinary lapse on Eisenhower's part that he should have taken an initiative, so loaded with political implications, without even consulting the Combined Chiefs of Staff, and it was a lapse that would greatly embarrass him in a later era, as President of the United States in the midst of the Cold War. Monty was shattered, describing it in a letter to 'Simbo' Simpson as 'very dirty work', and writing caustically to Brooke on 2 April, 'It seems the doctrine that public opinion

* One important factor in the American decision to leave Berlin to the Russians was their growing obsession at this time with the notional threat of a last-ditch Nazi 'redoubt' down in the Bavarian Alps. This proved to be a complete mare's nest, but sufficed to distract Ike into sending substantial forces in a southerly direction. One wonders whether the intelligence may not have originated in the Kremlin.

wins wars is coming to the fore again.' But such was the avalanche of events by the end of March, as well as the relative debility of the British position vis-à-vis the Americans, that there was absolutely nothing that could be done. It was no way to fight a war – or win it, let alone win the peace. In London Brooke and Churchill seethed, impotently.

At TAC Monty would frequently wonder aloud to Kit Dawnay, his senior staff officer, 'Why are they so hostile to me at SHAEF? Who are my enemies?' It was perhaps revealing that he still did not know. To Dawnay he dictated a note for the record, to the effect that:

> the Field Marshal considered that it was useless to continue to argue with the American generals as to what the correct strategy should be. They were unable to see his point of view, and were in any case determined to finish off the war in their own way.
>
> He therefore decided to make no comments of any kind on the American plan, and to adopt a policy of complete silence.*

It was a little like Achilles in his tent. Yet without any trace of self-pity, Monty the professional, decided simply to 'get on with his own job', writing to Ike with cold acceptance on 9 April:

> It is quite clear to me what you want. I will crack along on the northern flank one hundred per cent and will do all I can to draw the enemy forces away from the main effort being made by Bradley.
>
> Yours ever,
>
> Monty

But he was to write damningly in his memoirs, thirteen years later, reopening all the old wounds: 'Berlin was lost to us when we failed to make a sound operational plan in August 1944, after the victory in Normandy.'

As good as his word, Monty got on with 'cracking along', at an ever increasing speed. German resistance was diminishing rapidly. At the same time, as Peter Carrington with the Guards Armoured recalled,

* Quoted in Lamb, *Montgomery in Europe*, pp. 378, 380.

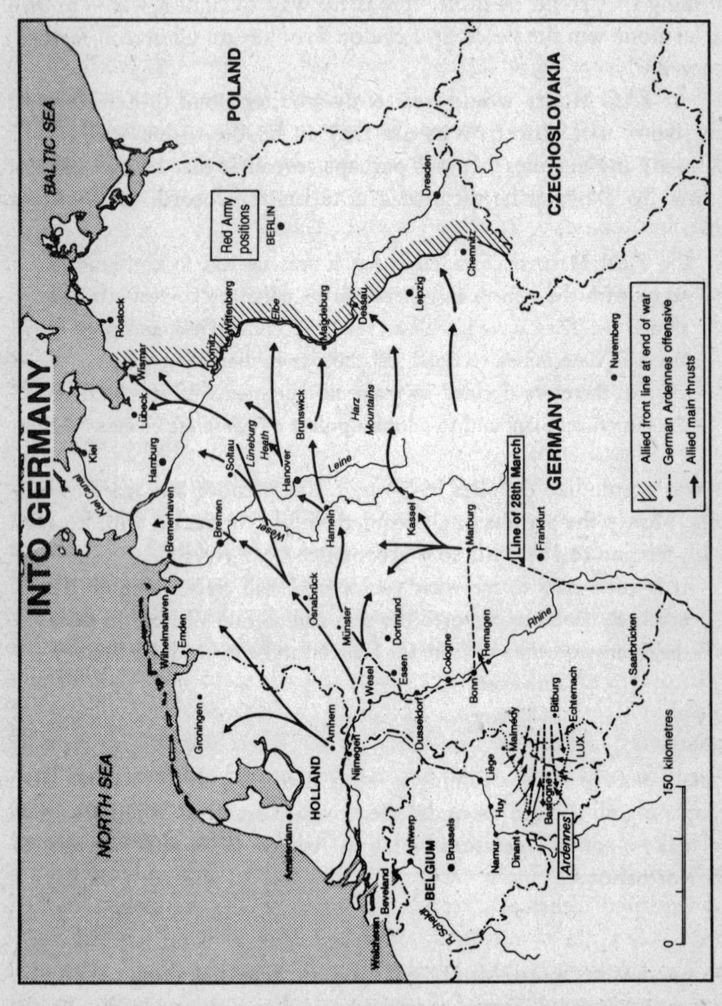

Into Germany

'everybody – including myself – was loath to indulge in unnecessary adventures when the end of hostilities and personal survival at last looked very likely'. Still, against all logic, the Germans fought on. It was not 1918 again. The Allied troops, noted Carrington, were constantly:

> astounded at the skill, tenacity and courage of the enemy. . . . Their discipline was remarkable. Their soldierly instincts, their tactical training and sense, were capable, right to the end, of teaching us a sharp lesson if we took liberties. They were superb fighting men, the men of the Wehrmacht against whom we fought; and my admiration and respect for them has never diminished.*

Members of TAC were shocked by the scenes of destruction they saw as they moved on through Germany. Sergeant Kirby recalled the ancient Westphalian city of Münster as a 'chaotic labyrinth' where 'our tyres and tank tracks crunched and pulverized the carved stone faces and limbs of medieval statues'. Hanover proved to be so extensively bombed that it was impossible to find a single unwrecked house for an officers' mess. Sergeant Kirby was moved by 'the wasted countryside, despoiled towns and gaunt faces of the people', but especially stringent security measures had to be adopted as 'everyone was a potential enemy'. At one halt his security section was mystified by a strange message from a sentry: 'Mabel is here. Will you come and sign for her. She is for the Chief and will need an escort.' Mabel turned out to be a new cow for the Commander-in-Chief's milk supply. There was chaos on the roads, choked with long columns of homeless German refugees 'displaced' by Allied bombing, or running westwards away from the Russians, with crowds of liberated French POWs and with unhappy runaway German soldiers. There were tales of fifteen-year-old SS officers of the Hitler Youth shooting their own soldiers who refused to fight, but more commonly of hordes of dispirited Wehrmacht troops longing only to be put behind barbed wire once again, to regain that specious sense of security which years of barrack service had given them. It was, the TAC personnel thought, like scenes out of Napoleon's retreat from Moscow – except that, mercifully, winter was over.

* Carrington, *Reflect on Things Past*, p. 62.

The remainder of the European war now took on the aspect of a parade, the Germans beginning to surrender in great bands. Monty wrote to Brooke on 8 April, 'A great deal of shooting up of enemy is going on. The whole area is covered with small bodies of enemy trying to get away.' But this was certainly not true of all the Wehrmacht. There were equally some pockets of fanatical Nazis who would fight on to the bitter end. On 4 April, TAC drove forward to a windswept site at Nottuln near Münster, deep in the heart of Westphalia, where the tents were 'entirely submerged in thick white clay, mud and water'. Once again each stop was of no more than a few days as Monty hastened to keep up with his advancing armies. From Nottuln TAC moved on 6 April to Rheine on the River Ems, one of the most sombre sites yet. Home was a badly bombed and filthy Luftwaffe camp alongside a railway siding. There was a pervading smell of decay and death, with one of the barrack huts, noted Kirby, resembling:

> a charnel-house – the floor was covered with what looked like charred bones, misshapen and almost liquefied by intense heat. Our joint feeling of horror at this dreadful place, with its giant slogans preaching sacrifice and obedience (*Gehorsam*), was given substance when our Medical Officer verified the presence of burnt human remains in that derelict barrack room.

In this grim place were to be found terrified civilians living in fear of the German Army returning or of armed raiding parties of liberated Russian slave labourers bent on revenge.

It was here, very late in the war, that Major Peter Earle, the Military Secretary to the VCIGS, at last fulfilled his longing to see action, finally escaping from the War Office to join Monty, the man whom he had regarded when he first set eyes on him at Caen as a 'raucous and bad actor'. He came as replacement for the wounded Carol Mather. A nine-hour jeep ride from Brussels had carried him

> through driving wind and rain, utterly devastated towns and villages, glum German civilians – homeless and completely wretched, the wrecks of tanks and guns, streams of refugees of all nationalities carrying their bundled possessions . . . fields littered with broken gliders. I have never seen such endless misery, such appalling destruction, and such wretched people.

Describing it all in a diary* which gives one of the best of all pictures of the final days of the war, as well as of life at TAC in April 1945, he arrived at Monty's map caravan where 'the incoming LOs were feverishly marking up the maps, preparatory to briefing the C-in-C on the day's work. They were coming in – some of them after ten hours' marching under appalling conditions.' Amid the evil stench of corpses at Rheine, Earle had the good fortune to find a captured German bed to sleep in. The following day, with Dick Harden he carried out his first LO job, to see General Horrocks, and came under 'desultory shellfire'. In the evening he and all the LOs reported to Monty: 'Two had crashed and not arrived.' The next evening, after travelling down sniper-ridden roads, when he reported, Monty (who had P. J. Grigg with him) 'to my surprise called me by my Christian name'. He found the work:

> mentally easy – provided one is not confused by detail. But physically exceptionally tiring job. Long drives in jeeps from dawn to dusk through battle areas. Pitted and cratered roads, past dust and noise, belching guns and tanks. Getting entry to all commanders and getting a concise picture is also difficult. The long grind back, not in the least knowing the way, and no one except enemy to ask; the sudden limelight of the caravan, with Monty as your audience – everything must be crystal clear by then.
>
> It is most peculiar driving through Germany now. We have only fought through certain areas, and only occupied quite small areas. On the road, as one dashes along in the jeep, one suddenly meets a German officer, Russians, French or Yugoslavs, or an organized band of German soldiers carrying a white flag.

The following day, the 8th, Earle paid a visit to his regiment, the King's Royal Rifle Corps, encountering more of the hazards that exemplified those last days of fighting. From his tank a brigadier:

> shouted to me as I went past which just – as he pointed out – prevented me from motoring into the enemy who were covering a blown bridge. I . . . went and saw General Hakewell-Smith, Commanding the Lowland Division, to find out why he was getting on so slowly. He said that he had had 350 casualties and taken 800

* In the keeping of the Imperial War Museum.

> prisoners in his six-mile advance and that all roads were blocked and covered, and all bridges blown. . . . Arrived XII Corps at 6.30, only to find the Commander at TAC HQ had moved on fifty miles. Returned flat out. Had a puncture south of Ibbenbüren. A small crowd of Germans gathered round the car. They smiled and the girls asked for chocolate and face make-up! We tried to take no notice but really fraternization was impossible to avoid. They asked if we were going to Berlin. I assured them we were. My face was black with dust as if I had emerged from a coal mine, with large rings round my eyes, where my goggles had been. I wore a tank suit, with the hood hanging down my back. I am now, partially only, clean again. Each day was like this.

On his return to TAC HQ he would rush straight to the map caravan, where he 'marked the maps, decided what to say, was black with dust, dashed back to my cabin, washed and changed and was in time to give Monty the picture at 9.30 p.m. "Very good, very clear", he said. "I have got the hang of it all." He always starts, "Well, Peter, where have you been?" ' Then would follow dinner at 10.30: 'Four fried eggs and bacon and two delicious bottles of looted Hock.'

During these days, Monty found more time than usual to write chatty letters to David, on writing-paper captured from the commander of the German VI Army Corps. On 8 April he was hoping David would steer clear of the mumps, but expressing disapproval of his going to Scotland with the convalescent Carol Mather:

> I think that your life during term time is so strenuous that you should spend the holidays quietly at home [at Amesbury School].
>
> The battle here goes very well, we are capturing enormous numbers of German soldiers; mostly very young, the ages varying from fourteen to eighteen as a general rule. . . .
>
> My very best love to you.
>
> Yr. loving Daddy

On the 10th, commenting sternly on David's reports from Winchester – with an appended note, 'Show this to Uncle Tom [Reynolds] – he wrote:

> I do *not* think this report is very good; except for the Chemistry. I

should say you have been playing the fool a good deal and wasting your time.

You are approaching the stage now when it is up to you to show your worth. . . .

Above all, you must cultivate a sense of responsibility; you must give up trying to dodge the rules, and fooling the masters. Anyone can do that, but it takes a proper chap to run straight down the course.

On the 16th:

I have sent home by this mail two parcels addressed to you:

1. Pictures of Rommel and Kesselring. This is for hanging in the passage at Amesbury.

2. A cake, a box of chocolates and a tin of sweets. This is for you. . . .

I hope all goes well. Here it is very cold. My HQ is now not far from Bremen & we get the cold east winds blowing from the Baltic.

It was with some delight that, after four days at dreadful Rheine, TAC moved on 10 April to what generally came to be regarded as 'the most idyllic resting place of our whole odyssey', the magnificent seventeenth-century mansion of Schloss Ostenwalde. Nestling by a lake in a cleft of the Teutoburger Hills just east of Osnabrück, and quite untouched by the ravages of war, Ostenwalde in the springtime of 1945 must have seemed to the weary members of TAC as the true *repos du guerrier*, a little Arcadian oasis of peace and beauty. After the owners, a very old Hanoverian noble family called Vincke (evidently related to the British royal family), had been summarily expelled, Monty and the LOs (now joined by Hereward Wake, Richard O'Brien and Tom Howarth) moved into the sumptuous quarters of the Schloss itself (there was, recalled Kirby, 'the *Mozartzimmer*, the music room with its white grand piano, the *Sonnenscheinzimmer*, the *Gartenzimmer*, the library and the Baroness's bedroom, with a magnificent bed in the shape of a swan'.* The Vinckes, added Peter Earle,

had left all their things. Everyone is busy furnishing themselves

* Kirby, *1100 Miles with Monty*, p. 114.

> with towels, linen, silk nightdresses, etc. In the attic we found a wireless transmitter and the old Ritter only handed over two guns he had secreted in his suitcase. It was impressed upon him that he would incur the death penalty. The prints in the house are nearly all English. Nelson, horse racing, Newmarket, view of Germany, our Royal family, etc. An old, heavily crested visitors' book has been found. All sorts of things recorded in it; a sentimental eulogy by an English girl who stayed here in 1936; photos of German tanks killing British soldiers, and entries by German 8th Panzer, whose HQ was once billeted here.... Monty... will write the next entry in the book! Typical of the man.

On his travels the following day, Earle heard a grim story of 'the lining up of fifteen British soldiers, captured by the Germans, and shooting against a wall'. That night Monty followed his description of the day's findings with his usual 'Very good, very clear. You obviously don't want a rest, do you? The others do; better take tomorrow off and do nothing. This is a little present for you.' He was then handed 'a copy of Gunn's exceedingly bad portrait!' Earle found it extraordinary that Monty should:

> be so personal – he called me Peter – and so generous in thought and so rich in self-advertisement, in which he loves to associate his staff, and when one reads a letter from Brookie, beginning 'Dear Earle' after twenty months. What an interesting contrast of personalities!

On the strength of the 'holiday' on the morrow, once the Field Marshal had retired to bed at his usual nine-thirty, a high-spirited rag was started by John Poston in the ancestral salon at Ostenwalde, in the form of a schoolboy cushion fight. A lot of glasses were broken, recorded Peter Earle, and then:

> attention in the room was focused – not without my assistance – on a vast gold frame swung high over the door containing a very bad, full-sized portrait of a German army officer, wearing the Iron Cross. He was the son of the house, and soon he was a target for a concentration of many coloured cushions.

Eventually, the painting was smashed,

> the head knocked out of the canvas.* In view of the promise that nothing would be damaged, the disposal of this vast frame presented some difficulty. At three in the morning . . . we walked it up to the lake – outside Monty's window, where, with much suppressed giggling, we put it into the water. Colonel Ewart said he must report the outrage to the Commander-in-Chief.

But, commented Earle, having removed 'so many books from the library, and a unique typewriter, I cannot think he can do much'.

It was not a very edifying story, but perhaps understandably typical of the high spirits prevailing in TAC in those last days of the war, among young officers who, in another age, would have barely left university. During the following day of complete rest, like some master at a boys' school, Monty organized a group photo, 'which he richly enjoyed':

> 'Now we will look at the camera,' he said. 'Now we will look to the right; now we will look to the left.' The LOs went through to the other side of the house where his caravan stands, and there we were photographed with him. Then he demanded we change into our travelling clothes – 'We are all too smart,' he said; 'take off your coat, John – is that my coat, by the way? And now I will be giving you the form, and I will point at the map and now we will look at Hanover, you'll be writing. . . . And now this will be for the *Illustrated London News*.' . . . And so it went on, Monty directing the whole affair.

A rare day of 'complete peace, seclusion and quiet' ended for Earle with a bottle of 'liberated' 1911 Pomerol shared with John Poston. The following night, he recalled a typical dinner with Monty, together with Kit Dawnay, Ray BonDurant, Johnny Henderson and Noël Chavasse:

> I sat on Monty's left. I described our trip to Burma, SEAC, Kandy, etc. His chief amusement was to deride Kandy, Staff College, the teaching, anything he could lay hands on. He recited the principles

* In the original of the Earle diary, lodged in the Imperial War Museum, the opposite page bears a fragment of the destroyed portrait – just the face of a German officer – glued into the diary, with the caption, 'Remains of the great portrait of Schloss Ostenwalde – a portion found in my pocket. A German officer – brought down 11 April.'

> on which war should be based, in his opinion. He asked me the first. I said 'concentration'. 'You have not been with me very long; it is all in my book. Have you read my book? I sometimes have three principles which I adhere to in all my battles – sometimes I have seven. Concentration is not among any of them. But all these old things like concentration, co-operation, are all wrapped up in my principles. The first is "win the air battle"; the second is "the initiative" and all that means; the third is "morale".'
>
> Then we discussed his decorations, whether they could hang on his pocket. He described how he had put the British honours on the first line, which he had left uncompleted in case he was given any more. He had added the foreign ones to the bottom line.

At the end of the evening, Earle's puzzled verdict was: 'A bounder: a complete egoist, a very kind man, very thoughtful to his subordinates, a lucid tactician, a great commander.'

On balance, he decided he was 'loving this job'. It was not unlike that of a fighter-pilot:

> Each day one goes out on a sortie – probably 200 miles in a jeep – this is quite a severe physical strain; forcing one's way through columns of tanks and driving on the pavements in towns, forcing the pace everywhere, heeding no signs from the Military Police or 'NO ENTRY' notices. . . .
>
> I was held up yesterday in a column of tanks near Uelzen. The woods were ablaze, the noise of tanks, the bark of anti-tank guns, sweet stench of dead cows, and here and there a dead horse, swollen and bloated, with its legs jutting stiffly upwards. The air filled with smoke and impenetrable dust; all this is tiring; nearer the battle, that special silence means danger and the absence of vehicles; or perhaps tanks deployed along edges of woods, and the savage clash of gunfire; corpses, shattered lorries and tanks; with clothing and litter hanging on the trees as though they were Christmas tree decorations. . . .
>
> I was for a moment hemmed in, as German Marine bazookas were fighting hard, with complete disregard for danger all round us. One such desperado appeared in the ditch, ten yards from the house in which we were sitting; we fixed him.

Meanwhile, Monty was so entranced by the charms of Schloss Ostenwalde that he was heard to declare, 'This is where I am going to live when we have won the war.' After only four days, however, the Vinckes heaved a sigh of relief and resumed their lives in the Schloss – little imagining that within a matter of weeks Monty would be back, and idyllic Ostenwalde requisitioned as the British Commander-in-Chief's residence for another twelve years.

It must have been a disagreeable contrast to move back to hard living, on 14 April, for a week out in the open again. This time it was damp meadowland in drizzling rain at Nienburg, just south of Bremen. In conformity with Ike's orders, the axis of 21 Army Group was now swinging ever further northwards, towards Lübeck and the Baltic (to prevent the Russians getting into Denmark) – and away from Berlin. TAC followed with it, and on the 21st, it reached its twenty-sixth and penultimate home in an isolated group of farm buildings outside Soltau, south of Hamburg.* The end of the war could only be a matter of days away now; the Red Army was battering its way into the eastern suburbs of Berlin, and the Americans shook hands with the Russians on the Elbe on the 25th. Model, Monty's unpleasant last adversary in Normandy and at Arnhem, had shot himself in the Ruhr on the 21st, and on the 30th, as the Russians closed in, Hitler committed suicide in his Berlin bunker. Yet it was still not a time for taking risks. In a tract of dense woodlands – known in a fleeting moment of fame as the Soltau Pocket – which had been bypassed by Dempsey's forces but was uncomfortably close to TAC, a subtantial group of diehard Nazis was still holding out.

In these very last days of the fighting there now occurred the bitterest personal tragedy for Monty of the whole war. The evening before leaving for Soltau, 'a beautiful hot day and nothing to do', Peter Earle recalled chatting with his friend John Poston, 'in his newly decorated German caravan – with his dachshund, surrounded by a looted wireless set and washstand. We discussed a plot for getting a couple of good cars from the Airborne Div. and getting them to Brussels.' That day, wrote Earle, 'I felt wonderful. . . . Never

* It was also little more than ten miles from Belsen concentration camp, the horrors of which had just been revealed to the world when liberated by British forces on the 15th. Monty was sickened when he inspected it from TAC at Soltau.

drunk so much, a bottle of wine each night for dinner and I have never felt so consistently well.' Major John Poston, a dashing Old Harrovian from the 'Cherry Pickers',* the 11th Hussars, was described as having 'steely blue eyes' in a 'hawk-like face'. According to Trumbull Warren, John Poston only had one speed, and that was flat out. 'Anything he did, he did at full speed.' At only twenty-five he had been with Monty since Alamein, had already won a bar to his Military Cross in Normandy and was the youngest of Monty's LOs, but he had also been with him the longest. Monty greatly valued the young Major's friendship and admired his ability. There was little he would not do for him, or that Poston could not get away with. Only a short time previously, Poston had asked Warren to get him to see Monty: he had fallen head over heels in love with a girl in London and wanted to marry her, but there was 'competition' and he urgently needed some leave. He was in 'Master's' office 'a long time', recalled Warren,

> and I thought, Holy smoke, what's happened? But when he came out, this young lad . . . had tears in his eyes. And I said, 'John, what's happened?' He said, 'I'm to take his aeroplane, fly to London and keep the plane there until the girl agrees to marry me – however long it takes.' And I said, 'Did he take all that time to tell you that?' He said, 'Oh no, he took two minutes. The rest of the time he told me how I was to go about it and what I was to say, and what I was to do.'

He returned, mission accomplished – but 'he never did marry the girl.' Generally the ringleader in the high-jinks at TAC (to wit the looted pig in Normandy and the rag in Schloss Ostenwalde), Poston was described by Odgers as 'the most vivid officer we had amongst us and his energy ran like a current through all our doings'. To Monty he was clearly the favourite among his young men, if not a kind of surrogate son.

If he had a fault, Poston was excessively incautious. Commented Dick Harden, also distinguished for his audacity, 'His mistake: he was a great one for driving his own jeep. . . . It was a silly thing which I *never* did. I always had "Tug" Wilson – a London bus driver,

* So called because of their magenta-coloured dress trousers.

an all-in wrestler in his spare time – drive me.' John Poston, wrote Alan Moorehead, 'would never take care'.*

Soon after arriving in Soltau, there was a disquieting sound of heavy gunfire near by and coming closer to the TAC HQ camp. A warning that a group of 4000 Germans was only two miles away sent into a fever some of the outlying units of TAC, who actually started burning documents and piling into their trucks. Thus on 21 April, little more than two weeks before the last shots were fired in Europe, Earle and Poston were despatched in a jeep to get through to 'Pip' Roberts' 11th Armoured Division, to find out what was happening. Earle was driving, his driver dismissed for the day. Both felt the mission 'a complete waste of time as 11th Armoured Division known to be resting', so they decided to take the shortest, uncleared route north of the forest. What followed was recounted in a typewritten report by Earle. In the morning they succeeded in getting through to the corps commander, General 'Bubbles' Barker, but it was on a short cut prescribed by Poston returning to TAC that they ran into trouble. Travelling at about 45 m.p.h. across open heath country,

> there were four isolated cracks, as of a carriage whip or cracker at close quarters. At the second or third, John said, 'What do you reckon that was?' 'Bullets,' I said; so I put my foot hard down on the accelerator. . . .
>
> From driving along on a summer evening, congenial company, dinner and a bottle of Hock not twenty miles ahead – the scene suddenly, like a clash of cymbals, changed.
>
> It was like standing in the butts at Bisley during a rapid shoot. The bonnet had been ripped up and the windscreen punctured, made opaque with bullets, and I found I had been hit in the right arm. The futility of it all; the inevitability of being late . . . for dinner and my appointment with the Commander-in-Chief. I saw ahead of me the same sordid end that had overtaken so many of my friends. . . . We had both fired our Sten guns from the side of the jeep until the bullets had run out. We did no damage, but may have kept their heads down. John was crouched down behind the level of the windscreen and I at once assumed – quite wrongly – that he was badly hurt. In point of fact, very sensibly he was

* Moorehead, *Montgomery*, p. 225.

taking cover from the bullets which I, as driver, could not do.

Earle, wounded in the right arm and unable to steer very well, nevertheless managed to drive straight at the German machine-gunner in front, killing him but crashing the jeep:

> The Germans closed in on us. John was now some three yards on my right; as I was slowly getting to my feet, I heard John cry out in an urgent and desperate voice, 'N-No – stop – stop.' These were his last words and were spoken as a bayonet thrust above the heart killed him instantaneously.
>
> At the time he was lying on the ground, unarmed with his hands above his head.

He was, added Earle, 'the most determined character for his age I have ever met and, I should say, knew no fear. . . . He would certainly have sailed with Drake.'

Patched up in a German field hospital, Earle was recaptured the following day with wounds in the arm and thigh, and Poston's body recovered. Bob Hunter, Monty's Medical Officer, had to tell the Chief the news; it was the only time, said Hunter,

> that I saw him truly shattered. John Poston was a son to him. The awful thing was, I had to tell him – and the details: 'John was bayoneted in a ditch.' He was terribly upset. . . . I had a feeling for days that I shouldn't have mentioned the details – but he asked me. . . . He just nodded, turned on his heel, and went into his caravan.*

Peter Earle was awarded an immediate MC, 'for great gallantry and devotion to duty'. Monty came into the hospital, and said, 'I am going to do a very unusual thing, because I am going to pin it now on to your pyjamas and we will have a photograph of us taken for your wife.' But for days Monty was inconsolable over the death of John Poston, and would see nobody. To Brooke he signalled a request for Churchill to be informed, 'as he knew them all and takes a keen interest in their work'. Churchill replied, 'I share your grief,' praising the 'marvellous service' of the LOs, while the King wrote a personal letter

* Interview 16 December 1992.

of condolence to Poston's father. For *The Times* Monty himself wrote an obituary, declaring, 'I was completely devoted to him,' and at John Poston's funeral a few days later he wept unashamedly – giving rise in a suspicious age to the unfounded suspicions of homosexual affections. For Monty the death of Poston went much deeper than that; it foreshadowed the end of 'family life', the loss of all his family of young men at TAC as the hostilities moved swiftly to a close, a family which – ever since El Alamein thirty long months previously – had given so much happiness to a thoroughly lonely man.*

At 6.30 a.m. on 1 May, TAC HQ moved to its final quarters in the war, its twenty-seventh since leaving England eleven months previously and 1100 miles from the beach at Courseulles in Normandy. The site was on a windswept bluff on Lüneburger Heide, above the small village of Deutsch Evern, with a great panorama over the barren heath to the south. By now TAC HQ had expanded to a considerable city of 200 vehicles, with 50 officers and 600 other ranks. Two days later Monty wrote to David:

> You will be back at Winchester now; I hope you will have a good term; next term I want to see you a prefect, or something of that sort, and you can easily do it if you take the trouble.
>
> I really think the German war is drawing to a close. We have taken one million prisoners in April, and the total since D-Day is now three million. Now that Hitler is dead I think we can expect large-scale surrenders on all sides. . . .
>
> I shall try and snatch a few days' leave, if I can; it has been an exhausting business. But I am very fit and well and the caravan life in the fields is very healthy. My present HQ is on a hill about five miles south-east of Lüneburg. . . .
>
> We reached the Baltic today, at two places – Lübeck and Wismar.
>
> My best love to you
yr very loving
Daddy

Later that same day, 3 May, the first German peace emissaries came, grey men in grey uniforms, with grey faces, on a grey evening to

* Chalfont, *Montgomery of Alamein*, p. 274.

offer the British Field Marshal the surrender of all their surviving forces. Thus, in a way, the last and greatest battle honour ironically came to Monty, not to Patton, Bradley – or Eisenhower – or even Zhukov.

As well as saving Denmark from the advancing Russians, British 11th Armoured's success in racing through to Lübeck had effectively sealed off at Flensburg Hitler's heir, Admiral Dönitz, from the remaining fragments of the Third Reich. This rendered capitulation inescapable. The German delegation of four, two admirals and two soldiers, were all big men. General Kinzel, Chief of Staff of North West Army Command, was described as 'a magnificent-looking officer' measuring six foot five inches; Major Friedl (believed to be the Gestapo representative and six foot six inches tall) had – according to Trumbull Warren* – 'the cruellest face of any man I have ever seen'. Though defeated, they looked overpoweringly sinister in their jackboots and (the two admirals) long black leather overcoats. In contrast, they were confronted by 'a rather short Irishman', recalled Trumbull Warren. Monty, deliberately, was dressed at his most casual, 'wearing a pair of corduroy trousers that had been washed so many times they were bleached white and had no crease; a grey turtle-neck sweater with a single American ribbon pinned to it', and the famous black beret ('which he was not entitled to wear') with its two badges. The charade put on by Monty must have been prepared for many weeks, if not years. A Union Jack was swiftly run up just outside his office caravan beneath its camouflage netting. Standing stiffly to attention the German officers were received by Monty, his head characteristically inclined to one side, hands behind his back, at ease. He bellowed at them 'in a very sharp, austere voice', 'Who are you? . . . I have never heard of you. . . . What do you want?' When he came to Friedl, Monty barked, 'Major! How dare you bring a major into my headquarters!' At this point, Warren whispered to Kit Dawnay that 'the Chief was putting on a pretty good act. Dawnay whispered back "Shut up, you S.O.B., he has been rehearsing this for six years!" '

Admiral von Friedeburg, Dönitz's successor as Chief of the Naval Staff, and the senior member of the German delegation, endeavoured

* Report on 'The Surrender of the German Armed Forces', unpublished, by Lieutenant-Colonel Trumbull Warren, PA to Montgomery, 48th Highlanders of Canada.

– for obvious reasons – to surrender to Monty all the German armies in the north, including those facing the Russians north of Berlin. Monty 'proceeded to tongue-lash them' on the subject of Belsen and the destruction of Coventry, told them that he had no sympathy for the plight of Germany, which she had brought upon herself, and that if an unconditional surrender was not forthcoming in twenty-four hours he would unleash on them '10,000 bombers, day and night'.

Sergeant Norman Kirby and Richard O'Brien,* almost a newcomer to TAC, and the Australian war correspondent Chester Wilmot (under the guise of a captain's uniform) accompanied the Germans back to their headquarters at Schleswig-Holstein to get Admiral Dönitz's and Field Marshal Keitel's† authority for the surrender terms. At the once mighty OKW's last hide-out in Flensburg, O'Brien recalled an even-tempered attitude of ' "Well, we have lost again" – they were charming, intelligent Rhodes Scholars – and "now we can face the real enemy [that is, the Russians]" '. The next day, 4 May, Friedeburg and his team returned, and – in a tent specially erected for the occasion – at 19.30 hours, British Double Summer Time, signed the unconditional surrender of all the German forces in the north. For this historic occasion Montgomery was sprucely clad in battledress, with his five rows of decorations, the small gold chain between his breast-pockets. Before the Germans arrived, Monty, at his jauntiest, told the journalists he had convened that the forces about to be surrendered to him would total 'over a million chaps. Not so bad, a million chaps! Good egg . . . !'‡ But during the signing all was solemnity and silence, a war correspondent (R. W. Thompson) recalling that the only sound was the flapping of the Union Jack outside. When it was all over, Monty leaned back and said simply, 'That concludes the surrender.'

That night he signalled Brooke in London: 'I was persuaded to drink some champagne at dinner tonight.'

Of those present, two of the German signatories subsequently committed suicide, Friedl died in a car accident, while Colonel Joe Ewart, a talented Scottish archaeologist and nephew by marriage of

* Interview 17 December 1992.

† Keitel was hanged at Nuremberg for war crimes.

‡ Press despatch by R. W. Thompson, quoted in Hamilton, *Montgomery*, vol. III, p. 513.

John Buchan, the intelligence officer who had so efficiently interpreted during the surrender,* was to die a few weeks later when his jeep hit a land-mine.

Although in effect this personal capitulation to Montgomery at TAC HQ signified the end of the war in Europe, the surrender formalities still had to be signed by Eisenhower, at his headquarters in Rheims, and by the Russians. To Monty's anger, the Germans managed to spin out the final signature for several days, so as to give the maximum number of Wehrmacht units facing east an opportunity to escape westwards, away from the fearsome and vengeful Russians. For one last time, he held the incompetence of SHAEF, and Ike, responsible. Ike, for his own reasons, refused to receive the German emissaries himself. Instead he left Bedell Smith to negotiate, while he waited in a next-door room. Pleading their desire to surrender only to the West, the Germans managed to procrastinate two days further; but at 0241 hours on 7 May the full military surrender was signed at Rheims, to be effective the following day. To an utterly exhausted Ike, somebody brought a bottle of champagne; 'it was opened to feeble cheers,' wrote his biographer, Stephen Ambrose.† Unlike Monty's rare tipple of three nights previously, it was flat.

On the 8th, VE-Day, Monty wrote to David:

> It is all over now. The last few days were very hectic; I expect you have seen in the papers all about my dealings with the German delegation that came in to surrender.
>
> I enclose a copy of my last message.
>
> I shall try and run over to England for a few days soon and, if so, will of course come to Winchester.
>
> yr very loving
> Daddy

* He had been with Monty since before Alamein; 'Bill' Williams said of him: 'He taught me all I knew.'

† Ambrose (2), p. 200.

EPILOGUE

> No one laughed. No one smiled. It was all over. We had won, but victory was not anything like what I had thought it would be. There was a dull bitterness about it. So many deaths. So much destruction. And everybody was very, very tired.
>
> (Kay Summersby, *Past Forgetting*, p. 194)

> I felt terribly sorry for my Chief, for he now looked completely nonplussed – I don't think I have ever seen him so deflated. It was as if a cloak of loneliness had descended on him.
>
> (Major-General de Guingand, 31 December 1944)

THE REVELRY of VE-Day over, an immense lassitude descended on all Europe. Half of conquered Germany and all of Eastern Europe would lie under the grim heel of another grim *Diktatur* for the next forty-five grey years. Britain was exhausted and bankrupt, Germany prostrate and destroyed. Among all those who had fought so long and hard, the one sensation common to all was fatigue. For the veterans of Normandy, hard to grasp in that first summer of peace was the novelty of being able to walk through a meadow or a cornfield without the dread of a Spandau or a Tiger lurking in wait at the next hedgerow. Of the mood at TAC as war ended, Major Paul Odgers closed his chronicle with the recollection that 'many of us merely felt very tired and suddenly anxious for the future'. Within the 'family', there was not much to rejoice about immediately. As if it were a sombre omen, only days after the burial of John Poston and the same week as the German surrender, another favourite LO of Monty's, Major Charles Sweeny MC, lay dying in hospital after a road accident when escorting one of the German peace emissaries to Flensburg. He had stood beside Monty on the beaches at Dunkirk, surviving all those years of war unscathed, and had only just been married. In an obituary for *The Times*, Monty demonstrated revealingly the same quality of bereaved affection he had felt for John Poston: 'Charles was an orphan and possibly it was that fact which drew us close together.... as if I was his father.... I loved this gallant Irish boy and his memory will remain with me for all time.'

On the first Sunday after the end of hostilities, following Thanksgiving Church Parade, Monty addressed his entourage. 'You will probably think, now that the war is over, that TAC will cease to function and that you can all go home. That is far from the case. Far from it.... Fighting Germans is easy', he observed to disbelieving laughter, 'compared with the job of dealing with the politicians, or statesmen as I believe they are called.' He would soon be finding out.

Occupied Germany had to be policed and administered. With a complete breakdown of any form of central government, it was something for which Monty the battlefield soldier was not prepared. 'Here was a pretty pickle,' he wrote in his memoirs. 'I was a soldier and I had not been trained to handle anything of this nature.' Nor, exhausted as he was, was his heart in it. As Alan Moorehead noted, although the British zone stood out as the best organized of the four occupation zones, Monty was 'not really interested in the Germans'. At the same time, he was 'quite unmoved by a sense of revenge or non-revenge. Abstract emotions – mass emotions – had never touched him in the least.' As after the elimination of Rommel in July, once the enemy had been defeated, he simply lost interest. His whole life an education in fighting battles, he had now manifestly fought his last one. If he wanted anything, it was to get back to reforming the post-war British Army, to teach again, but – more immediately – to look after, and enjoy, his 'family' at TAC. He was not yet fifty-eight, young in years – though not, at least for the time being, in spirit.

The last year, not surprisingly, had taken a great deal out of him. To his old friends, his slight figure seemed to have shrunk a little, the moustache was clipped back to almost nothing, the face thinner but still recognizably that of the subaltern who had sailed for India thirty-seven years previously. Major Terry Coverdale, who came out to replace John Poston, found him 'at sixes and sevens with himself . . . bored, at a loss, thinking about nothing else but waging war – and suddenly it was all over'.* Things were not helped by a minor plane crash shortly after the war ended, which caused a painful injury to his back. To Peter Earle, returned after recovering from his own wounds, he seemed already in those few months 'older and greyer, like some tired old vulture. . . . He neither likes nor understands the problems [of the Occupation] and has to shoulder the responsibility.' Earle's previous chief, General Nye, predicted, 'He will be CIGS, I am afraid, and retire a tired, worn-out and disillusioned old man.' And so it turned out, more or less.

Meanwhile, to the dismay of the Vincke family, as soon as he could move off from windswept Lüneburg Heath, in early June Monty headed back to idyllic Ostenwalde – as he had declared he would back in April. Here, just as it was on the brink of being taken away from him, and though he had lost the two members closest to his affections, Monty's surrogate 'family' took on renewed importance to him. In these last days, there seemed to be almost a febrile gaiety around the mess table. Major Sir Hereward Wake, who arrived at Lüneburg Heath as an LO just after the burial of John Poston, was struck by the almost childlike simplicity of the great man:

> He kept his medals in the top middle drawer of his desk, and would ask, 'Have you seen my medals?' Head on one side, like a bird as he often was. 'Which do you like most?' 'Oh, the Order of Suvorov.' 'Well, I think I like the Order of the Elephant!' This is not a story of conceit, but rather of straightforwardness and simplicity, like a boy with a new bicycle – lots of chromium plate. He wanted you to enjoy them – the medals – with him.

With many of the TAC staff recent arrivals, thus less integrated into the 'family', inevitably the atmosphere changed swiftly. Comments from the newcomers tended to be more critical, less reverential now the war was over. To many of them, intruding on the long-established customs of this inbred family, conversation at table must have seemed, though uninhibited, rather artificial. 'We never discussed his battles, or military history, or Marlborough, or the great commanders,' recalled Wake.

* Interview 16 November 1992.

> We were too young and ill-educated. We didn't talk about friends, shooting, fishing, hunting, riding, pictures, dancing – none of it. He was totally uncultured. He just loved getting us arguing with each other.... his one interest, soldiering.... At dinner we used to look at our watches and say, 'He's in bed now, we can enjoy ourselves!'*

Some of the more junior officers were shocked by the gusto with which Monty would criticize, and encourage criticism of, other senior commanders (with the one, eternal exception of Brooke). Even an officer with as much battle-experience as Richard O'Brien (he had won a DSO and two MCs, which made him the most decorated of all the LOs) was surprised at how Monty revelled in 'going over battles conducted by others. Oh yes – and he loved gossip.... But once you honed in on him, once you got near him, the climate changed.... He couldn't *stand* criticism of his battles.' Johnny Henderson could recall the conversation sometimes running to fantasies – icons of loneliness: 'He wanted to run the coal mines! "I told Attlee, 'I can get on with the Tyne and Tees boys!'" He was serious.'† Totally monastic, TAC seemed extraordinarily divorced from reality, especially to outsiders less susceptible to its purpose and style. O'Brien found it 'a strange set-up': 'He wanted to be kept away from the detail – and the starving Germans of course!... It was so remote, and there we were, this privileged corps, playing tennis on a summer's afternoon, and calm reigned.'‡

There were still battles, some of more comical than serious weight, which he fought – and lost – with the locals. A million Ostenwalde frogs, congregating in the lake just outside his bedroom, kept the Field Marshal awake at night with their amorous croaking. He mobilized all the local children to collect the offending batrachians in baskets and dump them humanely in a pond several miles away. For a few days there was perfect peace. Then the frogs all hopped back to their favourite quarters. The Vinckes were delighted.

The loyalty Monty would extend to his 'family' never failed, though the unforgiving penalties which he inflicted upon those get-

* Interview 25 November 1992

† Interview 29 November 1992.

‡ Interview 17 December 1992.

ting it wrong sometimes shocked. Major Terry Coverdale, who had served with distinction in Monty's 3rd Division since Dunkirk and was promoted to replace Kit Dawnay as his Military Assistant, was never forgiven. On Monty's way to the airport and home, he committed a breach of etiquette by climbing into the back of the car with the 'Chief':

> He said, 'You know my rules, don't you?'
>
> He never spoke to me again. . . . Never said goodbye, never thanked me. . . . I had made a mistake, and that was it. . . .
>
> He was a man of completely regular habits; a most extraordinary man.*

One who suffered, inevitably but unfairly, from Monty's attachment to his surrogate family at TAC in these last days was his own son, David. Two weeks after VE-Day, the conquering hero came to lecture at Winchester, the first time David had seen his father since his great triumph. He told the Reynoldses he had no time to stay the night and would fly direct to Winchester. David, aged seventeen, was approaching the end of his school career, and the Eton and Winchester cricket match was just coming up. The lecture was 'very impressive', David recalled, but then,

> apart from telling the school that he had asked the Headmaster for a half-holiday (he loved doing that sort of thing), he then announced that he felt it was important that we won this match, and so he was proposing to invite the Captain of Cricket out to Germany to visit him in the holidays if we won. After the lecture, when I teamed up with my father, I said, 'Am I included in this party?' and my father said immediately, 'Of course.' But I don't think he'd actually given the matter much thought. So I said, 'Well now, the Captain of Cricket is called Webb and I've never actually spoken to him in my life. . . .' He was a good year older than me, which made a difference then, and in another House.

David never complained (or, at least, only when a third boy was to be included on the visit), but it must have been most hurtful to a young boy who had only seen his famous father briefly and

* Interview 16 November 1992.

infrequently over the past six years, and clearly Monty could not understand this. Laconically he wrote to him on 25 May:

> I agree about the trip to Germany; two is company: and not three. It will be you and the Captain of Lords: if he wins the match. Work hard to become a prefect next term.
>
> yr. very loving
> Daddy

The episode sadly set the scene for the post-war relationship between Monty and his now adolescent son, very shortly himself to enter the army as a National Serviceman.

Soon after VE-Day, the TAC 'family' – some of whom had been together ever since El Alamein – began to disperse, as the wartime 'irregulars' (most of them) went home. The deaths of Poston, Ewart and Sweeny had predicated the break-up. Trumbull Warren returned to his law practice in Canada; Ray BonDurant rejoined the US Army in the Quartermaster Corps for another three years in Europe, then left the service as a colonel in 1968, still proudly wearing the MBE Monty had bestowed upon him, as well as numerous American decorations. Kit Dawnay left to go into the City, as did Johnny Henderson, later to become Lord Lieutenant of Berkshire. Paul Odgers returned to a desk in the Ministry of Education; Sergeant Norman Kirby became a teacher, Brigadier Bill Williams, Monty's inspired Chief of Intelligence, a History don at Balliol, Oxford, Warden of Rhodes House and a knight. Bob Hunter, Monty's medical officer, became an eminent doctor, Vice-Chancellor of Birmingham University and a peer; Richard O'Brien, an industrialist, was appointed head of the Manpower Services Commission and was knighted. Some like Peter Earle, Carol Mather and Dick Harden stayed on in the army; the last two both became MPs. Some, sadly, like Noël Chavasse, never quite managed to adapt themselves to the boredom of civvy life after the years of high tension at TAC. To the Chavasses, Monty bequeathed the last of his dogs, Tommy – 'born February 1945' – because, though ruler of the British Army, sadly he no longer had a home for it: 'I always hope that one day I shall be able to have him in a country home of my own, before we both get too old!!' He never did; Tommy stayed on with the Chavasse family. Among others Richard O'Brien stressed the loneliness that beset Monty as the war ended: 'But how could he *not* be lonely? . . . We all had our families to go back to, and jobs. He had none, only CIGS – which was a mistake.'*

Of the Allied generals with whom he served, and so often fought, most of the Americans returned home to fame and promotion. Patton, however, barely survived the war, dying ingloriously as a result of a car accident in December 1945. Two weeks later his adoring 'niece', Jean Gordon, committed suicide. The end of Ike's 'romance' with Kay Summersby was only marginally happier. Like Monty, from Frankfurt Ike found administering a shattered Germany tedious, and yearned to be back in the States. According to Kay, the war ended with further unsuccessful attempts to make love, with talk about marriage and having a baby. Then domestic responsibility, coupled with the power of the US establishment, reasserted itself. There were rumours (never confirmed) that he had contemplated divorcing Mamie and marrying Kay, but was sat on ruthlessly by Marshall and made to see sense. In November Ike left for Paris *en route* for America, dropping a heartbroken Kay like a hot brick. He published his *Crusade in Europe* in 1948, thereby launching the battle of the memoirs and greatly angering Monty. In 1952 he became President, under the implicit motto that nothing seriously bad could happen so long as Ike was in the White House. In those eight years not very much happened at all. He died in 1969. Kay died of cancer a few years later, leaving for posthumous publication her account of the affair with the Allied Commander-in-Chief, *Past Forgetting*.

Of the second generation, the sons of the arch-adversaries, of Achilles and Hector, both single children of almost exactly the same age, David Montgomery and Manfred Rommel, became close friends over the course of the years. Regularly they participated at the old soldiers' reunions. On the fiftieth anniversary of El Alamein, David read the First Lesson, Manfred the Second, at the special Thanksgiving Service held in Westminster Abbey in October 1992.

* Interview 17 December 1992.

Honours showered down on Monty: bejewelled medals, gold watches and silver swords, and honorary degrees from universities the world over. The Grande Croix of the French Légion d'Honneur, the American Legion of Merit and the coveted Order of the Bath joined the eight rows of ribbons on his chest. On New Year's Day 1946, along with Brooke, he was made a peer, choosing the title of Viscount Montgomery of Alamein. That April he returned to London to become CIGS, the highest post the British Army had to offer – marching into the staid War Office wearing the, quite irregular, black beret which was, as Alan Moorehead recalled, 'the symbol of it all'. (Because he still had no permanent home, the famous caravans went to lodge, like David, at Amesbury School.) As CIGS, he was not a success. When political acumen and diplomatic suppleness were called for, he showed just the same shortcomings that had let him down when dealing with his allies during the war. Certainly no previous CIGS had spent so much time out of England, travelling. His immediate associates (perhaps with the surprising exception of 'Mannie' Shinwell, the East End Jew who, under Attlee, became one of Britain's outstanding political bosses of the army) found him insufferable. Unashamedly, he entitled the appropriate chapter of his memoirs 'I Make Myself a Nuisance in Whitehall'.

If anything, success and honours had further sharpened that brittle insecurity and egotism which had first become so discernible on his triumphant return from El Alamein, and accentuated the bitter loneliness which descended after the dispersal of his wartime 'family' at TAC. His real family were the first to suffer. There was a deplorable scene just after the war, when the City of Newport in Monmouthshire had set up a ceremony to bestow on Monty the Freedom of all Wales. Thoughtfully, the Mayor had invited Maud, the Field Marshal's octogenarian mother, over from Ireland especially to attend the banquet – without forewarning him. In a fury, Monty declared, 'I won't have her here. If she comes, I go!' A compromise was effected, removing Maud's place-card from the top table to a distant corner. He refused to speak to her, and they never met again; nor did he attend her funeral a few years later.

'The Great Monmouth Scandal', as it became known within the shocked family, was a vicious and unseemly revenge for all the slights, real or imagined, of his lonely childhood. But it was not just Maud who was punished. His justly proud brothers and sisters all experienced similar snubs at one time or other as if some deep insecurity prevented him from sharing his honour with anyone else. No one suffered more than the ever faithful de Guingand, to whom Monty owed so much and whose health had been wrecked by his wartime labours. In refusing to have him as his VCIGS, Monty seems to have been insensitively brusque to the point of brutality. Even more incomprehensible was his refusal, in 1967, to allow an ailing de Guingand* to accompany him to the twenty-fifth anniversary celebrations of Alamein. How could he have thought the deferential de Guingand could conceivably have 'stolen the show'? Ike, himself bruised by the unmincing words Monty had reserved for his own memoirs,† consoled de Guingand by suggesting that 'more than a tinge of jealousy is at the bottom of it all. Most of us cannot understand such an attitude but it is something that is in character for that particular individual. I would not let it bother me in the slightest.'‡ Here was voiced all that Ike himself had put up with during the war.

One might have reckoned that deprivation of his 'family' at TAC would have brought him closer to his only son David. Although, at Isington Mill, Monty at last bought a home for them which he came to love, this was sadly not the case. David, always apologetic, felt in retrospect that he himself might have been 'too aggressive', recognizing all the complexities of 'a relationship between a young teenage son and an exceptionally famous father – one of the most famous people in the world at that particular time'. As he grew up, inevitably, David admitted:

> I started to have ideas of my own, and would of course argue with my father, which others couldn't do so easily. I considered, as he was my father, I could say what I damned well liked! This I think caused complications, especially for a man who was used to commanding over a million people, all of whom had to obey instantly everything he said. I think there was a dichotomy for

* David Montgomery was one of many who felt that de Guingand had been shabbily treated, and made a point of inviting him to be a pall-bearer at the Field Marshal's funeral, the only one not of five-star rank.

† Not untypically, when invited to participate in the BBC radio programme *Desert Island Discs* in 1969, apart from the statutary Bible and Shakespeare, his own *History of Warfare* was the book he chose to be cast away with.

‡ Letter of 21 February 1967, de Guingand Papers.

> him, which I can understand, and which I may have resented slightly at the time, but not a great deal; and he may have resented it more.

The advantage of all his 'surrogate protégés at TAC', David reckoned, was that 'They didn't really argue with him, and they were totally obedient, like all his staff; you only had to make one mistake and you were out.'

Fortunately for David, unlike his father he was always of a highly gregarious disposition and made friends easily. But it was more difficult for him to come to terms with the other surrogate sons whom Monty 'adopted' over the years, usually without telling him. Chief among these was the Swiss boy, Lucien Trueb,* whom Monty met on holiday at Sāanenmöser in 1946, showering him with photographs and letters and maintaining a warmly paternal and supportive friendship with him for many years. Although the letters were sometimes signed 'My love to you my little friend', 'je vous aime beaucoup: très beaucoup', or with similar displays of affection, neither David nor the Trueb family deduced anything in the least improper from the bizarre friendship. If anything it displayed pitiful loneliness. But the realization that here was a deficiency which he, his real son, could not fully requite was painful for David.

Nor was Lucien the only boy or young man in whom the ageing Field Marshal would suddenly show an interest:

> He was constantly providing scholarships to St John's.† He did all sorts of things and he took young boys in, and sometimes I knew about these and sometimes I didn't. It didn't really matter because he was a man very much of compartment minds; when he decided to devote himself or take an interest in his own son, then I was the exclusive property at that particular time.

* During the authors' joint recce of Normandy TAC HQs in the summer of 1992, at the Château de Creullet the present owners amiably showed them the family scrapbook; in it, dating from 1945, to David's amused surprise, was a group photograph of an unknown teenage boy with the late Madame Druval and Monty (visiting from Germany) wearing very continental long plus-fours and identified in the caption as 'David'. It was not Lucien Trueb or David – who he was remains a mystery.

† St John's School, Leatherhead, where Monty was a governor and always maintained a special interest.

Monty offered to these protégés generous help, encouragement and even financial support (which he could ill afford) – much the same kind of loyalty and kindness which he had shown to his lost 'family' during the war. Then, without warning he would suddenly drop these friendships.

With David there was, briefly (and literally), a honeymoon period at the time of his first marriage, in 1953, to Mary Connell. Monty was delighted, but took over the wedding as well as the engagement like a military operation. When it broke down twelve years later, Monty was ruthless in taking Mary's side, putting all the blame on David (quite unfairly, his many friends felt). The word 'adultery', an essential formula to obtaining a divorce at that time, was what outraged his father's puritan disposition. But he also took it personally, complaining to his fellow Field Marshal, Gerald Templer, 'It is hard to bear – particularly for a Knight of the Garter'*. He cut David out of his will, and only in his very last years was the breach healed when David was remarried in 1970, dynastically but happily, to Tessa Browning, daughter of Daphne DuMaurier and Monty's old friend from Arnhem days, General Sir Frederick ('Boy') Browning. But by then he had little time left.

When Monty retired after two years as CIGS, *Newsweek* claimed that the British Army had never been 'so incapable of going to war' since 1870. Possibly this may also have had something to do with the priorities of the ruling socialist government of Clement Attlee. However, the next ten years, first sharing an anomalous position of power with the haughty, anglophobe Marshal de Lattre de Tassigny at the head of Western Union Land Forces, then as Deputy Supreme Commander of the newly formed NATO (operating from SHAPE at Versailles), were not a great deal happier for Monty. He got on with contemporaries no better than before; and there was now no Brooke to curb his excesses or bail him out. Once again he found himself under his old wartime chief, Eisenhower. Ike was magnanimously prepared to bury the past, but Monty soon found that little had changed in the bureaucracy at Allied Headquarters since 1945. Nevertheless, it is generally accepted that he achieved wonders in turning NATO into a serious fighting structure.

* Quoted in Hamilton, *Monty*, vol. III, p. 929.

In 1958, aged seventy-one, after another decade of exile abroad, he finally retired – fifty years to the day since he had first been gazetted into the Royal Warwickshires. He now settled down to touring the world on peace missions, telling leaders like Mao, Khrushchev and Nasser how to run their affairs* and publishing his memoirs. Appropriately enough, the original (and better) title was to have been 'The Sparks Fly Upwards'. The sparks certainly did fly. Like the old Monty of the 1940s, he did not mince words in his autobiography; but there was little to be found of compassion or understanding of the vast, thankless task which had faced Ike. One felt that, in his eight years at SHAPE, he had learned little about coalition politics. Already showing signs of age, Ike was profoundly wounded, forgetting that it was he himself who had opened the battle of the memoirs ten years previously. (Monty had neither forgotten nor forgiven.) According to Stephen Ambrose, 'No one had ever made him so furious – not de Gaulle, not McCarthy, not Khrushchev.' In the midst of running America, the penultimate year of his eight in office, he actually contemplated mounting a ten-day seminar at Camp David to refute Monty's criticisms. It marked the definitive end of their friendship. The two old soldiers barely spoke again.

In a way, Monty had got his revenge for 1 September 1944, but was it worth it? He remained unrepentant, impervious to the damage done. Writing to console Kathleen Liddell Hart about some of the adverse reviews a book by her late husband, Basil, had recently received, twelve years later (Monty was then nearly eighty-three) he declared:

> It is a great pity that you worry so much; I never worry about anything, if people don't like what I say or write, I say it again!! I told Basil at Bournemouth that the critics would not like his book. But what does that matter? . . . One doesn't write to please people; one says what is true, and he has done that in his book; personally, I like it.†

* Leaders had 'no time to think' was one of his favourite themes, suggesting that rulers over billions of mankind would do better to run matters from the tranquillity of TAC HQ ivory towers, as he had done.

† Letter of 12 October 1970, Kathleen Liddell Hart Archives.

To the end of his life, his dedication to 'what is true' would remain the enemy of what was politic or what was sympathetic to the sensibilities of others. He himself reacted with remarkable equanimity to the wave of 'revisionist' history hostile to him, initiated by Correlli Barnett in *The Desert Generals* in 1960.

In the bleak winter of old age, he travelled less, spending more and more time alone at Isington Mill, tended, in restricted comfort, by the Cox sisters and surrounded by portraits of himself and curious little vanities such as the table napkins embroidered 'M of A'.* Relations with his son in a sad state of rupture, it was a life lonelier than ever. He made a few surprising new friends; one of whom was the then tetchy journalist Bernard Levin, who, perhaps curiously, found in him a total lack of 'pretentiousness or self-consciousness' and came to like him, 'because, so far from being the narrow puritan of popular legend, I found him warm, touchingly innocent and vulnerable, full of a crisp, positively sly, humour, and quite extraordinarily thoughtful'.

Otherwise, the closest friend in Monty's last years was the feisty military historian, and 'prophet without honour', Basil Liddell Hart, and his long-suffering wife-cum-secretary, Kathleen. Each January until Basil died in 1970, they would have a regular tryst in Bournemouth, fighting the battles of the past, Monty throwing out jibes about the 'Captain of History versus the Master of War', Basil growling back through the stem of his never-lit pipe. Monty's letters to both Basil and Kathleen are full of unsuspected warmth and concern – for Basil's health, or for Kathleen's finances after Basil died. It was all strangely at odds with his shabby, if not brutal, earlier treatment of colleagues like de Guingand.

The last years the old warrior spent pathetically bed-ridden, reconciled – though sadly very late in the day – with David. Among visitors at the end was Sir Denis Hamilton, then editor of *The Times*, who had served as a young brigadier under him in Normandy and who in Monty's old age had persuaded him to sell the bulk of his papers to his newspaper for a pittance.† To Denis he expressed

* Prompted, apparently, by that warlord of even greater vanity, Mountbatten of Burma, who had his monogram embroidered everywhere. Three sisters worked in the house, two brothers in the garden – all of them, in Monty's favourite phrase, 'quite useless'.

† On which his son, Nigel, subsequently based his three-volume biography.

concern about 'all those soldiers that I killed at Alamein, and in Normandy', and about it not being long before he joined them 'over the Jordan'. Early on 24 March 1976, he died, aged eighty-eight. His younger brother, Brian, and David were at his bedside. When David opened the safe at Isington Mill later, he found it empty but for Monty's service revolver – 'pointing at me' – and a note stating that all Monty's documents had gone to *The Times*. David handed the revolver to a policeman; he was told that it was unloaded.

Tributes poured in; so did, soon, the reassessments. Britain's greatest field commander since Wellington? Since Marlborough? The comparisons are hard to resist, though as A. J. P. Taylor remarked sardonically, they might be 'not much of a compliment', insofar as, since Wellington, there had been 'few competitors for the title'. In his introduction to *The Rommel Papers*, first published back in 1953, Liddell Hart had written:

> In seeking to upset the enemy's balance, a commander must not lose his own balance. He needs to have the quality which Voltaire describes as the keystone of Marlborough's success – 'that calm courage in the midst of tumult, that serenity of soul in danger, which the English call a cool head'. But to it he must add the quality for which the French have found the most aptly descriptive phrase – '*le sens du praticable*'. The sense of what is possible, and what is not possible – tactically and administratively.

In many ways all these attributes that Liddell Hart attached to Rommel belong yet more appropriately to Montgomery. Though he lacked Rommel's dash and capacity to strike with telling speed, Monty also suffered less from the 'artistic temperament' than Rommel, the tendency to swing from exaltation to depression. He was better balanced. (And, of course, he defeated Rommel – twice.) Correlli Barnett, the fiercest critic of Monty's desert campaign, and also a biographer of the great Marlborough, accords him high praise for having fought Normandy 'in Marlborough's style', his:

> persistent attacking on one sector, round Caen, forced the enemy to weaken other sectors of his front . . . exposing him to the final breakthrough by the Americans. . . . There was probably no other Allied commander who could have conducted and won this particu-

lar kind of battle – the most decisive fought by the western allies in the Second World War.*

Like Marlborough, it could be said that Monty never lost a battle. Like the Old Corporal, he never forfeited the affection of his soldiers or the respect of his officers, in that he never asked more of them than they could be expected to perform. But, unlike Marlborough, he would have been a disastrous coalition leader, totally lacking in the genius which he would never recognize in Eisenhower. Parallels to Wellington might be more exact – up to a point. Even if one were to ignore El Alamein (the numbers engaged were small, but it was the battle which marked the turning of the tide against the Axis), certainly in Normandy Monty brought Britain her greatest victory since Waterloo. Yet those fatal flaws of character which made him so difficult a colleague really remove him from the same class of greatness as either Wellington or Marlborough. 'No, he wasn't a nice man,' remarked his Chief of Intelligence, Bill Williams, who perhaps saw him more clearly than most. In his treatment, in victory and triumph, of his mother and his siblings and David, and of his associates like Freddie de Guingand, Monty indisputably revealed himself on occasions to be 'not a nice man'. But, as Williams went on to add, 'there was no place for a nice man in a war. . . . Nice men don't win wars.'

The unmistakable truth is that without an Ike to weld the coalition together, and keep it together, and without a Monty to convert OVERLORD from a blueprint into reality, victory might never have been achieved. No higher tribute could have been paid Monty than the judgement voiced by Ike's hard-nosed Chief of Staff, often a bitter critic of the Field Marshal: Bedell Smith said of D-Day, 'I don't know if we could have done it without Monty. It was his sort of battle. Whatever they say about him, he got us there.† D-Day was probably, as we have seen, a nearer-run thing than is generally realized. The almost miraculous luck with the weather, the total success of the FORTITUDE deception and the absence of Rommel are all things we have come to take for granted. The OVER-

* *Sunday Telegraph*, 28 March 1976.

† To Drew Middleton, 'Montgomery, Hard to Like or Ignore', *New York Times*, 25 March 1976.

LORD plan, as well as the equipment and the troops (especially Monty's own veteran divisions), had their flaws – as we have seen. Not least were the flaws within Monty himself: his isolation, his inability to tell Ike what he was doing, his capacity to fudge the record and delude himself with that pathological insistence that 'everything had gone according to plan',* his deadly conviction that he alone was always right, his blind refusal to accept the *realpolitik* of American military predominance. In all this he was, quite simply, 'his own worst enemy'.

And yet, no less simply – despite the costly setbacks before Caen, despite the terrible failure of Arnhem and the Ardennes – the Allies won. It may seem now like eulogy to claim, as Alan Moorehead did so soon after the events, that the OVERLORD plan was 'pure gold'. It was certainly less than twenty-two carat, but then the Germans fought harder, more skilfully and more tenaciously than anyone could reasonably have expected. Nevertheless, it was basically Monty's plan – persisted with in the face of so much carping criticism both at SHAEF and in the Allied press – which brought about the victory in Normandy, which liberated Paris and Brussels, and brought the Allied armies to the frontier of Germany. Without the unglamorous work of the Picador – those grinding battles fought by Monty's Anglo-Canadians round bloody Caen – Patton would never have made his triumphant, almost painless, scamper across France. What comes through, repeatedly, in Monty's record in Normandy is the sheer professionalism of the soldier, which saved his troops – as he so often had promised them – from unnecessary losses. By comparison the Americans, steeped in a belief in limitless reserves of manpower (which the Ardennes proved they did not possess), sometimes seemed almost profligate with their casualties – particularly on the tragic, and all too frequent, occasions when the airmen bombed their own troops, or in Patton's costly and pointless attacks on fortress Metz.

The ultimate tragedy of Monty was his inability to accept the dictates of arithmetic in not grasping that, following victory in Normandy, the baton of command would inevitably have to pass to an

* Though, as Liddell Hart observed, all 'eventually went according to plan, but not according to timetable', except that the Allied armies *did* reach the Seine well ahead of the famous phase-line date of D + 90.

American general. And here he was not helped by his boss, and friend, Alan Brooke, long regarded as the one paragon of British military wisdom in the Second World War, but who also has a lot to answer for in sustaining Monty in his less well-advised anti-American sorties. Both of the British generals fell short in being unable to grasp or respect the full measure of Ike's greatness. But then, equally, Ike was at fault in not having been a more decisive supreme commander from the very beginning, not having wielded a stick over the heads of his refractory subordinates. As for the still unresolved issue of 'broad front' versus 'narrow thrust', the verdict remains 'unproven', with the balance tilting away from Monty. Even disregarding American claims of numerical predominance, was either Monty or the British 21 Army Group – by the end of 1944 – the most suitable steel tip to the weapon that would strike with a great, single phalanx into the heart of Germany? 'Monty would have needed at least six months to prepare' was the prevailing view at SHAEF.

Finally, there is Hector, the defeated Rommel – so brilliant on the attack, a pessimist to the point of defeatism on the defensive (where Monty most shone). In judging that the only way to defeat the Allies after D-Day was on the beaches, not allowing them to consolidate and move inland, he got it right. But his judgement was countermanded by his superiors – fortunately for the Allied cause. No less fortunately, he let his virtues as a good husband deflect his gaze from Normandy on that one historic, longest day. He also got it wrong, in underrating the Americans and admiring his old adversary to such an extent as to persuade himself that the breakthrough, when it came, would be led by Monty at the head of a British force. Thus did Rommel play into Monty's hands by allowing all his Panzers to be concentrated against that eastern flank round Caen.

Some battlefields retain their peculiar flavour better, or rather longer, than others. Waterloo, a tiny field, is supremely well preserved. Little, however, remains of the murderous killing-fields of the Somme; much better delineated is the grim battlefield of Verdun, 1916, owing to the survival of those indestructible forts around which the fighting seethed. From the Second World War, virtually nothing remains in

France to remind one that the Germans passed by in 1940 – because they passed so fast. The battles of 1944–5 lie somewhere in between. The famous beachheads – UTAH, OMAHA, GOLD, JUNO and SWORD – lead one to contemplate once again the fate of ancient Troy, where those treacherous, destructive gods left not a trace of the great Greek invasion, entrusting it all to human imagination. Soon the beaches of OVERLORD will be the same; already the tides and sand have removed all but the caissons of the MULBERRY harbour, lying like a line of great dead whales off Arromanches. But the pounding sea, which could so easily have wiped out OVERLORD before it even reached Normandy, will eventually remove all trace. There are the little plaques, already decaying under the weather; there is the huge Cross of Lorraine at Courseulles marking where General de Gaulle landed, which – as the British–Canadian–American mementoes disintegrate – may to future generations of French schoolchildren suggest that his Free French legions swarmed ashore supported only by a handful of Anglo-Saxon battalions. To Monty there is to be found just one memorial in all Normandy, at Coleville-Montgomery, and one feels that in time the hyphenation, added after the war, will disappear, reverting to simple Coleville. In the grandiose new museum to War and Peace in Caen, the Gunn portrait (with 'Montgomery' misspelt) has been shunted off into a siding. Sadly even the famous Pegasus Bridge, captured by British 6th Airborne, was not allowed to survive until the fiftieth anniversary, scrapped in the autumn of 1993, against fierce resistance from British veterans, to make way for a widening of the Orne Canal – which had been fought for so hard in June 1944.

Less ephemeral are the great concrete gun emplacements, at Merville and the Point du Hocq, where the American Rangers scaled its 100-foot cliffs with such exceptional courage,* lying askew where the Allied bombardment left them, like obelisks from Easter Island. Enduring too, and deeply moving, are the numerous British Commonwealth cemeteries scattered throughout Normandy, all neat and superbly tended. Above the deadly dunes at OMAHA, looking out over the lashing seas, stands the one great American cemetery, row upon row of alabaster white crosses, intermingled with the occasional

* Two hundred and thirty Rangers came in; ninety went out.

Star of David and set off by an imposing inscription from the Battle Hymn of the Republic. Sprinkled about are the equally well-tended, simple black stones of the many German dead. Almost as moving is the small museum at Bayeux, with its lovingly collected mementoes of uniforms, mess-tins and poignant letters home, carefully assembled by the private initiative of a Frenchman, M. Benamou. Many towns and villages, totally destroyed in the fighting, have been rebuilt. Glorious Bayeux, with its famous tapestry of another invasion, was captured almost unscathed; Caen, on the other hand, shattered by Monty's heavy bombers, has little left except its cluster of medieval buildings around the ancient Abbaye – and an impossible traffic problem.

Over it all, to remind one what it was really like that summer of 1944, and to emphasize just how lucky Monty and his team were, is the vile, wet and foggy weather that still plagues Normandy on so many a June day.

As for the lethal bocage, sitting on a hidden oxbow on the gentle stream of the Seulles during a rare idyllic August afternoon, with grazing cattle, haywains and the distant sound of farmyard dogs and geese, it is hard now to conjure up an image of all the fear and the horror of just two generations ago. But here were positioned the eighteen-year-old Germans, fighting for their lives, fearfully anticipating what that beautiful weather, at last, would mean: the pulverizing bombing of Allied planes, the incessant shellfire, the dust, the sound of clanking tracks as British tanks moved up from the north, the fear, the unremitting losses – and yet another retreat. And, on the other side, the dry-mouthed anxiety of the infantry advancing across the high cornfields, towards those well-concealed machine-gun nests, the tank-crews' dread of what might lie behind each hedgerow. Some of the decisive moments of Normandy, for instance (as we have noted) Wittmann's destruction of the British 'A' Squadron at Villers-Bocage, are not difficult to trace, even today, with the aid of a good map and the right book. Less readily visible, but still detectable, are the pit-marks of the bullets with which 'Panzer' Meyer's Hitler Youth murdered the forty young Canadians, against a wall yards from the swimming pool of a luxury hotel.*

* Fifty years on it has become accepted that atrocities were committed in the heat of battle on both sides in Normandy; but this particular deed stands out in scale from all the rest.

Only a few miles from that grim reminder at Ardrieu, at the Château de Creullet, a small bronze plaque recalls that here de Gaulle, on 14 June 1944, 'retrouvant le sol de la France', came to confer with General Montgomery in his command post. In the recce, or the 'filial pilgrimage', in the summer of 1992, the authors encountered unexpected success in pinpointing all but one of the sites of Monty's twenty-seven TAC HQs in north-west Europe. Only the Holy Grail itself, the surrender site on Lüneburg Heath, proved tantalizingly elusive.

At many of the TAC HQ sites, there were people who remembered – warmly – the little British General. At Creullet, the Marquis de Canchy, the great-nephew of the sequestrated Marquis de Druval, produced tea and photograph albums. Near by, on the Seine at Vernon, the precise location of the pontoon where Monty crossed was easy to fix; so, indeed, later on, was the point where he, Brooke and Churchill crossed the Rhine at Wesel. At Dangu, close to Vernon, David Montgomery's old colleague, Charlie Pozzo di Borgo, vividly remembered the arrival of TAC, and his father's fuss about his lawns. Arriving unannounced at the Château de Saulty, near Arras, whose grounds had housed the caravans during the sweep across France, we were spontaneously invited to join a family birthday lunch by the present owners, M. and Mme Dalle.

Crossing into Belgium, the Princesse de Merode at Everberg recalled the 1940 outrage on her cellar. More happily, from 1944 she remembered Monty's dogs. At Zonhoven, of unhappy winter memories to the denizens of TAC, no plaque to Monty has ever been erected; by way of reparation, an elaborate banquet was set up in honour of the son of the famous former resident. At the Villa Mommen, where Monty had passed that long, frustrating winter, little seemed to have changed.

In Germany, at Schloss Ostenwalde, we were greeted most warmly by the present owner, Sabine, Gräfin Perponcher-Sedlnitzky, who remembered (without rancour) at age twenty being summarily expelled from her home in April 1944, and then again in June – this time for twelve years. She recalled her first sight of Monty, mistaking him, as he strolled in the garden in his normal unmilitary dress, for a simple private, 'scowling and looking unfriendly'. Finally, there was Lüneburg Heath. Here, the long build-up of excitement and the hubristic certainty that we would find the cairn constructed to commemorate the surrender evaporated in disappointment. It was not to be found. There was a noisy, and vinous *Schutzfest* going on near by to the accompaniment of a German oompah band. Interrogating the natives, we found no one who knew where the cairn might have been. It certainly did not exist any more; possibly it was inside the nearby Panzer firing range of the Bundeswehr. They seemed, understandably, hazy about the capitulation. Finally, a plump, half-shaven corporal in the Recce Corps led us, helpfully but with some embarrassment, to the broken fragments of a plinth inside the tank ranges. It was all too clear what had happened to it, the last casualty of Monty's battles.

Select Bibliography

This is by no means a comprehensive bibliography, but chiefly comprises works used in this book or directly quoted. Of particular general use, of course, was Nigel Hamilton's three-volume biography, to which we have constantly referred and to which we are indebted, Max Hastings' *Overlord*, Richard Lamb's *Montgomery in Europe, 1943–45*, and John Keegan's *Six Armies in Normandy*. Among the pioneer works, particular value was derived from Alan Moorehead's *Montgomery* (1946), from Chester Wilmot's *The Struggle for Europe* (1952), and from Milton Shulman's *Defeat in the West* (first published 1947, reprinted 1988). Nearer to the source, of course we have used (but with caution) Montgomery's own autobiographical writings, notably *Normandy to the Baltic* (possibly the most reliable, as written closest to the events), and *Memoirs*, as well as Brian Montgomery's vivid account, *A Field Marshal in the Family*. Among many excellent US sources, most useful are the various studies on Eisenhower by Stephen Ambrose, and Carlo D'Este's objective *Decision in Normandy*.

BOOKS

Ambrose, Stephen E. (1): *The Supreme Commander: The War Years of General Dwight D. Eisenhower* (London 1971)

——: *Eisenhower: Soldier, General of the Army, President Elect, 1890–1952* (New York 1983)

—— (2): *Eisenhower: Soldier and President* (New York 1990) [an abridged edition of the above two volumes]

——: *Pegasus Bridge* (New York 1985)

Baldwin, H. W.: *Great Mistakes of the War* (London 1950)

Barnett, Correlli: *The Audit of War* (London 1986)

Belchem, David: *All in the Day's March* (London 1978)

Bigland, Tom: *Bigland's War: War Letters of Tom Bigland, 1941–45* (Liverpool 1990)

Blake, Robert (ed.): *The Private Papers of Douglas Haig* (London 1952)

Blumenson, Martin (ed.): *The Patton Papers*, vol. II (Boston 1974)

——: *Break Out and Pursuit* (Washington 1961)
Blumenson, Martin; *The Battle of the Generals, The Untold Story of the Falaise Pocket* (New York 1993)
Bradley, Omar: *A Soldier's Story* (London 1951)
—— and Blair, Clay: *A General's Life* (New York 1983)
Bramall, Edwin, and Jackson, William: *The Chiefs* (London 1992)
Brett-James, Antony: *Conversations with Montgomery* (London 1984)
Brett-Smith, Richard: *Hitler's Generals* (London 1976)
Bryant, Arthur: *Triumph in the West* (London 1959)
Butcher, Harry C.: *Three Years with Eisenhower* (London 1946)
Carell, Paul: *Invasion: They're Coming* (London 1962)
Carrington, Peter: *Reflect on Things Past* (London 1988)
Carver, Lord: *The Apostles of Mobility* (London 1979)
Chalfont, Alun: *Montgomery of Alamein* (London 1976)
Churchill, W. S.: *Marlborough* (London 1933)
——: *The Second World War*, vol. VI: *Triumph and Tragedy* (London 1954)
Connell, John: *Wavell* (London 1964)
Davies, W. J. K.: *German Army Handbook, 1939–45* (London 1973)
De Gaulle, Charles: *Mémoires de la Guerre* (1954–9)
De Guingand, F. W.: *From Brass Hat to Bowler Hat* (London 1979)
——: *Operation Victory* (London 1947)
D'Este, Carlo: *Decision in Normandy* (London 1983)
Dupuy, Colonel T. N.: *A Genius for War* (London 1977)
Eisenhower, D. D.: *Crusade in Europe* (New York 1948)
Fraser, David: *Alanbrooke* (London 1982)
——: *Knight's Cross: A Life of Field Marshal Erwin Rommel* (London 1993)
Grigg, John, *1943: The Victory that Never Was* (London 1980)
Hamilton, Nigel: *Monty*, vol. I (London 1981), vol. II (London 1983), vol. III (London 1986)
Hastings, Max: *Bomber Command* (London 1979)
——: *Overlord: D-Day and the Battle for Normandy* (London 1984)
Herbert, A. P.: *Independent Member* (London 1950)
Hodgson, Godfrey: *The Colonel* (New York 1990)
Horne, Alistair: *To Lose a Battle: France 1940* (London 1969)
Horrocks, B. G.: *A Full Life* (London 1960)
Howarth, T.: *Montgomery at Close Quarters* (London 1985)
Irving, David: *The War Between the Generals* (London 1981)
Jacobsen, H. A., and Rohwer, J.: *Decisive Battles of World War II: The German View* (London 1965)
James, M. E. C.: *I was Monty's Double* (London 1954)

Keegan, John: *Six Armies in Normandy* (London 1982)
Kennedy, Major-General Sir John: *The Business of War* (London 1957)
Kirby, Norman: *1100 Miles with Monty* (London 1989)
Lamb, Richard: *Montgomery in Europe, 1943–45: Success or Failure* (London 1983)
Larrabee, Eric: *Commander in Chief: Franklin Delano Roosevelt* (New York 1987)
Lewin, R.: *Montgomery as Military Commander* (London 1971)
Liddell Hart, B. H.: *The Memoirs of Captain Liddell Hart* (London 1965)
——: *History of the Second World War* (London 1970)
——: *The Other Side of the Hill* (London 1970)
—— (ed.): *The Rommel Papers* (London 1953)
MacMahon, J. S., *Professional Soldier: A Memoir of General Guy Simonds, CB, CBE* (Winnipeg 1985)
Mather, Sir Carol, *Aftermath of War; Everyone Must Go Home* (London 1992)
Mellenthin, W.: *Panzer Battles, 1939–45* (London 1955)
Montgomery, B. L.: *Normandy to the Baltic* (London 1946)
——: *A History of Warfare* (London 1968)
——: *Memoirs* (London 1958)
——: *The Path to Leadership* (London 1961)
Montgomery, Brian: *A Field Marshal in the Family* (London 1973)
Moorehead, Alan: *Montgomery* (London 1946)
Moran, Lord: *The Anatomy of Courage* (London 1945)
Patton, G. S.: *War As I Knew It* (Boston 1947)
Pitt, Barrie, and Pitt, Frances: *The Chronological Atlas of World War II* (London 1989)
Pogue, Forrest C.: *The Supreme Command* (London 1954)
Rees, Goronwy: *A Bundle of Sensations* (London 1960)
Richardson, C.: *Flashback: A Soldier's Story* (London 1985)
——: *Send for Freddie* (London 1987)
Ruge, Admiral F., *Rommel in Normandy* (London 1979)
Ryan, C.: *The Longest Day* (London 1960)
——: *A Bridge Too Far* (London 1974)
Shulman, Milton: *Defeat in the West* (London 1947; new edn 1988)
Speidel, Hans: *We Defended Normandy* (London 1970)
Stacey, Colonel C. F., *The Victory Campaign: The Official History of the Canadian Army in the Second World War* (Ottawa 1960)
Summersby, K.: *Eisenhower Was My Boss* (London 1949)
——: *Past Forgetting* (London 1977)

Tedder, A. W.: *With Prejudice* (London 1966)
Thompson, R. W.: *Montgomery the Field Marshal* (London 1969)
Urquhart, Sir Brian: *A Life in Peace and War* (London 1987)
Westphal, General S., *The German Army in the West* (London 1951)
Wilmot, C.: *The Struggle for Europe* (London 1952)
Woollcombe, Robert: *Lion Rampant* (London 1970)

DIARIES

Harry C. Butcher diary, Eisenhower Library, Abilene, Kansas
Peter Earle diary, Montgomery Collection, Imperial War Museum
Johnny Henderson diary, property of John Henderson CVO, OBE
Paul Odgers, 'A TAC Chronicle', Montgomery Collection, Imperial War Museum

ARCHIVES

Ray BonDurant, unpublished notes, property of David Montgomery
De Guingand Papers, Montgomery Collection, Imperial War Museum
Grigg Papers, Churchill College, Cambridge
Kathleen Liddell Hart Archives, property of Lady Liddell Hart
Montgomery Collection, Imperial War Museum
Trumbull Warren, unpublished tapes, property of David Montgomery

INDEX